HOW PLAYS WORK

How Plays Work

Reading and Performance

MARTIN MEISEL

OXFORD
UNIVERSITY PRESS

OXFORD

UNIVERSITY PRESS

Great Clarendon Street, Oxford OX2 6DP

Oxford University Press is a department of the University of Oxford.
It furthers the University's objective of excellence in research, scholarship,
and education by publishing worldwide in

Oxford New York

Auckland Cape Town Dar es Salaam Hong Kong Karachi
Kuala Lumpur Madrid Melbourne Mexico City Nairobi
New Delhi Shanghai Taipei Toronto

With offices in

Argentina Austria Brazil Chile Czech Republic France Greece
Guatemala Hungary Italy Japan Poland Portugal Singapore
South Korea Switzerland Thailand Turkey Ukraine Vietnam

British Library Cataloguing in Publication Data
Data available

Library of Congress Cataloging in Publication Data
Data available

Typeset by Laserwords Private Limited, Chennai, India
Printed in Great Britain
on acid-free paper by
Biddles Ltd., King's Lynn, Norfolk

ISBN 978-0-19-921549-2

1 3 5 7 9 10 8 6 4 2

For Sarah and Luke

Prologue

This book began with the perception that many persons, some of them my students, wonderfully adept at novel reading and readily responsive to poetry, were far less confident and intuitive when it came to reading plays. Since it was my business to teach plays in classroom and seminar, plays in printed form for a start, I found that every such course in the literature of the theatre that I had a hand in, whether dealing with plays from Renaissance Italy or yesterday's Off-Off Broadway, became more or less the same course. Ever and always, I found that what one needed to absorb as the path to imaginative response was how the play before us worked. Every course, then, became an extended exploration of how plays worked. This was not anatomizing the art of the play for its own sake to arrive at a Poetics of the Drama, or developing practical formulas for writing one's own play as in the once ubiquitous Handbooks on Playwriting, but something closer to learning a language in order to take part in a conversation—a conversation, like that between stage and audience in the theatre, that is active on both sides.

Learning a language is not a bad analogy for how I imagine this book might work. It begins with matters that offer a way in, first, through a look at coding and convention in print and on the stage; and then, under the rubric 'Beginnings', at the business of entering the invented world of the play. Each additional aspect taken up in the succeeding chapters, such as 'Seeing and Hearing', 'The Role of the Audience'—I would call them 'elements', only they are more than that—is a gesture at enlarging the field of understanding. Each is a negotiation between the particularities of the plays I turn to for help (how *they* work) and something more general. It is a little like making the leap to the deeper structures of language from a modest collection of instances, which we do when we discover we are prepared to recognize sentences we have never heard before. As the scope enlarges from chapter to chapter, I would hope it also deepens, not least because the proceedings are recursive. I often bring back plays that have served to make some other point—a useful approach, not only to learning a language (building upon what one has already absorbed and in a sense owns), but to a richer understanding of any complex human creation worth remembering and revisiting.

There are many things this book does not do. I do not try to say everything or include everything in my reach. The kind of play I talk about, and draw upon for illustration and exploration, is almost entirely from the Western (European and American) tradition. I do not try to be fair in distributing attention by language, nation, period, or gender. I draw from the range of plays I have actually taught, though by no means the whole range, and some plays and playwrights turn up time and time again. I favour English language plays only where the play of language is especially important, and too much would be lost or transformed in translation. I do not pay much attention to how the play, written for live performance, differs from its great modern competitor (and some would argue supplanter), the motion-picture film, equally given to enacted narrative, and also, in its mature form, a complex union of seeing and hearing. I do not say much about the modern phenomenon of the strong director who in effect becomes co-author, inserting himself or herself between the script and the audience and—to put it accurately—*re*directing the play. Production, as everyone knows, entails making choices, by actors, directors, designers, from the inherent potentialities of the script, thereby putting flesh on the bones. That is a project more diffident, if in fact often more difficult, than adaptive co-authorship, which at its best *can* create a dialogue with the scripted progenitor, but often means overriding rather than engaging its voice and design. In an odd way, adaptive co-authorship follows in the track of what comes naturally to film. The product of the camera and the cutting room, of *auteur* and editor, close-up and tracking shot, is a much more controlled kind of seeing than is possible in the theatre. There is a point at which strong redirection can prove limiting and coercive in the theatre, in contrast to the kind of realization that is expansive and enhancing, that opens the play to a richer imaginative response. I cite two marvellous examples of what I mean by such enhancement near the end of this book, in stagings of Shakespeare's *Tempest*. Opening plays in some measure to such response, both as art and experience, in print and on the stage, is all that I would wish such a book as this one to achieve.

One more thing. When Ben Jonson in 1616 published his plays, masques, entertainments, and poetry in an imposing folio volume entitled *The Workes of Beniamin Jonson*, the jesters, riddlers, and rhymesters of the age (it often came to the same thing) had a field day. In the first place the weighty and expensive format was one deemed suitable for magisterial histories, the literature of antiquity, and collections of sermons by eminent divines. But the cream of the jest was in the title. One joker inscribed his drollery on the elaborately engraved title page of the folio itself, drawing a line through the title and substituting a couplet:

These are Ben Johnson's *Workes*, the Printer says:
Printer thou ly'st, They are Ben Johnson's Plays.[1]

The joke was in the claim of weight and seriousness for things so inherently ephemeral and frivolous as 'Plays'. At the time there was a strong disposition to seek a meaningful congruence between words and things. To ask, 'What's in a name', as Juliet does, shows a temperamental and intellectual daring that can get you into trouble. The 'truth' that spoke in the ordinary name for Jonson's glorified achievements was that pieces written to be put on the stage by persons in dress-ups pretending to be not themselves for the entertainment of other persons out for a good time were in nature unserious, all 'play'.

I mention all this because I have a related title concern, the mirror reverse of what should have been Ben Jonson's. I worry that a volume called 'How Plays Work' is liable to end up making them seem all work and very little play. Anyone who tries to write seriously about what makes one laugh, to take a painful example, knows the problem. The comedy mysteriously evaporates, the joke falls flat, sayings and doings under scrutiny lie prostrate before the prospect of analytical vivisection. Perhaps there is not much one can do about it, other than acknowledge the handicap and hope there will be compensations. In my case it requires acknowledging, or perhaps insisting, that *play* in all its many human senses is the soul of what I mean to be talking about. For it seems to me beyond dispute that all art and imagination, however charged with weighty tasks like forming the self and provisioning the well-being of society, for which they are indispensable, are in their deepest nature play.

In bringing this book to term, I have accumulated debts. The most imposing is to the generations of students who taught me how and what to teach, first at Dartmouth College, then at the University of Wisconsin, and last and longest at Columbia. You know who you are.

A number of colleagues read the whole of this book in manuscript. Their commentaries, in assorted shades of severity and encouragement, proved invaluable, saving me from some embarrassing slips and extravagances, and stimulating sensible compressions, but also unanticipated elaborations. My thanks to Michael Goldman, Robert Hunter, Karl Kroeber, Susan Manning, Martin Puchner, and Alex Zwerdling, whose point-to-point commentary was especially generous and demanding. The manuscript also had the benefit of Joseph Meisel's disciplined historian's eye and vigorous standards for grounded argument, of Andrew Meisel's gift for imaginative association, theoretical complexity, and stylistic lucidity, and of Maude Meisel's acute literary sensibility and enviable language talents—especially where Russian texts were concerned. Helene Foley gave aid and comfort in navigating scholarship on classical texts. Readers' reports shared by the press also helped me arrive at a final shape, in telling me what was getting through and what was not. Only Russ McDonald of the University of North Carolina shed his anonymity, but all have my thanks. The notion that there might be some point in writing such a book as this was first set going by Andrew McNeillie, now Senior Commissioning Editor for Literature at Oxford. He may be called to account as its onlie begetter.

Professor Gloria Beckerman graciously gave permission to quote from the late Bernard Beckerman's essay, 'The Odd Business of Play Reviewing'. The staff of the Billy Rose Theatre Division, The New York Public Library for the Performing Arts, was especially helpful in plumbing its rich visual holdings, and enabling reproduction for Figures 3, 4, and 9. I am grateful to the Daumier Register and Lilian Noack for Figure 6. Rowena Anketell's scrupulous editorial eye is everywhere at work in what follows.

Karl Kroeber, who seems to invent a new field of literary study every year, and in consequence is always ahead of the trend like those 'premature anti-fascists' of the nineteen-thirties, has had a half share in a forty-year conversation, sometimes harmonious, frequently insulting, but always alive and invigorating, on narrative and drama, film, painting, poetry, modernity, children's literature, and Lord knows what else. I have stolen from him more than he knows.

On a previous occasion, glancing at what I owed my wife and partner Martha in the way of love, insight, accommodation, and understanding, I wrote of its being mostly unacknowledged. I said I would not apologize since in fact we were much in each other's debt. That remains the truth of the matter, only more so.

This book is dedicated to the future in the special and distinctive persons of Sarah Emma Meisel and Luke Ramella Meisel. They give the best reason for hope.

MM

---

[1] Preserved in *A Choice Banquet of Witty Jests* (1660), and cited in Gerald Eades Bentley's *Shakespeare & Jonson: Their Reputations in the Seventeenth Century Compared* (Chicago: University of Chicago Press, 1945), ii. 111. Bentley describes the ridicule Jonson's publication inspired as 'endless' (i. 10 n.).

Contents

List of Figures

1

Introduction: The Art of Reading Plays

One of the lasting successes of the prolific playwright Carlo Goldoni—written for an eighteenth-century Venetian audience—was a comedy called *The Servant of Two Masters*. The title already tells all. It names a situation where the protagonist, pulled both ways to satisfy two incompatible sets of demands, has to juggle and stretch, double himself in some ingenious fashion, find ways to reconcile the competing claims. Comedy lurks in Truffaldino's impossible dilemmas, his desperate running from pillar to post, his inevitable sowing of confusion; but also in his serendipitous escapes and solutions. Where there is scope for comedy, however, there is also potential for tragedy. Raise the tone, and the figure caught in a conflict between unyielding master imperatives—between Love and Honour, say, or the commands of the heart and the mandate of the gods—may find no way of reconciling these claims, and so go down to destruction along with his or her world.

The situation of the printed play is not quite that parlous. It can be every bit as awkward as that of the *Servant of Two Masters*, thanks to the double bind that reflects a problematic identity. But like Truffaldino in his comic world, the printed play, the play that we read, has proved itself adept at finding ways to perform its double role, if at the price of some inherent and irreducible confusion.

Reading plays has much in common with reading musical scores; and yet, what score is designed to be read, like a printed play, for enjoyment, as an end in itself? At the same time, like the musical score, the printed play exists as a manual or a blueprint for performance. It exists as a manual *and* as a representation, in its own right, of that which is to be performed—whether it ever is performed or not, whether it is performed many different times in many different productions, guided and enacted by many different minds, or only once under the eagle eye of the author. Reading plays in the fullest sense, then, means being able to read the dialogue and descriptions as a set of directions encoding, but also in a measure *enacting*, their own realization. It means bringing to bear something of a playwright's or director's understanding of how plays work on an imagined audience in the circumstances of an imagined

Figure 1. Arlecchino (otherwise Truffaldino) between the travelling trunks of his two masters, discovering he has mixed up their things. From Giorgio Strehler's production of Carlo Goldoni's *Il servitore di due padroni*, Act III, Scene i, Piccolo Teatro di Milano, 1956–7.

theatrical representation. A book that presumes to offer advice on how to read a play—as this one does—is really a book that is obliged to describe 'How Plays Work'.

But the printed page, as 'a representation in its own right', apart from any production, has to have its own way of conveying meaning and registering effects. And that requires a set of agreed-on, or at least intelligible, conventions that ideally fade into unobtrusiveness. Useful, and indeed necessary, as these conventions are, they should not be taken for granted, however; for they are by no means the same for all texts or all times and places. In fact, not even making the play into a something inscribed on the page as an object of literary interest fit for private perusal is historically to be taken for granted.

What, then, are these conventions?

We are used to passages of dialogue separating the speakers and introduced by speech tags (names of characters), preceded by or interspersed with descriptions of scene and action. Sometimes the description includes the external appearance and differentiating traits of the characters. Often the individual speeches are rhetorically inflected, their tone, feeling, or emphasis indicated parenthetically. We are used to divisions marked 'Act' and 'Scene'. Mostly we read these divisions as implying a break in time or a shift in place—unless what we have before us is a printed play using French conventions, a play by Molière or any French play well into the twentieth century, and now matters begin to get complicated. There *scène* is defined, not by location, but by participants. A new scene is indicated every time a character enters or leaves the stage, and each scene in the printed text starts off with a list of those present. In the reading of such texts, the conventional divisions can suggest a rhythm of discontinuity, a rhythm that is likely to disappear in performance using the same text as script or score. That is because French classical drama required what was called *liaison des scènes*—at least one actor carrying over from one scene to the next, linking them in a chain of encounters through each of the conventional five acts, and so reinforcing a sense of continuity in an unfolding action within a fixed, generic setting. To further complicate matters, in the nineteenth century (where scenery and spectacle took on a new importance and specificity), playwright and printer often add a third term, namely *Tableau,* intermediate, as it were, between *acte* and *scène*, to indicate a continuous locale and to mark the changes. (For additional confusion, 'Tableau' was also used, notably in English and in both comedy and melodrama, to indicate the actors' momentary freeze into a stage picture.)

But even what seems to be basic in the form and layout of the play text—like separation of speeches, and identification of speakers—is not to be taken for granted. The oldest surviving manuscripts (papyri) of Athenian drama, presumably for reading and circulation, are blocks of lettering (all capitals) without marked divisions or even word separation, let alone discrimination of the various verse forms actors and chorus employed. There are hardly any stage directions and often no identifying speech tags; only a dash or double stop to indicate a change of speaker.[1] Elizabethan playbooks use act and scene designations haphazardly, or in some cases (as in the posthumous 'First Folio' to which we owe the text of many of Shakespeare's plays) formally and arbitrarily, at odds with the uninterrupted flow implicit in the playwriting. In some texts, where we would expect the name of the character speaking, the name of the actor for whom the part was written or by whom it was performed appears. (In the Italian comedy of the era, there was often no distinction between the actor's stage name and role name. Ruzzante was 'Ruzzante'.) The use of stage directions for elaborate description of setting, atmosphere, and characters was minimal before the end of the nineteenth century, the playwrights incorporating what they wished the audience to know or imagine in the dialogue. So, Shakespeare has Bernardo, taking up his post in the opening of *Hamlet,* tell Francisco, ''Tis now struck twelve. Get thee to bed

Francisco,' who then replies, 'For this relief much thanks. 'Tis bitter cold and I am sick at heart'—behavioural instruction for the actor, as well as evocation for Shakespeare's open-air daylight audience of another atmosphere: of night, cold, loneliness, and depressive anxiety. As for characterization, it was typical in the comedy of the next few centuries for a character's foibles, quirks, and qualities to be sketched in conversation before his or her first entrance, frequently concluding (as if in happy coincidence) with the entrance cue, 'Look where [he/she] comes!'

The change to more elaborate and discursive stage directions in printed plays was not a sudden revolution, though in the English-speaking drama George Bernard Shaw let himself in for both the credit and the blame. Having been little produced, he decided in the late 1890s to reach (and create) an audience through print, and to make his scripts reader-friendly. He did so by abandoning some of the notation that, in the ordinary printed play of the time, served the purposes of production more than those of pleasurable reading. Shaw resolved to avoid indications such as the following, from a successful contemporary comedy:

SCENE. *Same. Evening.*
Battens checked slightly; lights down outside window; blue lime through window; sofa and desk as in Act I.[2]

—or (for something more complicated) such as the following, from the published version of a once famous mid-century melodrama:

SCENE SIXTH. *A Cave; through large opening at back is seen the lake and moon; rocks* R. *and* L.,—*flat rock,* R.C.; *gauze waters all over stage; rope hanging from* C., *hitched on wing,* R.U.E.[3]
                    Enter MYLES *singing, top of rock,* R.U.E.[3]

In the first passage, the lighting directions ('*Battens*', '*blue lime*') are the practical form of 'EVENING'. In both passages, place and atmosphere are treated as lighting and scenery ('*large opening . . . lake and moon*', '*gauze waters*'), with special attention to what had to be 'practicable', not simply decorative (the '*flat rock*'; the rope), and with stage positions encoded in abbreviations (R.U.E. = Right Upper Entrance).

Shaw shifted from a language descriptive of means to a projection of the intended results. So, he opens *Arms and the Man*, one of his earliest plays, with the direction:

Night: A lady's bedchamber in Bulgaria, in a small town near the Dragoman Pass, late in November in the year 1885. Through an open window with a little balcony a peak of the Balkans, wonderfully white and beautiful in the starlit snow, seems quite close at hand, though it is really miles away. The interior of the room is not like anything to be seen in the west of Europe. It is half rich Bulgarian and half cheap Viennese.[4]

Figure 2. Setting and action in Act II, Scene vi of Dion Boucicault's *The Colleen Bawn* (1860), showing cave, lake, moon, rocks, and waters as in the playbook stage directions. Danny Mann, attempting to drown Eily O'Connor (the said Colleen Bawn), is shot in the act by Myles na Coppaleen, just visible on the rocks at right, behind the rope he will use to swing to Eily's rescue (contemporary print).

What follows is a detailed description of the room and its furnishings, establishing (in its hybrid dissonance) the world that the action will concern, but also including details that will come directly into the action (the enshrined portrait of a dashing soldier, a box of chocolate creams). The practical aspects, in other words, are clothed in the descriptive, atmospheric, and even symbolic characterization of the projected scene. The practical mechanics of a later entrance by a climbing intruder, for example, are carefully prepared in a passage introducing the reader to the sole occupant of this opening scene:

The window is hinged doorwise and stands wide open. Outside, a pair of wooden shutters, opening outwards, also stand open. On the balcony a young lady, intensely conscious of the romantic beauty of the night, and of the fact that her own youth and beauty are part of it, is gazing at the snowy Balkans. She is in her nightgown, well covered by a long mantle of furs, worth, on a moderate estimate, about three times the furniture of her room.

After a second character enters, the directions are essentially concerned with the dynamics of what is said and done—the activity, expressive and interactive, of the dialogue and the speakers. The directions make manifest for the reader those values a director (as middleman) might seek to elicit from the bare words; values the authors of an earlier day would mostly have left implicit in speech and situation for the actors (often with the author's hands-on coaching) to mediate, or realize. Thus, as the young lady's picturesque reverie '*is interrupted by her mother . . . a woman over forty, imperiously energetic*,' the action proper of *Arms and the Man* begins:

CATHERINE (*entering hastily, full of good news*) Raina! (*She pronounces it Rah-eena, with the stress on the ee*) Raina! (*She goes to the bed, expecting to find Raina there.*) Why, where—? (*Raina looks into the room.*) Heavens, child! are you out in the night air instead of in your bed? You'll catch your death. Louka told me you were asleep.
RAINA (*dreamily*) I sent her away. I wanted to be alone. The stars are so beautiful! What is the matter?
CATHERINE. Such news! There has been a battle.
RAINA (*her eyes dilating*) Ah! (*She comes eagerly to Catherine.*)
CATHERINE A great battle at Slivnitza! A victory! And it was won by Sergius.
RAINA (*with a cry of delight*) Ah! (*They embrace rapturously*) Oh, mother! (*Then, with sudden anxiety*) Is father safe?

Here, where much of the conversation is telegraphic ejaculation, the directions make vivid for the reader what the actor must otherwise supply, and incidentally steer the actor to what in the situation waits to be supplied. The result on the page is a melding of reading and performance—a script that becomes performance in the reading. The direction, '*entering hastily, full of good news*', for example, goes beyond cueing the bare physical action, to clueing attitude and expression (the actor's), heightening the reader's/audience's anticipation for what comes next. The impulsion is not just to the actor's bustling entrance, but to the drama itself. Moreover, there is additional drama in the contrast between Catherine's energetic eruption and Raina's contemplative reverie, which she is reluctant to leave. She answers '*dreamily*', clinging to her mood. For the moment, they are two presences diametrically at odds, a minor dissonance that needs to be resolved. Raina's inertial resistance to her mother's motive force ends abruptly with the news of the battle. The direction, '*her eyes dilating*', may not be something an audience will note directly, but it tells both actor and reader of the sudden awakening, the heart-stopping arrest of attention that is implicit in Raina's 'Ah!' It begins the rapid, rising play of emotions charted in the subsequent directions for expression and action, climaxing in what for audience and reader is sheer comic release in the infectious spectacle of their enthusiasm:

RAINA. Tell me, tell me. How was it? (*Ecstatically*) Oh mother! mother! mother! (*She pulls her mother down on the ottoman; and they kiss one another frantically*.)

Shaw then gives away the essentially musical model for his scenic and rhetorical dynamics in the operatic direction that launches Catherine's description of the battle:

CATHERINE (*with surging enthusiasm*) You cant guess how splendid it is. A cavalry charge! think of that! . . . Cant you see it, Raina: our gallant splendid Bulgarians with their swords and eyes flashing, thundering down like an avalanche and scattering the wretched Serbs and their dandified Austrian officers like chaff. . . .

—a description that, dramatically, sets up the radically opposite, deflationary account of the very same battle by one of its scattered survivors who will soon enter in the dark through those very same balcony shutters.

Having done all he could to make his scripts comfortable for the reader, Shaw often wished for the means to enhance his text as a score for performance. He wrote, in a commentary on the editing of Shakespeare's plays:

But I must repeat that the notation at my disposal cannot convey the play as it should really exist: that is, in its oral delivery. I have to write melodies without bars, without indications of pitch, pace, or timbre, and without modulation, leaving the actor or producer [director] to divine the proper treatment of what is essentially word-music. I turn over a score by Richard Strauss, and envy him his bar divisions, his assurance that his trombone passages will not be played on the triangle, his power of giving directions without making his music unreadable. What would we not give for a copy of Lear marked by Shakespear 'somewhat broader', 'always quieter and quieter,' 'amiably,' or, less translatably, 'mit grossem Schwung und Begeisterung,' 'mit Steigerung,' much less Meyerbeer's 'con esplosione,' or Verdi's *fffff* or *ppppp*, or *cantando* or *parlando*, or any of the things that I say at rehearsal, and that in my absence must be left to the intuitions of some kindred spirit?[5]

No modern editor of *King Lear* is liable to be so foolish as to try to supply what Shaw longs for, nor even the compromise he invents for his own plays. But generations of readers and interpreters have consoled themselves with the thought that so much of the expressive music and drama is already in the words as given. Take the great recognition scene (IV. vii) between Lear, waking from his madness, and his banished daughter Cordelia, where her kneeling for blessing, his attempt to kneel to her, her uncontrollable tears, his touching them (perhaps tasting them), her overwhelming emotion, are all to be read in the words spoken, not least in Cordelia's reiterated, scarcely articulate monosyllabics:

CORDELIA.   O! look upon me, Sir,
   And hold your hand in benediction o'er me.
   No, Sir, you must not kneel.
LEAR.   Pray, do not mock me:
   I am a very foolish fond old man,
   Fourscore and upward, not an hour more or less;
   And, to deal plainly,
   I fear I am not in my perfect mind. . . .
                . . . Do not laugh at me;
   For, as I am a man, I think this lady
   To be my child Cordelia.
CORDELIA.   And so I am, I am.
LEAR. Be your tears wet? Yes, faith. I pray, weep not:
   If you have poison for me, I will drink it.
   I know you do not love me; for your sisters
   Have, as I do remember, done me wrong:
   You have some cause, they have not.
CORDELIA.   No cause, no cause.

To all appearances, there is a world of difference between what we are obliged to do when reading a scene so fully articulated and annotated as Shaw provides in *Arms and the Man* and a scene as it more or less comes down to us from Shakespeare. Arguably, the reading experience for Shaw's successful hybrid of spoken word and descriptive amplification (the latter with its own distinctive pleasures of wit and style) takes us a bit closer to the reading of stories and novels. But is it really less connected to the theatre, less rooted in the conditions of dramatic unfolding in the theatre, than a bare-bones Shakespeare script? The fact is that in both instances the reading that pays off, that provides the most understanding, not only of the play's artistry, but of what is trying to take shape before the eye of the mind, is the reading constantly alert to the *how* of how plays work.

While some conventions that shape the texts we read come from what scribes, printers, and readers have found convenient, others come directly from theatre practice in a given time and place, as absorbed and embodied by the playwrights. The contingency of such convention is brought into relief when a playwright, departing from an established practice, consciously attempts to substitute an alternative whose formalized character calls attention to itself. Such a playwright is W. B. Yeats, from whom I have lifted the phrase 'eye of the mind'. It appears in *At the Hawk's Well*, Yeats's self-styled 'Play for Dancers', where he brings to a Western audience some of what he saw as the form and style of a type of Japanese theatre. For the private spaces where Yeats envisaged the performance of *At the Hawk's Well* and its like, he designed a substitute for the convention of the opening and closing curtain: a black cloth unfolded and refolded by a trio of Musicians, behind which, initially, the well (symbolically) and its uncanny Guardian may be established. Meanwhile the Musicians, singing, evoke the locale and its atmosphere, and the approaching disturbance:

> I call to the eye of the mind
> A well long choked up and dry . . .
> A man climbing up to a place
> The salt sea wind has stripped bare.

The mingling of narration and enactment that this opening then employs, and the musical underscoring, borrow from conventions of Noh theatre; but the unfolding and refolding of the cloth at start and finish is the playwright-poet's invention, one that, if unfamiliar, is readily grasped by analogy, and once established is ready to be used again. The cloth recalls a ubiquitous convention much taken for granted, at least in the West: the rise and fall of the stage curtain. It recalls it even as Yeats departs from it.

Like all conventions, it is subject not only to modification and displacement as here, but also to self-conscious ('theatricalist') exploitation. In Peter Handke's *Kaspar,* for example, where the entering audience has found the front curtain already open, what might be called the action begins as the clown-like figure representing Kaspar Hauser struggles to find and get through the slit in a closed curtain-like backdrop—a sort of birth struggle. At the other end of a performance, in Genet's *The Blacks*, where conventionally 'the Curtain Falls', the black velvet curtain that has served as a backdrop rises to reveal a play going on behind the play we have been seeing, now, as it were, beginning again. Perhaps most tellingly, at the very end of Jean Giraudoux's *The Trojan War Will Not Take Place,* where it appears that the war has been successfully averted and the final curtain begins to come down, it is arrested in mid-descent as the unforeseen incident that will after all trigger the war erupts—and then it rises again '*little by little*' as the consequences go out of control.

In earlier theatres without a curtain to close off the world of the play, other means developed to punctuate and underline the ending, some of them persisting as genetic legacies in texts of much later date. The *exodos*, the final song and recessional of the chorus in Athenian tragedy, served such a function, as did its Elizabethan-theatre analogue, the dead march that empties the stage, like the funeral procession, punctuated by cannon fire, that bears off Hamlet's body and the several other corpses littering the scene. In lighter fare, a celebratory dance and/or a joyous exit to a wedding feast signalled the end of a large body of hymeneal comedy from the classic period forward, as did the *plaudite*, when the actors turn to the audience and ask for its noisy approval. A regular thing in Roman comedy, Shakespeare adapts it in the last words of *As You Like It, All's Well that Ends Well, A Midsummer Night's Dream*, and *The Tempest.* 'Give me your hands, if we be friends,' says Puck; and Prospero pleads, 'But release me from my bands | With the help of your good hands.' For later theatres, with and without a front curtain, playwrights would contrive a final flourish by bringing all the cast on stage for a punctuating tableau (stage picture), or by having an actor step forward with a sententious moral, preferably a sententious moral that restates the name of the play. Oscar Wilde happily reverts to this antiquated cadence when he gives Jack Worthing the last word in his comedy of names, *The Importance of Being Earnest.* As the various happy couples embrace, Lady Bracknell reproves him: 'My nephew, you seem to be displaying signs of triviality.'

JACK: On the contrary, Aunt Augusta, I've now realized for the first time in my life the vital Importance of Being Earnest.

TABLEAU

CURTAIN

With title, tableau, *and* curtain as his signals of closure, either Wilde is absurdly overdoing it, or just taking no chances.

We read the dramatic literature of the past because, fortunately, it is not only contemporary plays that prove to be the most profound or interesting. And there is no gainsaying the fact that drama that is profound and interesting long ago lost its claim to be understood *sui generis* and has instead been co-opted into the imperium of Literature. That shrewd and weighty critic Samuel Johnson, in the Preface to his edition of Shakespeare (1765), roundly declares, 'A dramatic exhibition is a book recited with concomitants that increase or diminish its effect. Familiar comedy is often more powerful in the theater than on the page; imperial tragedy is always less. . . . A play read affects the mind like a play acted.'[6] The context of Dr Johnson's argument here is that in neither venue is the play likely to be mistaken for reality, involving real constraints of time and space, and that therefore arbitrary rules like the so-called unities of time and place are beside the point. But his formal definition with its logical priorities rolls over both history and practice in the making of a dramatic text, not to mention any unresolved ambivalence in the claims upon it for a twofold service. And yet history and practice are bound to have left their deep traces on what we read and on what constitutes the play. What we find when we read is, among other things, a buried archaeology of how plays were designed to work in material circumstances that are no longer current or self-evident. To take a prosaic example, in plays from Dr Johnson's era and after, from a theatre using movable scenery with masking wings and painted flats run in from the sides, we may find a pattern of brief scenes ('front scenes') with two or three people, set in a shallow space, alternating with populous scenes in large, even spectacular settings using much of the depth of the stage, scenes that require some preparation. In such cases, the path of the drama in its unfolding is not simply the reflection of an organic inner logic, but a result that accommodates the bygone conditions of scenic representation. The result may *also* be a triumph of plotting and dramatic rhythm, where the particulars, as in much fine art, are 'overdetermined'. Yet, keeping an eye on the practicalities—as the playwright was obliged to do—can add considerably to a present understanding, general and particular, of the playwright's art and of what is achieved in the individual play. Consequently it too has a role, not all-important perhaps, but quite important, in practising that seemingly paradoxical but richly rewarding skill,

'THE ART OF READING PLAYS.'

2

Beginnings

A strange thing happens in the opening of *Translations* (1980), Brian Friel's touchstone historical play. The play is set in nineteenth-century Ireland, and the scene is the classroom of what was known as a 'hedge school', a former barn and stable, shortly before the evening session is supposed to begin. Manus, assistant to his father the schoolmaster, is patiently teaching a young woman, Sarah, with a disabling speech impediment, to speak. Jimmy, an unwashed perpetual scholar in his sixties, sits apart, happily reading Homer and occasionally quoting passages in Greek, supplying his own translations and commentary. Well into the scene (five pages into the text), they are joined by another young woman, Maire, also a student, bringing the milk. As she flops down, worn out with the toil of the harvest, Jimmy addresses her in Latin:

JIMMY: *Esne fatigata?*
MAIRE: *Sum fatigatissima.*
JIMMY: *Bene! Optime!*
MAIRE: That's the height of my Latin. Fit me better if I had even that much English.
JIMMY: English? I thought you had some English?
MAIRE: Three words. Wait—there was a spake I used to have off by heart. What's this it was?
  (*Her accent is strange because she is speaking a foreign language and because she does not understand what she is saying.*)
'In Norfolk we besport ourselves around the maypoll.' What about that!
MANUS: Maypole.

Jimmy then admits (forgetting for the moment his Latin and Greek), 'Sure you know I have only Irish like yourself'—except, he adds, for one English word: 'Bo-som.'[1]

This revelation comes as something of a shock for both audience and reader. It comes after considerable conversation in English, including Sarah's triumphant struggle to get out a sentence ('My name is Sarah'), and after the audience, without having to give it much thought, has had a chance to acclimatize to the world on the stage, and settle in. Revising what we have taken to be the rules that govern and define this stage world is disorienting.

We have innocently assumed that the languages we hear are the languages the characters are supposed to be speaking. If we hear English, then they are speaking English. And yet, if the play were set in rural France or a town in Norway we would have assumed, with no indication to the contrary, that the characters are supposed to be speaking French or Norwegian, not English. The shock requires the revision, not only of the stage world and the rules of representation that shape and govern our relation to it, but of the thinking that led us to assume, with no indication to the contrary, that persons conversing in the depths of rural Ireland in 1833 would not be speaking in Irish.

As the shock is absorbed, the rules of representation are being reset. In this revised stage world, words spoken in English—even with a noticeable dialect inflection (e.g. 'a spake')—can represent either English or Irish. We will hear spoken Irish only in an etymological discussion of Gaelic place names whose standardization and Anglification is part of the task of the British military surveyors who have suddenly appeared in the district. The rule on representing *both* languages as English yields notable dramatic dividends in Friel's hands, apart from its novelty. It supplies humour and insight where Manus's brother, adept in both worlds and the mapping detachment's translator, deliberately mistranslates the military commander's inept explanation of the project to the community, neutralizing his gross insensitivities. And it provides the vehicle for one of the transcendent love scenes in modern drama (looked at later), between Maire and the English Lieutenant Yolland, neither of whom knows the other's language, but whose minds and hearts, converging, understand each other brilliantly.

2.1. DEFINING THE STAGE/ENLISTING THE AUDIENCE

As Friel's variation makes plain, the first order of business for any play is to define the stage. Put another way, the start of a play is a first pass at inventing and evoking the play world, though not exactly from scratch. Among other things, the serious playwright will invent with an eye to the actual stage of the time, with its practical limitations and known capabilities—unless, like a Shelley in *Prometheus Unbound* or Byron in *Cain* or Hardy in *The Dynasts*, he or she intends to write for a theatreless theatre of the mind. Writing, he said, for 'mental performance', Hardy sought a freedom of treatment 'that was denied where the material possibilities of stagery had to be rigorously remembered'.[2] Be that as it may, *any* stage, platform, or arena, whatever its physical arrangements and the demands of stagery, remains open to endless possibility, like a painter's blank canvas or a sculptor's lump of clay.

A corollary is that every play, however modest its claims, defines or redefines the stage in a general sense; not just as a locale—'*the Jones's living room*'—but as a medium and a practice. For one thing, no body of dramatic conventions, no set of audience expectations about content or representation, will of itself *wholly* accomplish the work of definition in any given play. But beyond that, the most compelling and inventive plays will enlarge, redefine, the realized capabilities of the stage so memorably that the practice of playwriting can never be the same again. The creative impulse either to depart from what has been done before or to add something to it is not special to any particular era or culture; but it is perhaps more to the fore, more overt and compulsive, in the modern and contemporary theatre than in most earlier (and more tradition-bound) times and places, characteristically taking the form of a project to undo and remake the relation between the stage and the audience. Audiences themselves, traditional and otherwise, are torn, between the perpetual appetite for novelty, and the tendency to take comfort in familiarity.

Initiating the play world is also initiating the audience into the play world. But then the question arises, when and where does that process begin? When and where, for that matter, does a play begin? The easy answer is: with the first things we see or the first things we hear from the stage, signalled traditionally by the rising of the curtain. But as we have already noticed, such signals—like the lowering of the houselights, or the three thumps on the hollow stage of the Comédie-Française—are far from universal, and less and less to be counted on in modern performance. The playwright Arthur Laurents recently explained in an interview why he loves musicals: 'It's one of the few forms of drama left in our theater where there is a curtain, which is a mystery. You don't know what's behind it. This bloody thing today of no curtain is giving away half of the taking you into another world.'[3] Nevertheless, curtain or no curtain, the process of defining the stage, that is, specifying and evoking the world of the play, may have already begun. It may have begun, even if one discounts real-world conditions, with descriptive reviews, seductive advertising, word of mouth, prior knowledge of the playwright's predilections or the theatre company's, all going to create prior expectations. For one thing, both the reading and viewing audiences are almost certain to come armed with the title of the play. In the instance of *Arms and the Man*, many of those encountering its initial scene would have brought with them the title's allusion to the opening line of Vergil's *Aeneid*, where love and war compete in an age of epic heroism—a suggestive frame of reference. For another thing, there is generally a playbill or a programme for the audience to peruse before the lights dim, often specifying the place and time of the action and listing the cast—the equivalent of the dramatis personae that usually precedes the opening scene of the printed text and begins to populate the void. That these count for something is made plain in two modern instances. In one, Anthony Shaffer's mystery thriller *Sleuth* (1970), whose plot uses disguise and impersonation, the story is that the playbill had to be redone and a false actor's name inserted because the cast list gave away the disguise and so undercut the effect of the revelation. (The subsequent printed editions give false 'original cast' lists.) In another, Michael Frayn's farce *Noises Off* (1982), where the action entails the staging of a play called *Nothing On*, the programme in a recent revival came in two booklets, each complete with cast list, actor biographies, (cod) advertisements, etc. Indeed, *Nothing On* was the title revealed (on an inner curtain) when the front curtain rose. Which, then, was going to be the 'real' play? That is, what was the organizing premiss of this play world, its ontological order?

As for titles, they too reveal their power, that is their predisposing effect, in instances of misunderstanding and contretemps. There is no qualitative misunderstanding in the title *Nothing On*, which has the generic ring of bedroom farce; or for that matter in *Noises Off*, a conventional stage direction which here promises a play whose subject is theatre, and probably theatre askew. But both Yeats and Shaw write about the mistakes of those who thought that Ibsen's *A Doll's House* (in its first proper English production) would be a nice family play, and brought the children; and there is a theatre legend about the unhappiness of those South Asians who came to see Kenneth Tynan's sexually explicit review, *O Calcutta!*—with its francophone pun in the title (*O quel cul tu as!*)—in search of nostalgia. Titles work in many different ways: as advertising a celebrity subject (*The Tragedy of Hamlet, Prince of Denmark*; *Antony and Cleopatra*; *The Man of Mode, or, Sir Fopling Flutter*, the last not the hero of the comedy, but its principal novelty attraction); as an epitome of the whole (*Much Ado about Nothing*; *Heartbreak House*; *Waiting for Godot*); or even as a teaser, asking to be illustrated and/or explained (*The Importance of Being Earnest*; *Life is a Dream*). In any case, a title is more than a convenience for buying tickets or dropping names; it primes and colours expectation on the way to creating the world of the play.

The transformation of the stage into the play world is not a one-way transaction, nor is it a cerebral exercise, all logical inference. However skeletal the means employed in text and production, and even where these are deliberately anti-illusionistic—that is, where the stage is supposed to remain the stage—the work of definition and transformation is accomplished for the most part by evocation, and by enlisting the audience in what is really a joint enterprise. The opening of *Hamlet*, which we already have glanced at, written for a generalized stage that is mostly bare platform, acknowledges the imperative in being designed, above all, to capture a buzzing, unsettled audience's attention and imagination, starting with that arresting challenge and exchange between extremely nervous sentries:

Enter BARNARDO *and* FRANCISCO, *two Sentinels.*
BARNARDO. Who's there?
FRANCISCO. Nay, answer me. Stand and unfold yourself.
BARNARDO. Long live the King!

It is significant of the tension that the first to challenge is the relief. Barnardo, corrected, then gives what passes for the password, and with a few more hints in the dialogue, the fraught, uneasy atmosphere of the royal battlements, cold, dark, and lonely, is collaboratively evoked.

What is really at stake is made plain when Shakespeare, daunted for once by the ambition of his enterprise, lays his cards on the table in the Prologue to *The Life of King Henry V*, and appeals directly to the audience. Since he cannot bring the thing itself before them—'A kingdom for a stage, princes to act'—but must depend instead on 'this unworthy scaffold' and mere actors to act, he asks that his auditors

> . . . let us, ciphers to this great accompt,
> On your imaginary forces work.
> Suppose within the girdle of these walls
> Are now confin'd two mighty monarchies,
> Whose high upreared and abutting fronts
> The perilous narrow ocean parts asunder:
> Piece out our imperfections with your thoughts;
> .   .   .   .
> For 'tis your thoughts that now must deck our kings . . .

Of course the speaker of this apologetic appeal (originally, according to tradition, Shakespeare himself) manages to infuse it with enough evocative imagery to lead his auditors into the world of the play even as he enlists their active collaboration. He reappears before each succeeding act, as 'Chorus', more evocative narrator and presenter than commentator, supplying continuity between events, effecting the transitions, preparing the scene, and reiterating his collaborative plea to 'Still be kind, | And eche [eke] out our performance with your mind.'⁴ In a different medium—some say the medium Shakespeare here tries to wish into existence—the imaginative dependence is much reduced. In Laurence Olivier's great film of *Henry V*, after an opening in the Elizabethan playhouse with made-up actors and manifestly limited resources, Olivier has the camera and the soundtrack take over the audience's collaborative function, moving the play out of the playhouse, Shakespeare's 'wooden O', and into the natural world, camera-ready, epically expansive, literally displaying what the Prologue wistfully names 'the vasty fields of France'. Yet, in the theatre itself, the modern theatre, the immensely influential Bertolt Brecht would argue for an 'epic theatre' that does not conceal its artifice as performance. Among his models is *Henry V*, Shakespeare's most conspicuous assimilation of epic and dramatic modes, if also a play where exposing the inadequacy of the artifice becomes a stroke of high artifice and of sophisticated co-option in creating the world of the play.

2.2. SETTING THE DEFAULTS/BREAKING THE RULES

No doubt there is a measure of pedantry in making a problem of 'When does a play begin', since the main work of creating the world of the play depends almost invariably on the presence of the characters on the scene. That is certainly so in what is still the normative model for drama in the Western tradition, despite the innovative challenges of Modernism and the example of Non-Western traditions where presentation and representation are often less differentiated. The model is most to the fore in the theatre of mimetic realism that in one form or another dominated the end of the nineteenth century and much of the twentieth. The premiss of such a play, whether it be set among Chekhov's provincial Russian gentry, for example, or Ibsen's middle-class townsmen and professionals, or Noel Coward's urban sophisticates, is that its world will be a convincing simulacrum of some sufficiently recognizable part of our own, without that evident strangeness or departure from the common rule that calls attention to an invented or pointedly exotic otherness. But as in any play, naturalistic or not, establishing its world in terms of when and where is only part of the story. And that is so even where the wish to replicate the familiar surfaces of life means that style, selection, the rules of action, of thought and behaviour, are supposed to remain invisible, tasteless like water (to use a favourite Shavian analogy) because it is always in our mouth.

The opening of the play addresses a set of implicit questions and sets the defaults. How do people speak in this world? In measure and rhyme? In ordinary prose? In dialect? To music? Are they allowed to express their deepest thoughts and most powerful feelings in commensurate language? Or is speech channelled into witty 'persiflage', a highly stylized polite exchange; or limited to the banalities and commonplaces of everyday; or to an impoverished monosyllabic street lexicon? Are gestures large, movements sweeping, and attitudes eloquent, as befits heroic and ideal figures? Or are they constrained and suggestive only, appropriate to cramped lives, cold climates, and domestic interiors? Is this a world keyed to laughter, where the consequences of misbehaviour are unlikely to be serious? Or to romance? Or to suffering? Is it an observable social world, where the drama lies in complex interaction? Or is it the projection of an inner world of feelings and desires? Or a parabolic world of embodied ideas and arguments? As these questions are answered, they establish the law and logic—perhaps the grammar and syntax would be a better analogy—of the stage world. And as they are answered, they launch whole sets of expectations about what is to come, and about what would be 'in keeping'—a phrase from the practice of painting—and what would not. Some of these expectations are clustered in what are thought of as 'genres', like Comedy, Tragedy, Melodrama. But some are better thought of as belonging to a 'mode' or a 'key'. Expectations, however, are precisely the stuff that the playwright has to work with: promoting them, teasing them, deceiving them, and finally disappointing or fulfilling them, though often in ways unexpected. What is called plot is usually a matter of anticipation and deferral, resistance and resolution, within a framework of managed expectation.

But since no play that is wholly predictable is likely to make it to a second night, freshness and interest have been sought, not only within the rules, but often by pressing their limits. And in a revolutionary or iconoclastic climate, like that of Modernism, breaking the rules, or standing them on their heads, can become a framework of expectation in its own right. And yet, even apart from such considerations, there is a feature of drama, all drama, that is naturally subversive of a static or stable definition of the world of the play. Inherent in the form of the drama is the possibility, indeed the expectation, of transformation: a transformation of the situation of the personages as we originally find them; a transformation of state, in the audience no less than in the personages, from ignorance to knowledge, from innocence to experience, from desire to fulfilment (or loss). Transformation is what happens between the beginning and the end of a play as a temporal, progressive form, except perhaps where that form is called on to represent a world in which nothing much happens. Such is the case in *Waiting for Godot* (at least as it concerns Vladimir and Estragon), where the second act substantially repeats the first with variations, and the end takes you to the prospect of beginning again. But then, *Godot*'s inertial subversion is a case in point. If transformation is something that is expected to happen *within* the limits and choices and traditions that define the particular world of a play, within the premises that create and confine our expectations, why not transformation of the premises themselves?

Bringing the rules into play, as in *Translations*, even in some instances challenging the very idea of such rules, can happen in endless ways. Let me note several. One is by a change in midcourse, or more likely towards the end of the play, through a sudden and unexpected shift in key; another is by purposeful mystification, a deliberately ambiguous or even deceptive opening that defers a stable definition of the stage; a third is by breaking the rule about rules, a subversion of all expectation and dramatic logic except the expectation that anything goes.

2.3. MODULATIONS

A shift in key is what occurs in the last-minute darkening of the world of Shakespeare's *Love's Labour's Lost*, a world of elaborate wit and high artifice, games of courtship and romantic expectation, where a sudden and unexpected messenger of death breaks the genre premises and alters the logic of the ending. As one of the lovers says, 'Our wooing doth not end like an old play; | Jack hath not Jill.' And when he is told that there still might be the prospect of a comedy (marriage) ending after a twelvemonth of penitential mourning, he replies, 'That's too long for a play' (V. ii. 864–8).

The title of *Love's Labour's Lost* can be taken as fair warning, however; and so can the subtitle of Friedrich Dürrenmatt's *The Visit of the Old Lady* (1956), 'A Tragic Comedy'. Neither rubric is self-explanatory, but both make sense in retrospect; and both call attention to the shift in key that will transform the world of the play. That world in *The Visit*, as established in the opening, has the character of a broad, almost cartoonish satire: a hapless town of venal and platitudinous stereotypes being put to the test by the visit of an egregiously rich and outlandishly grotesque *Alten Dame* and her bizarre entourage. But by the climactic event of the last act, the community's ritual murder of a gradually transformed and transfigured fellow townsman, the comic world has given place to a tragic scene of the utmost seriousness and power, impervious to the now deeply ironized satire. In a play whose progressive logic is in transformations, transformations both elevating and degrading, purging and corrupting, from the physical scene that represents Place to the character and appearance of its inhabitants, the most momentous transformation is in the genre of the play itself.

Other instances of a sometimes radical change in key come at the end of Frank Wedekind's once unproducible *Spring Awakening* (1891) and Shaw's duly sanctified *Saint Joan* (1923). Wedekind's play of youthful oppression, rebellion, and tormented sexuality, of parental and educational failure and adolescent tragedy, establishes itself in a generally realistic if comically inflected mode, with a few episodes of broad satire. The play ends, however, with a peripatetic corpse in a cemetery, its head tucked underneath its arm, talking to itself. Moritz, the corpse, a suicide, has just failed to persuade his erstwhile friend, Melchior, driven by remorse and desperation, to join him. He is forestalled by the sudden appearance of an otherwise unidentified 'Man in a Mask', speaking for life and guiltless moral autonomy. In this last scene, the world on the stage has shifted from objective, mimetic representation, to a subjective world, where inner crisis, ambivalence, and internal argument are projected expressionistically and fantastically, in theatrically concrete images and actions, in a tone less tragic than macabre—at once funny, grim, and sad.

Saint Joan follows the model of the chronicle history play, whose benchmark in English is Shakespeare, dramatizing notable events in the life and death of its protagonist and evoking her fifteenth-century world. In Shaw's hands, the play raises both world-historical and timeless issues; but for all its imaginative invention and discursive reach, it takes care not to contradict the historical record, and makes use of authentic costuming and decor. While its dialogue avoids antiquated locutions, is modern and idiomatic, and sometimes teeters on the edge of anachronism, it thereby gives recognizable life and reality to this imagined historical world and its inhabitants. The play progressively deepens and darkens, following the arc of Joan's own rise and fall, so that the opening scenes, flavoured with medieval farcical comedy and nineteenth-century melodrama, yield to scenes giving voice to the play of historical forces and to the timeless clash of the heretical (or visionary) individual and established institutions. Nowhere, however, does the play break the rules of a world governed by ordinary cause and effect, even in representing what some, in the play and out, are prone to label miraculous. The great trial scene, which concludes with the report of Joan's offstage immolation, is the most conscientiously historicist, lifting whole passages from the record, and achieving, in Joan's heroism and humanity, notable tragic power and pathos. With a final hint that perhaps all is not over with Joan even in this world, her death would seem to be the fitting conclusion to the play. But then Shaw provides a gloss, an extra scene that he labels an Epilogue, where Joan and a parade of other spirits and emanations (including an English 'goddam' who gets a day off from hell every year, and a dignified visitor in the laughable dress of the twentieth century) appear to the French king in his bed and reflect on the fact of the heretic's rehabilitation a quarter of a century after her burning. All are full of praise for the Maid, and visions of her future sanctification bring them all, former friends, enemies, and judges, to their knees—until Joan asks if she should return from the dead as a living woman. Great consternation. All jump to their feet and depart seriatim, once more forsaking her to her radiant solitude and despairing cry: 'O God that madest this beautiful earth, when will it be ready to receive Thy saints? How long, O Lord, how long?'[5] The end of the play has abruptly shifted from historically grounded action and discourse to satiric fantasy, making free with space and time. 'Do not', Shaw wrote to the actor playing the former Dauphin, 'be too tied to naturalism in the scene, which will have something of the insanity of a dream.'[6] The shift, from a fundamentally realistic premiss to symbolic extravaganza, from life-and-death contentions with tragic results to satire without direct consequence, annoyed many critics as characteristic 'Shavian' mischief, spoiling things for an audience that has been deeply moved and sufficiently instructed by Joan's heroic martyrdom. But for the playwright and the play, the shift in key completes the story of the troublemaking heretic as saint, and brings home to an audience only too ready to congratulate itself on its happy superiority to the benighted past its own ongoing complicities.

2.4. PUZZLE PICTURES

Mystification—teasing the audience (and the reader) with a deliberately ambiguous or deceptive opening—can add to the pleasure and interest, and indeed is typically comic in effect. It is also typically modern, amalgamating Modernist games concerning theatricality with cognitive uncertainty concerning what is really real. What is puzzling or deceptive in such openings is not a matter of plot—an unknown family relationship, or the meaning of a cryptic message—but rather the frame of reference for what is unfolding before us, the *kind* of reality it belongs to and how that defines the stage. The game is one Tom Stoppard loves to play, cognitive uncertainty having much in common with the ambiguities of natural language that inform his dialogue and provision his wit. Witness the opening of *Jumpers* (1972). With the voice of an unseen MC, the sound of audience applause, a failed spotlit performance by someone identified as a star of musical theatre, giving way to a striptease by a lady in a swing flashing between darkness and darkness, the scene is not likely to be read by the theatre audience as belonging to the pedestrian world of a philosopher's flat; not even when the philosopher himself appears, to complain about the noise. And then there is the opening of Stoppard's mischievously titled *The Real Thing* (1982), a play about love and marriage. The fraught opening scene, in the living room of Max and Charlotte, enacts the collapse of a marriage with no clue as to its belonging to a play within the play. Though we assume otherwise, it is *not* 'the real thing'. As far as defining the stage, it is deception rather than ambiguity. Ambiguity enters with the second scene, in the living room of the playwright and Charlotte, his actress wife; for it takes a little time for audience and reader to pick up the clues and sort out the relationships, not just of the characters, but within the structure of reality embracing these two scenes, each rendered in the convincing common idiom of domestic realism. Having mistakenly accepted the first scene as really real and put that first collaborative task of defining the stage behind us, it is hard to readjust. And even after the satisfaction of sorting it all out, we are likely to remain residually mistrustful, as indeed we should be, given the shifts in and out of performance in this particular play world, which is partly a world of the theatre.

Uncertainty about the character and laws of the play world surfaces as early as the opening, '*in a place without any visible character*', of Stoppard's first success, *Rosencrantz and Guildenstern Are Dead* (1966). Two Elizabethans (Rosencrantz and Guildenstern) are passing the time by tossing coins. Before they stop, the toss has turned up heads ninety-two times in a row. Faced with this fact, Rosencrantz and Guildenstern are in the position of the audience—trying to find the logic of a universe in which such things are likely to happen. That the world of the play is the world of *Hamlet*, seen from the wings as it were, is a lifeline for the audience, but not for the hapless protagonists, who haven't been there before, don't know the plot, and remain mired in the apparent arbitrariness. In *Arcadia* (1993), Stoppard's masterpiece to date, duplicity gives way to duality. The stage world is rendered, in successive, alternating scenes, as two times in the same room a century and a half apart. There are artefacts that remain and function in both times, and echoes and cross-currents in the dialogue and elsewhere. The creation of a stage world that allows such intercut presences means that the reader and viewer sees as reality what the inhabitants of the later period can only grasp, misconstrue, as history. But for the poignant last scene, in a bold stroke of theatre poetry that pays off beyond all reasonable expectation, couples from the two times, blind to each other, are on the stage simultaneously, in the same room, dancing to the same music. This radical break with the premises that have so far governed the play, its rules of representation, comes off as the revelation of another logic, a higher logic perhaps, consonant with thematic concerns: about loss and recurrence in the pattern of things; about iterated algorithms in a 'geometry of nature'; and how 'the unpredictable and the predetermined unfold together to make everything the way it is',[7] which is not a bad description of the progressive form of a play.

2.5. *DÉMONTAGE*

Breaking the rule about rules, a radical subversion of *all* expectation and dramatic logic, has an honoured place in the history of the Modernist avant-garde. It can be seen as avant-garde thinking merely pushed to its logical extreme, following the rigorous injunction to go beyond one's predecessors, to 'make it new'. But so fundamental a rejection of *any* ordering principle goes beyond the commandment of radical innovation. It is a declaration of war on art itself. Such was the programme of Dada, the collection of artistic bomb throwers who mounted performances in the purlieus of the Great War, and of their precocious progenitor Alfred Jarry in his prodigy of irreverence, *Ubu*

Roi. The legacy of their challenge to dramatic logic, including the very premiss of this chapter, that the first duty of a play is to establish the premisses of its stage world, may be found, qualified and modified, in various successors: in those aspects of Brecht's practice of 'estrangement' that challenge dramatic illusion; in Peter Handke's rejectionist *Offending the Audience*; in the brilliant inventions of Ionesco's early plays, for better or worse labelled 'Absurdist'.

The first of these Ionesco plays, *The Bald Soprano* (1950), is a case in point, starting with its irrelevant title, the product, according to Ionesco, of an actor's slip of the tongue. The play opens in what appears to be the most unremarkable of settings, evoking the most ordinary of dramatic worlds, the theatre of domestic realism. In the printed text, the stage directions underline the banality of the scene in the reiterated emphasis on its Englishness, telegraphing the view that the ordinary, in sufficient concentration and under attentive scrutiny, can be revealed as bizarre, even monstrous.

SCENE: *A middle-class English interior, with English armchairs. An English evening. Mr. Smith, an Englishman, seated in his English armchair and wearing English slippers, is smoking his English pipe and reading an English newspaper, near an English fire. He is wearing English spectacles and a small gray English mustache. Beside him, in another English armchair, Mrs. Smith, an Englishwoman, is darning some English socks.*

The giveaway comes next, after we (as audience) have a chance to take the scene in:

A long moment of English silence. The English clock strikes 17 English strokes.[8]

At this point, the assumptions invited by the ordinariness of the scene are shattered; and the one-sided dialogue that commences does not restore confidence:

MRS. SMITH: There, it's nine o'clock. We've drunk the soup, and eaten the fish and chips, and the English salad. The children have drunk English water. We've eaten well this evening. That's because we live in the suburbs of London and because our name is Smith.

MR. SMITH (*continues to read, clicks his tongue.*)

It is not only the woodenness of Mrs Smith's speech and the disconnect between the clock and her report, but it is also its blatant crudity as exposition that push it into comedy. Neither the Smiths nor the dramaturgy so far can be taken seriously. But the assault on the rule of rules, on anything that could pass for the logic of this stage world, or logic *in* this stage world, is just beginning. The clock will strike through the scene with arbitrary impertinence, filling silences and underlining speeches, and including a moment (after successive bursts of seven and three strokes) where the stage directions read, '*The clock doesn't strike*' (p. 11), and another, where '*The clock strikes as much as it likes*' (p. 19).

Ionesco subtitled *The Bald Soprano* an '*Anti-Pièce*', that is, an *Anti-Play*, and he describes his vertigo during the writing, the panicked feeling that his couch, with him lying in it, would 'founder in the Void.'[9] His ambition, he said was to *démonter*, that is to derail and/or dismantle, the theatre. His inspiration, notoriously, was a manual for learning English, and his sudden epiphany on the mad quality of the phrase lists and model dialogues when taken on their own, detached from their pedagogic function. Further, he discerned in their inanity a distillation of the stultifying vacuity of conventional bourgeois life and culture, including, of course, the art it countenanced. He saw his anti-play as a smack in the eye, as disengaging the gearbox of the theatre mechanism even as it exhumed the grotesque and the monstrous under the banalities we carry round and take for granted every day.[10]

Ionesco's assault on the theatre mechanism entails a direct assault on some of its hoariest conventions, but also a subversion of the logical basis of coherence in the manufacture of stage worlds. *The Bald Soprano* offers an extended parody of the classical recognition scene, when Donald and Elizabeth Martin, a long-married couple who, among other things, arrive together, live in the same room, sleep in the same bed, and boast a daughter named Alice with one red eye and one white eye, discover their relationship and fall into each other's arms. Only then are we informed by the maid that actually Donald's Alice has a white right eye and a red left eye, whereas Elizabeth's has a red right eye and a white left one, with the result that 'all of Donald's system of deduction collapses'. As for inductive logic, Mrs Smith pronounces, after three futile trips to the door, 'Experience teaches us that when one hears the doorbell ring it is because there is never anyone there' (p. 23); a conclusion whose validity she defends in the face of a fourth ring when there is somebody there, on the grounds that 'the fourth time does not count' (p. 25).

The assault on formal logic and the assault on anything that can pass for a delimiting rule of this stage world go hand in hand, along with a third term in this anti-play's programme of unmaking, the dismemberment of language, reducing it to syllabic nonsense in the vociferous climax. But in an odd way it is the assault on logic, both formal and contingent, that marks the play, and its play world generally, as comedy. For despite the descant of moderation and the voices of earthbound common sense that accompany the egregious obsessives and fantasists of so much of our best comedy, it is the release from logic—the inexorable logic of cause and effect, of act and consequence, of life and death, or of sensible norms and expectations so constraining in ordinary society—that is fundamental to laughter. Whether it is the logic of experience denied—the cartoon survival of the cat flattened by the steamroller, springing back into three dimensions—or logic driven to improbable extremes, as in the runaway Rube Goldberg machinery of bedroom farce, the pleasure and surprise of release from the logic of life in the world produces the sound of explosion.

The challenge to particular rules, like unity of place, or propriety of character, is an accepted thing in the history of the drama, and there is no difficulty in incorporating such a challenge in any number of plays. It is only a matter of writing (or rewriting) the rule. But an assault on the rule of rules, and even on the very idea of transforming the empty stage by means of rules into a fictive world, the world of the play, is quite another thing, far more difficult to bring off in the medium in question. The attempt to do so is nowhere more rigorous and more 'pure' than in Peter Handke's provocatively titled *Offending the Audience* (1966). Like Ionesco's *anti-pièce*, the play or *Sprechstück* (talk piece) denies its identity as a play. But unlike Ionesco, Handke refuses the help of parody and representation. *Offending the Audience* is not the representation of an audience being insulted, but an enactment. Its four speakers address only the actual audience, not each other; and among other things, they declare:

This is no play. . . . You are sharing no experience. . . . You don't have to imagine anything. . . . You don't need to know that this is a stage. You need no expectations. . . . What is the theater's is not rendered unto the theater here. . . . No spark will leap across from us to you. . . . These boards don't signify a world. They are part of the world. These boards exist for us to stand on. This world is no different from yours. . . . You are the subject matter. The focus is on you. . . . The emptiness of this stage is no picture of another emptiness. The emptiness of this stage signifies nothing. . . . This stage represents nothing. It represents no other emptiness. This stage *is* empty. . . . The stage apron is not a line of demarcation. . . . There is no magic circle. There is no room for play here. We are not playing. . . . We have no roles. We are ourselves. We are the mouthpiece of the author. . . . This is not the world as a stage.[11]

The irony is that in its vast litany of negatives, its rigorous, exclusionary permutations declaring what it is not, and despite its final descent into cascades of abusive epithets aimed at the audience in its manifold and/or comprehensive humanity, the piece is at the same time a sustained analysis of great force and intelligence—dialectical, it calls itself—of the fundamentals of the theatrical experience and of drama for performance. While vehemently insisting it is not a play, and systematically naming and depriving its audience of everything that belongs to plays in performance, it joins the company of analytical treatises and metatheatrical pieces emanating from the likes of Aristotle and Molière that have created the language and provided the insights for coming to grips with the nature of drama and its practice. It too is a guide to how plays work.

2.6. THEATRE UNVEILED

If theatre has a primal scene in a proper Freudian sense—a spectacle that takes us back to origins, and perhaps evokes a transgressive shiver at seeing what should not be seen—it is when the World of the Play is unmasked as the theatre itself. Why otherwise, in the days when stage banners were painted all on one side only, was it the gravest of sins for a hapless supernumerary to present the seamy side to the audience? On the other hand, the something risqué and irreverent in dropping the veil of representation has made the so-called illusion break among the hoariest of comic devices, and a voyeuristic, self-reflexive theatre about the theatre is nearly as old as the thing itself. When the play is set in the theatre and is about putting on a play, we have reached some kind of limit.

Reminders that we are in the theatre need not always depend on defining the stage as the stage, however. There is a measure of theatricalization, as we have already seen, in the bare consciousness of the relation between offstage and onstage; in the consciousness, for example, in reading or seeing *Rosencrantz and Guildenstern Are Dead*, that the play we know as *Hamlet* is mostly happening offstage. That characters identified as stage players enter both these worlds, and manage to demonstrate their art, further complicates our pleasures. An interesting hybrid is Leonid Andreyev's once popular theatricalist tragedy, *He Who Gets Slapped* (1915), where everything happens in a circus green room—normally an offstage transitional space, an airlock between the 'real' world and the performance world of slapstick, skill, and danger, the world of art. Here, the circus sounds of the official performance filter in from offstage throughout; but in a reversal of perspective, offstage (the green room) becomes onstage, for the green room is where the real drama plays out, both as conscious performance (by the eponymous clown, 'He Who Gets Slapped') and tragic reality.

When the theatre itself takes on the role of the play world, the giveaway game that the playwright exploits is liable, even at its most farcically entertaining, to problematize more than itself. Like Socratic introspection, such looking into one's innards tends to raise awkward questions—about what is real, what is good, what is knowable, what is art. The playwright among the Moderns who made such theatrical introspection his trademark was Luigi Pirandello, above all in his 'trilogy of the theater in the theater'.[12] But then, Michael Frayn also tries his hand, in his now classic send-up of the lesser stage, *Noises Off*, where one would be hard put to pin down a philosophical implication. The first act—as we learn after the confusing preliminaries already noted—takes place on a stage that represents the stage, disguised as the interior of a modernized country villa. The second act is backstage, or behind the set (the seamy side), before which the play we have just seen in the throes of rehearsal is now being performed. It is a Wednesday matinee out front, and most of the backstage action—romantic entanglements and jealousies among the actors—has to be carried out in pantomime, in concert with the blunders, lapses, wilful sabotage, scrambled entrances and exits, and desperate improvisations that are affecting the 'real' play going forward. The third act, once more seen from the front, is supposed to be the last performance of the same play. It turns into a progressive catastrophe, a demolition derby ending in the collapse of the set, the 'play', and the stage itself. The cast cries beseechingly, 'Curtain!' and the curtain begins to fall:

Except that it jams just above the level of their heads. As one man they seize hold of it and drag it down. A ripping sound. The curtain detaches itself from its fixings and falls on top of them all, leaving a floundering mass of bodies on stage.[13]

At a distant remove in its scale and ambitions, Peter Weiss's *Marat/Sade* (to use its convenient abbreviation) purports to offer a play in an improvised theatre, normally the tiled baths of a lunatic asylum, with the inmates for actors. The scene itself is fixed, unlike that in Frayn's theatre farce, but then unfixed in its nested identities: Revolutionary France at the time of Marat's assassination (1793), centred on the famous scene in Marat's lodgings of Marat in the bath (or rather, on its famous image as painted by David); nested within the Charenton asylum, where the production proceeds under the direction of the Marquis de Sade (1808); nested within the actual present-day theatre where the whole is being witnessed (originally 1964). At the end of the play, the revolutionary mob/the excited inmates/the actors who play them, now on the march, turn their attention to the actual audience (there is a stage audience: the asylum's Director, Coulmier, and his family, who flee their perch as the patients overwhelm the attempts of the staff to restrain them and advance shouting revolutionary slogans). As the imaginary 'fourth wall' between stage and audience threatens to dissolve before the advancing chaos, the signal is given for the curtain to fall.

But that is only a barebones account of the complex functioning of this stage world. The presence onstage of Coulmier and his family and Coulmier's alarmed interruptions point up the dissonances between imperial 1808 and 1793. Revolutionary Paris as the scene of the convergence of Marat in his bath and his assassin, Charlotte Corday, is flexibly multi-local, the stage accommodating both the stationary Marat and a scene of public execution simultaneously. The characterizing disabilities of the principal 'actors'—erotomania, narcolepsy, paranoia, megalomania—mesh appropriately or ironically with their roles. At one point—an episode titled 'Faces of Marat'—the stage takes on the character of a fevered projection from Marat's inner world: a procession of abuse from parents, schoolmaster, figures representing society's institutions, and even such notables as Lavoisier and Voltaire. Elsewhere the stage functions as an extra-temporal forum of ideas, with the Marquis from his directorial tribune (the play, after all, is an emanation from *his* inner world) and Marat (in character) from his position in the bath speaking across the arena in debate. One of the things that makes *Marat/Sade* so interesting dramaturgically—and so useful for a book on how plays work—is that in creating its play world, defining its stage as a medium and an instrument, it incorporates all three of the fundamental dramatic modes. These are *not* the conventional genres, such as comedy, tragedy, romance, but the use of the stage to create a theatre of social interaction and representation; a theatre for psychological projection; and a theatre of ideas.

Despite its complexities as theatre in the theatre, Weiss's representations are in no way bewildering. For all its several levels of purported reality, nested fictions, interactions that would seem to breach the ordering premises, we are never in danger of losing our bearings, of not knowing what is happening to what and where. Wholly at odds with such an outcome is the practice of one of the most theatre-obsessed of post-war playwrights, Jean Genet, in those plays of his that define their milieux as havens of pretence and illusion. The result is at its most disconcerting in *The Blacks* (*Les Nègres*, 1958), where the world of the play is a literal theatre, not so much nested this time within an accepted reality, but seeming or claiming to draw all reality into its blatant artifice. The stage is defined as a playing space in the midst of tiered platforms and a gallery, a disjointed reflection of the presumed actual audience chamber. A stage audience, 'The Court'—black actors in white masks representing the Queen, her Valet, and robed and uniformed officials—occupies a high tier, while below other blacks, mostly in evening clothes, dance around a catafalque heaped with flowers to music from *Don Giovanni*. Costume among the latter group is garishly stagy, and among the Court, superb. The signature of the opening is the incongruous note—the giveaway that says 'theatre'—a shoeshine box beside the solemn catafalque, tan shoes with evening dress, skin showing around the Court's masks, and disturbing orchestrated laughter from the supposed players, one of whom presents the others to the audience (the stage audience *and* the actual audience, indiscriminately). One of the players resists, however, when asked to bow, and Archibald, the Presenter, has to remind her, insistently, 'It's a performance.'

The effect of this exchange, along with other hints, glimpses, innuendoes, is that something is happening or is intended to happen that is *not* a performance; something real, or at least *more* real. The performance, we learn, involves the victim of a ritualized crime—the corpse of a murdered white woman—and the re-enactment of this crime, perhaps requiring a fresh corpse for every performance. The Queen asks anxiously, 'Are they going to kill her?' and has to be reassured: 'But madam . . . (*a pause.*) She's dead!' On another tack, something seems to be happening offstage. There is a capital trial of some sort in progress, black on black, with an imminently expected result. There are hints of an actual covert conspiracy afoot, a disciplined rising threat, with the performance before us (and the Court) no more than a deliberate distraction. At times the 'actors' show more engagement than we expect, speaking as characters, even persons, non-actors with offstage lives, rather than as ritual performers—as in one woman's jealousy and another's pained distress over the seeming involvement of the actor, Village, with the figure represented by 'the Mask', the white woman Village is supposed to have strangled. When obliged to narrate and re-enact her seduction and murder (with a black Uncle Tom in cartoonish skirt and mask as her stand-in), is there not more to Village's fear and fascination than performance? Elsewhere, the actors show less engagement than we might expect, as they give away the pretence—or seem to. After the murder, the others question Village:

ARCHIBALD [the Presenter]. Is it over? Did you have much trouble?
VILLAGE. Same as usual.
SNOW [who has been jealous]. Nothing happened, did it?
VILLAGE. No, nothing. Or, if you prefer, it all went off as usual, and very smoothly.
When Diouf ['the Mask'] entered behind the screen, he kindly offered me a seat.
SNOW. And then?
NEWPORT NEWS [one of the company]. Nothing else. They waited on a bench, off stage, and smiled at each other in amusement.[14]

So then, it is nothing but theatre after all—though we also hear that theatre, where performance is the norm, is more real, less false, than the life outside where performance is the black person's everyday burden and lie.

The net result is something that attempts to keep the audience (actual) unsettled, not just because there are complex layers of reality (or even, for whites, intimations of overt menace), but because the performance frame is constantly shifting, the degrees of sincerity and pretence confounded, along with the structure of the reality that constitutes the stage world. There is at work an almost sadistic determination to destabilize all those judgemental, categorizing certainties used to build up coercive normality and institutionalize injustice in the familiar outside world. In the end, with the catafalque exposed as merely a sheet over two chairs, and with the white Court, first unmasked, and then destroyed in a burlesque massacre, the backdrop rises to reveal a theatre—or a 'reality'—behind the theatre; a repetition or possibly a new beginning:

> . . . *All the Negroes—including those who constituted the Court and who are without their masks—are standing about a white-draped catafalque like the one seen at the beginning of the play. Opening measures of the minuet from Don Giovanni. Hand in hand, Village and Virtue walk toward them, thus turning their backs to the audience. The curtain is drawn.* (p. 128)

In *The Blacks*, Archibald speaks of the theatre as the place where, paradoxically, he and his fellows can escape living in a lie, the daily performance imposed by white society. 'Now, this evening—but this evening only—we cease to be performers, since we are Negroes. On this stage we're like guilty prisoners who play at being guilty' (p. 39). In contrast, performance, not as a counter-poison neutralizing the falsity of the everyday, but as a deeply pervasive and potentially redemptive feature of ordinary life, is the burden of Nikolai Evreinov's *The Main Thing* (1921).[15] Evreinov theorized the existence of a 'theatrical instinct', otherwise an 'instinct of transformation' in human beings, a will to transform life, which is anyway performative—full of role playing to ourselves and others. In its inventive aspects, this instinct resists '*as is*' qualities, the merely necessary and the factual. In the play, the character who frankly identifies himself as the author's spokesman, the *raisonneur*, describes 'the official theater, the actual theater, as a sort of laboratory of illusion'. But life at large—for actors who recognize their calling as 'masters of the art of salvation through illusion'—he pitches as a theatre without encumbrances: 'no sets, no curtain, no footlights, and not a trace of a prompter' (p. 66).

Dr Fregoli preaches his gospel of all the world's a theatre in a play world that is on the whole familiar, as ordinary, even tawdry provincial life, prosaic and limited, depicted within the bounds of mimetic realism. That holds even for the second of the four acts where the stage is defined as the stage of an actual working theatre, with a company engaged in rehearsing a dramatic version of that notable historical romance of pagans and Christians in Nero's Rome, *Quo Vadis?* The action begins before the curtain, with the Director dressing down the Electrician. In the scene that follows—the first attempt at a dress rehearsal on a stage supposedly still bare of scenery—we get bits of the play, the regisseur-adapter's interventions, assorted mishaps, and much backstage rivalry and misbehaviour. When Nero, for example, delivers the line in which he passes judgement on the Christian captive Lygia as 'Too narrow in the hips', Poppaea remarks, '(*with a demonstrative sneer*) Some narrow hips!'

NERO. Sorry, is that your line?
POPPAEA. No, it's my opinion. (p. 60)

Figure 3. Theatre unveiled. The dress rehearsal of *Quo Vadis?* in Nikolai Evreinov's *The Chief Thing*, from the Theatre Guild production, New York 1926, directed by Philip Moeller 'with the coöperation of the Author . . . Settings and Costumes by Sergi [*sic*] Soudeikine' (playbill). On stage with the costumed Actors at their revels, but in contemporary dress, are (at right) the Director (Edward G. Robinson) and the Prompter (Lee Strasberg); and (at left) the Electrician and 'the Actor Who Plays the Lover' but who claims that his costume won't fit.

At several points, the theatre folk turn on the (actual) audience—thrust into the role of interlopers at rehearsal. The net result is as hilarious as any of the classic burlesques of the theatre in the theatre (Buckingham's *The Rehearsal* (1671); Sheridan's *The Critic* (1779); Frayn's *Noises Off*). But it is also here that Evreinov's Messianic alter ego enlists some of the actors for his venture in the theatre without walls. They are to be a missionary force, Doctors Without Walls, to bring healing and perhaps transformation to unhappy lives through illusion, by acting a role: as jovial companion; as romantic lover; as cheerful and flirtatious serving maid—parts that correspond to the actors' theatrical *métiers*.

The subsequent acts are in the boarding house where Fregoli's unwitting patients reside (he himself combines a producer's role with that of a record salesman who travels).[16] The relocation is also a redefinition: the boarding-house world, a microcosm of the ordinary and the actual, is also no less a theatre. At one point Evreinov unblushingly has the supposed record salesman play the familiar speech from Shakespeare's *As You Like It*, 'All the world's a stage', on the boarding-house gramophone. Before we are through, however, the prosaic rooming house is physically transformed, on the eve of Lent and the end of the players' contract, into a phantasmal Carnival scene. Moreover, for the occasion, the theatre proper—cast and management from the *Quo Vadis?* production, many still in costume—joins the 'real world' scene, carrying the fusion one step further. Meanwhile, the missionary task force, including Fregoli, their work mostly done, are revealed in their true character and costume, as the principal figures in that archetype of theatre, *commedia dell'arte*: Harlequin, Columbine, Pierrot, and the Doctor from Bologna. Among the many plays that drop the mask by defining the world of the play as the place of performance, no play goes further than Evreinov's *The Main Thing* to turn the tables, and stake its claim for the theatre as nothing less than the whole of life.

I began with the opening of *Translations* because of the shock that makes us conscious of what we generally take for granted: how play and audience work together to establish the world of the play amid the endless possibilities that lie in wait in the undefined stage. Since that collaborative act has to be what I called 'the first order of business', the whole matter of beginnings came to the fore, and proved more problematic than one would think. So did the matter of 'expectations', about which there will be more to say later on. But already we see that expectations may lead us on, or lead us astray, whether auto-induced or foisted upon us, much as in Dickens's novel on the subject. Moreover, it soon appeared that even the rules of representation—the laws that govern each particular play world as initially established—are not beyond breach of contract and sleight of hand, through shifts of key, sustained ambiguity, even wholesale rejection of rule. In the last category, the only surviving rule would seem to be (Handke's proscriptive negativity excepted) that of the Abbaye of Theleme: *fay ce que voudras*, or as the theatre translates it, *Anything Goes*.

2.7. WORLDS WITHIN

When it comes to uncovering the working premisses of an art, self-exposure can be at least as effective as anarchic assault (the two are not unrelated), as we saw in those ventures into reflexivity where the world of the play is the theatre itself, and performance is 'performance'. Among such plays, Peter Weiss's *Marat/Sade* claimed particular attention, not only for its self-conscious theatricalism, but for its layered deployment of dramatic resources in creating its complex stage world, so that it offers a veritable three-in-one compendium of what I proposed as three primary dramatic modes. To repeat, these are: where the stage—and thus the play world—is defined as primarily a locus of social interaction; where it becomes a space for psychological projection; and where it functions as an arena of ideas. The first is much to the fore in the varieties of realistic representation that have dominated the theatre in more recent times, but one can fairly say it pervades the broad stream of Western drama, including the play worlds of such diverse strains as Roman and Restoration comedy; the *capa y spada* drama of contemporary dress and mores in the Spanish Golden Age; Elizabethan domestic drama and social satire (e.g. Ben Jonson); historical drama and costume melodrama of high politics and low intrigue. For all its latitude, it is what 'holding the mirror up to nature' is usually taken to mean, and what various audiences have long regarded as normative.

Much of the discussion in later chapters draws on drama in this mode and how it operates, notably in 'The Action of Words'. 'Reading Meanings', on the other hand, takes up, not just the general question of how plays make themselves intelligible and 'meaningful', but also the special case where ideas, metaphorically embodied or dialectically engaged, configure the world of the play. That leaves the use of the stage as a space, a holographic platform as it were, for psychological projection, where the play (or part of it) functions as a form of psychodrama. And it is that way of defining the stage and the world of the play that I wish to conclude with here.[17]

Theatre is physical, its means material, belonging to the order of bodies, objects, things. When a play dramatizes inner states, inner conflicts, it does so through corporeal means, principally the speech and behaviour of actors, and the cues for doing so are what we find in the script. The skills that can realize such inner life and commotion on the stage are what we have come to value most highly in the actor. Moreover, the skills to read each other's latent thought and feeling are what we, the potential audience, practise every day of our lives in the everyday world. In both venues, the soul (or some part of it) emerges socially and indirectly, through expressive (or dissembling) signals and clues. The playwright, however, also has the option of rendering the inner, psychological realm directly, still with the proviso, here paradoxical in the extreme, that it be rendered through 'practicable' means. That which belongs to the interior world, to the immaterial subject—conflict, division, memory, desire, imagination, state of mind—can be objectified, materialized, and projected, to constitute the world of the play.

How the psychological is actualized naturally reflects how it is understood. One view, the self as a contested ground for metaphysical forces and divided faculties, found externalized embodiment in such early-modern 'Morality Plays' as *Wisdom* (also known as *Mind, Will, and Understanding*, fifteenth century) and other plays with a debt to the common trope of a contention between the Virtues and Vices.[18] In *Wisdom*, 'Anima as a mayde', in symbolic white and black, shares the stage at various times with her own five senses, and with the three powers of the soul, Mind, Will, and Understanding. These in turn—when led astray by that dangerous gallant Lucifer—bring on stage their own sets of liveried retainers or attributes, such as Mind's Sturdiness (stubbornness), Malice, Hastiness, Discord. The didactic purpose and action of the play is incorporated in the discursive instruction of Anima, the soul, by the figure of Wisdom, or Christ. The illustrative drama is that of the temptation and fall of the soul's three powers, and the soul's twofold redemption, as at first from original sin, so now from commissioned sin, through repentance and grace.[19]

But projecting an unruly self-division through multiple figuration can serve a very different set of psychological assumptions, so that the Morality Play's use of the stage has its counterpart in the age of psychoanalysis, as in some of O'Neill's experiments for example, or with less fuss in Brian Friel's *Philadelphia, Here I Come!* (1965), in the doubling of the protagonist, Gar O'Donnell. Friel writes in a preliminary direction:

The two Gars, Public Gar and Private Gar, are two views of the one man. Public Gar is the Gar that people see, talk to, talk about. Private Gar is the unseen man, the man within, the conscience, the alter ego, the secret thoughts, the id.[20]

Played by two actors, Gar O'Donnell is in a constant dialogue with himself in a stage world whose rules permit Private Gar to remain invisible and inaudible to all but his other self and the audience.

Marlowe exploits and extends the legacy of the Morality Plays in *Doctor Faustus* (*c*.1592), not only in equipping Faustus with a good and bad angel at each ear, but also in deploying more affective forms of psychological projection. The initial scene of Faustus in his study, where he serially embraces and rejects the disciplines of logic, medicine, law, divinity, bringing him to the brink of his venture into dark knowledge, enacts the temporally compressed study and thought of a lifetime. Such temporal compression through externalizing representation returns at the end of the play in Faustus's last hour, as he yearns for but despairs of grace and feels the terror of the approaching midnight when his contract with the Devil expires. What he feels within is here externalized both in speech and in the marking of time. As he pleads that time might cease, or the hour be stretched to a year, a month, a day, the clock strikes eleven, then the half-hour, and finally the hour, in the fleeting space of fifty lines. We are in a stage world that later would be called 'expressionistic'.

It is arguable that Prospero's island in Shakespeare's *The Tempest*, the site of his fantasy of revenge and restoration, of his externalizing magic (the raging storm), and his restless agents (the earthbound rebellious Caliban and the quick and rarified Ariel), is a staging of the self writ large.[21] Later, the heightened world of Gothic and other kinds of melodrama also may be said to fall into the ambit of psychodrama, as does the mental theatre of Romantic egoism—most notably *Manfred, Faust, Peer Gynt*. Ibsen's *Peer Gynt* (1867) modulates between outer and inner realities, the latter projected in the Kingdom of the Trolls, the Boyg, the Button Moulder, even in the redemptive atonement of Peer's return to Solveig. The world of the play derives from what it means to be (in the words of the ex-Master of the Cairo Madhouse) 'ourselves with a vengeance; | Ourselves and nothing whatever but ourselves,'[22] though (paradoxically) in the form of the protean Peer, the archetypal escape artist. It so takes its logic, not from sheer fantasy, but from the commerce of the self and the world as psychodrama.

But it is with the challenge to mimetic realism in the modern theatre, and the vigorous deployment of alternatives, that the inventive use of the stage for the projection of inner worlds again comes fully into its own. The programmes of the movements labelled Symbolism and Expressionism make much of such externalized inwardness, realized in a diversity of forms. The graveyard scene in Wedekind's *Spring Awakening* gave a taste of the possibilities. In the early plays of Maeterlinck, however, prototypes of Symbolist theatre, the world of the play programmatically takes the colouring of the prosaically ordinary. In plays like *The Intruder* (1890) and *Interior* (1894), language, decor, the commonplace domesticity of uneventful lives in modest surroundings, suggest a naive, even minimalist realism. But Maeterlinck's virtue is in transforming this ordinariness into a poetic theatre of great intensity where, in the arrest of the moment, the interior life, magnified by each tremor, perfuses and transcends the externals. In *The Intruder*, for example, a blind old man's paranoia in a house stalked by death manifests itself in sounds and silences—the stillness of the birds, the sharpening of a scythe, the mysterious slamming of doors, approaching footsteps, the insistent pushing of the wind in the door, the sense of an uncanny presence at table, and even the accelerated striking of the hours, as in Marlowe's play of three centuries before.

Symbolist theatre, as a projection of interiority but freed from the semblance of a grounding in the ordinary, would find something like terminal expression in Russia, where the impulse had a vigorous presence in literary polemics and production before the Revolution. In Nikolai Evreinov's tragicomic and part tongue-in-cheek *Theatre of the Soul* (1912), the presented scene is a literalized human interior, the seat of the soul in the breast, inhabited by the Rational Self (M1), the Emotional Self (M2), and a sleeping benthic figure (M3) who wakes in the end and goes his way. Meanwhile the Rational and Emotional selves quarrel over the latter's infatuation with a music-hall singer. They evoke different versions of the collective subject's Wife and would-be Mistress, both of whom appear before us in their alternative forms and also fall to quarrelling. Both M1 and M2 send orders aloft through a telephone, for brandy or for valerian (the Valium of the day); their quarrels jangle the stretched wires (which are the nerves), and affect the audible heartbeat. Finally, in a convulsion of rage, M2 strangles M1; but then, rejected by his glamorous version of the singer, and silently reproached by the noble, maternal version of the wife, he telephones the command to take a revolver from its drawer and send a bullet into the pulsing heart. After some urging, there is a loud report that '*echoes through the vault of the soul*'.

A great hole opens in the diaphragm from which pour out ribbons of blood. Darkness half hides the scene. M2 struggling convulsively falls under the heart drowned in the streamers of red ribbon. The heart has stopped beating. The lung has ceased to respire.

M3 stretches wearily, and told by a porter that he has reached the last stop and will have to change, puts on his hat, takes up his bag, and follows, yawning, to his next destination, leaving the now silent and peaceful scene.[23]

Despite its modern communications and histrionic extravagance, *Theatre of the Soul* recalls much that descends from the psychology and devices of the Morality Play. Other rules and another logic govern the expressionistic projections of August Strindberg, in a series of plays that dramatize a spiritual journey in action and settings that echo the logic of dreams. Attuned to current psychological preoccupations, both occult and scientific, Strindberg brought to the dramaturgy of *A Dream Play* in particular (1902) the operative capabilities that, in *The Interpretation of Dreams* (1900), Freud collectively termed 'the Dream-Work'.[24] Strindberg's prefatory note to *A Dream Play* asserts that

the Author has sought to reproduce the disconnected but apparently logical form of a dream. Anything can happen; everything is possible and probable. Time and space do not exist; on a slight groundwork of reality, imagination spins and weaves new patterns made up of memories, experiences, unfettered fancies, absurdities and improvisations.

The characters are split, double and multiply; they evaporate, crystallise, scatter and converge. But a single consciousness holds sway over them all—that of the dreamer.[25]

In the play, the scenography is fluid and transformational. The elements that constitute the alley and doorkeeper's lodge outside a theatre, for example, change before our eyes to the makings of a lawyer's office, and then to those of a church interior. Days and seasons pass with the flickering of the lights. A grown man finds himself on a schoolhouse bench, suffering the humiliations of that condition, at once schoolboy and adult. The principal male figures—Officer, Lawyer, Poet—constellate as shards of some fragmented whole, connecting to and through 'the Daughter of Indra', whose incarnate pilgrimage in the world, and rough sampling of the stages of life, thread and connect the whole. Later, O'Neill would do something similar with the male figures in *Strange Interlude* (1928), the men in the life of Nina, the play's secular Alma, who speak to and reflect aspects of her layered psyche. In Strindberg's *A Dream Play* and its like, the world of the play enacts what Freud calls the '*sacro egoismo* of dreams'; for 'the dreamer's own ego makes its appearance in every dream, and plays the principal part, even if it knows how to disguise itself completely as far as the manifest content is concerned'.[26]

O'Neill's projections in the vein of psychodrama are restless in their means and ambitious in their experimental artifice, from the hallucinatory evocations in *The Emperor Jones* (1920), to the complex masking of *The Great God Brown* (1925), to the audible inner voices that complicate the dialogue in *Strange Interlude* (1928). In the instance of *The Emperor Jones*, both sight and sound engulf the protagonist in his own externalized nightmare, starting as he stands at the edge of the night-time forest in his flight from danger and death, and '*the Little Formless Fears creep out from the deeper blackness*'. [27] Brutus Jones, an American Negro who has bullied and conned his way to empire over a West Indian backwater and now faces deadly revolt, has set off on a prepared track for the coast. Once entered, the forest itself transforms to accommodate the spectral scenes that succeed each other: a cheating Pullman porter, announced by the 'queer clickety sound' of the dice, whose throat Jones had once cut and whom he tries to kill again; the convict road gang where Jones, drawn into the action, again tries to strike down the overseer with his non-existent shovel (and failing that, fires one of his precious bullets, giving away his location). Jones attempts to rationalize and dismiss the uncanny, manifest to us as to him in what we see and hear. Of the dice-thrower, he tells himself, 'Dat was all in yo' own head. Wasn't nothin' dere. . . . You jus' get seein' dem things 'cause yo' belly's empty' (p. 1049). As he goes deeper into the forest, the succession of encounters also takes him deeper into the self, in a penetrative regression through memory and history. The succession is from conscious, individual memory to an unconscious core of collective memory: being sold at a slave auction; suffering confinement in the claustrophobic hold of a slave ship; and finally, with Jones stripped of his glorious uniform and civilized trappings and down to something like a mere loincloth, his terrifying encounter with the chthonic rituals of the primeval African source and with the Savage God. Throughout he is pursued by the voodoo beat of the tom-tom, both responsive to his emotions and implacable. When we return at the end of the play to daylight experience and the forest's edge, Jones, having fled in a circle, is now only a sound crashing in the underbrush, and then—following shots from an ambush and the sudden silence of the tom-toms—only a limp, soulless body carried on to the social stage.

The modern theatre has assimilated much that once challenged expectation and the canons of realism, to the point where incorporating contrivances for direct psychological representation can be taken in stride. So it is in Friel's *Philadelphia, Here I Come!*, where the split and doubled protagonist is readily accepted as soon as it registers. And so it is in the spate of recent 'memory plays', like Tom Stoppard's *The Invention of Love* (1997), where the aged classical scholar and poet A. E. Housman, recently dead, calls to mind on the banks of the Styx the young man he once was and his world, in a series of scenes that eventually allows for the direct encounter and conversation of Housman young and old. Arthur Miller's earlier *Death of a Salesman* (1949), for all its force as social drama and immediacy as domestic drama, is in good part such a memory play, once titled *The Inside of His Head*. The inspiration for that title persisted, Miller wrote, in the wish 'to create a form which . . . would literally be the process of Willy Loman's way of mind'.[28] The result is a form in which the psychodramatic mode competes for the stage—as it competes in Willy's mind—with present objective reality. The setting, representing a house crowded by city apartment buildings, bears the marks of dream-like simplification and expressionistic distortion, but it also accommodates the divided modes, so that the blank apron serves '*as the locale of all Willy's imaginings and of his city scenes. Whenever the action is in the present the actors observe the imaginary wall-lines, entering the house only through its door . . . But in the scenes of the past these boundaries are broken, and characters enter or leave a room by stepping "through" a wall onto the forestage*' (p. 131). On this contested platform Willy's intrusive memories and imaginings, shaped and coloured by wishes, guilts, and illusions, are fully present as ongoing events, as fully present as they are to his unravelling mind.[29]

Where the inner world competes for the stage in a theatre conditioned by naturalistic premises, it is still possible to stretch beyond what is comfortably accommodated within the enlarged horizon of expectation. In Adrienne Kennedy's intense and disorienting *Funnyhouse of a Negro* (1964), the shattered self of the protagonist, successively identified as NEGRO and as SARAH, plays out its breakdown in the figuration of dream and imago. The stage slips between Sarah's room and '*the place for herselves*', changing character according to its inhabitants—a Duchess of Hapsburg, Queen Victoria, Jesus, Patrice Lumumba—all of them '*One of herselves*'. Sarah speaks through them, as do some more deeply internalized voices: Lumumba in monologue is also her father. External characters appear under distortion—Sarah's white landlady and white lover appear as Funnyhouse clowns whose commentary sometimes qualifies the polyvocal interior dissonance. Everything is rendered in the tension of black and white, from the cheap white satin that is ubiquitous, to the dark sarcophagus of a bed, to Sarah's black, missionary father who supposedly raped her now asylum-bound, unreachable mother, straight-haired and almost white. Sarah and the projections of her fragmented self are all losing the '*wild kinky hair*' that connects them, by the handful and bagful, bizarre symptom of the dissociative breakdown that will end in Sarah's suicide. A powerful and concentrated projection of a crisis of interiority, the play seeks to externalize, as psychodrama, something that is both intensely inward as experienced, and yet exemplary of a condition of race in America.[30]

After *Look Back in Anger* (1956), celebrated for its unwonted truth to contemporary social reality in Britain, John Osborne threw off its naturalistic signature in plays like *The Entertainer* (1957), with its music-hall interludes and design, and *Inadmissible Evidence* (1964), which begins in '*The location where a dream takes place*', with its protagonist, Bill Maitland, '*the prisoner of this dream*', and in the dock—a solicitor on trial for the failure of his life.[31] When the play modulates to the ordinary world of a law office, the boundaries between thought and expression, one client and another (all played by the same actress), between speaking to someone on the phone and speaking to no one, blur, as Maitland descends into breakdown and isolation. In *Luther* (1961), Osborne mines a recent psychobiography of the protagonist,[32] but goes beyond translating its insights into character and action. In a still astonishing scene, the stage becomes a dreamscape out of Hieronymus Bosch:

A knife, like a butcher's, hanging aloft, the size of a garden fence. The cutting edge of the blade points upwards. Across it hangs the torso of a naked man, his head hanging down. Below it, an enormous round cone, like the inside of a vast barrel, surrounded by darkness. From the upstage entrance, seemingly far, far away, a dark figure appears against the blinding light inside, as it grows brighter. The figure approaches slowly along the floor of the vast cone, and stops as it reaches the downstage opening. It is MARTIN, *haggard and streaming with sweat.*[33]

Speaking of the lost body of the child he once was and of his bowel-clenching fear of unworthiness, Martin Luther waits in his cell as a procession of monks, carrying the paraphernalia for his first Mass, passes by and disappears into '*what is almost like a small house . . . a bagpipe of the period, fat, soft, foolish and obscene looking*'. At the end of the scene, as the Mass is heard, Martin returns to the stage through the cone, '*carrying a naked child*'. It is the image of a second birth, wherein Luther, mastering his paralysing guilts and fears, has managed, as it were, to father himself. The surreal setting, its imagery at once phallic and cloacal, emblematic and psychosexual, sixteenth-century and modern, shifts after this scene to a more public theatre of action, ending on a note of domesticity, a conscious shift in mode and register. Osborne says in a comment on decor, 'After the intense private interior of Act One, with its outer darkness and rich, personal objects, the physical effect from now on should be more intricate, general, less personal; sweeping, concerned with men in time rather than particular man in the unconscious' (p. 56). It is still Luther's world, but a social and historical world that now holds the stage, not his inner world.

It is not Osborne's '*particular* man in the unconscious' who is objectified in Beckett's theatre—where one also finds interiority embodied in concrete metaphor—but rather glimpses of the general conscious experience of being in the world, something inherent in the human condition. Beckett's take on existence as strained through the workings of memory and the burden of consciousness finds dramatic expression in an extensive run of resonant images and situations that exteriorize the chronic heartburn of 'How It Is', to borrow one of Beckett's non-dramatic titles. Among them, a number of his shorter plays appear to give scope to the dialogue of consciousness with itself, in stagings of solipsism. *Embers* (1959) takes advantage of the radio medium to set voice against a background dominated by the sound of the sea. Here the monologist evokes ghosts, to be hearers for the story he uses to fend off vacancy, and calls into being sound effects—hooves, the slam of a door—and voices and exchanges from a past, whether real or imagined, but in any case brought into sound and consciousness, in the hopeless effort to shut out the inexorable lapse and murmur of 'the sea'. *Not I* (1972) shows only a mouth, both narrating herself and distancing herself (as 'she') in a nearly uninterrupted associative monologue, and with a silent, nearly motionless auditor. *That Time* (1976) lights up a face in the dark listening to three voices, all his own, picking up from each other in fragments of remembering. *Rockaby* (1981) sets a woman in a rocking chair, moving mechanically in time with a recorded voice (her own), which she joins occasionally in an echoing phrase. From the voice emerges a narrative of seeking connection with 'another like hersel' (or even 'a little like') until she gave it up, settling for being 'her own other' until that time when the rocker will finally 'rock her off'.

Among the longer and better-known plays, figure, locale, and predicament, ever resistant to historical specificity or allegorical transfer, make vivid the ungainly cohabitation of body and mind and the stratagems of beleaguered consciousness. So *Endgame* (1957), whose setting hints at the interior of a skull looking out on the world, hints as well at a schematic division of faculties in its inhabitants, with Hamm, Beckett's terminal Prospero, at the centre, blind and wheelchair-bound, issuing orders; Clov, his stiff-legged servant, agent, eyes, and auditor, resentfully carrying them out; and Nell and Nagg, Hamm's senile progenitors, stored in their bins of remembrance and forgetting. In

Krapp's Last Tape (1958), the single character moves in and out of a spotlight to listen to himself on a tape recorder—namely to some of the yearly birthday reviews that bring his younger voice, notions, and once fresh memories before him—preparatory to recording his present reflections. To these avatars of himself he responds with impatience, laughter, and occasional brooding anguish, the encounters enabled by the device that gives him plausible multiple presence. He is a persisting consciousness, but fractured by time. In *Happy Days* (1961), Beckett sets in a blazing light, with a '*Maximum of simplicity and symmetry*', the image of a determinedly cheerful Winnie, buried to her breasts in a mound (*mamelon*) in the first act, to her chin in the second, progressively deprived of her means for getting through the day, subject to the implacable offstage authority of a bell, and speaking her upbeat near monologue even as she sinks. (She has a terminally laconic partner—Willie—behind the mound.) The poignancy and the dark comedy are in the gap between how things are—a symbolic concretion that could fit any number of actualities—and how they are voiced, largely to oneself, with the starkest moments occurring when Winnie's voice falters and another awareness shows through.

Discriminating a mode where the stage is defined as a theatre of the soul surely does not mean that thought, feeling, ambivalence, and the psychology of the individual are absent in plays whose stage world adheres to the conventions of mimetic realism, and whose overt drama lies in social interactions. In a playwright like Beckett, however, it is the phenomenon of consciousness *as such*, and the human strategies for coping with and evading its burdens, for which he seeks an adequate imagery, and that makes a difference. Yet, there is a common ground which appears most tellingly in the process of enactment, in performance. Billie Whitelaw, one of the great Beckett performers, suggests something of that common ground. She speaks of doing *Rockaby*, where she has only a word to say (apart from choral echoes of her recorded voice): the word 'More', which starts and restarts the rocker and the Voice. Nevertheless, Whitelaw reports, she also said all the words in the taped monologue over to herself as they were spoken by the machine. She said the words because:

It's in my head. I think they're my thoughts. I put the tape in my head. And I sort of look in a particular way, but not at the audience. Sometimes as a director Beckett comes out with absolute gems and I use them a lot in other areas. We were doing *Happy Days* and I just did not know where in the theater to look during this particular section. And I asked, and he thought for a bit and then said, 'Inward'. And it was the most marvelous, succinct piece of direction I've ever been given.[34]

Whitelaw thinks of herself as taking the tape of her voice 'in with me, everything in with me,' even as she responds to it. In so doing, the actress is reversing the analytical projection whereby figure and voice, listener and speaker, are divided in *Rockaby*, and the dialogue within—or better, the reflexive monologue within—is made manifest. But at the same time, while leaving intact a stage world defined by rules that would seem to be designed above all to abstract and objectify the implacable burden of looking 'Inward', she reconstitutes (on Beckett's authority) the integrity and reality of a living woman, a whole person, facing her unmitigated lonely end.

3

Seeing and Hearing

Towards the end of Bertolt Brecht's *Mother Courage and Her Children* (1939/41), Courage appears—dish of soup in hand—just in time to prevent the last of her grown-up offspring from running off. Kattrin has overheard a conversation between her mother, who makes a living with her sutler's wagon following the armies of the Thirty Years War, and Lamb, a disreputable ex-regimental cook. Lamb has just succeeded to a tavern in Utrecht, away from the miseries and uncertainties of the battlefield, capable of supporting two, but not three. Kattrin would be one too many. In the temporary absence of her elders, gone to beg food, Kattrin takes up her bundle to depart, leaving an emblematic message (cook's trousers and mother's skirt side by side). But Courage, returning with the soup, stops her, holding her back by main force, and berates her, saying 'And don't go thinking I've given him the gate on your account. It's the wagon. I won't part with the wagon, I'm used to it, it's not you, it's the wagon.'[1] In a production record known as 'The Mother Courage Model', Brecht includes the following note: '*A detail.* While saying the words "Don't go thinking I've given him the gate on your account," Courage puts a spoonful of soup into Kattrin's mouth' (p. 376).

Here is a moment where what we see and what we hear are clearly at odds with each other. What we see contradicts what we hear, in this case the harsh spoken word. Brecht makes the effect even clearer in a summary where he characterizes Courage's action: 'Feeding her as one would a child, she assures her that it has never occurred to her to desert the wagon' (p. 375). Kattrin is functionally mute, confined to inarticulate cries in other circumstances, and to symbolic language. (The ultimate expression of her compassion and humanity will be in raising an alarm by heroically beating a drum.) Her silence as she listens and is fed adds to the poignancy of the dissonance between Courage's angry monologue and her eloquent maternal gesture.

Most of our language about the theatre, in English at least, favours the visual side of our experience. We go to *see* a play; we take in a *show*. 'Theatre' (from *theatron*, akin to *theasthai*, to see) is itself etymologically a matter of seeing. On the other hand, we use two terms for when we come together at a performance:

'audience' and 'spectators', with 'audience' the favoured playhouse term. And that part of the playhouse assigned to our use is 'the auditorium', the place of hearing—from whence, however, we contemplate 'the scene'.

'Audience' points to what one hears, 'spectators' to what one sees; and what one hears and what one sees constitute the grid of the play. They are coordinates like x and y, extensions like length and breadth, between them generating the play as a shape developing through time. They are the *stuff* of the play, the currency of the transaction between stage and audience wherein the play lives. There are of course modifications and enhancements that can qualify or enrich the fundamental grid. Other senses may be enlisted. Henry Irving used incense to generate the heady atmosphere of the church scene in his *Faust* (1885).[2] Sam Shepard and Nicholas Wright embed the flavour of domesticity in their scripts through actual food-making: the comforting morning smell of toast wafting through the audience from a battery of stolen toasters on the stage of Shepard's *True West* (1980); the background of kitchen preparations in the opening of Wright's *Vincent in Brixton* (2002), where 'The smell of roasting lamb enfolds the audience like a grandmother's embrace.'[3] Touch came to the fore in the Living Theatre's famous production of *Paradise Now* (1968) where, in the spirit of the times, the audience was invited to shed its clothes and join the cast on the stage to bring on 'The Exorcism of Violence and The Sexual Revolution'.[4] Mime plays (and narrative dance) are all about seeing, though forgoing speech does not mean forgoing music. Radio plays are all about hearing, though in their flourishing heyday most were designed to create a 'soundscape', a virtual space, using sound effects and microphone distance. Beckett, as a playwright given to subtracting dimensions to discover what he can do without, provides admirable examples of both: of speechless mime in his *Act Without Words I* and *II*; and of soundscape in motion (first forward, then in reverse) in his radio play *All That Fall* (1957).

Nevertheless, the standard model of the drama is an orchestration of what you see and what you hear, with hearing most heavily invested in the word, whether spoken or chanted or sung. In the nature of things, it is easier for a reader of plays to attend to the words, and even to experience them in relative vividness and immediacy (especially if one habitually reads by ear, as about half of us do—and all should try to do when a play is in question). But it is harder in following a printed text, for the most part nothing but words, to keep the visual dimension well in mind. Does that mean that in reading a play full blast one should consciously visualize a stage and its setting, with the characters/players moving within it, changing positions and making faces? I don't think so (though in *writing* a play, surprisingly many notable playwrights would habitually construct models and move waxen or cardboard figures about, if only to keep track of entrances and exits). Rather I believe that without thinking much about it, a competent reader of plays will experience a *sensation* of visuality, tied less to an idea of the mediating stage than to the world directly evoked by the play text. Such a sensation of visuality makes for a virtual space constituted as of the moment by what is immediately pertinent; a space more or less intimate, depending on what is going forward, while the rest of what would make up a complete visual world is felt, not as an absence or incompleteness, but as a vague potentiality. The visuality of dreams is somewhat analogous; and I would argue that in much admirable and even great drama, especially that written for a generalized stage like the Elizabethan where movement in time and space is not much constrained by physical markers, such limited visuality—character and actor centred—is inherent in the playwriting as well as in the text.

Still, if the art of reading a play demands an attention to how plays work, there are pitfalls in what I have described as the competent reader's unthinking experience. It is easy, for example, to lose sight of a silent presence even when that is the crucial element in the scene. The classic example, once more, is *Hamlet*, the second scene, where Claudius, recently become king of Denmark following his brother's death, enters in state with Queen and courtiers to preside over his Council. The procession enters, say the texts, with a '*Flourish*' on the brasses, and once in position, the King proceeds to business. Claudius summarizes the state of the crown and nation—their grievous loss, his succession sealed by taking the late king's widow to wife as 'imperial jointress'. He notes an opportunistic threat from the Norwegian prince and dispatches ambassadors to quash it, and then turns to local matters, notably Laertes' petition for leave to return to France. Only then, several minutes into the scene, does he—and the text—turn to Hamlet, registering his nephew and stepson's presence as more than part of the crowd. Yet Hamlet's silent presence has to be a locus of uneasiness throughout the opening, a jarring note—as yet unidentified—in the music of the King's eloquent and efficient assumption of command, a second centre of attention in the eye of the audience, creating expectation. Though nothing in the primary texts indicates staging, that Hamlet's silent presence is intended as conspicuous, an essential dissonance in the drama of the scene, is implicit in what the text tells us about costuming. The court is in appropriate rich and colourful dress, perhaps even festive in honour of the recent wedding; Hamlet is in mourning. After the King's ambiguous query, couched in metaphor ('How is it that the clouds still hang on you?'), the Queen more explicitly asks her son to 'cast thy nighted colour off'; whereupon what Hamlet calls 'my inky cloak' and 'customary suits of solemn black' become the text of his barbed discourse on the difference between inward feeling and outward show. For the reader, then, an awareness of Hamlet's anomalous presence (which staging would make conspicuous) is essential to grasping the underlying drama as Claudius passes from acknowledging 'our late dear brother's death', and his own swift marriage with 'our sometime sister and our queen', to business, including his flattering attention to Laertes and Polonius, Laertes' councillor-father, who perhaps helped bring King Claudius to the throne.

Presence is then an element in the interplay of what we hear and what we see; and when it is silent, it may even count for more than when it sounds. Absence too may count for something. Absent characters feature in the opening of many plays, where their appearance in the dialogue generates expectation. (Important actors liked a big entrance to themselves, and playwrights wrote to suit them.) In O'Neill's *The Iceman Cometh* (1939), the first act hangs on the anticipated arrival of the overdue Hickey on his annual bender among the down-and-outs of Harry Hope's saloon (and then on developing the difference between the anticipated Hickey and the man who finally arrives). At the limiting extreme, absence in a climate of ever-decaying, ever-renewed expectation is the fundamental contribution of the title role to *Waiting for Godot*.

3.1. SOUND THAT IS NOT SPEECH

Seeing embraces gesture, facial expression (including the fixity of masks), costume, charged objects, movement, configuration, all of which claim attention from a reader when they are more than simply illustrative of what the spoken words convey, and especially when they qualify the spoken word, or signify on their own. Hearing takes in music, noise, and of course silence, which like absence can have a telling dramatic effect. Sound that is not language can operate both to convey some concrete message, and less explicably, to qualify the moment or even the whole dramatic world of the play. There is, for example, the sound, pure sound, with no obvious source, identity, or evident meaning, that Chekhov calls for in the second act of *The Cherry Orchard*—a mysterious reverberation like that of a breaking string, filling the twilight with poignant mystery and changing the scale of the human events we have been witnessing. There is hardly a moment in modern drama more charged with uncanny effect, an effect that bridges to the end of the play when it recurs in an orchestrated cadence of sound and speech (the coach departing; the dying words of the old servant, inadvertently left behind; the sound of the axe cutting down the orchard; the sound of the breaking string). Hardly less effective, though wholly opposite in its signifying concreteness, is the sound that qualifies the final words of Ibsen's *A Doll's House*, the sound of a slamming door. It comes after Nora Helmer's explanation of what sends her away: her discovery that she is 'a stranger' both to her husband and to herself; and it speaks to her husband's desperate grasp at the straw of a possible future reunion. On her way out Nora had allowed the glimmer of a hope in the possibility of 'a miracle of miracles' happening: that she and Torvald Helmer might *both* change, making possible something like a true marriage—though she simultaneously chills the thought with the barbed comment that she no longer believes in miracles. Helmer, left alone, sinks into a chair, covering his face with his hands, and calls her name:

Nora! Nora! (*He rises and looks round.*) Empty! She's gone! (*With sudden hope.*) The miracle of miracles . . . ?
(*The sound of a door being slammed is heard from below.*)
CURTAIN

The sound is definitive. It is the last word.[5]

A sound-script for Ionesco's political fable *Rhinoceros* (1960) would plot the path of the action: the transformation of Beringer's world, from one where the offstage thunder of a passing rhinoceros is an entirely freakish and bizarre event, to one where the trumpetings and thundering passage of herds and armies of rhinoceros confirm that Beringer is now the freakish exception, the only human being who has managed to remain himself. Brendan Behan's *The Quare Fellow* (1956), which plots the daily routines of a prison in sound, reaches its climax in the offstage execution of the unseen title figure, registered in a crescendo of noise. What we see on the stage is the prison yard, occupied by two of the warders, waiting for the hour to strike. The voice of a prisoner starts up from the cells, describing, in the style of a race-track commentary, the procession to the hanging place and, as the hour approaches, the final moments:

MICKSER'S VOICE . . . (*A clock begins to chime the hour. Each quarter sounds louder.*) His feet to the chalk line. He'll be pinioned, his feet together. The bag will be pulled down over his face. The screws come off the trap and steady him. Himself [the executioner] goes to the lever and . . .
The hour strikes. The WARDERS *cross themselves and put on their caps. From the* PRISONERS *comes a ferocious howling.*
PRISONERS. One off, one away, one off, one away.

Finally, '*The noise dies down and at last ceases altogether.*'[6]

Behan's *Quare Fellow*, which bears the traces of its origins as a radio play, opens with a ballad, sung by an invisible prisoner, about prison sounds. Against the background of closed cell doors and (on the wall) the single word 'SILENCE', the voice sings:

> To begin the morning
> The warder bawling
> Get out of bed and clean up your cell,

> And that old triangle
> Went jingle jangle,
> Along the banks of the Royal Canal.

And as '*A triangle is beaten, loudly and raucously,*' a warder appears. Here, words, music, and extrinsic sound complement and reinforce each other, despite the contrast between the plaintive voice and the shock of the signifying noise.

But in the sound-script embedded in many of our play texts, music and noise are commonly at odds, practically as well as conceptually, an antithesis inscribed in the *dramma per musica* that was imagined as the revival of Greek tragedy, but instead turned out to be the invention of modern opera. At a critical moment in Monteverdi's *Orfeo* (1607), on a libretto by Alessandro Striggio, a stage direction reads, '*Here there is a loud noise behind the backcloth*' ('*Qui si fa strepito dietro la tela*'). Orfeo, by the power of his music, has liberated his beloved wife Euridice from death, and is permitted to lead her from Hades to the upper world on condition that he not look back at her. The sudden noise interrupts his walking song, both celebratory (of music) and anxious, and it provokes his fatal turn—a victory (however temporary) for anti-music, the malign forces of strife and disorder.

In *Orfeo* generic noise is laden with thematic meaning, but also with strong sensory effect. Such a partnership is at the root of much of the powerful impact in the theatre of Sophie Treadwell's expressionist tour de force, *Machinal* (1928). In Treadwell's printed text, each scene, and the play as a whole, is prefaced by a sound plot. Sound, notably the cacophonous noises of the modern urban industrial world, evokes the soul-destroying, mechanical social and economic environment that is the true antagonist in the drama. In their insistent clamour, the office machines, the routinized speech of the workplace, the construction noises that pour in from outside the lying-in hospital, radios, buzzers, footsteps, telegraph instruments, airplane engine, newspaper chatter, generate almost reflexively an empathic understanding of the young female protagonist's desperate and nerve-battered state. Like *The Quare Fellow*, *Machinal* culminates in an execution, here by electric chair. In the original staging, and in the play as we read it, it happens in the dark, a matter of sounds. '*The scene blacks out*', whereupon a counterpoint of the obligatory prayers of the Priest and the witnessing commentary of the Reporters evokes the action that is terminated, finally, by the voice of the protagonist:

YOUNG WOMAN (*calling out*) Somebody! Somebod—
    (*Her voice is cut off.*)

Later productions have been less careful of the spectator's sensibilities, the best of recent revivals, for example, showing the actress Fiona Shaw strapped in the grim chair and racked in an unbearably sustained convulsion.[7] Such a change points to a cultural shift in theatrical sensibility and decorum—what an audience deems appropriate or even tolerable for visual representation. It also acknowledges the greater impact of the visual within the weave of sight and sound. As a result, where the violent event *had* to happen offstage, as in much earlier drama, the task of language often became something more than conveying the news. It became that of visual evocation—indirect seeing.

3.2. INDIRECT SEEING

The report of the Messenger in much drama in the classical style is designed for just such scenic evocation. A powerful example is in the seventy-three lines that (echoing Euripides) describe the terrible death of Hippolytus in Racine's *Phaedra* (1677)—his horses panicked by the horrific monster from the sea, and he dragged off and torn to rags behind his runaway chariot. The bravura description is evocative of both sound and sight, but is above all virtual seeing. Additionally, the power of this evocation is reinforced in the dramatic circumstances of its delivery. Intensifying the pity and terror of the reported scene, the Messenger is not just anyone, but the victim's devoted tutor and friend; and the listener is Hippolytus' now partly enlightened father, whose misdirected curse has brought the catastrophe down upon the head of his innocent son.

The identity of the reporter makes a difference; but so does the staging of the report. Among the most effective evocations in the dramatic canon of an offstage execution is that of the beheading of Maria Stuart in Schiller's 1800 tragedy of that name. What charges it with an exceptional dramatic intensity is the situation of the reporter and the immediacy of his witness. That is, we do not hear of the death of the Scottish Queen as something already in the past tense being told to onstage auditors. Rather, as in *The Quare Fellow*, the account comes to us as it happens, but from Mary's betraying lover, the Earl of Leicester, trapped in a room above the execution chamber, and deducing from the sounds of the ritualized event precisely what is happening as it happens. Ordered to witness the execution, he halts on the way:

> Impossible! I cannot see this horror,
> I cannot watch her die—Ah! What was that?
> I hear them down below; beneath my feet
> They are preparing for their dreadful work.
> I hear their voices—Oh! let me be gone
> Away from this abode of death and terror!

(*He tries to escape through another door, but finds it locked and draws back.*)
What god or demon nails me to the ground?
And must I hear what I so dread to see?
That is the Deacon's voice—exhorting her—
She cuts him short—and now—she prays aloud—
Her voice is firm. Now it is quiet—quiet—
A sound of sobs—the women are all weeping—
Now they disrobe her—now, they move the footstool.
Now she kneels on the cushion—lays her head—

(*He has spoken the last words with mounting terror, then stopped for awhile; he suddenly gives a convulsive start and collapses, fainting. A muffled roar of voices is heard from below, which goes on reverberating for a long time.*)[8]

At the climax, speech fails. Leicester's collapse, and the sudden muffled roar that breaks the silence, are the visual and auditory signs that the deed is done. Meanwhile, we as audience and spectators have been participants, sharing in the relayed immediacy of the event, our feelings prepared by Mary's loving and noble farewells in the previous scenes; her bootleg confession, putting away earthly hates and loves; and her taking the sacrament while dressed in the festive white of a first communion. But along with the drama of the execution itself, a further layer of drama plays out before us in visual immediacy, in the spectacle of the trapped and conscience-struck lover who mediates and evokes the death.

Schiller gains effect from the little shock in the shift, through a momentary silence, from our dependence on Leicester as the reporter and interpreter of the sounds from below, to our hearing the sound for ourselves. In Brecht's *Life of Galileo* (1938/53), a concurrent event offstage, filtered through an onstage audience and terminally announced by a sound, similarly creates the drama of a climactic scene, that of Galileo's famous recantation. Here, however, the sound and its significance are foreknown to the audience(s), and become the focus of expectation. This enables Brecht to exploit the difference between the knowledge of the onstage audience, with divided hopes, and that of the actual audience, on how this test of Galileo's fortitude will come out. A quasi-official figure announces, 'Mr. Galilei is expected to recant at five o'clock before the plenary session of the Inquisition. The big bell of St. Mark's will be rung and the wording of the abjuration will be proclaimed publicly.'[9] But five o'clock comes and the bell is silent. A foreshortened three minutes pass, and nothing happens. Galileo's students and disciples are ecstatic, and proclaim the victory of Man. But '*At this moment the big bell of St. Mark's begins to boom,*' freezing them, and releasing Galileo's pious and now joyful daughter from her knees, while '*From the street*' (offstage) an announcer's voice is heard reciting the text of Galileo's recantation. In this scene, the drama of Galileo's invisible, inaudible encounter with the Inquisition is displaced to the proxy drama on the stage. The agon plays out between the two groups, his daughter praying for a saving recantation and his students fearing for him but hoping for some monumental heroic defiance, both groups torn between faith and doubt, and both in fact performing rituals of faith. The false resolution—the silence of the bell—serves to release the true feelings and beliefs of the Galileans, now free to articulate the dire consequences for Truth and Light of a recantation. And it serves to disconcert the expectations of the actual audience, intensifying the drama of the foregone conclusion and also refocusing it on the blow to the Galileans, so that the delayed sound, the booming of the great bell, will be experienced as a shock, not just by the stage audience, but by the theatre audience as well.

3.3. VISIBLE SPEECH

Of matters that belong to the realm of seeing, gesture, facial expression (including the use of masks), costume, movement, and configuration, all implicated with the actor's art, are most important. In the actor's repertory of skills, gesture has mostly been thought of as reinforcing the meaning and feeling that lies in the words; and indeed, the actor's art and the orator's were long conflated in manuals on rhetoric and handbooks on acting, and even in treatises on painting expounding the art of depicting the passions. However—crucially in eras of sparse or non-existent stage directions—significant gesture embedded in the spoken texts may be what the words are about, as during Lear's attempt to kneel to Cordelia (see above). And in one famous Shakespearian moment where the earliest text supplies a rare gestural stage direction, the gesture—made in silence—carries in itself the full import of the drama. In *The Tragedy of Coriolanus*, Caius Martius Coriolanus, having been driven into exile by his fellow Romans, returns at the head of an army of his city's enemies and is met outside the walls by his mother, wife, and child. Son, husband, and father, he is much moved in this reunion by conjugal love and filial love and respect. But, with his honour pledged to his new allies, and hardened against personal entreaties, Coriolanus declares his inflexibility. He turns away ('I have sat too long') from his mother's eloquent account of the impossible situation in Rome of those bound to him by blood and marriage, but he stays to hear her plea that he find another way, that he make Rome's peace rather than execute her ruin. He is *silent* through over fifty lines, a silence emphasized by his mother's urgings to 'Speak to me, son', 'Why dost not speak?', 'Daughter, speak you', 'Speak thou, boy', 'here is no man in the

world | More bound to's mother, yet here he lets me prate'. Finally, having
ordered all to kneel to his averted figure, she declares an end:

> Yet give us our dispatch:
> I am husht until our city be afire,
> And then I'll speak a little.
> [CORIOLANUS] *Holds her by the hand silent.*[10]

The yielding is all in the gesture; and the stipulated silence gives scope for
the women to begin to respond, visually, and for the audience to take in
the meaning of what it has seen and some of its implications. All this has
passed in the even more silent presence of the enemy Volscians, who soon will
return laconic answers when pressed, and Coriolanus understands his danger.
When he finally speaks—'O mother, mother! | What have you done?'—it is
to comment on what has already happened. The action that transformed the
situation, the turn, was all in the gesture, in the realm of what we see.

I began with an instance of gesture that neither dispenses with words nor
reinforces them, the action whereby Mother Courage feeds her daughter while
berating her. Such undercutting of speech, ironizing how characters present
themselves, is a tool ready to hand for the playwright or the interpreter, apt for
comedy or pathos, and inherent in the duality of seeing and hearing. It serves
to ironize the scene, for example, in Arthur Schnitzler's album of erotic life
in *fin de siècle* Vienna, *Reigen* (best known as *La Ronde*, 1897), in the episode
where the Young Gentleman and the Young Wife meet in a shady hotel. Both
play to the other in the style of high romance and noble passion, and—in the
case of the Young Wife—innocence as to the purpose of their tryst. When
she enters, veiled, closing the door, she '*remains standing there for a moment
while she brings her left hand to her heart as though to master an overwhelming
emotion*' (gesture here tells us she is no stranger to the theatre). Having been
drawn in, she allows the Young Gentleman to divest her of hat and veils.
Seated, the Young Gentleman covering her hands with kisses, she announces,
'And now . . . now I must go.' As he '*takes off her cape and places it beside the
other things on the divan*', as instructed, she resumes, 'And now—adieu—'.
But the chief ironizing instrument in the scene is the consumption of the
delicacies that Alfred, the Young Gentleman, has thoughtfully provided. While
waiting for Emma's arrival, he tries a marron glacé. As he is striking the right
sympathetic note by sharing his keen perception that Emma is unhappy, that
life is so empty and so short, and 'There's only one happiness . . . to find
another person who will love you,'

(*The* YOUNG WIFE *has taken a candied pear from the table and puts it in her mouth.*)
YOUNG GENTLEMAN. Give me half!
(*She proffers it to him with her lips.*)[11]

Gestural inflections of a less blatant sort are at work in Chekhov's *The Cherry Orchard*, as when, in the hour of dissolution, Lopakhin is given a last chance to propose to Varya. Some gestures are characterizing, or rather 'characteristic', in the way that a reiterated phrase can serve as a character's distinguishing tag (Jörgen Tesman's 'think of that!' for example, in Ibsen's *Hedda Gabler*; Joxer Daly's 'It's a daarlin' [whatever]' in O'Casey's *Juno and the Paycock*). Gayev, whose sister, Mme Ranevsky, has just returned from abroad to her Russian estates in the opening of *The Cherry Orchard*, has such a characteristic gesture, which manifests itself when he is embarrassed, or evasive, or preoccupied. He makes it at first entrance, while his sister recalls the customary accompanying phrases:

As he comes in, GAYEV *moves his arms and body as if making billiard shots.*
MME. RANEVSKY. How does it go now? Let me remember. 'Pot the red in the corner. Double into the middle.'[12]

In this same scene of reunion, Lopakhin, whose people were serfs on the estate, also displays a characteristic if less bizarre tic. He is present to welcome Mme Ranevsky, but also to explain his plan to save the estate, encumbered with debt and slated for auction. Conscious of time, and unlike Gayev, a man with somewhere to go, he punctuates the difficult scene by three times glancing at his watch. Late in the play, the gesture returns. When persuaded at last to offer marriage to the decent young woman who loves him, he telegraphs his ambivalence gesturally even as Varya is summoned and he reiterates his determination to speak:

LOPAKHIN (*with a glance at his watch*). Yes.

Despite his good intentions, the words are never said.

Reading gesture is critical when it takes on more than illustrative and expressive function, when it conveys meanings beyond the dialogue, which it can qualify or condense into something that feels definitive, like the kiss that seals the union of lovers in stage and film. (It was long excluded on the French stage, where its symbolism was culturally defined as too explicitly sexual.) Reading some texts discloses a *pattern* of gesture, and where that happens, there is a fair likelihood that the gesture itself is invested with a structural and thematic importance that performance would only accent. Such, for example, is the culturally charged gesture of the pledge of the hand that recurs throughout the progenitor of all subsequent Don Juan plays, Tirso de Molina's *Trickster of Seville and the Stone Guest* (pub. 1630). Don Juan is a dangerous delinquent in this play, a sadistic prankster lavish of hand and word for seduction and deception. The gestural motif is cumulative, and with every repetition builds the charge that will culminate and discharge in the machinery of retribution. At the very opening, his cover of darkness blown, Juan seizes his lady-victim's hand, having previously sworn to honour their mutually pledged word. Later, to the seaside Diana who has revived and sheltered him after a near drowning, he promises marriage ('Here is my hand and faith'), while she bows down 'beneath the word and hand of husband'. Again, to the peasant bride whose wedding he has invaded, he swears marriage and begs the hand that will signify her yielding:

AMINTA. You are not deceiving me?

DON JUAN. I'd be the one deceived.

AMINTA. Then swear you will fulfil your promised word.

DON JUAN. I swear by this white hand, señora, a winter of white snow, to keep my word.[13]

The gesture of giving and taking hands, as pledge of honour and acceptance, as disclaimer of duplicity, as synecdoche for the giving of one's whole self in its integrity, prepares for the spectacular comeuppance that gave the Don Juan legend its immense popularity. Keeping out of the way of his pursuers, Don Juan has stumbled on the sepulchral monument to the father of another of his deceived ladies, Don Gonzalo, whom he had killed while fleeing the premises. With his usual cynical disrespect, Juan invites the statue to dinner; and to the terror of all but Juan, the statue comes. Owing honourable satisfaction, Juan gives his word to do whatever the statue requires of him. '*Speaking slowly, as if from another world,*' the statue asks:

And you'll keep your word as a gentleman?

DON JUAN. As a man of honour and a gentleman, I keep my word.

DON GONZALO. Give me your hand, have no fear.

DON JUAN. What are you saying? I afraid? If you were hell itself, I'd give you my hand. (*He gives his hand*)

DON GONZALO. Pledged are word and hand. Tomorrow at ten I will look for you at supper. (p. 241)

And though Juan reports that when the statue took his hand, he gripped it so that it seemed he was in hell, he keeps his pledge. In the return of hospitality at the tomb, the macabre feast concluded, the statue again asks for and receives Juan's hand. Unable to free himself from the fierce grip, the Trickster cries out that he is burning, roasting, until—unconfessed and feeling the rigour of God's justice—he falls dead, whereupon the whole tomb sinks in violent thunder, carrying the statue and the corpse below. The transformation of the gesture of the freely given hand, of the deceitful pledge, into the uncanny grip of retributive punishment is embedded in the sensational theatricality of the story, and so persists in later versions, in Molière's *Don Juan*, for example, and Mozart and Da Ponte's *Don Giovanni*, where, as a bonus, a supremely musical rendering of seduction is embodied in the duet '*Là ci darem la mano*', on the joining of hands.

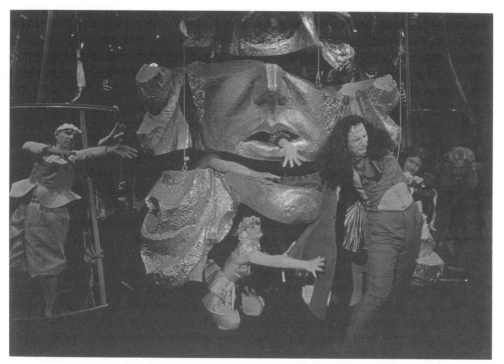

Figure 4. Don Juan's comeuppance in Molière's *Don Juan, ou Le festin de Pierre*. Responding to the Statue of the Commander's demand, Don Juan for the last time pledges his hand ('La voilà'), in a production that brings this persistent motif to a retributive climax. In the midst of the many hands reaching out to him, the Don's arm is held in the crevasse between fragments of the giant stone head, that and the hand reaching out from the mouth proper perhaps recalling the Roman *Bocca della Verità*, as immortalized in the film *Roman Holiday*. The photograph, in the New York Public Library for the Performing Arts, is identified only as '*Don Juan* by Molière'.

As part of a repertory of symbolic gestures used to flesh out a text in production, not every instance of the meeting of hands carries the same weight. When it is explicit in the text itself, however, it is rarely without dramatic point. Moreover, like other actions felt to be 'natural', but perfused with cultural significance, in certain plays the gesture can take on pivotal importance in the web of signification. Among them is *Götz von Berlichingen* (1773), Goethe's youthful history play built on English models that helped launch the great age of German drama. An early sixteenth-century 'free knight' at odds with the changing times, Götz wears an iron prosthesis in place of his right hand, lost in war. Much is made of it throughout; but the gesture of the hand, as gift and bond, becomes the pivot of the drama when it

condenses the central relationship of the play, between Götz and his fellow
knight and erstwhile friend, now become courtier and modernizer, the divided
and susceptible Hamlet *manqué*, Weislingen. Captured by Götz and held as
a valuable hostage, he is then enfranchised, Götz asking for 'nothing more
than your hand' as a pledge of neutrality.[14] Weislingen thereupon raises the
ante, and adds to the parties in the bond, by asking for Götz's sister. The
action is explicit in the spoken words. Weislingen says to Götz, 'Here I grasp
your hand. From this moment on, let friendship and trust be between us
unalterably, like an eternal law of Nature! And let me take this hand as well (*he
takes Maria's hand*) and with it possession of this noblest of maidens.' Götz
turns this triune configuration into a figure of betrothal: 'Give each other your
hands, and so I say Amen. My friend and brother! I thank you, sister!' But
then he reports a fearful dream that featured his friend and brother, newly
confirmed: 'Last night it seemed to me I gave you my iron right hand, and
you held me so fast that it came out of the vambrace as if broken off.' Had he
not, terrified, awakened, he now believes, 'I would have seen how you affixed
to me a new living hand.' That hopeful reading predictably comes to nothing,
as Weisingen, seduced, betrays his friend and abandons the marriage. In the
end, suffering the price of his anachronistic trust and the historical fate of his
class, the free knight is stripped of identity and posterity, figuratively castrated
and literally confined. 'Were you looking for Götz? He is long since gone. Bit
by bit they have mutilated me—my hand, my freedom, my property, and
my good name,' this name that bespoke both honour and power: 'Götz von
Berlichingen of the Iron Hand.'

3.4. MASKS AND MARKINGS

In the history of the theatre and in the vast majority of plays written for it,
most of the work of characterization is done through physical appearance.
Where typifying mask and signature costume prevail—as in Noh plays and
commedia dell'arte for example—nothing could be more evident. But even
without such overt formalizations, plays and playwrights draw upon common
cultural associations and fixed theatrical conventions for their sheer efficiency,
as a kind of visual shorthand—a godsend for the actor liable to specialize along
certain lines and perhaps playing a different role each night, and a convenience
for the spectator tuning into the play. Often these external conventions lie
implicit in the texts we read, though some are no longer familiar or acceptable,
and all are almost certainly changed in register, like the vocabulary of any
time-bound vernacular. They take on an extra measure of interest when the

play overtly challenges them—as Shaw, for example, challenges the language, behaviour, and external appearance of the conventional stage Irishman in the opening scene of *John Bull's Other Island* (1904).

Contrast and complementarity in appearance can have an importance beyond their convenience for remembering who is who on stage. So, for example, in a recent production of *Little Eyolf* that ignored the physical contrast between the two principal female roles Ibsen calls for in the script—between the earthy, impassioned wife of Allmers and his sensitive, repressed sister—the performance laboured under a handicap in conveying the dynamics of the dysfunctional family that is the subject. In populating a play, dramatists like Shaw and Wilde are fully as conscious of how elements of colour and timbre set each other off and work together as a composer would be in choosing voices and instrumentation, and indeed Shaw frequently made the analogy.

Though the one is fixed and the other may be fleeting, physiognomy and expression play their part, no less than age, bodily type, gender, and dress. For the reader of plays, the face of the actor as a register of emotion and intent remains for the most part buried in the lines, and in whatever parenthetical but non-visual inflection the script's directions may supply. But physiognomy and emotive expression can unite in the fixity of a mask (the enraged expression of a Japanese demon, the suffering mouth and eyes of a Greek tragic heroine), while there is an uncanny apparent mobility even in such fixity, thanks to a capacity in audiences for imaginative projection. What a masked actor says and does affects the reading of the mask. The use of masks in the modern theatre is always self-conscious, however, and marked with special purpose. Yeats, for example, much influenced by Japanese theatre in his 'Plays for Dancers', uses masks in his legend-based drama, *The Only Jealousy of Emer*, to discriminate between orders of being. The heroic figure of Cuchulain *'wears a heroic mask'* (distorted when assumed by an inhuman impersonator). A 'Woman of the Sidhe' who embodies a beauty and perfection at odds with ordinary mortal capacity wears a metallic mask *'so that she seems more an idol than a human being'*. The musicians sitting on the stage who provide the narrative and the accompaniment have *'faces made up to resemble masks'*.[15]

Something similar in the way of ontological discrimination operates in the use of masks in Pirandello's *Six Characters in Search of an Author*, the canonical modern exemplar of theatrical self-consciousness. In the play proper, actors supposed to be rehearsing a Pirandello play have their stage invaded by a group of 'characters' seeking enactment of their own story, imagined but then abandoned by a shadowy author. The actors appear as ordinary figures from ordinary life, however italicized by theatrical temperament. The 'characters', however, wear partial masks as recommended in the stage directions:

The masks will help give the impression of a face constructed by art and fixed immutably each in its own fundamental emotion, which is remorse *for the Father,* revenge *for the Stepdaughter,* disdain *for the Son,* sorrow *for the Mother with tears of wax fixed in the dark circles around her eyes and down her cheeks such as one sees in the carved and painted images of the* Mater dolorosa *in church.*

The contrast, Pirandello argues, will speak to the deeper meanings of the play, which have to do with alternative realities, the nature and stability of personal identity, the creations of the mind and of art.[16] As Wilde's Lord Henry Wotton says, 'It is only shallow people who do not judge by appearances.'[17]

3.5. DRESS CODE

In some theatres, like the Elizabethan, lavish investment in dress furnished a principal means of creating spectacle, always an attraction in its own right. But in its uses, dress can be merely a decorative enhancement; or it can be a means of refreshing a familiar classic (transposing a drama of Troy, for example, into the grinding futility of the 1914–18 war); or it can be a means of creating a dissonant dialogue with the present. Still, these are production choices that, while they may enhance and facilitate staging a script, do not inhere in its essential drama. Yet costume or dress *can* convey the action of the essential drama, as a few examples can show. Hamlet's contrariety and isolation in the court of Claudius is stated in the contrast of dress, as we have already observed; and his subsequent 'antic disposition', put on or otherwise, is registered (in Ophelia's report) by 'his doublet all unbrac'd' and his stockings down about his ankles (II. i. 78–80). But there is a later momentous turn in the drama that is also visibly and forcibly conveyed through dress. While still in black, Hamlet has gone on to disturb the court and make serious mischief, including one fatality, but he has also been ineffectual as a man charged with carrying through a particular piece of work. As coded in the conventions of the time, his black clothing betokens, not only mourning, but melancholy, a recognized disabling pathology. He is sent abroad by Claudius to be killed, but on the journey turns the tables on his conveyers, and after other adventures has returned with a difference. Hamlet, no longer in black, returns in practical, perhaps even nautical, travel gear (he speaks later of his 'sea gown', precursor to a pea jacket). The court, processing to the burial of Ophelia, would, despite her 'maimed rites', be cloaked in Hamlet's 'nighted colour', now put off (and here, as the colour of mourning, proleptic of more to come). The change in the relation between Hamlet and his world, and the turn in the action towards what will now be conclusive, is marked in Shakespeare's dramaturgy by a radical reversal of the earlier contrast in dress.

A somewhat comparable exchange over time occurs in Pushkin's great historical drama. *Boris Godunov* (1825), a play that distils from the chronicle of events a meditation on the nature of history. Boris, through force and cunning, ascends the throne as czar at the beginning of the play, but towards the end, at the point of death, troubled in conscience and set round with enemies, he puts on the cassock and tonsure of a monk. Meanwhile Grigory Otrepev, whom we first encounter as a young monk, assumes the garb of a warrior and prince. The historical figure known as 'the false Dimitry', he takes power at the end as the 'rightful' czar. The crossing of trajectories structures the play; but the iconic interchange of the czar turned monk and the monk turned czar says more. At the end of the play, where the new czar is proclaimed by the Boyars, the brutal murder of Boris's family, especially his son and heir, repeats the critical events in Boris's ascent to the throne. The People, asked to shout 'Long Live Czar Dimitry Ivanovich!', stand *'silent in horror'*. In character and temperament, Pushkin's Grigory Otrepev and Boris Godunov could not be more different. But personal qualities make no difference, and their eclipse, marked by the trappings of their interchanged roles, speaks to the ascendancy of the role over the man, the price of power, and the suffering of the realm and the people in the flux of history.

More than a century later, Bertolt Brecht uses costume for a similar perception of the power of institutions and interests to override identity by staging the investiture of a pope. In Brecht's *Life of Galileo*, Cardinal Barberini has been a sophisticated, intellectually inclined, and sympathetic interlocutor with Galileo. Now he has become pope. Between Galileo's enforced dispatch to Rome and his offstage trial, a scene shows the Pope giving audience to the Cardinal Inquisitor while preparing to address a waiting crowd of churchmen and the learned. As it opens, Barberini is adamant:

THE POPE (*very loud*). No! No! No!... I won't permit the multiplication tables to be broken. No!

However, *'During the audience the pope is being dressed'* in the elaborate garments that bespeak his office and function, his social and institutional role. While the investiture is taking place, there is an extended argument on the practical implications of the new astronomy and mechanics, and the many interests involved. Then there is a brief stillness:

(*Pause. The pope is now fully robed.*)

THE POPE. At the very most the instruments [of torture] may be shown to him.

THE INQUISITOR. That will suffice, Your Holiness. Mr. Galilei is well versed in instruments.[18]

The Inquisitor's argument, which we hear, is complex; the action, which we see, is elaborate but simple; and it is the action (the investiture) that tells.

When dress surfaces in a text, in conversation or preliminary description, it has more to do than cover nakedness. Costume may be enlisted both to conceal and to reveal: to conceal, by characters forwarding their private ends; to reveal, by the playwright adding layers of signification. *Disguise* on the one hand and *emblematic dress* on the other complicate the action and signpost character and thought in countless plays. Disguise, useful in melodrama, is especially keyed to comedy, where besides facilitating confusion, it enacts a vicarious carnival liberation from everyday, buttoned-up selves. Accordingly, a staple of comedy has been cross-dressing, as in the so-called 'breeches parts' in plays like Farquhar's *The Recruiting Officer* (1706), a speciality of some actresses. Earlier, when adolescent boys did the work of actresses on the English stage, parts for boys dressing up as girls dressing up as boys (Rosalind in *As You Like It*, Viola in *Twelfth Night*) planted even richer confusions in the dramatic text—and in Shakespeare's hands, opportunities for exploring crossing the divide.

Disguise and emblematic dress are sometimes combined in a single stroke. Edgar's disguise as a madman in *King Lear*, for example, is also emblematic, at once concealing and revealing (and since it consists chiefly in dirt and nakedness, revealing nearly all). In Lear's emblematic reading, the revelation is of 'unaccommodated man', the bare, forked animal stripped of its trappings, in a play where divestiture, the process of stripping—as of a kingdom, affectations of virtue and the ties of nature, even of one's wits–furnishes the spine of the action. Shaw knew what he was about in *Heartbreak House*, the play that he called his *King Lear*, when he has his shocked and exasperated man of business cry out, 'Look here: I'm going to take off all my clothes (*he begins tearing off his coat*) . . . Let's all strip stark naked. We may as well do the thing thoroughly when we're about it. We've stripped our selves morally naked: well, let us strip ourselves physically naked as well, and see how we like it.'[19]

Emblematic dress as a visual key to understanding takes several forms in Calderon de la Barca's baroque masterpiece, *Life is a Dream* (1635). When we first encounter Segismundo—son of the Polish king, put away in infancy like Oedipus to confound the dire predictions at his birth—he is dressed in animal skins and heavy chains, a solitary brute raised away from his kind in an isolated prison, which is all that he has ever known. He is, in this philosophical drama rooted in the culture of Christianity, an image of fallen man, imprisoned by the legacy of sin and prey to his animal nature; and his first words, accordingly, are a meditation on the inexplicable crime of being born. He is, he says, 'a human monster', a man-animal and an animal-man. In the course of the drama, he will be taken from his cell, transported to the royal court, and dressed in the elaborate finery appropriate to his royal station—and, when he acts according to his nature, be returned to his prison confinement and animal dress, a life's journey in little, as it were, from womb to tomb. But then, unexpectedly resurrected and put at the head of a rebellion, he turns out to have learned from his experience. Still dressed in his feral skins, he masters his unregenerate condition, and, in the moment of triumph that humbles his star-reading father, redeems both himself and the kingdom from their sins of pride and passion, their errors of heart and head.

Another figure in the play offers a somewhat simpler, secular version of such emblematic dress. In the opening action, Segismundo is discovered in his isolated prison by Rosaura, a woman in pursuit of her lost honour, and in that anomalous condition wearing man's dress. Later she is persuaded to resume woman's dress and entrust her vindication to others. Finally, her honour still not redeemed, she appears on horseback as, in her words, 'a monster of both sexes', in the riding dress of a woman, but bearing arms, the sword and shield of a man (III. x). In Segismundo's case, the symbolism of dress reaches towards the allegorical; in Rosaura's, she uses it to externalize her state metaphorically. Segismundo's dress and condition draw upon a fund of contemporary imagery: folklore's Savage Man of the European forests; the numerous accounts of the inhabitants of the New World; the imagery associated with Cain after the Fall. As for Rosaura, more socially than metaphysically transgressive, involved with the niceties of honour in its sexual manifestations, her emblematic dress draws on Amazonian associations. But in so far as gender and its expression are bounded by an idea of what is 'natural', her condition shares with Segismundo the stigmatizing epithet of monstrosity, an unnatural mingling of separate kinds proclaimed in her androgynous dress before the final resolutions.

For the most part, dress is complementary and supportive, its coding a clue to rank and character. In traditional historical drama, however, the splendour, exoticism, and purported authenticity of dress were commonly what people came to see, as part of the gorgeous spectacle. And in the work of the two great purveyors of Romantic drama in nineteenth-century France, the elder Alexandre Dumas and Victor Hugo, there was often something more. In Hugo's *Ruy Blas* (1838), a play of court intrigue set in the decadent Spain of the 1690s, costume is so intrinsic and thematized as to become the prime vehicle of both the drama and its politics. In earlier periods not yet forgotten, sumptuary laws demanded a correspondence between place in society and the character and richness of dress. In the liberal nineteenth century, Hugo uses the impress of such social rigidity to attack the notion that extrinsic indicators of any kind—like name, rank, or fortune—can measure and decide a man's worth. The principal action of the play pits the villainous Don Salluste–an arrogant grandee fallen from power for abusing a woman, and now plotting revenge against his nemesis, the Queen—against Ruy Blas, 'born of the people', who in hard times has taken service with Salluste and wears his household livery. In a sudden inspiration for furthering his plot, the master turns his servant into a counterfeit of Salluste's very own missing cousin, Don César de Bazan, by throwing his own cloak over Ruy Blas's tell-tale garb, hanging a sword upon him, and covering his head as Royalty approaches, as is the right of 'a grandee of Spain'. In the same opening act we have met the real Don César, dressed in the rags and exaggerated gear of an outlaw bravo, but—in keeping with his eccentric and quixotically honourable character—sporting a resplendent doublet (regrettably stolen) of rose-coloured satin and gold beneath his patches. Known only by his *nom de crime*, he and Ruy Blas, it turns out, have been friends; and in Don César's egregious but emblematically revealing get-up is a hint of their Romantic affinity.

Hugo provides elaborate costume descriptions in the text we read, not to save the producers thought, but because dress is so integral to the play. At their first entrance, in the magnificently furnished '*Hall of Danaë in the King's palace at Madrid*',

Don Salluste is dressed in black velvet, court costume in the time of Carlos II. He wears the Order of the Golden Fleece. Over his black garments, a rich mantle of bright green velvet edged with gold and lined with black satin. Sword with a large shell guard. Hat with white plumes. . . . Ruy Blas is in livery. Brown breeches and body-coat. Beribboned surtout, red and gold. Bare head. Without sword.[20]

Later, at the height of his fortunes, as Chief Minister, Duke of Olmedo, and in train to reform the corrupt and suffering kingdom, Ruy Blas enters the Council Chamber where he presides dressed, like Salluste previously, '*in black velvet, with a mantle of scarlet velvet. He has a white plume in his hat, and wears the Order of the Golden Fleece*' (p. 1576).

As the merest servant, Ruy Blas was romantically and impossibly in love with the Queen. Now, raised to a sublime height by the Queen's acknowledgement of her love for him, he is brought crashing down by the return of Don Salluste, who drops his cloak to reveal himself '*dressed in flame-coloured livery gallooned in silver, like that of Ruy Blas's page*'. The exchange of signifying dress between master and man is now complete. But Salluste, his plan now ripe for harvesting, holds power over his intended cat's-paw, and reasserts his authority cruelly—by interrupting Ruy Blas's high policy concerns with bored commands for menial services: to open the window, pick up his handkerchief. Consequently, for the final act, where Salluste's trap closes, Ruy Blas resumes the livery that he wore at the beginning. Revealing it climactically to both the Queen and Salluste, Ruy Blas speaks the line that galvanized audiences and pulls all together: 'and as for the two of us, my lord, we make an infamous pair. I have the clothing of a lackey, and you have the soul' (p. 1652). Though an impossible love and an impassioned remorse dictate Ruy Blas's own tragic demise, he still manages to kill Salluste beforehand (and save the Queen) quite satisfactorily. Swordless as befits a lackey, he seizes his tormentor's weapon, laughs at his call for an equalizer, and butchers him:

DON SALLUSTE (*disarmed, looking about full of rage*). On these walls, nothing! Not a weapon! (*to Ruy Blas*) A sword at least!

RUY BLAS. Marquis, you [*tu*] jest! Why, master! Am I a gentleman, me? A duel! Faugh! I am one of your servants, flunkies dressed in red and braiding, a scoundrel to be scolded and whipped—and who kills! Yes, I am going to kill you, my lord, understand? As a villain! as a coward! like a dog! (p. 1655)

In Hugo's sublimation of historical 'costume drama' in *Ruy Blas,* the integral play upon dress goes considerably beyond the Salluste–Ruy Blas seesaw that has been traced here, and its implications are fully elaborated in copious spoken interchanges. But the thrust of the drama lies in the action of what you see: the costume transformations and their ironic accretion of a meaning that is subversive; subversive of all those trappings of rank, privilege, and convention that, taken as the counters of human value, give cover to baseness and stifle true worth and natural capacity.

3.6. THE OBJECT IN VIEW

At one point in the complicated intrigue of *Ruy Blas,* a detached fragment of clothing becomes something else: a performing object. The Queen has found a scrap of lace stained with the blood of an invisible sympathizer, who daringly climbs the defended walls of her park to leave her the flowers of her native land, and finally a letter. Later, when the Queen is struck by the handwriting in a dictated message from the King brought by a brand-new courtier (Ruy Blas), and notices the ruffle on his sleeve and his bandaged left hand, she inadvertently pulls the scrap of lace from her bosom. It is the token that leads to an overwhelming mutual recognition, not just of identity, but of reciprocated feeling. As a signifier, it is more than equal to the task, combining in itself lace's rich delicacy with the heart's blood.[21]

Performing objects, symbolically charged with meaning, value, or danger, stand out in the visual field of many a play, often as the linchpin of the intrigue. Othello's handkerchief, strawberry-spotted, comes immediately to mind: his gift to Desdemona, stolen for Iago, seen in the possession of Cassio, and clinching evidence to Othello of his wife's betrayal. The hand-prop in the title of Wilde's *Lady Windermere's Fan* (1892) serves a similar purpose, as a token of unfaithfulness, though in Wilde's comedy the catastrophe is successfully evaded. Through its presence in bachelor quarters, the fan stands for the concealed person of Lady Windermere herself—a kind of metonymy—until claimed, falsely, by the demi-rep she knows as Mrs Erlynne (actually her mother). In the economy of the situation, the compromising token may be redeemed for one (plausible) female body. Mrs Erlynne comes forward, while Lady Windermere slips away, unseen.

The surrogate function of objects can work through their mere presence, as in the case of '*some new boards standing by the wall*' in the Aran Island cottage that is the setting of J. M. Synge's *Riders to the Sea* (1904).[22] They turn out to be coffin boards, bought for Maurya's son Michael whose drowned body has not yet been recovered from the sea. While a bundle of clothing taken from a body found in the far north awaits scrutiny by Maurya's daughters, her last son, Bartley, is going into danger. In the condensed action of the play, the white boards stand as the constant presence of death in the lives of these people—the very condition, according to Synge, that makes possible his modern tragedy. In the end it is both Bartley's body, brought up dripping from the sea, and the bundle of clothing, Michael's object-surrogate, that together will occupy the coffin to be made from the boards, in a condensation and consummation of *all* her losses that it is Maurya's grandeur to accept and articulate. The effect of the boards through their visible presence is underlined in dialogue that calls them to our attention. For a play in performance there is a presumption of functionality when an object is given prominence, and there are no prizes in the theatre for useless clutter (as in conscientiously 'naturalistic' productions), or for objects that are merely decorative or possibly even misleading—unless misleading for a purpose.

The role of the charged object is not always so passive or initially discreet as in the instance of Synge's white boards—witness not only the loaded guns and other weapons whose stage appearance is a promise of their eventual use, but objects whose dramatic function is to signal change. One such occurs in *R.U.R.* (1921), Karel Čapek's fantasy of a world gone wrong. In the third act, a global revolt of industrial robots has reached the corporate headquarters of Rossum's Universal Robots, the island that is the place of their original creation and manufacture. A small band of company managers and scientists have gathered in the home of the General Manager, Domin. Fabry, in charge of technical matters, has hitched electric cables to the garden railings and switches on a light to test the current and see if people are still in charge of the generators. 'Ah, they're still there, and they're working. (*Puts out lamp.*) So long as that'll burn we're all right.' Later, after the fence has proved its worth, and as the siege reaches its climax, Fabry again lights the lamp:

FABRY . . . The dynamo is still going, our people are still there.

HALLEMEIER. It was a great thing to be a man. There was something immense about it.

FABRY. From man's thought and man's power came this light, our last hope.

HALLEMEIER. Man's power! May it keep watch over us.
ALQUIST. Man's power.
DOMIN. Yes! A torch to be given from hand to hand, from age to age, forever!
(*The lamp goes out.*)

The action of the lamp—its failure—has been prepared, along with what that failure signifies:

HALLEMEIER. The end.
FABRY. The electric works have fallen![23]

Other meanings with which the lamp is charged have been invoked in the celebratory litany that precedes its going out. The effect is to overlay the melodrama of the moment with a large dramatic irony, turning boast and retrospect into epitaph.

In the approach to this last stand of humanity and in the subsequent denouement, a significant role is assigned to another physical object, the piece of paper on which is written old Rossum's initial discovery, the essential formula for the manufacture of the robot substance. Like the proprietary formula for Coca Cola, it is imbued with an improbable importance; but it is destroyed before it can be put to use as a bargaining chip, or for further good or ill. Such an object, usually contested, often a piece of paper—a letter, a will, a formula—comes into its own in the nineteenth century, both in melodrama and in the ingenious plotting of what is too often patronized as 'the well-made play'; and it has an afterlife in film, decaying into what Alfred Hitchcock labelled 'the McGuffin'. Though material proofs play a part in earlier drama—as in the tokens that authenticate identity, that trigger recognitions and reunions—they take centre stage as contested keys to knowledge and power (or as objectified value and truth) in an age struck by the successes of the scientific method and credited with the invention of detective fiction. The exemplary comedy that came into English as *A Scrap of Paper*, Victorien Sardou's *Les Pattes de mouche* (or 'Fly Tracks', 1861), where the contest is over a compromising billet-doux, even makes reference to Poe's seminal story 'The Purloined Letter'.[24] In Sardou's play, the value of the letter is less in its contents (long undelivered, time has mooted its message) than in its continued bodily existence, and that materiality is reflected in its vicissitudes. The play tracks the letter's perils and humiliations. It is rescued from oblivion, concealed in plain sight (as in Poe), singed, twisted, tossed from a window, torn, turned into a beetle-holder, and eventually burned to ashes. In a comedy where no one gets hurt and lovers find happiness (notably the worldly wise pair who compete for possession of the letter), it suffers for all, tragically as it were, its disruptive potential fatally marking it as a scapegoat sacrifice for the greater good. Unlike Othello's handkerchief, which acts on an Othello already convinced and transformed and whose role is thus non-essential, Sardou's scrap of paper is the indispensable heart and soul of the dramatic action—the Object (a visible hand-prop, renewed each night) as protagonist.

In the theatre, an object has presence. If it is large, it requires accommodation in the staging. If it is invisible, as sometimes happens, pantomime and gesture can give it virtual presence. Properly identified, it is able to evoke presence beyond itself, like the Count's spurred riding boots waiting to be polished in the manor-house kitchen in Strindberg's *Miss Julie.* In Ionesco's brilliantly theatrical *The Chairs* (1952), the eponymous object, progressively multiplied, serves as the anchoring reality for a stage densely populated with an imaginary audience; that is, the furniture is real, the people—except for the Old Man and Old Woman who greet them and converse with them and bring on the multiplying rows of chairs—virtual. The play dramatizes the assembly of this virtual audience within the circular walls of the ancient couple's isolated island home, to hear the Old Man's long-gestated message for mankind. The arrivals, introductions, flirtations, *politesses*, ringing of the doorbell and fetching of the chairs, accelerate frenetically to produce a 'packed', waiting stage, climaxing in the arrival of the (invisible) Emperor in a burst of blinding light and sound. This is followed, at last, by the arrival of the Orator, a real person/actor, but in manner and appearance—according to the text—made to appear histrionically unreal.[25] The Orator has been hired for the occasion, to deliver the Old Man's message to the world. But after the Old Man delivers an elaborate introduction, he and his wife hurl themselves from opposite windows in a surprise joint suicide, whereupon the Orator (a deaf mute, it turns out) makes inarticulate noises, writes cryptically on the blackboard, and departs disappointed, leaving an empty stage except for the chairs—and a crescendo of human noises, the invisible crowd, now heard for the first time. It is the apotheosis of the performing object, the chairs—or *what we see*—having in effect summoned into being the crowd—or *what we hear*.

3.7. MOVEMENT AND CONFIGURATION

Modern production likes to keep the stage in motion (a director's common vice), and audiences expect no less of the actors, even when they ought to keep still. The role of configuration in the experience of the play tends to get less attention, though movement and configuration together constitute the substance of 'blocking', that ordinary prologue to mounting a play. As far as reading plays goes, much that has to be decided for the staging of a script does not appear even as an issue in the text, nor should it. But certain particulars of the movement of actors in relation to each other, and of their positioning in sustained configurations, will speak from the script's notation, and it is these that are liable to prove meaningful or even illuminating in the unfolding drama.

In some ages of the theatre, where actors lined up across the stage and declaimed, movement was undoubtedly less significant than the rhetorical and expressive play of language in marking the turns of the drama. But comedy is always an exception, and here Molière's *Le Bourgeois Gentilhomme* (1670) is instructive. In this *comédie-ballet*, performative movement is thematized through the scenes of instruction designed to qualify M. Jourdain for aristocratic society: how to dance the minuet, how to make a bow to a marquise ('a marquise named Dorimène'), how to fight a duel without getting killed, even how to pronounce the vowels and consonants—sound reduced to the movement of lips, tongue, and jaws. The dancing master gives instruction on the bow:

DANCING MASTER. If you wish to greet her with a great deal of respect, you must first make a bow stepping back, then advance towards her with three forward bows, and to conclude you bow down to her knees.
M. JOURDAIN. Give me a sample.[26]

—which he does. (When Jourdain applies his lesson, however, he is obliged to ask the lady to step back, to give him room for the third bow.)

Similarly, the master of arms puts Jourdain through a severe fencing drill, keeping up a running commentary as he demonstrates, with impeccable logic, the whole secret of his art: 'to give, and Not to receive'. Then, in one of the best-known scenes in the French theatre, Jourdain—wishing to show off his invulnerability—fences with his servant maid, Nicole, who, ignoring Jourdain's '*raison démonstrative*' and the art of fencing by the numbers, scores numerous hits. In all this, Molière is acknowledging and ridiculing a notion of gentility that identifies it with a vocabulary of dress and physical behaviour, and certain hallmarks of language, among them specious titles to which one has no claim.

Elsewhere in the same play, Molière gives a sample of how movement can structure a scene in the *commedia*-like encounter of the young lovers, Cléonte (echoed by his servant, Covielle) and Lucille, Jourdain's daughter (echoed by Nicole). The men, indignant at having been ignored in public, turn away from the women and retreat, until the women decline further explanation and apology, whereupon the pursuing movement is reversed, all ending in the explanatory reconciliation that brings the two couples together, at a stand. In its patterned movement, its complementary doubling of partners, its turn and counterturn and final configuration, the scene is a tightly choreographed quadrille whose sublimated eroticism generates comedic delight. A similar scene in Molière's *Tartuffe* (1664) has the offended male lover, Valère, making for the door and returning repeatedly for one last word, until he is momentarily pinned down by the sensible servant, Dorine. It is then Mariane's turn to make the moves towards departure, forcing Dorine to run between them until, pulling each by the hand, she successfully draws them together. To conclude, she demands a hand from each—each professing bewilderment over her intention. Hands joined, they stand for a little time, looking elsewhere, before turning to each other for reconciliation—only to restart the cycle of reproaches, which Dorine has hastily to cut off.

The choreography of these scenes, a lover's dance, involves both movement and configuration, ending in an image emblematic of union. Configuration is the foundation of the much stronger comic episode where Elmire sets out to prove to her Tartuffe-besotted husband, Orgon, the gross hypocrisy of the supposed saint. Arranging the scene, Elmire plants Orgon under a table, where he remains, while beside it Tartuffe, with increasing freedom, presses his suit, and Elmire, with increasing desperation, coughs and raps for Orgon's attention. Ultimately he will emerge, nonplussed, though only after Tartuffe is dispatched to check his whereabouts. He will emerge once more, from behind his wife, when Tartuffe, returning, advances upon Elmire with open arms; whereupon all movement briefly freezes in a confrontation.[27]

Movement and configuration here carry the action. They are integral to the collaboration of sight and sound and to the reading of the scene as comedy, but are not charged, in the orchestration of signals from the stage, with providing further meanings or perspectives. The image, in other words, carries no additional symbolic burden, as it does, for example, in the configuration Brecht contrives when Mother Courage, grieving, numb, and reluctant to surrender the corpse of her daughter Kattrin (killed by soldiers while raising the alarm that saves a town), holds Kattrin in her lap like the Virgin Mother cradling the dead Christ in the traditional arrangement of a *pietà*.[28] Without such clear iconic reference, but still suggestively symbolic, is the evocative configuration with which Cocteau ends his reimagining of the Oedipus story, *The Infernal Machine*. It is a configuration that reflects on and extends the original riddle of the Sphinx, whose solution (erotically charged in this version) was Oedipus' ticket to fortune and Jocasta's bed. Now, before Antigone leads her blind and bleeding father off the scene into exile, Jocasta appears to him as a ghost, no longer wife, she says, but only mother. 'Your wife is dead, Oedipus . . . hanged.' Mother on one side, daughter on the other, they guide his steps, *'speaking in perfect unison'*.[29] The solution that Oedipus found to the original riddle—whose clues were in locomotion—was 'Man'. But what then, in himself, is 'Man'? In this final configuration, Cocteau embodies his coded answer: a figure in pain, helpless and dependent, between mother and daughter; a subject for poetry, bracketed and comforted in an embracing love purged of sexuality.

Less evocative than clarifying and reinforcing, is Shaw's ironically revelatory index to the action of *Candida* (1895), a configuration recalling and revising an earlier one from the play itself. In the third and last act, Candida has been left by her husband, the radical preacher and moralist Morell, in the company of the very young Shelleyan poet Eugene Marchbanks, who is desperately in love with her. To match Morell's handsome gesture of trust, Marchbanks confines himself to reading Candida his sonnets. We find them seated on either side of the hearth, where there is a comfortable armchair on one side and '*a miniature chair for children on the other*',[30] now occupied by Marchbanks, reading aloud. Shortly thereafter, Morell returns, and in the face of his solemn nobility and masculine presumption about their marriage, Candida ostensibly holds an auction of herself, poised between the man and the boy. After Morell, mastering himself, places his dignified bid, and Eugene offers only 'My weakness. My desolation. My heart's need,' Candida makes her choice: 'I give myself to the weaker of the two' (p. 138). Eugene understands instantly, but Morell is struck to the heart; and then, incredulous, learns that it is he who is intended in that description.

CANDIDA (*smiling a little*) Let us sit and talk comfortably over it like three friends. (*To Morell*) Sit down, dear. (*Morell, quite lost, takes the chair from the fireside: the children's chair*). Bring me that chair, Eugene. (*She indicates the easy chair. He fetches it silently, even with something like cold strength, and places it next Morell, a little behind him. She sits down. He takes the visitor's chair himself, and sits, inscrutable. . . .*)

In this new and eloquent configuration, Candida's loving but devastating explanation to Morell—she '*leaning forward to stroke his hair caressingly at each phrase*'–is a revelation, and a reduction, to which he responds '*quite overcome, kneeling beside her chair and embracing her with boyish ingenuousness*' (pp. 139–40). And it sends the poet, who speaks now '*with the ring of a man's voice—no longer a boy's*', out into the night, alone. The exchange in the roles of man and boy, their ages irrelevant, is now complete.

The image of an enthroned Candida, embraced by a kneeling Morell, until then officially master of the house, in the shadow of a sidelined Marchbanks, has a curious but perhaps not entirely fortuitous echo at the end of Pinter's *Homecoming* (1965). In a final tableau Ruth sits '*relaxed in her chair*' as the newly installed queen-mother-mistress and off-site sex worker, dominating the survivors of the male primal horde that surround her. She has displaced the nominal patriarch, Max, and chosen not to return to her arid life in America with Teddy, her husband and Max's respectable prodigal son. If *Candida* is an inversion of the marital dynamics of *A Doll's House*, *The Homecoming* takes it one step further. Here, it is not Nora or Marchbanks, wife or potential lover, who leaves, but Ruth's husband. Like Nora, 'TEDDY *goes, shuts the front door.*'

And on that note, the final configuration takes shape. Joey, the youngest son, a burly boxer, walks across the room, '*kneels at her chair. She touches his head, lightly. He puts his head in her lap.*' Lenny, also a son, pimp and voyeur, stands silently by, while Sam, Max's ineffectual brother, lies unconscious on the floor. Moving about, anxious and mistrustful, Max makes a final bid to exert his authority. Failing,

> *He falls to his knees, whimpers, begins to moan and sob.*
> *He stops sobbing, crawls past* SAM's *body round her chair, to the other side of her.*
> I'm not an old man.
> *He looks up at her.*
> Do you hear me?
> *He raises his face to her.*
> Kiss me.
> *She continues to touch* JOEY's *head, lightly.*
> LENNY *stands, watching.*
>
> Curtain[31]

If, in this unholy family configuration, Pinter provides opportunity to exploit recollections of the iconography of the Virgin enthroned and worshipped by pious donors and saints, Shaw brings such enriching imagery explicitly to bear. He calls for '*a large autotype of the chief figure in Titian's Assumption of the Virgin*' over the hearth, attributable to some '*fancied spiritual resemblance*' to Candida. Like language, visual imagery, notably in composed configurations like Pinter's here, is liable to carry a history of connotation and association inseparable from both meaning and effect.

The conclusiveness of Pinter's final configuration also takes its force from the chaotic contest for dominance (the underlying drama in so many of Pinter's plays) that fills the first of *The Homecoming*'s two acts. A memorable episode plays out between Ruth and Lenny, in movements that centre on a glass of water. Lenny starts out as the aggressor, hovering about the seated Ruth, and he has poured her the unasked-for glass of water. Then—after stories conveying his sexually charged violence and unpredictability—he declares she has had enough, and moves to take the glass away. First Ruth calls his sexually threatening bluff—'If you take the glass . . . I'll take you'—and then presses him to sip from her glass, sit on her lap, and then—while '*She stands, moves to him with the glass*—' to open his mouth, lie on the floor, and let her pour the water down his throat. With Lenny paralysed, she drinks, smiles, puts down the glass, and leaves the field. The pattern of movements, including the circling dance, advances, reversals, and retreats, is not so formal or so schematic as in Molière's lovers' minuets, but (like the object whose control is contested) it is no less fundamental to the scene.

Equally pertinent to Max's abjection and displacement at the end of the play is its contrast with the end of the first act, where, in a flurry of violence, Max re-establishes his primacy to his own satisfaction. Once again, the movement resolves in a configuration. After Joey, apologizing for his father's bad behaviour, describes him as 'an old man', Max unexpectedly hits him in the stomach with all his might, strikes down his brother Sam with his stick, and, recovering from his exertions, calls Ruth to him (who comes). Having asserted himself, he is now prepared to accept his prodigal son Teddy and his unknown wife, and calls on Teddy for a cuddle and kiss with his old father (p. 44).

TEDDY. Come on, then.
> TEDDY *moves a step towards him.*
> Come on.
MAX. You still love your old Dad, eh?
> *They face each other.*
TEDDY. Come on, Dad. I'm ready for the cuddle.
> MAX *begins to chuckle, gurgling.*
> *He turns to the family and addresses them.*
MAX. He still loves his father!

Curtain

The come-on and positioning is like that of street or schoolyard brawlers squaring off. In the original production, Teddy took off his glasses, ready to engage. Though Max is once more in charge, the act ends with neither a blow nor the promised cuddle, only a suspension of hostilities. The next act will open, however, with a configuration indicative of domestic tranquillity, with Ruth at Max's invitation presiding over the coffee service (in the local phrase, 'playing Mother'). In this delegation and the tranquil scene are the foreshadowings of the end of Max's disputed patriarchal authority.

The plays we are ordinarily likely to read are nearly always those whose distinction is in the language spoken, combined with some meaningful overall action—some change of state or situation or relationships (or in some instances a circuit through the possibilities of change that only brings us back to the beginning). In any case, it is easy to read a play as a narrative in dialogue, and to understand it more as something to be heard than as something to be seen and heard. But if in fact the play was written for the stage, which is usually the case, and has been worked and shaped by trial and error on the stage, as is often the case, it is important to incorporate the stage and performance in our rational and imaginative understanding. That means, when we are readers, an extra measure of attention to the visual dimension implied or adduced in the text; paying heed to its part in the drama of tension and release, its work as

counterpoint or inflection, its capacity for structuring understanding and for
focusing feeling.

Not that such conscientious attention will resolve all difficulties. At the
end of Shakespeare's *Measure for Measure*, a play in which stunned silences
have dramatic point, and scripted gesture and configuration—e.g. the act
of kneeling—have shaping force, there is a silence not easily accounted for
in dramatic terms, unlike those of Hamlet or Coriolanus, or of Angelo in
this same play. Angelo has by now been condemned to death by the Duke
of Vienna for his acts of misgovernment while the Duke was supposedly
absent. These include his plot against Isabella's virtue and his supposed
execution of her brother, Claudio. Mariana, once betrothed to Angelo and
Isabella's substitute in bed, now newly married to Angelo for form's sake, but
nevertheless unmoved by the prospect of becoming a rich widow, begs for her
new husband's life. And she begs Isabella—who does not know that Claudio
is still alive—to take her part:

> Lend me your knees, and all my life to come
> I'll lend you all my life to do you service.
>
> (V. i. 429–30)

Isabella resists mightily. After all, it is she who, enraged at Claudio's begging
her to yield to Angelo's infamous proposal in exchange for his life, had cried
out:

> Die, perish! Might but my bending down
> Reprieve thee from thy fate, it should proceed.
>
> (III. i. 143–4)

But now, finally, even as the Duke rubs in the supposed fact of her brother
Claudio's death and the justice of Angelo's punishment, she kneels with
Mariana and pleads for mercy.

From Isabella's plea for Angelo's life to the end of the play, she says no
word, a stretch that includes the revelation of Claudio alive after all, Angelo's
pardon, and the Duke's declarations of intent to take Isabella to wife ('Give me
your hand and say you will be mine'). Though her silence invites explanation
galore (as the would-be nun's unspoken resistance, for example), its dramatic
function is not apparent, and in fact it poses an awkwardness. Excluding
textual losses, which I think unlikely here, it may be that the strain between the
literal and the parabolic, the tacit framework of religious metaphor that peeps
out at various points in the play, here becomes too great, and nothing Isabella
could say would ring true. But that is speculative. The true moral is that seeing
and hearing do not, after all, tell us everything, just as everything is not always
successfully enshrined in the script. One way that reading plays differs from

producing a script is that actor and director have to decide what to do with this silence—how to present it, how in effect to fill it (though Shakespeare helps cover it with the Duke's busy dispensing of punishments and rewards). The reader of plays, however, need not make these choices. The reader is free to treat Isabella's silence as a field of possibility—or even as a lapse, in a play that, like many or most, is less than perfect, a game of solitaire that doesn't quite work out. To return to first principles, if reading a play means reading it in terms of how plays work, that means recognizing when and how they might not work. The next step is thinking about how they might be made to work—and that way theatre lies.

4

The Uses of Place

Duration and location are features of performance; time and place are intrinsic to the play. Of the latter two, place would seem the simpler matter, as less essentially 'dramatic'. The dramatic uses of time are manifest: in the familiar notion of suspense, for example, where we have to wait and see; in the melodramatic (now cinematic) race against the clock; in the one-thing-leading-to-another succession of events, culminating in revelation or denouement. In contrast, the work of place in the modern theatre tends to be equated with 'setting', which suggests torpidity and fixity. In a common view, it can contain, colour, and condition the action, and help the audience get its bearings on what sort of play to expect, but considered as drama it is for the most part inert; merely appropriate packaging.

But place can be much more than that. It can actually give shape to the drama, not just the visible scene. It can include movement and direction, articulating the path of change. It can take on an indexical function, shaping understanding through its progressive transformations or its juxtapositions and contrasts. It can, as it were, become the protagonist of the drama. Indeed, though they have their own distinctive potentialities, place and time, in sustaining the lineaments of the representation, work together to constitute the coherent, apprehensible whole—like seeing and hearing.

In thinking about the uses of place in the art of drama, as in what follows, there is no harm in starting with some of its *static* workings, simply as a 'setting' defining and characterizing the space in which things happen. More ambitious because more various is place in its *active* workings: manifesting a visible transformation, for example; or offering a meaningful succession of locales; or embodying in division and difference the dialectical movement of the play. And finally, place has to take its place in the evocation of imagined worlds as the less fugitive face of the conjoined twin, *place/time.*

4.1. STATICS

The uses of place have undergone large shifts in Western drama, shifts that go hand in hand with a transformed subject matter. Including the early modern plays and cycles offering a *Theatrum Mundi* and using multilocal stages and simultaneous settings, the broadest overall change has been from a drama, comic or tragic, played out in public places, to one whose norm is a domestic interior. The trends have been from public space to private space, from outside to inside, and from general to specific. Fixed architectural settings in Classical and Renaissance theatres lent themselves to place generically conceived: before the king's palace; a street with several houses from which persons emerge and encounter. Place in Greek drama bespeaks the *polis*, the city, its public character reinforced in its choruses. But even in much later drama, generic interiors, from an audience chamber to a lady's dressing room, were likely to have a public character or at a minimum enter into a dialogue with park and field. Even in such a domestic tragedy as *Othello*, while the catastrophe doesn't spill out of the bedroom into the street, the street and the public realm spill into the bedroom.

Place, even as fixed generic setting, conditions expectations, and does so the more as it takes on greater specificity. In the Renaissance, a schematics of place defined (and limited) genre expectations, as in Serlio's famous illustrations of the Tragic, Comic, and Pastoral scenes, all exterior settings, the first two urban and differing in the relative dignity of the façades and the depth of the perspective. Generic settings lived on in stock and repertory companies even in the age of movable scenery; and the identification of place with a recognizable kind of play, conditioning expectation, continues in the labels 'Drawing-Room Comedy', 'Kitchen-Sink Drama', not to mention 'Bedroom Farce', displaced more often than not, however, to the raffish restaurant with private dining room or the seedy hotel. Finally, place at its most specific, made particular to the play, can present an ambience conditioning and expressing its inhabitants—as we saw, for example, in Shaw's description of the Petkoff establishment and Raina's boudoir in *Arms and the Man*, or that we find in the sultry, funky French-Quarter setting of Tennessee Williams's *Streetcar Named Desire* (1947), a play unimaginable out of its particular ambience.

Place then moves into the foreground, even in its passivity, in such plays as Gorky's *The Lower Depths* (1902) or Elmer Rice's *Street Scene* (1929), where locale is a constant and the individuality of the inhabitants is absorbed into the commonality of the milieu, the direct object of representation. In *The*

Lower Depths, the flop-house setting in all its grim particularity cannot change significantly because it is at the gravitational nadir, and there is nowhere else to go. One scene—where change for some of the inhabitants seems possible until the moment explodes in violence—moves out into the cellar's yard. But in the end we are back inside where things are much the same, despite the new management, the comings and goings, the deaths and dispersals. Place, the expression of an intransigent social pathology, prevails.

The specificity of place in *The Lower Depths* does not prevent it from carrying beyond itself into broader social, and even metaphysical, implication. But the naturalistic elaboration and concreteness which gives it such specificity contrasts with the uses of place in another dramatist of the intractable dead end, Samuel Beckett. Beckett's bent is to strip away the limiting specificity that inheres in place and time, leaving the bare bones, a kind of concrete abstraction. He vigorously opposed the attempt to amplify the precisely detailed minimalist generality of his definition of place in *Endgame* (1957), for example, when the director, JoAnne Akalaitis, and her designer, Douglas Serin, thought they would specify what she not altogether unreasonably saw as a play in an imagined post-nuclear holocaust world. Place became a burned-out metro tunnel under vast structural remains, broken girders, two charred full-scale railway cars, mud, water, a burnt body.[1] This, in contrast to Beckett's:

Bare interior.
Grey light.
Left and right back, high up, two small windows, curtains drawn.
Front right, a door. Hanging near door, its face to the wall, a picture.
Front left, touching each other, covered with an old sheet, two ashbins.
Center, in an armchair on castors, covered with an old sheet, Hamm.
Motionless by the door, his eyes fixed on Hamm, Clov. Very red face.
Brief tableau.[2]

The two windows look out on the sea (leaden, empty) and the land ('corpsed') as Clov reports them; greyness everywhere. Many more implicit scenarios of desolation, outer and inner, material and spiritual, can be accommodated in the impoverished enclosure and neutral emptiness of place in *Endgame* as Beckett imagined it than in a locale like that of Akalaitis, dominated by the spectacular furnishings of a fully specified place and time, historical if only by anticipation. And yet, place is not wholly neutral in Beckett's conception. The enclosure has the vestigial traits of a shelter, an observatory, a fortress, an outpost, a domestic enclave (the ashbins domicile Hamm's legless parents, Nagg and Nell), and a skull. Beckett specifies just enough to create a structure for the grim, often hilarious, entropic comedy of a universe, a humanity, a single consciousness, at the end of its rope.

4.2. DYNAMICS

Place takes on characteristics of a protagonist in *The Lower Depths* by its inertial persistence. Whatever the vicissitudes of its inhabitants, it remains the same. But elsewhere, in several of O'Casey's plays for instance, place pointedly shares the vicissitudes of its inhabitants, so that its fortunes map their trajectory and serve as an index of change. Place is dynamic. Moreover, in what has been called O'Casey's 'Dublin Trilogy',[3] place is also (in contrast to *Endgame*) both historically and locally specific. Constancy and change are not mutually exclusive, however, in plays that encourage wider reflections on the patterns of human life, and so it is in O'Casey.

Set in the Civil War of 1922–3 that followed hard on the creation of the Irish Free State, O'Casey's tragicomedy of the Dublin slums, *Juno and the Paycock*, seems nevertheless fixed in an interminable round of reciprocal slaughter marked by cruelty and folly. Within that condition, it is place that dramatically alters. O'Casey charts the destruction of the House of Boyle as Aeschylus did of the House of Atreus, and Sophocles of Laios. In the Boyle catastrophe, 'House' takes literal form. The Boyle family—Captain Jack, a 'resting' construction labourer, his wife Juno, grown daughter Mary, and son Johnny, a maimed, nerve-shattered freedom fighter, inhabit a two-room Dublin tenement flat whose principal room is before us. It is sparsely utilitarian, with fireplace, essential cooking implements, tin bath, partly concealed bed, long-handled shovel, a few books (Mary's), and picture of the Virgin with votive light. In the course of the first act, the family fortunes suddenly seem to take a turn for the better. Boyle comes in for an unexpected legacy, sheds his parasitic drinking partner Joxer Daley, and declares himself 'a new man from this out', while Mary, with a pick of suitors, has caught the eye of a young man of a better class. In the second act—a few days have elapsed—the scene and place are *'The same, but the furniture is more plentiful, and of a vulgar nature. A glaringly upholstered armchair and lounge; cheap pictures and photos everywhere. Every available spot is ornamented with huge vases filled with artificial flowers. Crossed festoons of coloured paper chains stretch from end to end of ceiling.'*[4] In the course of this act, more is added—a gramophone, complete with horn. The occasion turns into a festive celebration, interrupted by the funeral of a recently killed diehard Republican from upstairs, and shaded by Johnny's terrors.

The third act dramatizes the fall of the House of Boyle in the active degradation of the scene. The will proves flawed, and Mary, abandoned by her preferred suitor, proves with child. To recover a temporary loan, a neighbour makes off with the gramophone. Repo men begin to carry out the furniture.

The votive light before the image of the Virgin goes out, and two gunmen with revolvers enter the scene and drag off Johnny Boyle as a suspected informer. 'Sure, the house couldn't hould them lately,' says Joxer, Boyle's treacherous parasite, 'Sure, they were bound to get a dhrop!' And later Boyle rages, 'That's more o' th' blasted nonsense has the house fallin' down on top of us!' When the curtain rises again, '*most of the furniture is gone*'. News comes that Johnny's body has been found. Juno and Mary leave, 'never [to] come back here agen'. When Boyle and Joxer return, drunk and philosophical, the space, now stripped, degraded, and abandoned, is no longer a home, the family as it was no longer a family. What remains, as Boyle remarks, is universal 'chassis'.

In *Juno*, the changes that befall a defined locale serve to mark the arc of the action with both tragic and comic effect. In O'Casey's next major play, *The Plough and the Stars* (1926), place—given more complex embodiment—serves more complicated ends. Taking a wider circuit but retaining a local specificity, the play presents an alternative view of Dublin and its people at the time of the abortive, weeklong rebellion of Easter 1916, the founding event of Irish independence. The larger scene is captured in a spatial progression that loops back upon itself and encapsulates the interplay of private and public, outside and inside, in a dialogue that overwhelms those antitheses. The space of the first act is again defined as the domestic enclave, the once stately drawing rooms of a partitioned Dublin tenement, now the Clitheroe flat, whose furnishing, we are told, '*suggests an attempt towards a finer expression of domestic life*'. At the opening, Fluther Good, carpenter and fellow tenant, has just finished repairing the lock on the door at the behest of the aspiring young wife, Nora Clitheroe. This attempt to secure the domestic enclave elicits great scorn from an aggressive top-floor neighbour, Bessie Burgess, who threatens violence as she pushes her way in. The enclosure, in fact, is under constant threat of invasion and disruption, from fellow tenants with no notions of privacy and from the senseless quarrels of live-in relations. Quarrels, disorder, uniforms, weapons, supply unending centrifugal impulsions; but the final threat to the Clitheroes' little world comes from without, in the form of a paramilitary messenger who disrupts a scene of loving intimacy, exposes Nora's defensive manipulations, and summons her husband Jack to the masculine arena of politics and war.

The second act is a displacement from the tenement to the outskirts of a great outdoor meeting, spilling over into a public-house bar. The scene is the bar into whose activities the dark silhouette of the orator against the window, and his voice preaching the glory of war, rhythmically intrude, so that the intoxicating words of the speaker without and the drink-fuelled eruptions among the tenement dwellers within form a counterpoint. The third act loops back to the tenement, but sets before us the tall, multi-storey façade at the interface between outside and inside. It is some months later; the rebellion is in full swing, and the tenement's occupants emerge and return, making forays into the offstage public action, both venal and heroic.

The final act takes us back into the tenement interior, but it is now Bessie Burgess's mean attic rooms where all the neighbours have taken shelter. The first-floor Clitheroe flat, exposed to heavy gunfire, is now uninhabitable. There is a coffin in Bessie's room, holding little Mollser, dead of poverty and tuberculosis, as well as Nora's stillborn infant. Nora is in the next room, her wits astray. The space, '*with a look of compressed confinement*', is at once claustrophobic and ineffective as a protective enclosure. There are cries from the street, a window starred by a bullet, and a sky reddened by fire. Before long, the room will suffer both invasion and evacuation, with Jack Clitheroe reported dead and the inhabitants and their community, such as it was, shattered and wholly displaced. In the end, only a British corporal in full war kit and his sergeant are left in possession of the emptied-out domestic space, along with the body of its legitimate occupant, Bessie Burgess, shot while attempting to push the distraught Nora away from the window, and mistaken for a sniper. One soldier pours out the tea they find on the hearth in a parody of domesticity, while from the distance comes '*a bitter burst of rifle and machine-gun fire, interspersed with the boom, boom of artillery. The glare in the sky seen through the window flares into a fuller and deeper red.*' It is the general attack on the Post Office, headquarters of the rebellion, followed by cries for ambulance and the voices of soldiers on the street outside singing that sentimental song of the Great War, about the men who are called to fight and the women who love them but send them off bravely: 'Keep the Home Fires Burning.' With Dublin in flames, the irony is ferocious; and as the soldiers sipping tea in company with Bessie's corpse join in the chorus, inside and outside, hearth and holocaust, private and public lose all distinction. At this point, represented place and the play's conceptual space are joined, in the nested horizons of the room, within the tenement, in the slum, in the half wrecked city of Dublin, in the greater holocaust of the World War, in the everlasting contest between generation and destruction, the seeds of life and the seeds of death, the latter now in the ascendancy—the expanding array that ultimately structures meaning in O'Casey's drama of place.

Friedrich Dürrenmatt's *The Visit* (1956) is another play where place is thrust to the fore as the register of dynamic transformation. In this play it is the town itself, Guellen, that is at stake in the moral contest that fuels the drama. Guellen in its near isolation is the object of Claire Zachanassian's vengeance, both the place and its inhabitants; and the measure of her success is its transformation, apparently—ironically—for the better. The play is framed by her arrival and departure, reception and send-off, at the town's railway station: to '*a tumbledown wreck*' of a townscape in the first instance, and from a glittering, prosperous scene in the last. The price is the soul of the town. Mme Zachanassian, who turns out to own most of the place already, and has brought it to near ruin, offers Guellen *eine Milliarde*—five hundred million for the town, five hundred million to be shared out to each family—for justice on the man who betrayed and belied her when she was the young and pregnant Klara Wäscher. 'The world turned me into a whore,' says Mme Zachanassian, now more a collection of durable prostheses than ordinary flesh and blood; 'I shall turn the world into a brothel.'[5] And Guellen, in the play, is the world.

Through the play, we witness a gradual process of change as the community trades on its expectations from Mme Zachanassian's conditional bounty—the index of a temptation and fall, in a trajectory that crosses the rise to moral clarity of the once-guilty designated scapegoat, Alfred Ill. Within Guellen—staged using a flexible, multi-local setting, at times reminiscent of the early Mansion Stage—are two principal locales: the Inn where Claire sets up headquarters and waits for the town to accept her terms, and the grocery-shop dwelling where her former lover and his family live. Ill's desperate movement within the defined space of the town and its immediate environs is circular. He makes the rounds of those with civic and communal responsibilities—policeman, mayor, priest, schoolmaster, taking in even the railway station itself, where the crowding of the townsfolk inhibits his departure. Later, sending his family off in their newly purchased motor car, he accepts his need to stay. A private time of reflection on the irretrievable, between Claire and Ill in their old haunt, the village wood, then gives way to the climactic public meeting in the inn auditorium, ritualized and rhetorical, on the acceptance of the gift, all broadcast and recorded by the media of the day. After a solemn canvass (repeated for the cameras), the hall is cleared of outsiders while the Guelleners perform their ultimate communal act of 'justice'. Ill, unresisting, is strangled, the town is purged of its sin, and justice is acknowledged in a mighty cheque from Guellen's Fairy Godmother, the once bewhored outcast whose simple commercial principles now dominate the world. For the final scene, once more at the Railway Station, and marked by a chorus of townsfolk now in evening dress, Dürrenmatt provides a measure of the distance Guellen has come from its Cinderella life among the ashes. The stage has gradually grown '*more inviting, while rung by rung it scales the social ladder and metamorphoses into wealth*' (p. 98). Now with flags and streamers, posters and neon lights surrounding the renovated station,

the epitome of that ascent occurs in the concluding tableau. The erstwhile grey and dreary world has been transformed; it has grown rich and dazzling new, a flashy incarnation of up-to-the-minute technics, as if the world and all were ending happily.

Like O'Casey's domestic enclaves, Durrenmatt's village *Heimat* proves vulnerable to intrusion and dispossession. A latent fear of bodily invasion, a primitive dread of bodily extrusion, are ready to hand in the contest over any self-identified space, one's carapace or lair. The figure of the intruder as a plot precipitator, upsetting a stable environment, and the actions of displacement and purgation that drive both tragic and comic outcomes are related to this nervous territorialism. The modern playwright who has most nakedly and effectively tapped these insecurities is Harold Pinter, notably in such earlier plays as *The Birthday Party*, *The Dumb Waiter*, *The Caretaker* (all written 1957–9); but such a figuration of place is still potent in, for example, *No Man's Land* (1975). Pinter's first play, appropriately titled *The Room* (1957), grounds its enigmatic action in the rising tide of such anxieties, set against a pathology that reveals itself in the sudden violence that explodes in the end. The agoraphobic Rose, unlike her silent, lorry-driving husband, Bert, keeps to the room that is her space, safe from the inhospitable cold outside. 'We're very quiet,' she recites, using the national cliché: 'We keep ourselves to ourselves. I never interfere. I mean, why should I? We've got our room. We don't bother anyone else. That's the way it should be.'[6] But Rose is anxious about the basement quarters, once on offer. The room they occupy, their landlord says, was once *his* bedroom. And a room-hunting couple found on the landing say a man in the basement dark reported a vacancy:

MR. SANDS. . .. One room. Number seven he said.
    Pause.
ROSE. That's this room. (p. 112)

Much agitated, Rose tries to speak to the landlord, who, however, is deaf to anything apart from the message he must deliver, from the man in the basement who has been waiting to see her without Bert, and will not leave until he does. Rose resists—denies all knowledge of who it might be—until a worse fear, of Bert's return with the stranger still on the premises, brings a precipitous reversal. Entering the room, the stranger proves to be a blind Negro who—in the face of frantic resistance and denial—summons Rose home on behalf of, or perhaps as, her father; not as 'Rose', but as 'Sal'.

ROSE. I've been here.
RILEY. Yes.
ROSE. Long.
RILEY. Yes.
ROSE. The day is a hump. I never go out.
RILEY. No.
ROSE. I've been here.
RILEY. Come home now, Sal.
    She touches his eyes, the back of his head and his temples with her hands.
    Enter BERT. (p. 119)

In the end, after Bert's brutal account of his run—

BERT. . . . I drove her down, hard. They got it dark out.
ROSE. Yes.
BERT. Then I drove her back, hard. They got it very icy out.
ROSE. Yes.
BERT. But I drove her. (p. 120)

—he kicks Riley into insensibility, perhaps to death. And Rose, clutching her eyes, goes blind.

The end, from Rose's exchange with Riley through the violence and stigmatic transfer (the blindness), serves as a revelation that inferentially reverses the character of the room: from protective shelter (under threat) to prison cell, with the prisoner lost in the pathology of her fears and habituation. The change—and so the dynamism of place—is cognitive, in the eye of the beholder. Rose's blindness is a retreat into a still narrower space, into the exclusionary darkness of the mind.

A threat to the self, to its individuality and humanity, operates in the progressive retreat and confinement of Ionesco's *The Rhinoceros*: from public square, to office workplace, to Berenger's rooms, his all-too-permeable private lair. Ionesco's interest here is more in social than individual psychology, and Berenger's drama is chiefly that of the incorrigible individual's resistance to the mass. But in an earlier work, the distinctly flawed *Amédée or How to Get Rid of It* (1954), the threat externalized in the dramatic premiss is more redolent of an inner world of secret guilts and intractable repressions. The brilliant theatrical metaphor in the first act of the play, of a living space under internal assault, gives nightmare shape to a complex of feelings in its mix of the ordinary and the fantastic. Amédée, a blocked playwright, and his wife Madeleine live, work, and quarrel in the living room they have not left for years, while in the bedroom, offstage, lies a corpse that grows like the mushrooms that have colonized the flat.

Suddenly, from the adjoining room, a violent bang is heard against the wall . . . The left-hand door gradually gives way. . . Then AMÉDÉE *and* MADELEINE, *dumb with terror, watch two enormous feet slide slowly in through the open door and advance about eighteen inches on to the stage.*[7]

Eventually the growing body threatens to fill all the available domestic space. And its disposal, slipped through the window '*interminably*' and dragged away by Amédée, proves also to be his liberation—from room, marriage, past, anxiety, even gravitation.

Where place under assault takes on the attributes of inner space, it makes a difference whether the audience feels the assault from the perspective of the besieged, as in the previous examples, or whether it looks over the shoulder of the invader. In the latter case, the progressive breach of the fortress and its citadel translates into a movement that can aptly be called penetrative. Such a movement, registering through place, governs the shape of Strindberg's experimental chamber play, *The Ghost Sonata* (1907), which begins outside, before the façade of a modern apartment house, with glimpses of the tenants' lives as they emerge from the doors and appear at the windows, an array more social than psychological. The scene then moves into the domestic interior, the formal 'Round Room' of the ground-floor apartment, with its closeted skeletons and secrets, for a musty routinized social occasion called 'the ghost supper'. And finally it enters 'the Hyacinth Room', the sanctum of sanctums holding the nubile hyacinth girl, which the Student, who is the protagonist and in some sense the audience surrogate, successfully attains. But that penetration, fraught with sexual overtones, into what at first seems an idyllic paradise, proves equally fraught with toxic, material encumbrances. As earlier the figures at the ghost supper had been systematically stripped of their social personalities and identities, so now—with Strindbergian infusions of Eastern philosophy—the veil of illusion falls away in this 'room of ordeals', with the intrusions of grossness and truth-telling. The room itself, the seeming paradise of love, dissolves in light, leaving only an image of the place of the dead.

The burden on place in creating progressive form is greater in this experimental play for the elision of other kinds of dramatic logic. The play depends, not on an exfoliation or concatenation rooted in causality—though the ghost supper scene, revealing truths from the past, mimics its strategies—rather, it follows the mind's transitions: sudden, epiphanic, and condensed, triggered by an image or rising like a modulation in musical key. The progressive penetration of a questing mind through successive veils of social appearances, domestic relations, and private illusion, is rendered as a journey inward through a progressive penetration of place. One difference from a play like *The Room*, where place is also figured as a citadel of the self, is in how the audience will experience this penetrative action, and that depends on the dramatic equivalent of point of view. Will the audience identify with the occupant of the threatened space or the invader? Is invasion destruction or liberation? Is the space a shelter or a trap?

Where place entails a progression that is distinctly directional, inward or outward, it serves a structural need in drama. But place, pluralized, can also provide structure through a pattern in its multilocality. For example, a vivid duality of place structures Schiller's *Maria Stuart*, composed after Schiller had abandoned his earlier Romantic sprawl for a dramatic architecture much more classical in conception. The alternation of place through the five acts encapsulates the complex contrast between the dual royal protagonists, Mary Stuart ('Queen of Scots') and Elizabeth Tudor (Elizabeth I of England), who meet (non-historically) only once, and disastrously, in the central act, the only one set outdoors. The progression, in its mirror-like symmetry—goes as follows:

   I. Prison: Fotheringay Castle (Mary)
  II. Palace: Westminster (Elizabeth)
 III. Neutral ground: Park, trees, open landscape (Mary & Elizabeth)
 IV. Palace: presumably Westminster (Elizabeth)
  V. Prison: Fotheringay Castle (Mary); with a Palace coda (Elizabeth)

Following the climactic events in the last act, in the chamber where Mary becomes reconciled to her death and from which Leicester reports her execution, the coda returns us to the palace room where Elizabeth had previously signed and dispatched the order of execution. In this final division and contrast, with Mary surrounded by love and sacramental blessing, intimating a personal transcendence, her prison becomes in effect a palace; while for Elizabeth, with lovers and faithful servants either banished or abandoning her in response to the execution and her deviousness, the palace has become her prison. At the curtain, now wholly the empowered ruler, but effectively alone, *'She masters herself and stands with calm composure.'*

The formal, structuring use of place in *Maria Stuart* creates a dialogue housing multiple subsidiary pairings and contrasts that complicate the initial polarities, between Mary and Elizabeth, the personal and the political, and more. But as the last act already intimates, the next step from dialogue is a dialectic of place, the emergence of a third term from the field established by the polarity of the initial two. A prime instance is in Rolf Hochhuth's forensic docudrama *The Deputy* (*Der Stellvertreter*, 1963), perhaps the most scandalous and widely controversial play of its time. The play concerns the role of Pope Pius XII in relation to the slaughter of the European Jews during the Second World War, and condemns his failure to take a strong public stand. It is a huge play whose numerous productions in many countries were inevitably of shortened versions, but it was written nevertheless both to be seen and read. Though presented textually in the traditional five acts of classical tragedy, its underlying organizing form is something else: a three-phased movement, as essential to its argument as to its dramatic effect. The first movement (Act I) is Berlin; the second movement (Acts II, III, IV) is Rome; the third movement (Act V) is Auschwitz. Auschwitz, the existence and character of the place as embodied evil, as the expression of hell on earth, is the dialectical result, the play asserts, of the failed, qualified, evaded antinomy between Rome and Berlin.

Within the threefold progression of Berlin-Rome-Auschwitz are fractal elaborations of the dialogue of place. The Papal Legation brings Rome to Berlin in the first movement; Gestapo Headquarters is a presence in Rome in the second. With mirroring symmetry, each urban locale includes both public and private spaces. The culmination of the Rome segment comes as we reach its heart, the Papal Palace itself, where, at a critical juncture, the Pope's fatal and definitive evasion occurs. It is, in the phrase Hochhuth borrowed from Dante, 'the Great Refusal'. Up to this point, the drama has suggested in everything a still fluid reality where the uncertain and the arbitrary, as opposed to the fixed and inevitable, still rules. After it, we are in the phantasmagoric death factory of Auschwitz.

A subtler dialectic sustains a play that, through its characters, foregrounds an acute consciousness of place, namely Chekhov's *Three Sisters* (1901). The antithesis of place lies here between the provincial garrison town that is the home of the Prozerovs, present to the life, and Moscow, its virtual other, informed with the remembered past and the imagined future but present only as the object of an intense yearning. To that persisting antithetical consciousness, framing a climate of inertia, Chekhov adds a directional flow of actual spatial displacement, as the sisters are crowded out of their family home by Natasha, their brother Andrey's cuckoo bride. From the sunlit drawing room and ballroom scene of the first act, darkened in the second, their space contracts to a single bedroom in the third act, and is moved outdoors in the last. Now fully dispossessed by Natasha, her children, and her lover, the invisible Protopopov, the scattering of the sisters is only momentarily stayed in the final recessional and diaspora, ending the polarity of place between the home of the Prozerovs-in-exile and the Moscow of memory and desire that has defined and sustained their world.

4.3. PLACE-TIME

Modern science brought the news that the world we live in happens in space-time. The play world is equally four-dimensional, and abstracting time and space from each other can only take one so far, as the prescriptive theorists of the three Unities—time, place, and action—learned long ago. How time in itself may be structured, and in turn can structure the experience of the play, will be explored in connection with 'The Shape of the Action' (Chapter 6, below); but no thinking about place and its uses would be adequate without a glance at the interactions of time and place in some of its more intimate collaborations.

A special occasion, the red-letter day that interrupts the ordinary flow of time even as it marks it, is a fundamental resource of the drama, weighting the ordinary with something momentous. In the making of the play world, occasion is to time what place is to space, concretizing and even spatializing it.

In *The Three Sisters*, along with the progressive displacement of the Prozerovs and the dialectic of place, occasion provides much of the structure that traditionally comes from the shape of 'the plot'. Moreover, in a play much concerned with the weight of time and its ever-receding promise, occasion serves to mark both its duration (the interminable present) and its passing.

The play opens with the oldest of the sisters speaking to the youngest:

OLGA. It's exactly a year ago that Father died, isn't it? This very day, the fifth of May—your Saint's day, Irina.

Olga goes on to contrast the days—the current sunshine and seasonal warmth with the severe cold and snow of the earlier fifth of May. Then, Irina had fainted, 'and [you] were lying quite still, as if you were dead. And now—a year's gone by, and we talk about it so easily. You're wearing white, and your face is positively radiant.'[8] To underline the dual character of the occasion, change registers through recurrence: '*A clock strikes twelve*,' and Olga notes, 'The clock struck twelve then, too.' Place is put in a temporal perspective as well, through its remembered other, for Olga recalls Moscow, and how everything there was in bloom by now. All three sisters are present in the opening: Olga, who was 17 when they left Moscow eleven years earlier, deepest in nostalgia for the past; Irina, only 20, looking to a different future; and between them Masha, settled in marriage, in Hamlet-black and silent (except for whistling), who is most intensely afflicted by the present and its limitations, and is most ready to rebel.

The occasion in the first act is the festive party celebration of Irina's saint's day; that in the second—a late evening in February more than a year later—is Carnival, with a party of celebrants expected. Some things have changed with the passage of time and some remain the same; and by the end, tellingly, the occasion is aborted, the celebrants turned away, and the stage emptied out, leaving Irina in her longing. The third act—the scene contracted to the bedroom Olga and Irina now share—occurs on another sort of red-letter day: a great fire in the town, disturbing the normal course of things and releasing much that has remained incipient or unsaid. It is again more than a year onward, and further along in the day cycle as well: after two in the morning. Much of the talk, the 'philosophizing', is the same, but there is also, as in Beckett, an inertial constancy in decline. Andrey, the brother, has gone from being the focus of hope for a livelier future into physical, moral, and intellectual decay. The play world itself is dissolving: the house mortgaged, the marriages foundering in adultery, the sisters' culture slipping away, the military rumoured soon to depart. Even Irina's positive curtain decision—to take a good man whom she doesn't love as her husband—registers the journey from hopeful expectation to weariness and verging despair.

The occasion of the last act is the departure of the regiment from this garrison town where their presence has brought something of culture and civility from the larger world. It is a time of farewells. It is also midday again, and autumn, soon to be winter, completing the cycles of the day and year; and it takes place in the garden now, completing the displacement of the Prozerovs. Like the Carnival celebration, Irina's marriage to the Baron and the 'new life' they were to begin together are aborted, with the news of his death in a pointless duel. To the jovial, receding music of the regimental band, an impoverished version of the status quo reasserts itself. And the sisters are left together, before their dispersal, to ponder the meaning of things: what it means to go on living and working, to begin and begin again, to endure with the years, and then pass into what is remembered and what is forgotten.

One of the minor characters in *The Three Sisters* is a camera bug, given on all occasions to taking snapshots (most, alas, burnt in the fire)—a gesture at fixing time, in a play that is like a series of snapshots, using occasions to mark a continuum. Another character, in a moment of unhappiness, deliberately drops a clock and smashes it, a futile gesture, since time is not halted nor the past so exorcized. As defining a location in time, occasion has much in common with place in establishing the coordinates of the play world. But in acknowledging that place has another dimension, in time, and time a subjective hold on experience, playwrights like Chekhov, Wilder, and Beckett raise the ante for audience and spectator, and open the way to those ultimate questions that engage our deepest reflections.

Occasion—a moment deserving pause and attention—helps give dramatic focus to plays whose premiss is ordinary life; but occasion, singular or successive, is the lifeblood of plays that take up historical events or whose premiss is public life. A powerful instance, where occasion increases the valence of the action from local event to universal history, is Jean Racine's play *Athaliah* (1691), built on a model of Greek choral tragedy, and drawing its subject matter from the Hebrew Bible. Place and setting are the Temple in Jerusalem; and the historical moment is the day of the overthrow of the tyrant Queen Athaliah—daughter of the wicked line of Ahab and Jezebel—and of the restoration of the anointed line of David in the person of the child, Joas (Jehoash), rescued as an infant from Athaliah's furious massacre, and brought up secretly in the Temple. The action is in the outer courts of the Temple, a defensible structure like a Chinese box, with its most sacred treasures at the core. It culminates in the revelation of some of those treasures, disclosed to the light of day.

Racine chose to set these events in train on a recurrent rather than a unique occasion, a special day in the sacred calendar: Pentecost. And, together with place, it is the subject of the opening dialogue. Abner, a commander in the service of Athaliah, but also bound to his faith, declares:

> Yes, I have come into this Temple now
> To adore the Everlasting; I have come,
> According to our old and solemn custom,
> To celebrate with you the famous day
> When on Mount Sinai the Law was given us.
> How times have changed![9]

The festival is observed as a day of sacrifice of the first fruits. It is also a day of revelation, not just commemoratively, of the Law of Moses, but prospectively: of the new dispensation that will come by way of sacrifice from the line of David, made manifest when the Spirit descends on the Disciples at another Feast of Pentecost, and endows them with the gift of tongues. On the occasion of the play, set between the occasions of the Mosaic and the Christian Pentecosts, revelation and ritual sacrifice will also be the order of the day.

The Temple, as the place of Racine's Pentecostal action, condenses an extended temporal significance. In a preface Racine points to a tradition 'that the mountain on which the Temple was built was the same mountain where Abraham had once offered his son Isaac in sacrifice' (p. 230). At several points in the play Racine invokes that association, as when the High Priest asks,

> Are we not here upon the holy mount
> Where Abraham above his innocent son
> Lifted obedient arm without complaint . . . ?

(IV. v. 17–19)

Now it is the boy, Joas, demanded by Athaliah, who is in Isaac's place as the candidate for sacrifice. The moment of revelation—a literal epiphany as a curtain is drawn and Joas appears in kingly regalia, enthroned—also reveals to Athaliah that she is the substitute sacrifice, the ram caught by the horns in the tangle of her confused emotions whose agency she cannot understand. As she is surrounded by ranks of armed Levites in the closed and bolted Temple, the High Priest, who has stage-managed everything, drives it home:

> There's no escape,
> And God has hemmed thee in on every side.
> That God thou bravedst has now delivered thee
> Into our hands.

(V. v. 29–31)

The moment of the revelation of Joas is staged as a sacred picture, suggestive of Christ in majesty, a sword-bearing angel at his side, saints kneeling on the steps of the throne, and angelic legions in attendance while Judgement (with the further revelation of the legion of armed Levites) is passing below. The tableau is thus also a vision of what lies latent in futurity in the Temple's treasures. The High Priest, possessed by the Holy Spirit like his Pentecostal successors, prophesies the Temple's destruction and that of Jerusalem, these places in the historical and dramatic present resonant with the sacred occasion, to be succeeded by a New Jerusalem, truly eternal, and by a universal, multi-local Church.

Such metaphysics of place embedded in occasion are not met with every day. Ordinarily, in drama, we tend to pay attention to the dimension of time only when the playwright wants us to, either by putting something at risk against a ticking clock or by blatantly altering the pace, direction, and succession of its linear flow. Certainly, consciousness of the subjectivity of our ordinary experience of time, and its relativity in the light of eternity, did not wait for the inspiration of Einstein, or even for the disclosure of the unimaginable lengths of geologic and cosmic time.[10] But it is no accident that a number of twentieth-century playwrights have brought something analogous to modern Relativity to the language or syntax of the stage, among them Thornton Wilder, J. B. Priestley, and Alan Ayckbourn. Wilder is the classic figure in this array, achieving that sort of transparency and elegant simplicity in at least one play that lights up the essential character of the place-time matrix, and transforms abstraction into human experience.

The Long Christmas Dinner (1931), a play in one long act, fixes place—like a ground bass or pedal point—in order to alter the perception of time. We are throughout in '*The dining-room of the Bayard home*' during a single sustained occasion. But as Wilder warns his readers, '*Ninety years are to be traversed in this play which represents in accelerated motion ninety Christmas dinners in the Bayard household.*'[11] The effect is rather like that of time-lapse photography. The dining room is of a self-evident typicality, with a normal entrance hall, but with two '*strange*' proscenium portals, one trimmed with garlands and fruits and the other draped in black velvet. Through one, characters enter in prams; through the other, having left the table, they depart for good.

Four overlapping generations sit at the table through the ninety years, growing and ageing, with a fifth generation announced, while throughout the table remains '*handsomely spread*', with a great turkey at the carver's chair. And through all the comings and goings, the dining room, the visible part of the Bayard home in a town somewhere in the heartland of America, holds all together—together with the occasion. But in fact, place is not so entirely fixed or unchanging, any more than the stream of many Christmas dinners that seem like one. For just as the diners are subject to a life cycle rooted in human biology, so too is the Bayard home subject to a life cycle of its own. There is a Mother Bayard, who remembers Indians on the site, and having to cross the

Mississippi on a raft to get to it. At the opening, pushing in her wheelchair, Roderick Bayard, her son, newly married to Lucia, asks her, 'Well mother, how do you like it? Our first Christmas dinner in the new house, hey?' Later, we hear 'it looks as good as new'; then that it needs a touch-up here and there; then that it is getting old and unfashionable, 'with all that ironwork filigree and that dreadful cupola', to be taken down and a new wing built; then that it is beset by factories and soot, and another kind of ageing. An unmarried daughter of Roderick and Lucia finds herself stifling: 'It's not only the soot that comes through the very walls of this house; it's the *thoughts*, it's the thought of what has been and what might have been here. And the feeling about this house of the years *grinding away*.' And at the last, through death and the dispersal of the young, only an ancient cousin is left at the table; while elsewhere, a daughter of the fourth generation and her husband are 'having their first Christmas dinner' in a brand new house, where her mother—now more comfortable in a wheelchair—has gone to live, and writes of an expected grandchild. When the cousin, grown from '*very old to immensely old*' totters at last into the dark portal, she is even murmuring of a 'Dear little Roderick and little Lucia'.

Place and time are less in dialogue here than in intimate conjunction; less simple coordinates here, like x and y, than embedded in a cascade of complex equations. Place too is temporalized, subject to a life cycle of its own, but one not wholly divorced from human and social temporality; while time is spatialized, in the fixity of occasion, and in the recursive track of human life in whose end is a new beginning.

In 'Beginnings', we saw how Tom Stoppard invents a stage world split between two distinct eras, but yoked through place. In Stoppard's *Arcadia*, place—a room on the garden front of a grand country house—is no less a constant than the family dining room in *The Long Christmas Dinner*. But instead of Wilder's time-lapse continuity, Stoppard's room alternates between two different times, two sets of events unfolding independently, two sets of characters—though with family connections. The first scene belongs to 1809; the second begins:

The lights come up on the same room, on the same sort of morning, in the present day, as is instantly clear from the appearance of HANNAH JARVIS; *and from nothing else. . . . The action of the play shuttles back and forth between the early nineteenth century and the present day, always in this same room.*[12]

Decor, books, papers, and other props serve both periods, and minor anachronisms are to be ignored. 'What triggered the [play], in a way,' Stoppard told an interviewer, 'was the idea of having a room which doesn't change, and you see what happens in the room in the past, and you see what happens in the room 180 years later.'[13]

But local change is not entirely ignored. In the earlier period, while the pleasing classicism of the park outside the windows is suffering a transformation to Romantic irregularity to the thumping music of a Newcomen engine, Newton's stable universe with its reversible equations is giving way to a universe subject to time's arrow and thermodynamic decay. Change is not ignored in either temporal locale. In fact a revolution is in progress, or rather several revolutions, in sensibility and thought; and where one embracing concern of the play as a whole is entropic loss and its inevitabilities, another is alternative pathways to renewal and regeneration. Moreover, there is an interplay between the two discontinuous eras. Some figures in the late sequence echo their predecessors, if in paler form and in combination. Some are consciously engaged in efforts at historical recovery, providing much of the comedy. The audience enjoys the gap between its direct knowledge and the historians' reconstructions and misconstructions. But some of the things lost to time can be identified after all, and others rediscovered. And the echoes and variant reiterations, even on a diminished scale, speak to that twentieth-century revolution in the understanding of the workings of Nature in time variously dubbed 'Chaos Theory' and 'Complexity,' but labelled by the precocious Thomasina of 1809–12 as 'The New Geometry of Irregular Forms', before she herself is lost to time so poignantly and prematurely.

In the last scene, as noted earlier, something wonderful happens: the two times converge. With no attempt at explanation or excuse, persons from the two alternating eras occupy the same space simultaneously, the modern characters mostly in Regency clothing for the occasion (a summer fête); and at the very end they all dance, one couple from each era, to the offstage music. In this singular space which constitutes the world of the play, they perform (to invoke the title of Poussin's pertinent visual allegory) nothing less than a Dance to the Music of Time.

Presentness is in the nature of all dramatic enactment, as Schiller long ago pointed out, but that does not obviate location in time. And, by the rules of ordinary experience, location in time (a feature of most plays) would seem to preclude having two times present in the same space. Presentness does not mean simultaneity. But then, as we have seen, when a play goes about its business of defining the play world, it is by no means obliged to incorporate the rules of ordinary experience. So, in *The Invention of Love* (1997), Stoppard has the aged A. E. Housman, very recently dead, strike up a seemingly ordinary conversation with his younger self. In *Time of My Life* (1992), where everything happens in a restaurant that is the site of a family birthday celebration, Alan Ayckbourn has a principal action going forward at a centre table, while at one side table, with some of the same characters, a second sequence is going backward into the past, and at another a third sequence is skipping ahead into the future. Our attention is directed by the lighting, but in effect we have three temporal locations in one place, present together.

Ayckbourn is an inveterate experimenter with resectioned time and space; but it would be selling him short to suggest that it is only for the novelty or the formal interest. The result of the symmetrical exfoliation of past and future in the locale and atmosphere of the present occasion in *Time of My Life* is a poignant, darkly ironic take on the nature of human happiness. The last scene returns us to the main table, '*to the night of the party, at the very start of the evening,*' an evening, as we now know, that ended in dire catastrophe. It concludes with a toast in which the head of the family remarks to his wife (whose birthday it is), to his two sons, and to their women, 'you know, in life you get moments—just occasionally which you can positively identify as being among the happy moments. They come up occasionally, even take you by surprise, and sometimes you're so busy worrying about tomorrow or thinking about yesterday that you tend to miss out on them altogether. I'd like to hope tonight might be one such moment.'[14]

Ayckbourn seems all the more inventive in that, aside from his radical management of place and time, he keeps to an acceptably naturalistic premiss. In plays where the supernatural or the acknowledged uncanny interfere, an easier legitimation is on offer, not so much for the resectioning of sequence and extension, as for the transcendence of the ordinary rules governing these dimensions. The most extraordinary instance occurs in an immensely successful nineteenth-century melodrama, an adaptation of a Dumas *père* novella, in which Dumas himself probably took a hand. Leaving the uncanny aside, it could almost be taken for a proleptic glimpse of some of the bizarre quantum puzzles of identity that Stoppard explores in his recondite espionage play, *Hapgood* (1988).

If Stoppard and Ayckbourn manage to give simultaneity to diverse times in one place, the authors of the dramatic version of *The Corsican Brothers* (1850) manage to represent the very same moment in diverse places. The first act, set in Corsica, climaxes in a vision of the outcome of a duel in the Paris environs. The bloodstained spirit of Louis dei Franchi—half of a pair of separated Siamese twins—rises through the floor, and presents a visionary scene:

He disappears—at the same moment the scene at the back opens and discloses an open clearing in the forest of Fontainbleau—at [one side] c. *is* CHATEAU-RENAUD, *who is wiping his sword, and on the other,* LOUIS DEI FRANCHI, *upon the ground,* R.C., *supported by a* SURGEON *and his* SECOND, *who are rendering him assistance.*[15]

The second act opens in the Paris Opera House on the night of a masked ball, and it leads, through contest and challenge in defence of a woman's honour, to:

Figure 5. Vision Scene from Charles Kean's production of *The Corsican Brothers*, Princess's Theatre, London, 1852. The ghost of Louis, rising through the stage at the end of Act I, shows the result of the duel in the forest of Fontainbleau wherein he was killed to his mother and twin brother Fabien at home in Corsica. Lithograph from the sheet music cover for the once ubiquitous 'Ghost Melody'.

A clearing in the Forest of Fontainbleau. — LOUIS DEI FRANCHI *on the ground* R.C., *wounded, attended by his seconds . . . a* SURGEON *is near him, and examines his wound—in the centre of the stage is* CHATEAU-RENAUD, *wiping his sword . . . It is an exact reproduction of the* TABLEAU *that terminated the First Act.*

Moreover, as Louis utters his last words,

the bottom of the stage opens slowly—the Chamber of the First Act is discovered, the clock marking the hour, ten minutes after nine; MADAME DEI FRANCHI *and* FABIEN [Louis's twin] *looking exactly as they did at the end of the First Act.* (p. 36)

In other words, the second act and the first act (as a note explains) *'are supposed to occur at the same time'*. They are not successive, but simultaneous, one passing in Corsica and one in France, each leading to the scene that ultimately unites them. The second act is nevertheless explanatory, enacting what led up to the event that culminates in the striking forest tableau, which in a less enterprising play might be relegated to retrospective narration.

In both sequences, much is made of the clock and the exact moment of Louis's death. Fabien in Corsica feels the blow that killed his twin in Paris at the very instant it occurs, annihilating the space that separates them (a macroscale anticipation of what is currently known as 'quantum entanglement'). Time as an inexorable, inelastic measure, however, drives the second-act incident that precipitates the duel, a bet against the (visible, moving) clock. The issue is whether the villain, Chateau-Renaud, will succeed in bringing the lady whose honour is Louis's concern to a compromising bachelor's supper by 4 A.M. on the night of the masked ball. (He does, by trickery.) But time, in relation to place, proves less linear, more recursive, after all. The third act takes place in the *same* clearing in the Forest of Fontainbleau that was the site of the original duel. Fabien has travelled to Paris to seek out his brother's slayer, and the play culminates in a third iteration of the scene in the forest, now however with Chateau-Renaud fighting Louis's identical twin. And this time—as in an alternative-world version—it is Chateau-Renaud who falls, once again shortly after the clock strikes nine.

Place has other functions in this play, aspects with critical, even political bearings. The manners of Corsica—its generous hospitality, bloody vendettas, vigorous customs and superstitions—are set in a contrast with those of Paris, its civilized pleasures, easy seductions, and polite heartlessness.[16] Each locale—for reasons of the heart—has claimed the adherence of a brother. In the final act, the Corsican brother equates the polite murders of an accomplished swordsman following the civilized code of the duellist with the assassinations of his native land. And the final duel itself turns into *'a violent bodily contest'* with broken sword blades tied to the duellists' wrists—Corsica in the Paris purlieus, the duel at one with the wild justice of the vendetta. It is the recursion in time and place, however, this fortuitous *déjà-vu,* that brings to the climactic outcome the feeling of 'poetic justice', and marks the invisible operations of the universal Providence that ultimately governs events in the world of melodrama.

From *The Long Christmas Dinner,* Wilder moved eventually to his ambitious *summa* of human life and history, *The Skin of Our Teeth* (1942), where place—the Antrobus home, and the tawdry carnival of Atlantic City—provides an anchoring base in present-day New Jersey for a series of overlays: of geologic time (the onset of the Ice Age, extinction of the dinosaurs); sacred time (the Flood, Armageddon); cultural-historical time (invention of the alphabet, the wheel); and transcending all these—though staged as the Procession of the Hours—the heritage of the great thoughts of the philosophers and seers. Like the place they inhabit, the much endangered Antrobus family, resilient but troubled, archetypal and ordinary, precariously surviving individually and collectively through the ages, grounds the sweeping cycles in something close to the tempo of human experience. Meanwhile, there are recurrent eruptions of theatre-in-the-theatre, when the actors slip their roles and supposedly speak for themselves with comic or serious effect (and with distinct correspondences between the actors and their Antrobus personae). This also throws out an anchor, with place reduced to theatre, the place of performance, and time to the time of enactment in the presence of an audience.

It is the role of the audience through its presence that now asks to be considered.

5

The Role of the Audience

In Shakespeare's *Tragedy of King Richard III*, at the end of a long scene where Richard woos and—just short of a 'yes'—wins Lady Anne, widow of the Lancastrian Prince of Wales, he turns to the audience in astonishment. He is amazed at his success; and indeed, it is hardly credible. But what scepticism we the audience might feel about its plausibility he undercuts, neutralizes, simply by agreeing with us. He in effect takes us into his confidence. Here he is, the murderer, not only of Henry VI whose corpse Anne is escorting for burial, but of Edward, Henry's son, who was actually Anne's husband. Here he is, ugly and misshapen compared to that paragon prince, 'Young, valiant, wise, and no doubt right royal'. Richard emphasizes every improbability:

> Was ever woman in this humour woo'd?
> Was ever woman in this humour won?
> I'll have her, but I will not keep her long.
> What, I that kill'd her husband and his father:
> To take her in her heart's extremest hate,
> With curses in her mouth, tears in her eyes,
> The bleeding witness of her hatred by,
> Having God, her conscience, and these bars against me—
> And I, no friends to back my suit at all;
> But the plain devil and dissembling looks—
> And yet to win her, all the world to nothing!
>
> (I. ii. 232–43)[1]

—and so on. We in the audience know that even before Richard's entrance Anne rained curses on his head. Then, when he outrageously declared that he had murdered out of love for *her*, and made offer of himself, she actually spat at him. Yet, there was something compelling even for us in his astonishing audacity, his shameless effrontery, his agile thrust and parry in the verbal exchanges, his challenge to Anne to stab him with his own sword, breast bare and on his knees. Nasty as he is, there is something flattering in his humorous confidences, his treating *us* as sophisticated and intelligent equals who can see the joke, so unlike the foolish innocent he has caught in the toils. Like those later villains, Iago and Edmund, he is something of a comedian, both in his irreverence and his self-deprecating humour (he says he will buy a looking-glass, and hire fashionable tailors to adorn his favoured limbs). He is a thorough charmer here, no doubt pathological, but adept at manipulating his auditors. And he succeeds with us no less than with poor Lady Anne, whose grim prospects, so coldly noted ('I'll have her, but I will not keep her long'), might help us keep our enthusiasm in check.

Co-opting his audience in some fashion is the job of the actor, director, and in the first instance the author, even if that means no more than taking quick advantage of what the audience brings to the play: readiness to pay attention and a set of latent expectations. Attention can be ripened into engagement with what is going forward on the stage. And expectations can be refashioned from what is brought to the occasion as the action unfolds. The script may be understood as a programme for creating and managing such expectations, and for managing sympathy, antipathy, curiosity, credulity, prurience, revulsion, shock, and deferred gratification—all that goes into response. Its working premiss, acknowledged or not, must be that every play aimed at performance is a transaction between stage and audience. 'Transaction', however, implies a two-way street, rather than passive reception and unqualified malleability. It means that in every performance the audience has a role to play, though its job may differ from play to play. And it follows that implied audiences also may differ, come with a personality, a distinct identity. Bizarre as it may seem, every listing of the dramatis personae in the printed text or the playhouse programme could plausibly include a line acknowledging, and perhaps characterizing, 'The Audience'.

Not surprisingly, there are plays that actually put 'an audience' on the stage, supposedly witnessing a performance, and in fact directly participating in it. Such stage audiences play the role of targeted collaborator, whose function is attention and response, while actually providing the real audience with an object of attention, whose 'responses' are intended to generate a response. All these plays reveal playwrights thinking about audiences and *their* performances, sometimes with mixed feelings or even hostile intent; for audiences do perform, and playwrights can be critical. At the author's curtain call on the first night of *Lady Windermere's Fan*, Oscar Wilde famously congratulated the audience for playing its part so well:

Ladies and Gentlemen: I have enjoyed this evening *immensely*. The actors have given us a *charming* rendering of a *delightful* play, and your appreciation has been *most* intelligent. I congratulate you on the *great* success of your performance, which persuades me that you think *almost* as highly of the play as I do myself.[2]

CROQUIS PRIS AU THÉÂTRE par DAUMIER

— On dit que les Parisiens sont difficiles à satisfaire, sur ces quatre banquettes pas un mécon-
tent — il est vrai que tous ces Français sont des Romains.

Figure 6. An enthusiastic audience, responding as one; but an audience plainly qualified for status as 'performer'. The caption accompanying the lithograph (from Honoré Daumier's series, 'Sketches Taken in the Theatre') reads: 'They say that Parisians are hard to please. On these four benches not one who is discontented. It is true that all these Frenchman are Romans' (i.e. members of a hired claque). *Charivari*, 13 February 1864; Delteil #3263.

And the custom on the Russian stage for the actors not just to acknowledge but to reciprocate the audience applause implies at the least degrees of audience merit and accomplishment.

In what follows, I shall first take note of a number of such staged audiences to see what the playwright makes of them. Then, after a look at some extreme ventures into transgressive mingling, I wish to consider, in the more ordinary case of the audience as an offstage presence, some essentials of its collaborative functioning—notably, how expectation and response enter the fabric of the play and govern our experience as readers and viewers. Finally I want to look at some instances of purposive co-option of the *actual* audience, extending the stage world, as it were, to include it, often when the playwright has designs on that audience that go beyond art and entertainment.

5.1. AUDIENCE ENACTMENTS

Two plays of the early modern era—the great age of the drama in England and Spain—take opposite tacks in staging an audience. In one, it is as if the stage comes to the audience; in the other, the audience seemingly invades the stage. In the first, Cervantes's *El Retablo de las Maravillas*, or *The Miracle Show* (earlier than 1615), a peripatetic performing group—the Manager (Chanfalla), his wife, and a musician—offer their show, replete with wonders, to the worthies of a country town, who contract a private performance to celebrate a wedding. The catch, the Manager warns, is that only those will be able to see the show who are of 'pure' blood and legitimate birth. Cervantes's satire is here directed at the first unequivocally racist mindset in early modern Europe, which distinguished 'old Christians' (*viejos Christianos*) from those with some Jewish or Moorish ancestry, and fetishized the difference as a matter of 'blood'. The scene is supplied with an interior curtain, and 'the audience'—all the notables and some of the townsfolk—file on expectantly. All are of course supremely confident that the announced disqualification could not possibly apply to them. And then, when it appears to each that indeed it does—as the Manager and his wife describe what is supposed to be passing before their eyes—all in this audience are desperate to conceal their presumed disability from their neighbours. Not that this audience is really a challenge. There is a delicate moment at the height of the supposed performance when the nephew of the Mayor compliantly joins the (invisible) biblical Herodias in a saraband:

BENITO. Go on, nephew, hold tight to that rascally Jewess. But if she's a Jewess, how can she see these marvels?

CHANFALLA. All rules have exceptions, Mr. Mayor.[3]

It is only when a billeting officer who has not been primed interrupts the show, questions everyone's sanity, and is accused of being 'one of *them*', that the imposture breaks up in a glorious free-for-all.

Apart from its telling social satire, Cervantes's playlet, designed for performance as an *entremès* or interlude between the acts of more serious drama, has something to say about audiences in general. Initially, it tells us, the audience is amenable to almost any premiss. It brings a latent appetite for wonder that translates into a willingness to be deceived. Moreover, once expectation is created, an audience can be unwilling to let go (unless it is trumped by something better, especially by something unexpected but—on second thought—already in the cards). As for the *real* audience, identification with the stage audience is by no means to be assumed. In fact the incentive to deny such identification, to put distance between oneself and these gullible, pompous, or stupid bumpkins, lets the play make its point. The play flatters the real audience by assuming its superiority, and by letting it in on the joke.

In Francis Beaumont's *Knight of the Burning Pestle* (1607), written about the same time as Cervantes's interlude, we have, not the stage brought to the audience, but rather the audience invading the stage. A self-conscious burlesque of theatrical taste and practice, it also has distinct affinities with Cervantes's great anti-romance *Don Quixote* (1605). In Beaumont's play, a Citizen, ostensibly a member of the actual audience, interrupts the Prologue and climbs on to the platform from the pit, complaining of the treatment his like receive on the stage of the day. He wants positive plays, 'something notably in honor of the commons of the city', something that presents its legends and history. He wants a hero of his own ilk, citizen and grocer.[4]

Soon Nell, the Citizen's wife, erupting from below, joins her husband. The practice of the time allowed for some privileged and fashionable members of the audience to sit along the sides of the platform that was the stage. 'Pray, gentlemen, make her a little room,' says George, the Citizen, enlisting one of these notables to help her up, she chattering amiably to all and sundry on her arrival. George calls for two stools, and there they sit with the other privileged spectators, bringing their tastes and fancies to bear directly upon the proceedings. George is not without some knowledge of the London theatre, but his taste leans to antiquated civic pageantry. Nell has a taste for chivalric romance, but is new to the theatre experience and naive in her responses. Both react and interrupt frequently. At their insistence, Nell's manservant, Rafe, is also plucked from the general audience, to play the lead as a knightly grocer-errant, and the players needs must suffer this chivalric action to cross and blend incongruously with the scheduled performance, a domestic play of parents and children, love and fortune, called 'The London Merchant'.

Beaumont's play appears to have been written for one of the Jacobean 'private theatres', catering to a more sophisticated audience, and for a professional children's company much in the fashion, whose competition the players in *Hamlet* found too much for them, and hence their travels. The play itself demonstrates that George's negative expectations—derived from the mere title—and his complaints on how citizens are treated in much Jacobean drama are not without warrant. That is, once more the playwright aims at complicity with an actual audience, *not* represented by the stage audience; an audience that will share the joke of George's preferences and Nell's naive credulity and misplaced sympathies. In Nell's enthusiasm, for example, for the silly suitor 'of gentle blood' that the rich merchant Venturewell intends for his daughter instead of the clever, impecunious, and worthy apprentice, she fails to read the coded signals and genre conventions, fails to play her prescribed (inscribed) audience part. But the opportunities for ridicule that the Citizen and his wife provide carry to targets beyond their unsophisticated class and kind. Indeed, neither the putatively superior and complicit real audience nor its taste and habits escape scot-free. Nell reproves the gentlemen she sits among for their filthy smoking. She sentimentalizes over the pretty children who do the acting. And the accepted conventions of dramatic style and genre, from rhetoric to closure, are brought under mocking scrutiny. As the play winds down, for example, George complains that everyone's part is come to an end but Rafe's, who has been left out. Nell has the solution: 'let him come out and die'. One of the regular company objects:

BOY. 'Twill be very unfit he should die, sir, upon no occasion, and in a comedy too.
CITIZEN. Take you no care of that, sir boy. Is not his part at an end, think you, when he's dead? Come away, Rafe.
    Enter Rafe, with a forked arrow through his head. (V. 276–81)

Rafe then proceeds to die at length, in blank verse, summarizing his knightly career, saying farewell to his 'prentice pleasures, and expiring in piteous groans. In so satisfying a concession to Nell and George's expectations, his performance, like much of the rest of the play, floats a genial critique, not just of the naive and sensational in audience taste and of the theatrical fare that suited it, but of theatricality itself, a preoccupation in an age much given to outward show and uneasy about it.[5]

Adding an audience not called for in the text to the *mise-en-scène* of a canonical play is now a not uncommon directorial ploy. But though sometimes enlivening, such anti-illusionist enhancements rarely give scope for the sort of engagement with the nature of theatre that staging an audience can give when it is part of the script. The appeal in such staging is made plain by the playwright Alan Bennett talking about possible influences on his *Forty Years On* (1969), which has a play within the play. He reports seeing Peter Terson's *Zigger Zagger* (1967) 'with the stage a crowded football terrace, which made me realize how theatrical a spectacle is an audience watching an audience'.[6]

Nevertheless, for the playwright, staging an audience is hardly ever a neutral act, free of critical animus or reformist zeal. Like the actor, whose dependence on an audience is both more immediate and more absolute (a Shavian resort to publication is not an option for the actor), the ambitious playwright may harbour a degree of resentment at how his dependence limits his autonomy. Speaking through the role of the Player in *Rosencrantz and Guildenstern Are Dead*, Tom Stoppard addresses such dependence, in the end as intrinsic to the playwright's art as to the performer's need. Earlier in Stoppard's play, the Player's company and Hamlet's old school friends had met on the road to Elsinore. There, when the actors launched into a wayside performance for this impromptu audience of two, the audience seems to have stealthily decamped.

GUILDENSTERN. Ah! I'd forgotten—you performed a dramatic spectacle on the way. Yes, I'm sorry we had to miss it.
PLAYER (*bursts out*). We can't look each other in the face! (*Pause, more in control.*) You don't understand the humiliation of it—to be tricked out of the single assumption which makes our existence viable—that somebody is *watching*. . . . The plot was two corpses gone before we caught sight of ourselves, stripped naked in the middle of nowhere and pouring ourselves down a bottomless well.[7]

On the other hand, Stoppard shows also a degree of (ambivalent) sympathy with the plight of the ordinary audience. Writhing on the periphery of the mysterious events at Elsinore, Rosencrantz, at the footlights, complains: 'I feel like a spectator—an appalling business. The only thing that makes it bearable is the irrational belief that somebody interesting will come on in a minute. . . .'

GUILDENSTERN. See anyone?
ROSENCRANTZ. No. You?
GUILDENSTERN. No. (*At footlights.*) What a fine persecution—to be kept intrigued without ever quite being enlightened. (p. 41)

—an effective, if jaundiced summation of subjection to an art that succeeds by stringing us along.

Aggression towards an audience channelled via representation looms large in a host of modern plays, especially those in an avant-garde tradition that flaunts its credentials by attacking an imagined bourgeois or philistine establishment—plays like Peter Weiss's *Marat/Sade* and Genet's *The Blacks: A Clown Show*, both already considered for how they bring complexity to the making of stage worlds. Weiss's staged audience, unlike Beaumont's Londoners and Cervantes's villagers, is placed in a historical perspective that presumptively distances it from the actual, contemporary audience. The play is in fact a history play as well as a drama of contending ideas with psychodramatic underpinnings, its premiss the performance of a piece written and directed in 1808 by the Marquis de Sade, in the asylum where he was for a long time confined, concerning events taking place in 1793. The onstage audience, the institution's director Coulmier and his family, prominently seated on a raised tribunal in the eye of the actual audience, wear the costumes of 1808. Coulmier, however, acts as a Prologue and host, welcoming the actual audience, but in terms that cast it (co-opt it) as contemporary, like the actual Parisians who found entertainment in the mad and visited the asylum to attend de Sade's spectacles.

Throughout the performance, Coulmier and his family, the onstage audience, serve as reverberators, reacting visibly and audibly to the complementary excesses of anarchic individualism (de Sade's and the madder actors') and revolutionary populism (Marat; the Jacobin, Roux; the mass of patients who make up the assemblies, armies, crowds). Embodying the middle-class, bureaucratic order and civility that had succeeded the revolutionary fervours, the liberal Coulmier and his family are the targets of de Sade's and the play's opportunistic provocations, and Coulmier frequently rises to the bait, to intervene where something threatens to go too far, where an invisible line is crossed. The risqué game that moves between the titillating and the transgressive (a Sadean though perhaps not a sadistic game, in that it is a challenge to authority rather than an exercise of power) is made manifest through the use of this staged and targeted audience. In such circumstances, the actual audience will be likely to want to distance itself from the targets, to share the superior position of the manipulator and ironist, as in the case of Shakespeare's Richard and Anne. But especially at the end, the play takes a turn intended to make this difficult. The volatile mob on the stage floor gets out of hand, and marches to the front, directly, frighteningly, at the real audience, chanting, shouting, and fighting. Coulmier's welcoming incorporation of the actual audience into the Charenton scene now comes back as an attack on the psychological distance in spectatorship. In Peter Brooks's famous production (Royal Shakespeare Company, 1964), now enshrined in the English-language text, the Jacobin Roux provides a choral refrain directed explicitly at the real audience:

> When will you learn to see
> When will you learn to take sides

—before he is swallowed up in the advancing ranks.[8] The aggression against the audience, the rebellion against its limiting control, ceases to be indirect as the action assaults and denies its defined and insulated role in the collaborative contract.

In *The Blacks*, the staged audience, viewing the action from a high gallery, is without the historical specificity of Weiss's audience. Rather, it has a collective archetypal character as 'The Court'—Queen, Valet, Governor, Judge, Missionary—emphasized by mask and costume. Its theatricality is further declared in that the masks, representing white persons, are contrived to reveal the black actors' dark skin and woolly hair. (The Dedication says the play was intended for an all black cast.) Their action is cartoonish, and eventually the

Court will die in a grand parodic massacre. But despite such blatant distancing, the Court also stands in for what was then the assumed white audience,
whose enlightened political views (likely in Genet's avant-garde following) are
not permitted to immunize it from the scorn and ridicule directed at these
typifications of folly, bluster, bloody-mindedness, and venality, these icons of
a racist colonialism. When Archibald, the black presenter, opens, he takes care
to obliterate the distinction: '[A]ddressing now the audience, now the Court,'
he declares inclusively, 'You are white. And spectators. This evening we shall
perform for you.'[9]

How does Genet know that his audiences will always be white? He doesn't,
of course, but in a preliminary note he stipulates: 'This play, written, I
repeat, by a white man, is intended for a white audience, but if, which is
unlikely, it is ever performed before a black audience, then a white person,
male or female, should be invited every evening. . . . The actors will play for
him.' Genet even makes provision, when no white person is forthcoming, for
creating a symbolic white audience through masks or a dummy. Such overt
specification of an intended real audience is unusual, if not unique, and it
tells us something about the particular dynamic at the root of *The Blacks*, on
which Genet built his tensions and effects. It also tells us something general
about how plays work. It tells us that every play's transactions between stage
and audience are of such calculated specificity that its moment-to-moment
workings can be affected, perhaps even fatally, and certainly altered, by an
unscripted audience. It tells us that, especially in approaching the inherited
text, it is useful to take account of the character of the audience that the
play first aimed to engage, and how it differs from that abstract, timeless, and
characterless entity sometimes called 'the audience'. It also tells us, however,
that a living audience can extend Coleridge's 'willing suspension of disbelief'
to aspects of its own contemporaneity, can open itself to alien mindsets,
compounded of imagination, expectation, and experience, of which it may
have little conception to start, but will absorb in the course of the play.

A genre matter of some pertinence is that playwrights, often working
with particular companies, particular theatres, in specific locales, are more
likely to write for particular audiences whose tastes, interests, and capacities
they know than are most novelists—even of genre fiction—whose audience of dispersed individuals encourages a vaguer, more generalized sense
of an implicit readership. I would include here the 'dear reader' of most
Victorian authorial asides, even though there is a certain affinity between
a Richard of Gloucester's audience confidences and a Thackeray's ironic
intimacies.

5.2. ILLICIT INTERCOURSE

Though the question 'What is theatre?' had engaged such great practitioners as Shakespeare, Calderón, and Molière as worthy of dramatic exploration, it was with the onset of Romantic subjectivism at the turn of the nineteenth century and the preoccupation with the intrinsic character and materials of the arts in the self-conscious twentieth that it claimed the entire foreground in ambitious work for the stage. Staging the audience in such work gave scope to representations, not simply analytical and critical of role and function, but iconoclastic—boundary dissolving and problematizing—as in the case of the two meta-dramatic playwrights who seem to embody most thoroughly the acute theatre-consciousness of their age. In Ludwig Tieck's *Land of Upside Down* (*Die verkehrte Welt*, 1798) and Luigi Pirandello's *Each in His Own Way* (*Chiascuno a suo modo*, 1924), the boundaries are tested, if not actually trashed, between the real world, inhabited by the actual audience, and the fictive world, inhabited by invented beings. And it is not only the boundaries as such that are put to the stretch, but the easy dualistic thinking that distinguishes the two realms in the first place.

Tieck's play—its title invoking the carnival imagery and the revolutionary impetus in the motif of 'The World Turned Upside Down'—opens with an Epilogue, addressed, as such epilogues always were, to the audience. (The play will close, needless to say, with a Prologue.) The Epilogue assures the audience that it can perfectly well skip the formality of seeing the play before passing judgement. After all, he says, you are presumably a thoroughly experienced audience (*schon geübt*), and one 'in the habit of accepting whatever's shown you'. Moreover,

You've given out enough opinions in your lives to tell what's what in our comedy without having to see it. The author's name—provided he's famous–or the views of a reliable friend—these are your usual guides.

The Epilogue then ventriloquizes, speaking *as* the audience:

Well, well, not a bad play—good enough for the old days—tolerable if you keep in mind its modest pretensions—but hardly first-rate, of course.[10]

Apart from skewering the audience's herd instinct and its patronizing vacuity, Tieck projects theatre-goers schooled—and limited—in their expectations, bored with familiarity, but by no means avid for originality. But he also buffers his indictment, and prepares his audience for further challenge, by setting this direct address at one remove. The opening stage direction reads:

The curtain rises, revealing a theater, whose curtain rises, disclosing the EPILOGUE, *who steps forward.*[11]

Having established a hierarchy of representations in receding perspective, however, the play proceeds to breach its lines at every turn. An argument between Poet (author) and actor soon involves a voice from the audience and turns into an argument between actor and spectator. The actor Pierrot, tired of playing, wants to be a spectator for a change, and jumps into the parterre. The spectator Grünhelm, who wants to act, climbs onto the stage. On stage, with the approval of the audience, the comic lead, Scaramuz, repudiates genre decorum and takes over the dignified, serious part of Apollo. To the histrionic despair of the Poet, the public—claiming authority from long experience—takes over responsibility for what goes. In practice, this means that the audience gets the effects and the outcomes it wants, much as in *The Knight of the Burning Pestle*. Some spectators, in the midst of a love scene, fancy a thunderstorm:

GRÜNHELM [now as actor]. Gentlemen, a thunderstorm is an excellent thing, but it doesn't fit into this particular play.
SCÄVOLA [a spectator]. It doesn't fit! We say it fits, so it'll fit!
PIERROT [now a spectator]. Bend or break, we want a storm.
GRÜNHELM Very well, come with me, my love, let us take shelter under a roof, since our cruel audience demands a thunderstorm. (p. 53)

Soaked by the rain, battered by the thunder and lightning, Scaramuz as Apollo swears at the technician for exceeding the script, while the technician in turn blames public demand. Scävola from the audience explains: 'It's because we want to take pleasure in your tragical situation,' driving the weather-beaten Scaramuz to Lear-like sublimities.

The transgressive mingling of representational categories, of 'theatre' and 'life', to the confounding of all distinctions, takes an inward turn with the appearance of an Innkeeper who is extremely conscious of his stake in the repertory and in theatrical convention. He speaks in character (not as an actor) about the innkeeper role, its utility, its variants, its fluctuating stock in theatrical fashion. He confounds role and representation, worrying, for example, over the current dearth of travellers, so unlike that 'time of prosperity once when you rarely saw a play without an inn and its innkeeper'. He suggests that had he anticipated such a slump in business, he would have taken up some other profession—a Court Official, for example, much in demand in the current theatre.

In the third act (of the standard five), some characters, with the help of the Muses, decide to put on a play for Apollo (Scaramuz) and his court. The scene is '*A hall with a stage*'. Grünhelm announces 'the audience', and, to the sound of trumpets, Apollo comes on with his retinue.

They sit. The stage curtain rises, disclosing a garden.
                    Enter GRÜNHELM *as* PROLOGUE.

As the new play unfolds amid comment, Scävola from the original audience exclaims:

SCÄVOLA. Say, this is tremendous! Here we are spectators, and over there are seated these other spectators too.
PIERROT. A play always has another one tucked inside of it. (p. 78)

The characters in the inner play announce they are about to put on a play. And now Pierrot asks, 'Which play should we be interested in? The earlier one, or the one that's going to be presented now?' Guests arrive for the entertainment, the scene changes to a room with '*a small private theatre*' where they take their seats, and the curtain rises on a charming pastorale. Each play has an allegorical bearing on its envelope, and eventually they collapse into each other, leaving the primary 'spectators' (planted among the actual audience) in an uproar.

SCÄVOLA. This is too crazy. Look—here we sit watching a show; in this show more people sit watching another show, and in this third show, the third actors are watching still another show!

Another 'spectator' asks, 'Imagine now—what if we were actors in a play, and somebody saw it all tangled together. Wouldn't that be the confusion of all confusions!'

SCÄVOLA. There are fearful dreams of this kind. And there are thoughts that spin and spin deeper and deeper inward. And such dreams, and such thoughts, can drive you mad. (p. 87)

Though the initial stage audience is confused, and the real audience ought to be as well, what with characters at one level playing characters and audience at another, nevertheless the scaling through receding planes is actually well worked out. What it points to, however, is cognitive collapse—of rational order into mental chaos, of the actor and audience functions into each other—and to the *Blick im Abgrund*, the terrifying glance into an ontological abyss.

In the end, Grünhelm, to avoid having to fight in the coming stage war, makes the harlequin's *salto mortale*, a perilous leap back over the footlights into the audience, framed and dramatized as a suicide. But such transgressive heroism, and the implication of a great gulf fixed between stage and audience, is once more undercut when the 'spectators' freely invade the stage to aid Scaramuz as the war goes against him. Reminded by the Director that the war and everything else are make-believe, the 'spectators' nevertheless make manifest their ultimate power. The Director was going to fire Scaramuz for his intransigent ways, but now is happy to change his mind: 'I'd be a fool if I let him go, seeing that he's so popular.'

Pirandello's *Each in His Own Way* was the second play in what he described as 'something of a trilogy of the theater in the theater'.[12] In all three plays, primary stakeholders in the partnership of the theatre are brought into conflict with each other. In *Each in His Own Way*, the conflict, he says, lies between the spectators, the author, and the actors.

The premiss of the action is that Pirandello himself has written a play that dramatizes the aftermath of a recent society scandal, an amorous triangle that resulted in the suicide of a gifted artist. Pirandello stages the audience for the first night performance of this play in two 'Choral Interludes', scenes representing the theatre lobby in the intervals between the acts. The play proper, a programme note warns, may be either in two or three acts, given the probability of some untoward incidents. In actuality, the second Interlude serves as a final act, for 'the play' and for the play about 'the play'.

The audience that Pirandello parades in the first Lobby Interval is a mixed lot. There are pro- and anti-Pirandello factions, the former very explanatory; a rival author or two; and a clutch of professional critics, since this is a first night. A number of ordinary playgoers voice their bewilderment and irritation. A number of sophisticates are ostentatiously knowing about the scandal the play is based on. There is considerable comedy, in the actions of one circulating magpie, for example, who retails the opinions of whichever group he last managed to overhear. The focus in this first interval is very much on the foibles, confusion, partisanship, varying responses of this ostensibly representative contemporary audience, with Pirandello calling it to account for its deficiencies and indulging his accrued animosities, while the real audience presumably takes the satire in good part, recognizing the types and the formulas with amusement, and discounting any personal application in the spirit of Cervantes's villagers.

The focus shifts, however, towards the end of the Interval, with the entrance of two of the irate principals (and their restraining friends) in the real-life drama 'the play' supposedly exploits. They are thus part of 'the audience' (they come from the offstage auditorium) as well as, by transfer, the persons in 'the play'. Actually, we may have seen these originals before. In the text he approved as 'definitive', Pirandello provides for an improvisational prelude to the first act: '*The representation of this play should begin on the street,*' he writes, '*or more properly in front of the theatre,*' with some newsboys crying an Extra featuring the immanent scandal of Pirandello's play based on the well-known recent tragic events. Meanwhile, some men in evening dress near the (actual) box office attempt to dissuade a distraught woman (the 'real-life' lady in the case) from purchasing a ticket; while in the (actual) lobby a similar scene erupts as a gentleman (the surviving lover) assures his friends that nothing will happen; he knows she will be there, but he only wants to see her.[13]

In the second Lobby Interval, after the second act, the audience is slow to appear, and there is audible turmoil coming from the invisible auditorium and stage. When the doors are thrown open and the crowd spills out, the continuing uproar is explained. 'The Moreno woman' has made her way backstage and evidently precipitated a series of assaults: on the actress who impersonates her, and possibly by that actress on the author himself. The drama in effect now comes out into the lobby, a drama in progress; and the crowd becomes the audience for, first, the revolt of the actors, who mostly go home, and then the end of the drama proper, as the 'real' subjects of the play encounter and more or less replay 'in life' the impassioned scene of violent hatred, consuming love, and convulsive union in self-discovery with which 'Pirandello' had concluded the second act of his reality-based 'play'.

With or without the preliminary sideshows near the box office and in the actual lobby (which concern the struggle of the 'real-life' characters to become part of the audience), the eruption of the models for this 'drama with a key' late in the first 'Choral Interlude' is also their differentiating emergence from the audience as staged. There are numerous mischievous paradoxes here. In as much as the inner society drama, whose first act we have just seen, puts these individual audience members, their society, their lives, on the stage, it is dramatizing the audience that the outer play also stages. But then it turns out that those members of the audience credited with living the drama originally take their cues, their understanding of themselves, even some of their language, from the dramatized and acted version of their lives, reversing the established relation of the real and the represented. A 'SPETTATORE INTELLIGENTE' underlines the fact that 'They have done, perforce, under our very eyes and quite without intending to, something that art had foreseen!' (p. 197). (One of the 'actors', reappearing, undercuts this pat conclusion, however, by hinting that more had taken place outside the theatre; there is, after all, a missing third act). Finally—the 'performance' having collapsed—theatre officials start clearing out the 'lobby', the curtain comes down, and the Manager of the company comes before it to announce to those still in their seats (the audience proper) that due to the unfortunate incidents that occurred at the end of the second act, the play is over for the evening.

Both Tieck and Pirandello are more interested in the collapse of distinctions, roles, and cognitive hierarchies than in rescuing them from confusion, though both are deeply engaged with the ways in which imagination and experience, inner and outer worlds, constitute our reality. Both also take pleasure in planting a few darts in the audience, so admirably positioned in its liminality to illustrate and respond to such unsettling concerns. Each stages an audience distinctly of his era, one popular, one urban and modern, and uses it to twist the tail of a putative real audience for its failures in competence and adventurous understanding, for its appetite for the sensational *and* the familiar, for the burden of an inertia that can weigh down and even derail the theatre's collaborative enterprise. One does so with an ebullient Romantic energy that hardly knows where to stop, dragooning its audience into a comic universe; the other with a modern qualifying scepticism whose involutions give way to impasse, implicating its audience in the comedic heartlessness of the spectacle, as bystanders in the presence of suffering.

5.3. AUDIENCE SURROGATES

There is another, less direct form of audience representation in the play text and the theatre, one that is especially convenient in plays that have an argument to make, or that have designs on the mental landscape of the auditors. In such plays there is often a figure, sententious or ironic, whose views come closest to articulating those of the author, a figure identified in the criticism of nineteenth-century French 'thesis drama' as the *raisonneur*. In Pirandello's *It Is So (If You Think So)* (1917), Lamberto Laudisi is such a figure, as is Cayley Drummle in Arthur Wing Pinero's fallen-woman play, *The Second Mrs Tanqueray* (1893). They are, in effect, *author* surrogates, and collectively, and probably deservedly, have a bad name. Such figures are at a far remove, however, from those that function as *audience* surrogates, whose role in the play is not that of a choral commentator, pointing a moral or furnishing futile advice, analysis, and wisdom, but rather that of a learner, open and vulnerable to experience, and typically suffering change. Shaw, who was often accused of ventriloquizing his views through all his unnaturally articulate characters, does no such thing. Rather, in his heterodox critiques of our social arrangements and mental furniture, he allows each character his or her own point of view. It is out of their encounter that knowledge and insight emerge—or failing that, the need for radical change. But if Shaw keeps clear of author surrogates, he makes frequent use of audience surrogates, figures whose learning curve, and whose progress from Romantic illusion to pained disillusion to a new grasp on themselves and the world, lays out the track Shaw has in mind for those who are following the play. Many of these audience surrogates in Shaw's plays are vital and energetic young women: Vivie Warren in *Mrs Warren's Profession*; Raina in *Arms and the Man*; Barbara Undershaft in *Major Barbara*; Ellie Dunn in *Heartbreak House*. Barbara, a tireless and magnetic Salvationist, is bereaved of her uniform, her vocation, and her innocence on encountering her father and discovering the complicity of war and religion, money and salvation, in the social fabric. When, still troubled, she begins to master her despair—and glimpse the possibility of using the devil's tools for her own purposes—Undershaft comments on the process: 'You have learnt something. That always feels at first as if you had lost something.'[14] In Shaw's hopeful design, something similar can happen to the audience, in parallel, vicariously. Of *Mrs Warren's Profession*, where Mrs Warren's daughter Vivie has to learn something about her complicity with prostitution, Shaw wrote that, finally, 'Nobody's conscience is smitten except, I hope, the conscience of the audience. My intention is that they shall go home thoroughly uncomfortable.'[15] Of *Widowers' Houses* (1893), the first of his 'Plays Unpleasant', he wrote that 'the didactic object of my play is to bring conviction of sin';[16] which it does, not by parading a repugnant antisocial villain, but by aligning us with the well-meaning, liberal, conscientious lover Harry Trench. Discovering that his father-in-law to be is a slum landlord, Trench rejects the money that was to come with the bride, upsetting the match. But his would-be benefactor demonstrates that Trench's own income, and that of his aristocratic relations, depends on the rents and high interest such property produces. Trench, staggered, asks, 'Do you mean to say I am just as bad as you are?'

SARTORIUS. . . . . If, when you say you are just as bad as I am, you mean that you are just as powerless to alter the state of society, then you are unfortunately quite right. *Trench does not at once reply. He stares at Sartorius, and then hangs his head and gazes stupidly at the floor, morally beggared, with his clasped knuckles between his knees, a living picture of disillusion.*[17]

Though Trench is revived in a sexually charged reconciliation with the slumlord's wilful daughter, he is left with the wreckage of his moral superiority, unable to see past the social realities. He becomes part of the general conspiracy. Here surrogate and audience are meant to part company. Where Trench becomes one with the present order, the audience is meant to be provoked to second thoughts by the residual, unresolved unpleasantness; to wish to reject the stigma of complicity in the prevailing iniquity.

In later plays, with other audience strategies, characters who can function as audience surrogates are not thus left in the lurch. Like Ellie Dunn, the naive, romantically inclined young woman invited into the strange, leisure-class bohemia of Heartbreak House, they tend to come out on the far side of disillusionment. In Ellie's case, involving public disaster—the Great War—as well as private catastrophe, it is to a vision of 'Life with a blessing'.[18]

Needless to say, Shaw did not invent the audience surrogate. The author of the great fifteenth-century morality play *Everyman*, for example, creates a protagonist whose job is to learn what the audience has to learn, in parallel, a protagonist who, facing Death, exemplifies the universal condition. Some of the choruses in surviving Greek tragedy provide, not just lyric interludes or responsive commentary, but the expression of an advance in knowledge or insight that aligns it with a responsive audience's experience. Shaw's successor in the creation of a modern heterodox forensic drama, Bertolt Brecht, uses variants of the audience surrogate: the Control Chorus asked to pass judgement on the fearsome decision of the three agitators to kill their comrade, after witnessing their enactment of what led to the decision, in *The Measures Taken*; Galileo's former pupil and disciple, his landlady's son, particularly in the final episodes of *Galileo*, where the meaning of the scientist's submission, for himself and the world, needs to be argued out. As in the Shaw plays, Andrea, the audience surrogate here, has something personally important at stake, and that is what validates his surrogacy, makes it dramatically tolerable.

W. H. Auden once wrote, 'Drama began as the act of a whole community. Ideally there would be no spectators. In practice every member of the audience should feel like an understudy.'[19] However drama began, whatever gives an audience a stake in the issues and outcomes serves to make the experience meaningful; and if we moderns are not up to playing Prince Hamlet himself, as another poet suggests, surrogacy is probably the quickest practical route to feeling like an understudy, Auden's second best.

5.4. AUDIENCE EXPECTATIONS

In the opening scene of Jean Cocteau's *Orphée* (1926), Orpheus, the archetypal poet and musician of Greek myth and religion, sits listening to the alphabetic tappings of an astonishing horse, like those carnival animals once used to tell fortunes and do sums. Orpheus, enraptured, believes he is channelling the spirit world. As the horse taps out the letters according to their position in the alphabet, the poet announces them to Euridice, his jaded wife: M . . . E . . . R . . . At this point the audience is caught up in aroused expectations concerning what comes next. It anticipates the letters that will complete the rude word MERDE. Instead The horse taps out: C . . . I . . . for MERCI, or 'Thank you'. Expectation has been deceived; but from another angle expectation has been fulfilled with the two letters that complete the word, only not as anticipated, and the result is rueful laughter.

The expectations of the particular audience Cocteau assumed are aroused in the play by the letters themselves, but they are reinforced by association with a notorious event in French avant-garde theatre and drama, the scandal of the first word (or near word) in Alfred Jarry's *Ubu Roi* (1896): 'Merdre!' They are further enhanced by the known predilection of Surrealist artists, Dadaists, and other moderns (with whom Cocteau was often at odds) for forms of automatic writing, the generation of poems out of randomness, and for giving offence. The audience, then, at the moment between the first three and the last two series of taps, is seized by an expectation with a threefold genesis: internal to the play (the build-up in the first three letters); the legacy of an earlier play (*Ubu* and its notorious opening stroke); and the wider cultural and lexical heritage (Surrealist poetics, the legendary *mot de Cambronne*, etc.).[20] But Cocteau isn't finished with this bout in the game of expectations. Having feinted successfully and scored with 'Merci', he unexpectedly scores again by delivering the avoided shocker. The horse had previously tapped out a magical sentence which Orpheus entered in an All-Thrace poetry competition. The sentence poem, we learn, is 'Madame Euridice reviendra des Enfers' (Madame Euridice shall return from the underworld). But as the Bacchantes and the Arcadian public eventually discover, the sentence contains an acrostic, its initial letters forming the word MERDE. This insult to public dignity precipitates the poet's violent dismemberment.

The play and the playwright create expectations, and so lead the audience on, teasing, deferring, fulfilling, and exceeding them, using expectation as a springboard for surprise. But expectation is by no means wholly in the playwright's hands. As in the case of the tapping horse, it also depends, inevitably, on what the audience brings to the play. And if playwright, actors, and audience are to be understood as collaborators, it is above all in negotiating the confluence of expectations that the work of collaboration lies.

That playwright, actors, and audience can find themselves tugging in different directions we have already seen dramatized in the rebellion of Beaumont's and Tieck's vociferous spectators with their non-negotiable demands. Modern playwrights, feeling constrained by the conservative bent of theatregoers (and producers), speak their unhappiness directly. Chekhov, subject to surviving genre conventions, complained about endings: 'The hero has either to marry or shoot himself'; and his major plays, culminating in *The Cherry Orchard*, can be seen as tracing a progressive elimination of those inexorable alternatives.[21] At about the same time Shaw noted, dismissively, 'we have plenty of dramas with heroes and heroines who are in love and must accordingly marry or perish at the end of the play'.[22] But when he attempted to evade such a Hobson's choice at the end of *Pygmalion* (1914), first the principal actor—who knew what his audience desired and expected, and what it meant for his own success—and then several generations of like minded producers, subverted or rewrote Shaw's ending to bring it closer to the romantic comedy norm.[23] Playwrights of a calibre to redefine the possibilities of drama have long engaged in genre stretching: Shakespeare does so, for example, in *Love's Labour's Lost*, Molière in *The Misanthrope*, Ibsen in *A Doll's House*. In *A Doll's House*, Ibsen actually teases his audience with outcomes that would meet genre-based expectations. He sets out both tragic and comic resolutions, and then snatches them away as they are found wanting. The tragic outcome looms when—helpless to avoid the exposure of her forgery, believing herself unfit as a mother, believing Torvald, her husband, will nobly take the blame for her crime if not prevented—Nora, exalted, rushes off to kill herself. But her exit is interrupted by Torvald, damning revelation in hand, who tells her to 'stop play-acting', 'Let's have no silly nonsense'; and then far from rising to a heroic self-sacrifice, looks for a practical, face-saving way out. The comedy ending is also dangled before the audience. The revelation of Nora's wifely crime—the forgery that saved her husband's life—has been set in train by the hard-pressed blackmailer and usurer Krogstad. But Nora's friend, Mrs Linde, reviving an old romantic affinity, so overwhelms him by proposing that they join their battered lives that he declares he will retrieve his damning letter to Torvald and presumably suppress the evidence of the forgery. All this recalls the plot mechanics of intrigue comedy and drama, where happiness or catastrophe is invested in a document—a will, a compromising love letter—or an object—a necklace, a fan. With Krogstad transformed by love and the fatal document suppressed, the Helmers' imperilled domestic bliss (sustained by ignorance) might be in the end secured. But, seeing a compelling case for truth within the Helmers' marriage, and wise enough to avoid leaving her own motives open to suspicion, Mrs Linde stops Krogstad from retrieving the letter, and thus the play from coming to rest with all domestic dissonance resolved. Krogstad does return the forgery, which Torvald joyfully destroys, professing the belief that all can be as it was, but it is too late for such a comedy conclusion, just as it is too late for tragedy. Instead, Ibsen surprises expectation with something else, something patently not of the theatre in its then current forms, and in that sense no longer, in Torvald's phrase, 'play-acting'. There is no fatal conclusion, no happily ever after, familiar to the well-trained audience. Instead, Nora explains herself, departs into a terrifying indeterminacy, and changes things for ever.

Expectation—with respect to language, behaviour, causes, and consequences—flows in from many sources, not all associated with the theatre, and neither the playwright nor the actor has to start from scratch. Expectation is principally a matter of norms rooted in experience, whether taken from art or life: what is conventionally said and done in the circumstances; how things are supposed to happen. When they happen otherwise, the effect can be either refreshing or thoroughly disconcerting—the latter a boon to an artist who wants to shock or, in Ezra Pound's famous watchword, to 'Make It New'. Or the effect can be terribly funny, as in W. S. Gilbert's Palaces of Truth, Joe Orton's parade of naked Ids, or Oscar Wilde's deformations of cliché ('Divorces are made in heaven'). In fact there is nothing that humans find more hilarious and more exhilarating than violations of the coercive logic of the ordinary and the necessary.

An exemplary demonstration of how the orchestration of an audience's evoked and diverted expectations can play into the unfolding of an action can be found in John Millington Synge's *Playboy of the Western World* (1907)—even though the riots that marked that play's first Dublin production and its subsequent travels to America suggest that Synge, who knew how to be provocative, here might have overplayed his hand.

Figure 7. The audience engaged (or the drama displaced). J.-J. Grandville's 'The First Night of [Victor Hugo's] *Hernani*', an illustration for Louis Reybaud's novel *Jérome Parturot* (1846). As with Synge's *Playboy* in its initial reception and other such playhouse events, the audience Grandville depicts, both partisan and otherwise, in fact disengages from the play proper, reducing it to the occasion of a (subsequently) famous politico-cultural happening.

The initial premiss of this great 'dark comedy'[24] is that the Playboy, otherwise Christy Mahon, in flight from the law, wanders into a community in the west of Ireland where his crime—when he confesses to having murdered his father—evokes universal admiration, and he is not only made welcome but made much of. This reaction—thoroughly at odds with all normal expectation—is comic in effect, the comedy enhanced and indeed licensed by Christy's extreme timidity. Christy has to be bullied into confession by the sharp-tongued Pegeen Mike, daughter of the public house where the play is set. (Had Christy been fierce and intimidating, had he *seemed* like a murderer, our response to his welcome would be different.) The comedy is further reinforced by Christy's improbable role in resolving the immediate difficulty concerning Pegeen Mike: what to do about her protection while her father and his cronies disport themselves at a distant wake, her suitor having declined to keep her company out of concern for the proprieties. To the locals, hiring Christy as a pot boy so that 'herself will be safe this night, with a man killed his father keeping danger from the door' seems the ideal solution.

Synge establishes Christy as '*a slight young man*' speaking '*in a small voice*'; in his terrors and timidities the very counterpart of Pegeen Mike's virtue-prone, cowardly suitor, Shawn Keogh. The task of the play is to effect the transformation of such unlikely material into the figure that by mid-play Christy becomes: champion athlete in the quasi-Homeric games, and heroic lover through the poetic power of his words and imagination. Stages in this transformation, progressively marked, constitute the path of the action. In one series, patterned and incremental in effect, whose recurrence we come to expect, Christy begins by telling how, badgered beyond bearing, he felled his father with the edge of a loy (a long, narrow spade). With every subsequent retelling the blow becomes mightier, from just 'dropping on the ridge of his skull', to halving it, to splitting him 'to the knob of his gullet'. Finally it becomes the feat of 'a gallant orphan cleft his father with one blow to the breeches belt'. As Christy achieves this exuberant climax, he opens the door of the cottage and staggers back, shattered by what he takes to be 'the walking spirit of my murdered da'.

Christy's boastful flight and crash landing are part of a deep-seated rhythm in the unfolding of his transformation, one that conditions our expectations without fixing them. With every rise in self-assurance there comes a fall, with every blossoming of self-regard there comes a frost. When timid Christy, left with Pegeen Mike, warms to her good opinion and begins to take it to heart ('and I a seemly fellow with great strength in me and bravery of . . .'), a vigorous knock at the door reduces him to terror, whereupon the Widow Quin, entering with a fresh clear eye, completes the taking down. ('Well, aren't you a little smiling fellow?') But from every setback—and there are many, comic in their deflationary timing—Christy bounces back, bolder and stronger, so that it is *after* the shocking reappearance of his unmurdered but bandaged Da that Christy wins all the prizes in the games—for running, leaping, riding—and then, by the power of his poetry, transforms the barkeeper's daughter ('and I the fright of seven townlands for my biting tongue') into 'the Lady Helen of Troy, and she abroad, pacing back and forward, with a nosegay in her golden shawl'.

More astonishing even than the transformation of Pegeen Mike is Christy's own transformation; but its permanence scarcely seems assured. Though the wise and now sympathetic Widow Quin succeeds in sending Christy's risen father on his way, we do not expect that we have seen the last of him; quite the contrary. And that instability in Christy's situation translates into the precariousness of his new persona, into inchoate future possibilities in the unfolding of the action, and into an incentive to see what happens next. Old Mahon, Christy's nemesis, returns again during his offstage triumphs in the games on the strand; but when Mahon thinks that he recognizes his worthless son in the glorious champion, the Widow Quin persuades him he must be mad from the blow on his head—'a sniggering maniac, a child could see'—and sends him on his way once more. Still, Mahon has aroused some local suspicions, and the threat of exposure (and the suspenseful expectation of a further return) remain.

One extra dividend in Old Mahon's reappearance is that he draws a picture for us of what the original Christy was like—timid, weakly, incompetent, a dreamer, terrified of a petticoat, and generally known as 'the looney of Mahon's'. Mahon's picture refreshes our first impression of Christy, and gives substance to the threat that now hangs over him, when the lie upon which his transformation is founded is finally (inevitably) exposed. All along Synge has reinforced the idea that what we are to the world, and indeed to ourselves, depends in good part on how we are construed. 'Didn't I know rightly I was handsome,' says Christy, looking into a mirror the morning after his engagement as potboy, Pegeen having meanwhile declared him 'a fine, handsome young fellow with a noble brow,' and likened him to the poets, 'fine fiery fellows with great rages when their temper's roused'. In contrast, 'it was the divil's own mirror we had beyond', Christy says, 'would twist a squint across an angel's brow'. His teenage fan club, the awed respect his deed seems to have earned him among the Mayo countrymen, and even Shawn Keogh's attempt to buy him off with natty new clothes—effecting Christy's *visible* transformation—contribute to what he increasingly *becomes*. And Christy's vision of Pegeen—even polishing her boots he sees as exalted service—appears to be similarly transforming.

Christy's apogee comes when he runs Shawn off and both coaxes and intimidates Michael James, Pegeen's father, into accepting and blessing the match with Pegeen.

MICHAEL . . . (*He joins their hands.*) A daring fellow is the jewel of the world, and a man
    did split his father's middle with a single clout, should have the bravery of ten, so
    may God and Mary and St. Patrick bless you, and increase you from this mortal day.
CHRISTY AND PEGEEN. Amen, O Lord!

    [*Hubbub outside.*]

[*Old Mahon rushes in, followed by all the crowd, and Widow Quin. He makes a rush at
    Christy, knocks him down, and begins to beat him.*] (Act III, p. 71)

From this catastrophic fall, hurled back all the way to where he started, reviled
by the crowd as 'a Munster liar, and the fool of men', Christy rises '*in shy
terror*'. But then Christy's increasing desperation turns to anger, into a scorn
of the crowd that had made so much of him, and into rage at his father,
once more the spoiler, whom—loy in hand—he chases off the stage. After a
moment Christy returns, dazed, having killed his father a second time, and
now, it appears, for real.

Synge had alternatives before him for the ending, which he and others subsequently discussed—embryonic possibilities in the turn of events, smacking of
different genres. One possibility was relentlessly tragic: Christy, like Oedipus,
has slain his father, not even inadvertently. The crowd turns nasty and—led
by Pegeen, the bravest, angriest, and most competent of the lot—ropes him,
pulls him down struggling to the floor, and eventually burns him loose from
the table he clings to, to give him over to the severity of the law. In fact all this
happens in the play, except the final result. For in the brief moment before
Pegeen successfully applies the burning sod to Christy's leg, Old Mahon has
crept in unnoticed on all fours, very much alive.

CHRISTY (*kicking and screaming*). O, glory be to God!

    [*He kicks loose from the table, and they all drag him towards the door.*]

JIMMY (*seeing Old Mahon*). Will you look what's come in?

    [*They all drop Christy and run left.*]

CHRISTY (*scrambling on his knees face to face with old Mahon*). Are you coming to be
    killed a third time, or what ails you now? (Act III, p. 79)

The inherent comedy in Old Mahon's third appearance, as unkillable as the
cartoon cat or coyote in their animated slapstick, is reinforced by the stage
picture of the confrontation, Mahon and Christy nose to nose on all fours. We
know then that, however violent and immanent the tragic outcome seemed,
it was never really on the cards. The wrench in tone and expectation, severe
enough as it is, would have been too great. And there was something other
than tragedy in Christy's anticipatory rise into gaiety as he clings to the table
and defends himself, not to mention his delight (and our unfeeling laughter)
when he bites Shawn Keogh in the leg.

The alternatives to this near tragic outcome Synge so alarmingly evokes are
all broadly comic, infused with different degrees of complex irony. Impostors

are indigenous to the whole inherited tradition of comedy (the *Miles Gloriosus* of Plautus, Shakespeare's Falstaff and Parolles, Molière's Tartuffe), and their exposure and deflation is the outcome their egregiousness calls for. A final deflation for Christy is well within the field of audience expectation. Synge's biographers write that in early versions of the play, 'Christy is dismissed as a coward and walks off tamely, with a ballad singer already at work on the incident.' Shawn is left in possession (alas for Pegeen), and when he tells the ballad singer to drop it, that this 'daddy man' was an impostor, the Singer first complains, 'God help me, and I after spending the half of me day making of his deed. But it's a lovely song. Well I'll sing it other roads where he's not known at all.'[25] So much for poetry and truth. The irony here, with a myth in the making, reinforces Pegeen Mike's much noted remark, 'that there's a great gap between a gallous story and a dirty deed'; between the marvel of 'a strange man . . . with his mighty talk', and 'what's a squabble in your back-yard, and the blow of a loy' (p. 77). It underlines the gap between romantic self-delusion and prosaic—even sordid—reality, a staple of comedy (cf. *Don Quixote*), but with serious and critical political bearings in the simmering Ireland of the day.

Synge considered another ending, one the writer George Moore urged on him, but which Synge noted he had already tried and rejected, 'as too commonplace'. It provided the generic happy ending for boy and girl that still conditions expectation, but at the price of a stroke more cynical and satirical toward the Irish peasant character than anything to which the initial audiences took violent exception. Moore wrote:

Your end is not comedy, it ends on a disagreeable note, and that is always a danger, especially when one chooses parricide as the subject of a jest. The comedy end and the end which would make it acceptable to an audience seems to me to be that at some moment the old man Mahon discovers that his son is about to marry a very rich girl; the peasant's instinct for money overtakes him, causes him to forget his wounds, and he begins to boast like [and of] his son . . . To the peasant anything is preferable rather than money should pass out of the family.

Mahon's reversal, and the grand picture of the Mahons that he paints, persuades Pegeen's father to take Christy as his son-in-law after all. 'This end would be in keeping with the facts.'[26]

Synge's chosen ending is much more original, and that means less conditioned by genre or our previous experience of plays in the theatre. Though unexpected, it follows from patterns and possibilities in much that we have just seen and heard. It is not inevitable, however; on the contrary, it determines the character of the action as a whole and gives it shape and meaning in retrospect. Christy and his father go off together to tell stories 'of the villainy of Mayo, and the fools is here', but with Christy now in charge, 'like a gallant captain with his heathen slave'. Christy blesses all for having 'turned me a likely gaffer in the end of all, the way I'll go romancing through a romping lifetime from this hour to the dawning of the judgment day' (p. 80). Figuratively speaking, he has once more slain his father, and this time for keeps. In retrospect then, for all his many ups and downs, with each swing wider than the last, Christy becomes the Playboy, becomes the illusion of himself, and that is the shape of the action. He embodies 'the power of a lie' (p. 74), the *real* power of poetry and the imagination, working—as even Old Mahon's descriptions of the old Christy have hinted—on a potential, a dramatic as well as characterological possibility that was already there. It is a new reality that, of those left behind, only Pegeen Mike, deprived like the audience of the standard comedy ending, sees and understands. So, as Synge brings down the curtain with a classic restatement of the title, it is rendered as Pegeen Mike's recognition:

PEGEEN (*Hitting* [Shawn Keogh] *a box on the ear*). Quit my sight. (*Putting her shawl over her head and breaking out into wild lamentations.*) Oh my grief, I've lost him surely. I've lost the only Playboy of the Western World.

The famous event in the history of the theatre known as the *Playboy* riots had roots in the militant paranoia of Nationalist politics and is not to be understood as simply the audience's spontaneous response to the dynamics of the play. Many in the first Dublin audiences came with a prepared mind and a readiness to take offence. But that is not to say that the play had no hand in provoking such a response, in an audience, urban and middle class though it was, that somehow saw itself and oppressed Catholic Ireland represented and insulted in the peasant community on the stage. The displeasure of the first-night audience was triggered by Christy's use of the plain word 'shift' (rather than the politer 'chemise'), and it is clear that the play's woman-led violence, where Pegeen Mike burns Christy's leg, was found especially indigestible. Among other things, it shocked genre-based expectations for comedy, as did the underlying grimness of the last movement, from Christy's murderous assault on the head-bandaged old man to his torment and repudiation by his erstwhile admirers. For the rest of the week, despite the scores of policemen lining the audience chamber, the play was largely inaudible, the audience thus vigorously repudiating any risk of engagement and collaboration. And yet the audience was not entirely off the mark. The play does create an unflattering portrait of a venal, fickle community whose failure is a failure in the quality of its imagination; a community open to escapist romance, but made queasily evasive by concrete reality; fearful of the authority of priest and policeman, and dissembling its cowardice in group action; quick to turn on its erstwhile heroes with vindictive energy or callous indifference. At the time of the play's opening, the history of Ireland's fallen leader, Parnell, still sat uneasy on the consciences of many, both Catholic and secular Nationalist. Synge had been attacked before for his representations of the back-country Irish. Now, having provoked his wilfully deaf metropolitan audience into repudiation of its collaborative role on prudish and patriotic grounds, he could have the satisfaction of seeing its identification with the crowd in Michael James's shebeen confirmed. For later audiences, however, in Ireland or elsewhere, reading or seeing this true modern masterpiece stirs up little in the way of conflict. Thanks to time and distance, there is no need for any audience to take the play personally, and politically there is little at stake, except perhaps pride in one of Ireland's great literary achievements. Freed from the immediacy of circumstance, the audience can relax into its role as the playwright's and actors' partner in the game of expectation and enjoy its superior discernment.

5.5. OUTREACH

Most plays try not to alienate their audience, even when they target some of its members or habits for satire. We are most accustomed to plays in which the role of the audience is veiled by an apartheid that seems to ignore its presence. One way around this limitation is the use of an audience surrogate. Some plays, however, like Tieck's or Beaumont's, just break the barrier, and some represent an audience directly, putting it on the stage. And then, without going quite so far, there is a notable set of plays that take the regular collaborative interaction of stage and audience and push it hard, reaching out to co-opt the actual audience, not just as Richard does in confiding his astonishment at his success, but pulling it right into the play, drafting it as a collective actor playing an audience. Weiss's *Marat/Sade* does something of the sort; but Peter Nichols carries it off more directly, and with great comic effect, in the abrupt opening of his play *Joe Egg* (1967), where Bri, a teacher in a minimum-security local English school, unleashes a tirade directly to the audience (some of whose members he singles out), thus abruptly made to stand in for his class: 'BRI *comes on without warning. Shouts at audience. . . .* That's enough! . . . Another word and you'll be here till five o'clock'—and so on at excruciating length.[27] John Patrick Shanley's *Doubt* (2004) begins with a homily on 'Doubt' delivered straight to the audience—thus cast as a congregation—to be followed later by another on 'Intolerance'. The preacher here and his priestly character are soon the focus of the contention between these discordant states of mind, their generality made specific in character and action and so brought home to the co-opted audience. After the curtain calls in the play's first, long-running production, that audience was asked to vote its own doubts or conclusions. Shanley's casting his audience in the role of congregation had notable precedent in the Christmas sermon of the Archbishop Thomas Becket that bifurcates T. S. Eliot's *Murder in the Cathedral* (1935), first presented (to further complicate the audience's involvement) in the Chapter House of Canterbury Cathedral, 50 yards from where the subject of the action, the murder of Becket, took place.[28]

No play that I know has pushed such audience co-option further than Clifford Odets's militant drama of the 1930s, *Waiting for Lefty* (1935), where the premiss is a taxi-drivers' union meeting with the leadership, corrupt and otherwise, on the platform stage debating whether to go on strike. The official leadership, goon supported, is opposed. The chairman of the rank-and-file Workers' Committee is missing, however, and as the meeting waits, members of that committee argue their case by invoking the critical moments in their own histories that brought them to their present militancy, moments that are enacted as if in flashback. At one point, a driver struggles up on to the stage from the audience to expose another member of the rank and file, who is counselling prudence, as a company spy—and his own brother. But it is the *whole* of the actual audience that stands in for the taxi-driver rank and file, the target of the arguments that get more heated as the play moves to its deferred and expected culminating action, the union's vote on whether or not to strike. In point of fact, with the rise in temperature, the last flashback episode and the final speaker have shifted the issue from simple strike to revolution. The moment of truth comes with news of Lefty, the missing chairman. Dashing through the audience on to the platform, a messenger reports that Lefty has been found—'Behind the car barns with a bullet in his head!' Agate, the final speaker, cries out then to all America, lacing his indictment with phrases from *The Communist Manifesto*, and putting the question straight to the audience 'Well, what's the answer?' Having been cast as the taxi-drivers' union, the audience (salted with a few 'Voices') now acts like it, spontaneously shouting their scripted words, caught up in an inspired revolutionary fervour, both in the initial production and in many that followed:

AGATE... (*To audience*) Well, what's the answer?
ALL. STRIKE!
AGATE. LOUDER!
ALL. STRIKE!
AGATE AND OTHERS (*on stage*). AGAIN!
ALL. STRIKE, STRIKE, STRIKE!!![29]

Odets, seated with the future director Elia Kazan—'we were one of the voices in the audience'—was himself carried away, author, actor, and responsive spectator as one, fusing into his audience. As he remembered it, 'the audience became the actors on the stage and the actors on the stage became the audience, the identification was so at one that you saw for the first time theatre as a cultural force'.[30] In so fully incorporating his Depression-era audiences into the performance itself, Odets achieved the ideal of agit-prop drama, to mobilize opinion and move it towards action. What carries the experience of the play beyond its moment, beyond the present prospects of reader or spectator confusing their role with that of the strikers or actors, are the more general and generous human and dramatic values. There is an affinity between idealism—here in its social guise—and melodrama, whose Manichaean clarity depends on the mobilization of powerful sympathies and antipathies. To empathize with the expression of those feelings, and to understand their genesis and management, is to understand how a play like *Waiting for Lefty* can continue to work.

Except that it also enlists the actual audience in the performance, Evreinov's *The Main Thing* would seem to be at the furthest remove from a play like *Waiting for Lefty*, both in style and substance. In the second act, where—as we have seen—the stage represents the stage of a theatre with the actors engaged in a rehearsal, when the audience comes into notice it is cast as unwelcome interlopers. The 'actors', or one of them, improves the occasion by disparaging both actor and audience roles in their collaborative enterprise. Far from embracing that collaboration, Evreinov's actors as 'actors' seek to drive the audience as 'audience' from the premises:

COMIC (*approaching the footlights*). But why all the strangers!.. Who let them in?.. (*Yells at the audience.*) Ladies and gentlemen, you're not wanted here!.. Leave!.. Well, hurry up then! Get a move on!.. Yech, look at 'em all!.. and who let you in?

REGISSEUR (*to the audience*). Be so kind, ladies and gentlemen, as to vacate the theatre, or I shall be obliged to be unpleasant.

ROMANTIC LEAD (*to the audience*). Ladies and gentlemen, nothing instructive, beautiful, or sublime will you see in our theatre. I hope you are already convinced. Please leave! This is a dreadful show. We ourselves recognize how pitiful and laughable our attempts are at portraying heroes when we haven't a trace of the heroic in our own souls. Don't shame us with your presence . . . What can be amusing in seeing people make fools of themselves over a crust of bread, people incapable of real, creative work? Make fools of themselves, imagining that they serve art, humanity, the lofty ideal of ennobling the human soul. Now you see how Melpomene's modern priests set about ennobling souls. I hope it is enough to drive you from the theatre forever. Leave then, please, and don't shame us with your presence.[31]

Presumably the audience proper is able to remember itself as distinct from the role in which it is cast, and the play, including the 'rehearsal', can continue—as Stoppard's Players, bereft of an audience, could not.

It is always instructive when the actors turn on the audience, breaking complicity sometimes with rude effect. There is such a moment at the end of John Osborne's theatrical undressing of post-Imperial Britain, *The Entertainer* (1957). This play too has pressed the audience into service, along with the playhouse itself, for the music-hall turns that alternate with the scenes of family drama. Archie Rice, as music-hall comedian and impresario, speaks directly from the front with the stand-up comic's risqué jocularity and cheerful aggression, punctuated by song and dance. By the time of his last turn—following a nude tableau of Britannia—all Archie's plans have collapsed (like the Empire, which also happens to be the name of the archetypal music hall). His Edwardian father is dead; and so is a son lost in the debacle of Suez. Archie gives his last tired monologue, sings his last bits of songs, and then:

He stops, the music goes on, as he walks over to PHOEBE [his wife], *who helps him on with his coat, and gives him his hat. He hesitates, comes back down to the floats.*
You've been a good audience. Very good. A very good audience. Let me know where you're working tomorrow night—and I'll come and see *YOU*.[32]

And he walks out of the spotlight, leaving the orchestra in the pit and the empty stage.

A similar reversal of actor and audience roles ends Jean Genet's *The Balcony*. Madame Irma, owner of a brothel which specializes in costumed fantasy, muses while steadily extinguishing the lights after a night in which revolution has lost out to role-playing. 'In a little while, I'll have to start all over again . . .' Then '*she stops in the middle of the stage, facing the audience*,' and memorably sends it on its way, to end the play: 'You must now go home, where everything—you can be quite sure—will be falser than here.'[33]

When the actors turn on the audience, breaking complicity, as in *The Balcony* and *The Entertainer*, they may be asserting a deeper affinity between theatre and how we live our lives. Violating the implicit compact between audience and stage is also to brush aside spectatorship as a shield resting on an acknowledged distance and difference. Turning on the audience, then, and turning to it, hardly makes a difference when both are an unwelcome reminder of a deeper complicity. Gogol's great satirical comedy, *The Inspector General* (1836), drives the point home in a supreme moment of that kind. Towards the end of the play, the Mayor of the town in darkest Russia where it is set discovers that not only have he and his fellow notables been taken in by a feather-brained idler whom they believed to be a government inspector, but they have taken themselves in. In a raging frenzy, he calls out:

Come and look, look, all the world, all Christendom, all of you, look how the Mayor's been made a fool of!

He shakes his fist at himself and imagines the nobody they all took for an important personage spreading the tale of his folly everywhere.

You'll not only be made a laughingstock, but some scribbler, some cheap hack, will come along and put you in a comedy . . . He won't spare my rank and calling. Everyone will grin and clap. (*To the audience.*) What are you laughing at? You're laughing at yourselves!

The audience, of course, has been *caught* laughing, worked up to it by the spectacle of the Mayor's impotent rage; and it is at that moment of evoked hilarity that Gogol chooses to attack its smug superiority.[34]

Max Frisch invents a protagonist who finds a different style for making a similar point. In *Herr Biedermann and the Firebugs* (1958), Gottlieb Biedermann turns to the audience defensively, by way of excusing himself. Unlike Gogol's Mayor, his resentment and anger are all but repressed. Despite a pattern of arson much in evidence in his town, through a mixture of caution, self-interest, cowardice, and wilful blindness Biedermann has allowed a pair of thugs to insinuate themselves into his household. Their increasing demands, including petrol storage and gourmet entertainment, will culminate in Biedermann's lending them his matches, as 'a sign of trust'. Before that, however, on a trip to the wine cellar, he takes time out for self-justification:

> *Biedermann comes to the footlights carrying a bottle.*
> BIEDERMANN. You can think what you like about me, gentlemen. But just answer one question:
> *The sound of raucous singing and laughter.*
>   . . . Tell me the honest truth, gentlemen; When exactly did you know for sure that they were firebugs? It doesn't come the way you think, gentlemen—it comes first slowly and then suddenly . . . Suspicion! I was suspicious from the beginning, one is always suspicious—but tell me honestly, gentlemen, what would you have done in my place, damn it all, and when?
> *He listens. There is silence.*[35]

A play in the parodic guise of a Greek tragedy (with a chorus of helmeted firemen) that is a parable of the triumph of gangsterism in the heart of Europe in the twentieth century, *Herr Biedermann and the Firebugs* makes vivid how it happens that one compromises with evil and, invested in denial, embarks on catastrophe. 'What would you have done in my place . . . and when?' The matter of timing is especially pertinent, given the century's history of appeasement and silence in the face of atrocity. Bridging the footlights, putting us all in the same boat, and making the audience self-conscious to the point of embarrassment, Biedermann lets us know it is a matter we should take seriously, and take home.

Less controlled in its effect, because of the oddly mixed feelings it evokes, is the sudden discovery and co-option of the audience at the end of Mayakovsky's Soviet-era satire, *The Bedbug* (1929). The play is set in two epochs, the imperfect post-revolutionary present of the 1920s, and the utopian techno-socialist world of the future. Its bumptious proletarian protagonist is an enthusiastic dupe of opportunistic bourgeois leftovers in the first half, and (emerging from accidental deep freeze, like Woody Allen's cryogenic hero in *Sleeper*) is studied scientifically and displayed as a specimen of an extinct parasite in the second half, along with a companionate bedbug. Prisypkin is greedy, boorish, sentimental, alcoholic, eager to betray his class and abandon his girl for fancier goods in the new Soviet reality, but appealingly and incorrigibly human in the gleaming, sanitized, Taylorized, techno-socialist world of the future. Unveiled in his cage, with vodka and guitar, he is invited to demonstrate to the stage spectators how cleverly he can imitate humanity. But Prisypkin—about to comply—

> (. . . *suddenly turns around and looks at the audience. His expression changes, a look of delight comes over his face. He pushes the* DIRECTOR *aside, throws down his guitar, and shouts to the audience.*)
> PRISYPKIN. Citizens! Brothers! My own people! Darlings! How did you get here? So many of you! When were you unfrozen? Darlings, friends, come and join me! Why am I suffering? Citizens! . . . [36]

Satire is often exceedingly time-bound, and there is no way in the reading or seeing that one could recapture precisely the responses of this play's initial and intended audiences. The play was produced in a climate of intensified control in the new Soviet Union, after the closing down of a period of liberalization which had its attractions as well as its follies and abuses. But some matters are timeless—the satire of bureaucratic processes, for example, and of academic and scientific pomposity. And there is no sell-by date for the contest, within and without, between anarchic impulse and desire and the demands of society and civility, between life and form. Knowledge and experience of such a contest is something that any audience, and therefore the responsive, collaborating sensibility that we conveniently call 'the audience', can be expected to bring to the play. But plays are written for enactment, and so in drama as in the theatre abstraction and generalization seek out concrete embodiment, in particulars. It is a particular audience that the boorish and now pathetic Prisypkin turns to and recognizes, and (like Gogol's Mayor) brings into the play, breaking through the shield of our spectatorship that makes it easy to laugh. What he recognizes is himself and his humanity in this audience. 'Citizens! Brothers! My own people! . . . So many of you!' What the playwright and the actors hope and strive for is that the audience recognizes its own humanity in Prisypkin.

I have talked about the functioning of the audience and the representation of the audience, but taken its existence *as* an audience as given. But of course that is not the case. However well disposed its members, and open to what comes when the proceedings begin, audiences are not born, but made. The challenge, not just before the actors and the production, but before the play itself, is to make out of a crowd of individuals—some quick on the uptake and some slow, some innocent and some jaded, fractured in gender, taste, years, and experiences—a collective able to fulfil its role, which is, to make one in a willing partnership with what is going forward, to take part as one in what is shaping and being shaped by its response.

And to start, that same audience puts itself in the way of seduction, for which the theatre itself—like Richard III—has had to endure much blame. Not that the liaison is without its complications, even perversities. We have seen that some plays dramatize the relationship by putting the audience on the stage, to a considerable degree even making the audience and its shortcomings the subject, as in Beaumont's burlesque and Cervantes's interlude. By staging an audience, playwright and actors readily find opportunity and excuse for turning the tables on those who normally sit in judgement, find scope for acts of aggression from which an actual audience may or may not be permitted to exempt itself, as in Weiss's *Marat/Sade* and Genet's *The Blacks*. Furthermore, exemption depends on keeping a certain distance from what is put on the stage; and though always subject to a breach for comic or histrionic effect ('I see . . . a multitude . . . in transports . . . of joy,' says Clov, as he turns his telescope on the audience in Beckett's *Endgame*), the decorum of the audience role, even in collaboration, stipulates such an established distance—or at least awareness of a status difference founded in a secure sense of what belongs to reality and what to mere representation. When Dr Johnson kicks the stone to refute Bishop Berkeley, he is demonstrating such an ontological security. Consequently, in Tieck's and Pirandello's radical challenges to the decorum of the audience role, the upshot is precisely a radical challenge to ontological security, in the one case through a chaotic mingling of spectatorship and performance, in the other of life and art.

Not quite a staging of the audience but closely related, the 'audience surrogate', I argued, offers the playwright an engaging means for leading an actual audience in the paths, emotional and intellectual, wherein it should go. Shaw here furnished the prime examples. Like the audience proper, the surrogate, however naive, is hardly ever a blank slate. He or she comes equipped with assumptions and expectations, and in the course of the play has to come to a new understanding. Expectations and their management constitute, from one perspective, the Whole Art of the Drama, along with the shaping of response. Expectation surely sits at the centre of our concern with what actually happens in the unfolding transaction between audience and stage. Here habit, genre, and convention have their say; but actuating expectation, through its creation and modulation, frustration and fulfilment, are integral to the very fabric of playmaking, and for that Synge's *Playboy* served as the chief exhibit.

Finally there is the play that draws the actual audience into the action as a performer, either standing in for other audiences—such as the rank and file of the taxi-drivers' union—or standing for itself. For the most part such performances involve a double consciousness of self and role, comparable to that attributed to the actor, which in some failed acting but also in rare moments of transcendence may wholly dissolve. Odets, Clurman, and others tell us that the latter is what happened in the audience at performances of *Waiting for Lefty* in the special time and circumstances of its original creation. However remarkable, however extreme, such an outcome represents the limiting curve of a response to the playwright's ordinary necessity: to provide the wherewithal for actors and production to create an audience, to make of many one. Away from the theatre, reading the script, we are of course one. For that matter, much as in Odets's account, we are of necessity audience and actors as one. But it is not given in such circumstances to experience directly the enormous release of fusion energy so revelatory to Odets of what theatre could be. For that one needs critical mass. Nevertheless, in reading a play it is possible to recognize, and even experience, as in a tuned string's sympathetic vibration perhaps, the nature and result of audience engagement—that is to say the role of the audience as *an* audience, however imperfectly responding as one, and as such indispensable to the workings of the play.

6

The Shape of the Action

There is a poignant moment in Pirandello's *Six Characters in Search of an Author*, whose premiss is that the dramatis personae of a work abandoned by its author come to a theatre to persuade manager and actors to perform their unrealized drama. So that the play can be taken down and made into a viable script, they attempt to enact, or re-enact, a critical episode, where the Father unknowingly attempts to seduce his Step-Daughter in a dress shop with a sideline in prostitution. The Mother, for the moment an agonized spectator, cries out, 'No! No! Don't permit it! . . . I can't bear it. I can't.' The Manager (an ordinary mortal) is puzzled: 'But since it has happened already . . . I don't understand!' To which the Mother replies, 'It's taking place now. It happens all the time.'[1] For the Mother, as a dramatic character, all time is present time, all experience present experience.

'All narrative forms make of the present something past; all dramatic form makes of the past a present.' So runs the epigrammatic generalization of the playwright, poet, and historian Friedrich Schiller when he sets out to identify what distinguishes tragedy from other forms and genres 'which only narrate or describe'. In tragedy, he writes, 'particular events are presented to our imagination or to our senses at the very time of their accomplishment; they are present, we see them immediately, without the intervention of a third person'.[2] Though one can think of various ways to qualify and complicate Schiller's formulation, such presentness and immediacy are inseparable from the idea of enactment or performance. In its design and intention, what is a play but an unfolding transaction between the mimed present of the actors and the real present of the audience?

'The theatre is a dangerous place,' says the late eminent director and man of the theatre Lloyd Richards. 'It's a place where anything can happen. It's *real*. It's not on film anywhere, it is happening *now*. Regardless of the fact that it's talking about something that happened a long time ago, the theatre itself is happening now.'[3] But what happens when the play is over? When it is no longer something happening now, a continuum unfolding before our eyes, but a completed whole that can be seen and grasped in retrospect? When we have before us, perhaps for the first time, not simply the ongoing action, but the entire shape of the action?

This consideration, as it bears on the reading and also on the *making* of plays, asks for another kind of twofold awareness. It requires that when we talk about the play as an action, we talk about it under two aspects: as immediately experienced and as perceived in retrospect—as if it were to be construed in two tenses, the one 'present progressive', the other 'present perfect'. In the present perfect, the play appears like a shape seen from above and all at once, a coherent, completed whole that embraces beginning and end. It is a God's-eye view. In the present progressive—a condition less seen than felt—we find ourselves in the midst of things, responsive to what is happening now, with questions, expectations, anxieties about what is going to happen next, about where it will all end, and how are we going to get from here to there. For the engaged playgoer, the present-progressive aspect is liable to be dominant, the moment-to-moment response more intense. For the engaged reader, the play as 'perfected' is likely to claim precedence—the entity that develops, achieves a shape, and is then present to reflection. For that very reason it is important to read experientially, attentive to the moment-to-moment responses and effects, the continuities in the continuum; and attentive also, if one is reading critically, to how the responses of the imagined theatre audience are being created and even manipulated, for (in the language of neo-classicism) our delight and instruction.

It should not be forgotten that part of the progressive experience, and part of our pleasure and engagement, is in seeing the play *taking* a shape—as when, watching an artist sketching an animal, the drawing becomes a rabbit before our eyes, emergent with the line of the back, a tail, an ear. There is gratification for the beholder as completion confirms anticipation; there is tension along the way in that the sketch might just turn into something else—a donkey, a camel. For that very reason, the endgame assumes a special importance. That is, the end of the play often has a shaping power that carries back over what went before, precipitating as well as punctuating the whole. Conscious of that power, in his metatheatrical masterpiece *The Main Thing*, with its missionary company of actors and exposed theatre-in-the-theatre, Nikolai Evreinov gives us our choice of endings. Fregoli, author and producer of the therapeutic scenario played out in the 'real' world of the boarding house, offers a range of possibilities whose effects would be to decide *ex post facto* the genre of the play: romantic comedy, with the couples reassorting and happily marrying; or serious drama, with consequences for individuals that are liberating or punitive. 'Or we could even give it a tragic ending', where Fregoli himself is exposed by the enemy of artifice among his boarding-house subjects, and his philosophy of benign illusion reduced to nothing.

The Theatre Director, on the other hand, takes a practical view of closure, believing that 'the main thing is to finish the play on time'; while the Play Director argues, 'The main thing is to have a smash ending . . . Everybody dance! . . . Apotheosis is always appropriate!'[4] An ending, he knows, needs a cadence, a flourish; something that says (even when there is no more to be said), 'This is the end. Curtain.' But it is also nearly always the ending of the play that is charged with resolving the final shape of the action, even if that means resorting to the fireworks of an apotheosis, or to a divine intervention, the dreaded and discredited deus ex machina. That formal demand grates on some modern sensibilities, nurtured in a climate of counter-culture resistance. The playwright and actor Sam Shepard puts it plainly: 'I hate endings, just detest them . . . the temptation towards resolution, towards wrapping up the package, seems to be a terrible trap'.[5] As a result, where there is a romantic preference for process, spontaneity, life over form, or a deep scepticism over meaning and coherence in our experience of the world, we find forms of cadence signalling 'The End' that also seek to evade being conclusive, that ask to be seen as open-ended.

Not that the playwright is in any case sure to know all along where his or her play in-the-works is going to come out, always having in mind the contours of the whole and chivvying things to their predestined end. In this respect the playwright's experience may even take on the presentness, the insecurities, and the epiphanic sensations of a witnessing audience. Caryl Churchill declares that the critical revelation of the mother–daughter relationship in *Top Girls* (1982) between the super-professional protagonist, Marlene, and her hapless 'niece' was not in her mind from the beginning, but 'was something that came very late'. It arrived in support of an essential thematic dimension; but it also brought the sanction and force of the long tradition of hidden relationships revealed in canonical drama.[6] And Bernard Shaw wrote, to set a critic straight, that 'A live play constructs itself with a subtlety, and often with a mechanical ingenuity that often deludes critics into holding the author up as the most crafty of artificers when he has never, in writing his play, known what one of his characters would say until another character gave the cue.'[7]

In the end, we are dealing with two faces of one imaginative construct, so that the distinction between the tenses is not always easy to maintain. Nevertheless, in what follows I emphasize, first some matters best understood as part of the play as an unfolding experience; and second, features that seem to emerge when the experience is complete and the play appears to us in retrospect. Both all that is immediate and progressive and all that is achieved and holistic constitute 'the shape of the action'.

6.1. ONE THING AFTER ANOTHER

There is no listening to music one note or one chord at a time with no
before and after. There is no music so mindless, so purely sensational, that
it does not depend on tension and release, recurrence and variation, the
making and breaking of patterns. And similarly the experience of the play
in its immediacy involves movement, relationship, the perception of change,
making waves in the fourth dimension. The 'present progressive' operates in
arousing expectation and evading or fulfilling it; in establishing a condition,
a character, a relation, and then destabilizing it; in enlisting dissonance and
resolving it. It makes use of adumbration, recognition, intrusion, surprise,
recurrence, revelation, to generate anticipations and deflect them, generate
patterns and depart from them, open possibilities and foreclose them.

On the face of it, the simplest form of progressivity in the action is to be
found in one of Bertolt Brecht's explanations of what he called Epic Theatre:
'one thing after another'. The complication comes with what connects, or
perhaps even contains, the parade of incidents. Do they lead one to another,
or simply seem to accrue? Do they depend on similarity to suggest cohesion,
or do they make an effect through emphatic difference? Does likeness register
as cumulative or intensifying, perhaps even constituting a shaping crescendo
effect? Is difference used simply to enhance the pleasures of variety and
surprise? or to disconcert, jarring complacent expectation? or for purposive
contrast? Shakespeare, with his open, minimally defined stage, makes much
use of purposive contrast—between scenes of action and reflection, for
example, between romantic lovers and their comedic counterparts—contrast
and parallelism often providing unspoken commentary.

Of his major plays, the one where Brecht took most pains in production
and argument to emphasize its exemplification of the linear directness of epic
theatre was *Mother Courage and Her Children*. Yet—as in that moment we
have looked at where Courage simultaneously scolds and feeds her daughter
Kattrin—nothing is quite so simple in human relations and human experience,
or in their meaningful representations. And where complexity sets in, often
as complication and contradiction in one and the same action, one and the
same moment, it complicates the workings of 'one thing after another'. The
one thing after another in this play includes the successive loss of Courage's
children, each taken, variously, by the war. First Eilif is lost to a recruiting party
(and later lost definitively to his ingrained aptitude for war, when he is executed
for carrying the habits he has acquired into a short-lived interval of peace).
Then Swiss Cheese is condemned by the enemy for his stubborn defence of

the regimental cash box. Finally Kattrin is shot while desperately raising the alarm that saves a city and its children from sudden destruction. The losses for Courage are cumulative; and in the end they constitute the progression that shapes the play. Its completion is reinforced by the retrospective reference of the final image: Courage pulling her now battered, near-empty sutler's wagon all by herself against a bleak cycloramic background, evoking the opening episode, where the fresh, newly stocked wagon is drawn on in the morning light by her two strong sons, with Kattrin and Courage aboard.

Such recursion, underlining difference, is one way of registering transformation while marking completion of the pattern that produces the change. As the incremental pattern of loss emerges, each episode creates expectation and reinforces dread of further loss. But Brecht doesn't depend entirely on our inferences. He adumbrates the pattern in the very first scene, where Courage, in order to counter the siren call of the military recruiters with a healthy fear, perpetrates a fortune-telling scam whereby all three of her children draw a black cross, signifying death, from the mingled slips in a helmet. (In Kattrin's case, Courage draws it for her, with appropriate histrionics.) The most adamantly rationalist playgoer understands the danger of such flirtation with ominous prediction, 'tempting fate', and how it affects the dramatic odds. It plants an expectation, along with a mixture of anticipation and dread and a residual hope of evasion, until the last grim piece of the pattern falls into place.

How the deaths actually come about, and how Courage will cope with them, is not in the prediction; and such circumstantial variation and uncertainty engage our continuing response and interest. (Courage is obliged to conceal her grief at Swiss Cheese's death even when confronted with the corpse; she remains ignorant of Eilif's fate; and she is numb with grief and lost in ineffectual denial as she cradles Kattrin's lifeless body.) We recognize pattern, and respond to variation.

Other patterns, recurrent and developing, help give life and meaning to *Mother Courage*, patterns more easily thought of as belonging to the texture of the unfolding action than as constituting a shaping structure. So it is that time and again Brecht puts Mother Courage in the situation of the double bind. Time and again she is torn between her economic interests and her domestic interests, her role as a merchant-entrepreneur and as a mother. The rub is that her buying and selling are for the purpose of providing bread for herself and her children, in a horrendously chaotic age. But it is a dangerous game, making a living out of war; and Brecht is interested (as he explained) in exploiting the contradiction between roles, between the Proto-Capitalist and the Mother.[8] Hence the recurrent situation of stress, even impasse, where Courage is pulled in two directions, suggesting a structural condition underlying the individual drama in the historical world of the play.

The first such dramatic situation comes at the very beginning, the recruiting episode. Courage is about to leave, her family intact, when she is distracted by the chance to make a sale to one of the recruiters. Meanwhile the other goes to work on Eilif. While her attention is divided between the bargaining and Kattrin's inarticulate cries of alarm ('Just a minute, Kattrin, just a minute. The sergeant's paying up'), Eilif falls into the toils. Other such moments reinforce the pattern; but the fullest articulation of the double bind in a dramatic situation is the episode (Scene 3) in which Courage needs cash for a bribe to save the life of Swiss Cheese. The only asset on which Courage can raise the money is the wagon and its contents, which she wants to mortgage, but is only able to sell. 'But what will you live on?' someone asks. Mother Courage replies: 'That's the hitch.' She is torn between the wagon—the indispensable instrument of their livelihood—and the desperately imperilled Swiss Cheese. And so she bargains—to keep at least some of her capital, for a peddler's pack. By the time she concedes the full 200 guilders demanded for the bribe ('Maybe I bargained too long'), the drums are heard, signalling that sentence has been passed, and that it is indeed too late.

As the scene proceeds—Mother Courage giving ground slowly—and the tension grows, the disposition of most audiences towards sympathy for someone in Mother Courage's position is liable to wane, curdling in the face of such unsentimental haggling while a son's life hangs in the balance. But her final desperate concession and upwelling anxiety work for her, as does her seated stillness under the terrible blow ('*It grows dark. The drums stop. It grows light again. Mother Courage has not moved.*'). Further, as she swallows the bitter dose and disclaims knowledge of the corpse (unable to speak, like dumb Kattrin, she manages to shake her head), the iron self-control she shows evokes admiration and compassion, but perhaps also a measure of reserve, an emotional distance that echoes the grip Mother Courage has to keep upon herself in the midst of her grief. Admiration and sympathy for an indomitable Mother Courage became an issue for Brecht in the light of the play's first successful production; and his efforts to qualify positive views by altering the text suggest both what is apt and what is insufficient in the notion of the playwright's art as one of shaping a stream of expectation and response. To the extent that it is apt, however, not only is the unfolding of events, involving expectation and fulfilment, to be managed in the evocative programme of the script, but so also is our feeling about the characters—whom to care about, for example, and whom to mistrust. A false note, a generous thought, a glimpse of vulnerability, a stereotyped phrase or gesture, can set us one way or another—or reset our previous assumptions. In the case of the figure of Mother Courage, Brecht's efforts to resume control of the balance of empathy and critical scrutiny, and his distinctly limited success, is most instructive.[9]

Figure 8. Managing the pathways of response (or not): Brecht's stage direction for the tableau opening of the final scene of *Mother Courage and Her Children* reads, '*Outside the wagon Mother Courage sits huddled over her daughter. The peasant couple are standing beside them.*' But Brecht and his collaborators comment on this '*Pietàbild*' representing a production in Dortmund, West Germany, 'This image (Mother Courage holds the dead Kattrin in her arms) demonstrates—however effective it may be—a false conception. It shows the mother animal [*Muttertier*], the Niobe figure of legend. In attitude and expression, we are given the naked horror over death. Death appears as elemental, unalloyed biological fact. In the play however it is above all a social fact. It is brought about by human beings. The business woman is by no means guiltless in the death of her daughter.' From *Theaterarbeit: 6 Aufführungen des Berliner Ensembles*, ed. Ruth Berlau et al. (Dresden: VVV Dresdner Verlag [1952]), 286.

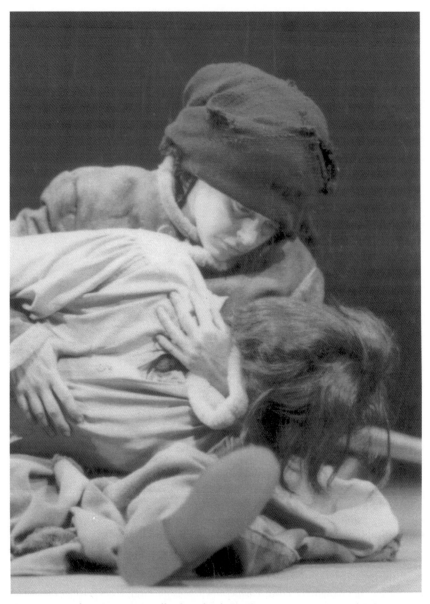

Figure 9. Mother Courage cradles her dead daughter Kattrin in a notably less iconic configuration, from a 1963 New York production of *Mother Courage* directed by Jerome Robbins. Rather than offering a draped lap as the altar of her pain and the sacrificial figure in more or less full frontal display, as in the conventional *pietà*, Courage (Anne Bancroft) sits flat on the floor, her legs awkwardly extended, and Kattrin (Zohra Lampert) is held to her breast like a nursing infant, giving the image an intimacy and a poignancy at once more painfully human and more directly evocative of the stricken *Muttertier*.

Though the script is indeed a programme for evoking and shaping response, what the audience brings to the play, and what it *wants* to find there, are precisely, if by no means exclusively, what the author and the production have to work with, and then have to reckon with.

Brecht's formula, 'one thing after another', probably emerged from the presumed structure of the chronicle-history play as established by Shakespeare and taken up by his Romantic emulators, a model suited to the serial enactment of the momentous episodes of an era or a life. But pattern and variation, intensification and relaxation (diastole and systole), and finally some cadence-like effect signifying completion, mark even the most episodic of plays, plays with no credible vestige of that strategic shaping of events tracing a logic of cause and effect that goes by the name of a plot. An extreme instance is that once notorious comedy of Viennese erotic life in the 1890s, Arthur Schnitzler's *Reigen*, one of whose seduction scenes, its postures undercut by marrons glacés, supplied examples of cross-talk between Seeing and Hearing. The play consists of a series of ten episodes, each dramatizing a sexual encounter whose further consequences, if any, are not the business of the play. Each encounter is self-contained; none can be said to lead to or depend on another; but one partner in each episode—always the new character—carries over into the next. The result is an extended chain, or—since one character from the first episode reappears in the last—a necklace, or a '*Ring-Dance*'. Though the play steers clear of any overt allusion to epidemiology, *Reigen* follows a path close to the threshold of awareness rather like the track of a venereal disease (Schnitzler was a physician, and the subject, much repressed, was one that loomed in the shadows of erotic life at the end of the nineteenth century).

Bringing back the prostitute who goes with a soldier (for free) in the first episode as the female partner in the last does give a sense of completion. It 'brings us full circle', as opposed to merely breaking off. But even such strong formal closure could very well seem arbitrary and unearned; and so, shaping our experience of the play towards this conclusion are aspects of the string of encounters that can register as progressive—a progress through the gamut of class, for example. We have whore and soldier, soldier and servant, servant and young master, young master ('Young Gentleman') and bourgeois wife, the wife and her older husband, husband and 'sweet young thing', extending finally into the outer social reaches of art and aristocracy—to the bohemian and relatively classless Poet and Actress, Actress and Count, and finally Count and Prostitute, a conjunction of highest and lowest.

But whatever is different and incremental in such a series—saving us from boredom—depends upon what is invariant, the sameness that enters the experience of the play as recurrence and its expectation. Sameness, however—fundamentally, the sexual act between a man and a woman—is also the foundation of further patterning and further variation, which we also come to expect. Pairing between the young, for example, gives way to a series with a younger woman and an older man. But the basic, reiterated structure of the episodes is Before and After, with a discreet blackout in between. There is comedy, and occasionally pathos, in the reversal of roles in the two halves of the scene, as when the urgency of the seducers—most often male—gives way to preening or a marked disposition to decamp, while their partners, previously reluctant, become tender and retentive. Poet and Actress are thus refreshing for their equality in narcissism and playful and unapologetic sexuality, their readiness to spoil each other's attitudes, and their general freedom from guilt and cant, while Actress and Count are notable in the reversal that makes him the delicate and squeamish partner, full of quirky formality and comic reluctance, and she the irresistible seducer.

The last episode, in the prostitute's room, breaks the structural pattern. It surprises in that it is *all* morning after, with the prostitute asleep and the Count unable to remember. For a while he believes there was no Before—that nothing took place—and he is oddly disappointed when he learns otherwise. In this final, asymmetrical variation, breaking and capping the pattern while bridging age and gender difference as well as social extremes, we are made conscious, partly through the musings of the jaded Count, of the great equalizers: sleep, death, and their cousin, sex, a melancholy post-coital note that shades the broad social and sexual comedy it so perfectly concludes.

6.2. SHAPING FORCES

Synge's Christy Mahon is an intruder in the locale of Michael James's pub. He comes into a community where he doesn't belong and upsets relationships and expectations. At the end of the play he is purged from the community, though he makes it seem the other way around. Like Shakespeare's banished Coriolanus, he says, in effect, 'I banish you. . . . There is a world elsewhere'. Departing, Christy leaves the community to pull itself together and return to its 'normal' condition the best it can. *Intrusion*, with the figure of the intruder, the outsider, disrupting the world of the play, is one of a number of agencies and devices that initially propel an action, and then help structure it. The intruder creates a dissonance that asks to be resolved, a dissonance that is not in itself shaping but is certainly propelling. As in the case of music, perfect harmony, absent all dissonance, would make for very short compositions. In drama dissonance is at the root of the broadest comedy (as 'incongruity', as slapstick, as misapprehended meaning) and the most gripping melodrama, driving the moment-to-moment experience. It is dissonance that stimulates our need to know what comes next. It engages us with what is going forward, and then works on our appetite for order, clarity, stability. It creates a tension and the need for resolution. Sometimes the dissonance lies in the realm of information. This can be defective or incomplete (as in the catastrophe of *Romeo and Juliet*), or arising in misconception. Misconception can be mutual (the duel scene in *Twelfth Night* and much other comic mistaking), or delusional (Orgon in Molière's *Tartuffe*); inadvertent (Goldsmith's *She Stoops to Conquer*), or deliberately foisted (*Othello*, *Much Ado about Nothing*, *Life is a Dream*). Nearly always, with clarification, the dissonance is resolved.

Thus, when the intruder's intervention terminates with that figure's departure, the emergent shape of the whole fits the more general, ternary pattern of Calm (perhaps an uneasy calm)/Storm (disruptive)/Calm (celebrative, desolate, or reflective) that governs the progressive shape of so many plays. A classic instance is in Ivan Turgenev's serious comedy *A Month in the Country* (1850). It is set in the circumscribed world of a country estate where Beliayev, hired to tutor the 10-year-old Kolya and a student himself, upsets everything and everyone by innocently causing most of the women to fall in love with him, from Kolya's mother Natalia Petrovna, wife of the estate's owner, to Vera, their nubile ward, to Katya the serving maid. 'What's happened?' Natalya Petrovna asks her long-suffering amorous friend Rakitin. 'I think everything used to be so calm, so quiet, in this house—and suddenly it's all got out of hand! I mean we've all gone out of our minds'.[10] In the end, Beliayev—altered himself, and no longer the emotional innocent—must leave. But his passage has changed other lives. Rakitin must also leave, Vera has accepted an elderly and ridiculous suitor to get away, and other departures are in the offing. The core family, shaken and depleted, remains, and things will no doubt settle into a new equilibrium, but they will not be the same.

The essential usefulness of the intruder whose presence unsettles a community and whose coming and going shape the action, allows for no end of variation. Staying with classic Russian drama, Nikolai Gogol's satirical comedy *The Inspector General* (1836) is built upon such a figure, a self-complacent featherbrain whose earthquake effect upon the officialdom of a provincial town is enabled by a case of mistaken identity. Chekhov, whose characteristic ambience and dramaturgy recall Turgenev's, often uses unwonted presences to upset his provincial worlds (e.g. Elena in *Uncle Vanya*). Much further down the social scale, Luka, the ambiguous holy-man tramp in Maxim Gorky's *The Lower Depths* (1902), stirs up the flop-house world he enters, only to disappear during the deadly convulsions his presence has one way or another precipitated. In a similar ambience in the New World, Hickey, the travelling salesman in O'Neill's *The Iceman Cometh* (1939), with his gospel of facing the truth, brings turmoil to the numb permanent denizens of Harry Hope's saloon. Tennessee Williams often enlists such figures, including 'the gentleman caller' in *The Glass Menagerie* (1944), Blanche DuBois in *A Streetcar Named Desire* (1947), and the magnetic Val in *Orpheus Descending* (1957). In the two latter instances, the disruptive presence is not eliminated without dire consequences to the outsider. No mere catalysts passing through, they become the sacrificial subject, scapegoats expelled or destroyed in the effort to defend and restore a 'normal' world.

While wreaking havoc, an intruder like Beliayev or Elena may do so unconsciously and inadvertently, mired in apparent passivity. Nearly always, however, the root of dissonance in a dramatic action lies in or between what can be thought of as the rival programmes of different characters, all seeking different outcomes, and producing what playwriting handbooks call 'conflict', that sine qua non of 'plot'. Actors may usefully be asked to approach their roles by conceiving their character's 'project'. That is, if they have any life at all, characters come equipped with plots of their own—with plans, goals, desires, and interests—each character wishing to shape the action towards a particular outcome. Such projects can be wholly or partly at odds with each other, and they can be wholly or partly reinforcing. The final outcome will be the result of these plots, these forces interacting, like the composition of forces in mechanics whose product one can chart in a vector diagram.

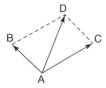

In this simplest of diagrams, Able Baker (AB) is moderately effective in exerting force in a given direction; Able Charley (AC) rather more so; and the result (or 'resultant') of their exertions, the extent and direction of movement, the true 'path of the action', appears as Able Dog (AD).

Actually characters adjust and improvise as matters develop, and another sort of diagram would show twists and turns, loops and tangles, generating the knot that unravels in what is aptly called the 'denouement'. Even that most self-conscious plotter, manipulator, and would-be puppeteer, Iago, has to improvise, which he does quite brilliantly. But in the end, even he gets both more and less than he expects, since other characters exert force and directionality too—his wife Emilia, for instance. Iago, a master stage manager and illusionist, fancies himself sole author of the *Tragedy of Othello*. But what emerges finally as the shape of the action is necessarily a collaboration. As a rule, no character's path is likely to run smooth and straight, and none of the collaborators with a plot of their own to realize is likely to get his or her way entirely, certainly not without much deviation, delay, and detour. As Hamlet observes, speaking from experience, 'There's a divinity that shapes our ends, | Rough-hew them how we will' (V. ii. 10–11). That divinity, as far as the design of the play goes, has to be the author; though most plays are the better for his keeping behind the scenes, and giving, or appearing to give, the characters/actors their heads. (Washing his hands of them, as in Pirandello's *Six Characters*, is probably going a little too far.)[11]

Perhaps we have now reached the point where clarifying and distinguishing some traditional terms should be put off no longer. The *action* of a play (not to be confused with 'activity', or business) is what happens. (There is a powerful preference rooted in Aristotle for an action that is unitary and comprehensive.) The *story* is the linear narrative that frames and includes the action. The *plot*, with all its convolutions and indirections, is the path of the action, and gives scope to the interplay of action and story. The *story* of Sophocles' *Oedipus Tyrannus* begins with the oracle preceding the infant's birth. The *action* of the play begins many years later, with his attempts as ruler of Thebes to discover the cause of the plague afflicting the city; and it concludes with his self-discovery, self-punishment, and exile. The *plot* follows the irregular, though inexorable course of Oedipus' investigations and discoveries, as he overcomes serious resistance (from Tiresias, Jocasta), leaps to erroneous conclusions, and integrates discrepant information as it accumulates into a coherent whole.

Plot is simpler in *Oedipus* than in a play like *The Marriage of Figaro*, for example, because the 'projects' of the characters are simpler (and fewer), and are not so much competing as keyed to one determined project, that of Oedipus himself: to find out. In Beaumarchais's *The Marriage of Figaro* (1784) there is also one overarching project that shapes the whole, posted in the title itself. But Figaro's and Susanna's intention, to marry, intersects and competes with the project of Figaro's master, Count Almaviva, to seduce Susanna; that of Marcelline, to marry Figaro; that of the Countess, to recover the affections of the Count; that of the adolescent Chérubin, to make love to all womankind, and the list is by no means exhaustive. The result is five acts of intrigue and error, plot and counterplot, concealment and discovery, in a mounting series of fraught situations that flirt with serious consequences. But in the end, with the help of darkness, disguise, mistake and revelation, the satisfactory outcome brings the Count to his knees before the Countess (dressed as Susanna), brings Figaro together with Susanna (dressed as the Countess, her virtue intact), in both instances at some cost to male conceit. By the final reconciliations there has been a shift in power relations, perhaps not entirely temporary, pointing to something more attractively egalitarian with respect to gender and class. Yet it is not at all clear that the outcome, the 'resultant' of the characters' projects, the various energies tugging with differential force in various directions, is more important in the play than the perils, ingenuities, and dilemmas of the plotters, whose convoluted track, as in the comedies and dramas of intrigue that for centuries dominated the theatre, constitute the experience as well as generate the shape of the action.

6.3. PENETRATIVE PROGRESSIONS

The nature of drama, historical or otherwise, Schiller intimates, is to inhabit a directly experienced progressive present; and allowing some latitude for challenging experiment, the model is a good one. But even where the action of the play inexorably drives forward in the present, as in the case of *Oedipus Tyrannus*, its plot may carry us back to earlier parts of the story in the form of momentous retrospective revelations. This is not the same as exposition—filling in what has gone before and preparing for what comes next—in that the revelation itself carries the force of the drama. Forward progression in such a case depends on a penetration of the past, so that the shape of the action is, properly speaking, Janus-like. Revelation, whether of what lies concealed in the present or of the truth that is buried in the past, is among the most powerful effects in the playwright's armoury, but it need not be sudden or unexpected. It finds fullest expression in a play like the *Oedipus* as a progressive penetration of the true conditions of the present through a progressive penetration of the past.

Oedipus is the archetype of such a play, and Ibsen's *Ghosts* is its modern cognate, where it is not the identity but the character of the dead Captain Alving that is at issue. Progressively, as in an archeological dig, layers of what constituted the true nature of Captain Alving are peeled back. Initially he is the deceased pillar of the community being memorialized by his widow in the new orphanage that will bear his name. Then, in his domestic character, he is revealed as a dissolute, lecherous, occasionally sadistic wreck of a man whose viciousness has been concealed through the heroic and selfless efforts of a wife who once almost left him. And finally he is understood as a man with a great and joyous appetite for life, frustrated, coarsened, and darkened in the cold, bleak, loveless climate of his community and marriage. Our guide in dispelling the social conspiracy that kept the Captain's reputation intact, and of which she was the mainstay, is Mrs Alving herself. It is she who at need reveals the Captain's depravity, and then has the intellectual courage to penetrate to the deepest understanding of what was. At stake in the present is how their son Osvald copes with his inherited disease, the congenital syphilis for which—encouraged to idealize his father—he blames himself and the freedom of his Parisian artist's life. His design, to marry the vital young servant Regine as his future euthanasiologist, precipitates one stage of the revelation concerning Alving. (Regine is Osvald's half-sister, and they have to be told.) But the final penetration to a deeper, more generous understanding is not thus compelled. Its achievement by Mrs Alving is both her liberation from the ghost of Alving and the ironic prologue to her retributive punishment. It puts her—heroic as the agent who penetrates to the deepest truth, including her own history of complicity in stifled emotion and the iron-willed effort to sustain a lie—at the moral centre of the action. It leaves her in the bleak, terrible situation where, her eyes now wide open to the past, she is suspended in the impossibility of choosing between effecting her own son's death according to her promise, and bearing the living death of his now manifest terminal paresis.

The action that comprises a progressive penetration to a core of truth takes on a different character in the light of modern developments such as the relativizing of the observable, the undermining of deterministic causality with quantum uncertainty, the attention to the cognitive and social construction of what passes for reality. That there *is* a foundational truth that can be reached through a progressive penetration of the past or of appearances on the model of *Oedipus* or *Ghosts* is precisely what is at issue in some of the classics of modern drama. Pirandello's *It Is So (If You Think So)* (1917) sets out to prove otherwise. The play works as a dramatic parable that has at its centre a tight family configuration of a man, his unseen wife, and his mother-in-law, surrounded by a circle of the curious in the community where they are newly arrived. That community is driven to try to get at the truth—that is, the facts—that would explain the peculiarities in the Ponza family's living arrangements and stand-offish behaviour. The family has come from a town devastated by earthquake with many killed and records destroyed. The issues come down to whether the wife is a first wife and the old lady's daughter or a second wife and nothing of the kind; whether it is the husband who is obsessed and delusional or it is the mother whose mind is afflicted, through grief. In the attempt to penetrate to the truth, each successive explanation of the situation and its history doesn't simply contradict the previous account, but incorporates it. And that goes for behaviour. If the husband falls into a mad rage at finding the old lady speaking of 'her daughter', he can turn it off instantly and explain that it was to preserve her illusions about himself and his madness and still protect his wife. The husband claims that his first wife was killed in the earthquake that destroyed the town. When the authorities send for the documents that would validate one account or the other, or for the testimony of survivors, they find that witnesses have dispersed, records have been destroyed, and whatever remains is inconclusive. To validate present reality through its derivation from a past that may or may not leave a trace on paper or in the memory of others becomes a doubtful proposition, if not, as here, an exercise in futility. In the end, all comes down to the testimony of Signora Ponza herself. It is a last best hope, as the play is organized, for eliciting the facts as to who she really is. Climaxing the progressive effort and successive failures to get closer to the core of truth, her revelation is expected to explain the human relationships to the satisfaction of the curious (including ourselves), to resolve the irritating ambiguities, and to satisfy the universal, if sometimes prurient, appetite to know. Of course it does nothing of the kind. The woman appears under a veil, declares herself the daughter of the old lady *and* the second wife of her husband, and for the rest of us, 'I am who you want me to be'. Her message is compassion, respect for the human need that has constructed this reality, this modus vivendi, and scepticism as to the attainability and even the value of an objectified truth.

Pirandello's challenge here is also to a foundational premiss of accepted dramatic logic and process: the attainability of truth and the validity of revelation. Most plays in the inherited canon take for granted our faith in what is disclosed, inadvertently or otherwise, in the progress of the plot. Lies, concealments, pretence and illusion are the stuff of the intrigue, and its unravelling. As the adage tells us, 'Truth is the daughter of Time', and Truth will out. When it is a question of the past, a climactic revelation is often also one of reversal, a transformation of the present. The past is a terrain that can be known, discovered or rediscovered, lying in wait with undiminished potency. The past is not 'a construct', but a reality.

There is no such past in the distinguished *oeuvre* of Harold Pinter, with one possible exception. Pinter takes the presentness in Schiller's characterization of the medium of drama a step further, in impressing it upon the world his characters inhabit. In that world, the past that we derive from the assertions and disclosures of its inhabitants is as unreliable and uncertain as the future. What was Stanley and what really happened to him before he came to rest with Petey and Meg in *The Birthday Party*? What were Goldberg's relations with his father? (What indeed is his right name?) What if any were Spooner and Hirst's previous relations in *No Man's Land*? What is imagined, what revised, and what remembered in the erotic rivalry of *Old Times*? ('ANNA . . . There are things I remember which may never have happened but as I recall them so they take place'.)[12] The exemplary figure here is Davies, the aged derelict in *The Caretaker*, a bundle of defensive grievances and evasions who could 'prove who I am! . . . could prove everything', if only he could get to where his papers once were, in Sidcup. Characteristic of the revelations and confidences that come through Pinter's characters is the absence of that seal of authenticity, that note of conviction, that validating circumstance, that authorial accreditation, which allows an audience to accept the truth of what it hears concerning what is not present, not immediate. A convention so useful for exposition and revelation is here stripped of its privilege. The exception, or perhaps the evasion of the liability such an austere dramaturgy creates for plays seemingly engaged in a progressive revelation of the past is to be found in Pinter's *Betrayal*, where he arranges the succession of scenes as a *regressive* present, staging the history of an adulterous triangle from epilogue to beginning, from two years after its dissolution to the opening flirtation.

Making the dramatic action a progressive series of attempts to penetrate the past takes another shape in Michael Frayn's dazzling probe of a critical episode in recent history, *Copenhagen* (1998). In this instance the problematizing of knowledge and memory has an immediate and appropriate scientific analogue, in the elusiveness of quantum reality. In the so-called Copenhagen Interpretation, whose prime movers were Niels Bohr and Werner Heisenberg, the radical notions of 'complementarity' and 'indeterminacy' displace the either/or of binary logic and other absolutes of knowledge and identity. The progressive premise of the play is the attempt to determine retrospectively the true nature of a particular historical encounter by replaying it until the three characters involved get it right. The event is the visit of Heisenberg, while in charge of the German atomic weapons effort during the Second World War, to his old mentor Niels Bohr in occupied Denmark. What is questionable are Heisenberg's motives in coming to Copenhagen, and his knowledge and intentions with respect to carrying out his wartime charge, as revealed—or not—in an after-dinner walk with Bohr. The dramatic reiterations are made feasible through something analogous to controlled laboratory conditions. These are dramatically enabling; but there is a further question, whether under *any* conditions penetration to a single truth embedded in a determinate reality can be achieved. The third party in the probe is Margrethe, Bohr's wife, and she opens the play by posing the initial question:

MARGRETHE. But why?
BOHR. You're still thinking about it?
MARGRETHE. But why did he come to Copenhagen?
BOHR. Does it matter, my love, now we're all three of us dead and gone?
MARGRETHE. Some questions remain long after their owners have died. Lingering like ghosts. Looking for the answers they never found in life.
BOHR. Some questions have no answers to find.[13]

Heisenberg is present and gradually engages, the characters' counterpoint speech and remembering conjoining until memory becomes the foreground and narrative and argument slip into enactment. As Margrethe says, with the opening of memory 'The past becomes the present inside your head', and so also in the limbo of this stage.

The iterations or revisitings begin more or less the same way, with Heisenberg coming to the door, and are signalled by the phrase 'one more draft'—Bohr's analogy with the progressive refinement of one of his papers in physical theory. But the progressive aspect has to be understood in the light of the Copenhagen Interpretation: 'that there is no precisely determinable objective universe. That the universe exists only as a series of approximations' (pp. 73–4). Since human sentiments and motivations are here at issue, Heisenberg's actions emerge as overdetermined, his intentions manifold and equivocal. At the same time, like Schrödinger's famous cat in a box, both alive and dead until someone looks, or the photon that can be in two places at once, or the electron that can exist both as wave and particle, Heisenberg's intentions in coming to Copenhagen remain indeterminate, in view of the fact that there was no German atomic bomb. The box never had to be opened.

Consequently, the last iteration is turned into a 'thought experiment'. Instead of breaking off the conversation in horror at the first hint of what Heisenberg was up to, this time Bohr lets it continue. This is counterfactual history; but as such it is a probe into the content, the unrealized potential, of the moment. What would have emerged had these human particles in momentary collision not flown apart, but had remained in an aggregate long enough to have started a chain reaction? If Bohr had asked the obvious technical question that Heisenberg had not thought (or did not want) to ask? In the first New York production (but not in London, if memory serves) the answer came with startling clarity and effect. As Heisenberg, jogged by Bohr, made the calculation—

HEISENBERG. . . . . The scattering cross-section's about 6×10^{-24}, so the mean free path would be . . . Hold on . . .

—there was a heart-stopping *boom and flash*.

BOHR. And suddenly a very different and very terrible new world begins to take shape . . . (p. 91)

The production effect is not present in the reading, even as a stage direction. Does it belong? Is it part of the play? It is implicit in Bohr's words ('And suddenly . . .') but only as an adumbration ('begins to take shape', he says). Its effect in the arc of the drama is hard to fault. It is the satisfying punctuating climax, emotional and conceptual, to a long, additive, exploratory quest. The play as an experience is poorer without it. But it is unbalancing. Even though it enacts what never happened, it is decisive in the realm of the undecided. It extracts an unrealized alternative world from the historical juncture in which it lay undecidably. Margrethe puts it in human terms:

That was the last and greatest demand that Heisenberg made on his friendship with you. To be understood when he couldn't understand himself. And that was the last and greatest act of friendship for Heisenberg that you performed in return. To leave him misunderstood. (p. 91)

The present, or what survives from the past in the present, can only take us so far into the world of the past, when *it* was the present, and still undecided. It is the undecidedness that counts. And so the dramatic action shaped as a progressive penetration to a nugget of pure truth, a disambiguated bedrock reality, here meets the knowledge of its intrinsic limits when it takes account of the reality of uncertainty.

6.4. FIGURES OF THE WHOLE

The ultimate shape of the action informs the ongoing experience of the play as a question or a promise, as a tantalizing uncertainty or as a dreaded or desired inevitability. But when the end comes, the achieved shape of the whole can be grasped in retrospect with the help of a range of schemata—patterns, shapes, figures available as the mind's regular way of making sense of the world, or as familiar master tropes within our cultural inheritance, such as belong to genre: Comedy, Tragedy, etc. The schema for the shape of the action that might best apply to any particular play could range from the most abstract and diagrammatic to what might be called 'natural', a found shape existing elsewhere in life and society. The novelist and playwright David Storey has a gift for exploiting the found shape, as in his locker-room play *The Changing Room* (1971), which takes its three acts (and emotional structure) from the preparations, half-time interval, and aftermath of a Rugby League football match. In *The Contractor* (1969), it is a job of work—the erection (on stage) of a complete tent-pavilion for a wedding and its subsequent dismantling after the fête—that makes up the *arsis* and *thesis*, the 'lifting up' and 'setting down', of the action (roughly, like the tent itself, a V shape upside down). Among the more abstract schemata are such figures as *displacement*, an action culminating in one personage assuming the identity and position of another (often visualizable as the crossing of two trajectories, one rising and one falling); and *convergence*, a structure where two narrative streams meet. To the diagrammatic X and Y of displacement and convergence one can add the O generated by *recurrence*, most notably when used to provide closure.

Pinter, who invests heavily in the intruder's disturbing agency (*The Care-taker*, *No Man's Land*, etc.), often assimilates it to an overall *displacement* figure. Displacement, or the threat of it, helps generate the intense atmosphere in the first of his plays, *The Room*, and it plays a part in *The Caretaker* and *Old Times*. It is the action, unqualified by explanation, of *A Slight Ache*, where Flora's husband and a strange tramp exchange places, clothing, roles. And it is the mechanism that ultimately shapes the action in perhaps the richest of Pinter's plays, the dysfunctional-family drama *The Homecoming*. To start it is Teddy, the escaped oldest son, returned from America with his stranger-wife Ruth (also British), whose 'homecoming' it is. By the end it is she who has come home rather than her husband, who returns to the clean, bright sterility of America without her. And in a vivid image (as we have seen), it is she who, enthroned, presides in the end over this all-male household, displacing Teddy's stick-wielding father, who kneels, a pathetic petitioner, at her side.

Ruth's enthronement is a reminder that a displacement action is often the armature of tragedy with a historical basis: Richard's displacement, for example, by Henry, Earl of Richmond, first of the Tudor dynasty, at the end of Shakespeare's *Richard III*—after Richard's own rise (like Macbeth's) through a series of ruthless displacements. Again, the figure is given an iconic embodiment. On the battlefield Richmond's father-in-law, Lord Stanley, enters holding the crown, plucked, he says, 'from the dead temples of this bloody wretch [Richard]', and he sets it on Henry's head. Other instances are the Czar's displacement by the fugitive young monk known as the False Dmitri in *Boris Godunov*, their crossed trajectories structuring the whole; and the displacement of Hoss by Crow in the prolonged convergence and Rock and Roll shootout that shapes Sam Shepard's *The Tooth of Crime* (1972).

The sense of immanent or necessary *convergence*—of characters on a collision course, of plot and subplot, of the story we know and bring to the play and the one unfolding before us—shapes the action even as it propels it. An instructive instance is the fatal meeting of Mary of Scotland and Elizabeth of England at the heart of Schiller's historical tragedy *Maria Stuart*. The event never in fact took place, but the drama, full of parallels and contrasts, played out in counterpoised locales (palace and prison), in effect demands the conjunction. It is the crux of the action, the necessary, anticipated encounter that precipitates the two queens' more radical divergence and ultimate fates. And it happens in the middle of the play.

No form of convergence, however, has quite the conclusive, shaping effect as that between the drama we have been following and the story we already know. It is the conclusion, for example, of Giraudoux's *The Trojan War Will Not Take Place*. We know the war took place; its naming in the paradoxical title even tells us as much. But the strenuous, almost successful contest for its avoidance waged by Hector, which constitutes most of the play, unites with the Homeric narrative only at the very end, when blood is spilled and Hector grimly states, 'It will take place'. In Peter Weiss's *Marat/Sade*, it is a famous image, one that has condensed the historical memory into itself, that marks the convergence of supposed dramatic enactment and familiar historical event. It is achieved, after a series of abortive approaches that raise expectation, as a tableau realization of David's familiar painting of *Marat assassiné* (Marat in the Bath). Just in case the image is not familiar enough, it appears as a reminder on the cover of the paperback editions and in the programmes and promotional imagery of most productions.

Often it is language with a familiar ring, the deeper ingrained the better, that provides the stroke that signals convergence with its special frisson. So it is in Byron's heretical cosmic closet drama *Cain* (1821), where the dialogue and action of the play join, at last, the familiar language of the biblical account:

A Voice from within exclaims, Cain! Cain! . . .
Enter the ANGEL *of the Lord.*
ANGEL. Where is thy brother Abel?
CAIN.   Am I then
  My brother's keeper?

—followed by a paraphrase of the biblical exchange that culminates in the Angel (standing in for the Lord) setting a mark on Cain's brow, as brand and protection. (Byron qualifies the comfortable familiarity of the convergence with orthodoxy by Cain's continued intransigence, and the interventions of Adah, Cain's extra-canonical wife.)[14] A more recent instance of exceptional force and brilliance is in Athol Fugard, John Kani, and Winston Ntshona's play *The Island* (1973), a play set in the notorious prison, Robben Island, in apartheid-era South Africa. The goal toward which the action drives, against resistances, is the performance of a distilled version of Sophocles' *Antigone* by the actors/prisoners John and Winston. The actors—much given to performing for each other scenes recollected and imagined—are subject to the foibles of ordinary mortality. But despite that, and despite the poverty of their improvised means, both they and the modern play rise to a heroic dignity and power in assimilating their resistance, their politics, and their suffering to that of the classical Antigone. In the very act of performing the *Antigone*, they, like Antigone, will pit themselves against the laws of the state, to honour Justice and 'those things to which honour belongs', otherwise the laws of God.

Winston and John's performance at the so-called prison concert of 'The Trial and Punishment of Antigone' ends the play. (We take the place of the audience, 'we' originally being their fellow South Africans under apartheid.) The scene is a condensed version of the forensic encounter between King

Creon and Antigone; but it ends with a shocking gesture that disrupts the
formal achievement, the convergence of the drama we are witnessing with
Sophocles' canonical play and text. Translations of Sophocles differ widely, so
it has to be, not the precise words, but their recognizable sense and prove-
nance that creates the exhilarating perception of the two strands locking into
place and becoming one. In the ancient text, after her condemnation to a
death by incarceration, Antigone speaks her farewell, directly to the Chorus of
Elders, and less directly to the Theban polis that the Athenian audience stood
in for:

> Men of my fathers' land, you see me go
> my last journey. My last sight of the sun,
> then never again. . . .
> . . . I go to the fresh-made prison-tomb.
> Alive to the place of corpses, an alien still,
> never at home with the living nor with the dead.

Her final words are:

> O town of my fathers in Thebes' land,
> O gods of our house.
> I am led away at last.
> Look, leaders of Thebes,
> I am last of your royal line.
> Look what I suffer, at whose command,
> because I respected the right.[15]

Fugard and his collaborators echo the language and reframe it through a
shocking action.

WINSTON. (*to the audience*) Brothers and Sisters of the Land! I go now on my last
     journey. I must leave the light of day forever, for the Island, strange and cold, to be
     lost between life and death.
(*Tearing off his wig and confronting the audience as Winston, not Antigone.*)
     God of our Fathers! My Land! My Home!
     Time waits no longer. I go now to my living death, because
     I honoured those things to which honour belongs.[16]

The violent gesture visually reasserts the duality of the two currents in the
convergence while at the same time insisting, through the words, on their congruence. And as Winston speaks the words of Antigone, the dissonance dispels
any chance of aesthetic complacency, forces recognition of the immediacy and
urgency of the tragic issues while capturing the heroism of resistance. Like
Antigone's, such defiance in the name of Right, a shocking action, theatrically
disruptive, could not be without consequences. So the curtain falls on the
pantomime of John and Winston at the punishing, programmed labour that

served as the prolonged opening—a form of closure by recurrence that carries infernal overtones even as it gives a qualified final shape to the play.

Whether through *displacement* or *convergence* or any other progressive scheme, completing the figure signals the moment where the present progressive gives way to the present perfect, the experiential to the retrospective. It is a moment for punctuating epitaphs and epilogues—Horatio's and Fortinbras's reflections on Hamlet, Albany's (or Edgar's) on the world of King Lear, Othello's on himself. One of the schemata that signify completion, however, can work in either of two ways. It can invite us to look back and so give force to the feeling of closure, or, on the contrary, to look forward for more of the same. This is the figure whose signature is *recurrence*, or return to the point at which things began. The circularity that gives definitive force to closure denies neither time nor change, but rather is in the nature of a revisiting that emphasizes the distance travelled, the pastness of the past. In Chekhov's *Seagull*, Nina's recitation of her speech as the Moon in Treplev's maiden play, performed in the first act and recalled and repeated in the last, has such an effect. The original speech, jejune in its high-flown symbolist ambition, is informed in repetition by all that has happened in between, especially to Nina. When she recalls the words in the last act and recites them, they are not made meaningful in the way of *Macbeth*, for example, where the puzzling words and pictures of the witches have their hidden sense revealed on their climactic resurfacing. The men, lions, eagles, and partridges of Nina's speech have not gained semantically on their recurrence. For Nina (and the audience) the words themselves are scarcely relevant. They in fact project a universal extinction of life, whereas Nina introduces the recurrence with: 'How nice it used to be, Kostya! Do you remember? How peaceful and warm, how joyous and pure, our life was then, what feelings we had—like tender, exquisite flowers . . . do you remember . . . ?' For Nina, the backward look is nostalgic, and the recurrence crowns her forceful efforts (in the long recitative leading up to it) to pull herself together, so that invoking the distance between then and now appears to strengthen her will and give her impetus to go on. For Treplev, it is only the measure of loss, the sound of his emptiness, and the prelude to his suicide. For the audience it evokes the mixed feeling of loss and stoical affirmation that belongs to Chekhov's modernity and greatness, and it also signifies closure, the completion that comes with perspective and retrospect and the accomplishment of the figure of the whole.

Musical analogies—like the return to the tonic, or the recapitulation of a leading theme, or what is called ternary form (ABA)—suggest themselves. In musical *drama*, however, we have, not analogies, but prime examples of what one writer on opera calls 'the principle of thematic recurrence' shaping the close of works from Verdi's *Otello* and Puccini's *Madama Butterfly* to Gilbert and Sullivan's *Yeomen of the Guard* and Kern and Hammerstein's *Showboat*. In *Otello*, the music planted at the climax of the Act I love duet is evoked with the kiss in the murder scene, and returns again with poignant finality when Otello kills himself. In opera, such recurrence best serves to recall a past state of feeling, a lost happiness or innocence, as a measure of distance and loss, though in at least one instance it becomes the stuff of apotheosis and release, in the expanding, transfigured return of the music of the love duet in the concluding *Liebestod* of *Tristan und Isolde*. In *Tristan*, the 'love death' also now achieves the cadence evaded through the interruption that shattered the mood of the love duet, so that recurrence and deferred resolution in the music now complete the figure of the action with extraordinary affective force.[17]

The circularity that uses *recurrence* to signal more of the same works on the perverse principle of simultaneously effecting closure and withholding it. It is a characteristically modern gesture, associated with the catastrophic twentieth century's rejection of ideas of transcendence and of meaningful design within the existing order of things. In most plays of the mainstream traditions, completion means the satisfactions of resolution, containment (or discharge) of the energy let loose by instability, and the achievement or the return to an equilibrium. Recurrence that signals such completion marks a return, not to the *same* place, but as on a helix to a corresponding point on a different plane, higher or lower, incorporating gain or loss. But *mere* recurrence is strictly circular, as in an endless loop or a treadmill that goes nowhere, carrying the implication of endless folly or futility. As a return to square one it emphatically announces closure, marking an end to forward movement, possibilities exhausted. But as a beginning all over again it denies closure, and much like the song about the dog and the tombstone that begins the second act in *Waiting for Godot* (or the interminable vistas of 'The Bear Went Over the Mountain'), it signifies endless recurrence, no end in sight. Ionesco has such endings in his earliest plays like *The Bald Soprano* and *The Lesson*. In *The Bald Soprano* he was inspired in production to reinforce his satire of middle-class modernity through a variation that implies robotic interchangeability:

Mr. and Mrs. Martin are seated like the Smiths at the beginning of the play. The play begins again with the Martins, who say exactly the same lines as the Smiths in the first scene, while the curtain softly falls.[18]

But it is Beckett who writes of 'the beautiful convention of the "da capo" as a testimony to the intimate and ineffable nature of an art [music] that is perfectly intelligible and perfectly inexplicable' (surely how he liked to think of his own work).[19] And it is Beckett who carries the convention furthest, in

Play (1963), where a penultimate stage direction reads simply, '*Repeat play*'. This he follows with a '*Closing repeat*' (or in the language of music, a da capo al fine), which can release the audience from its witnessing, but not the characters from their presumed eternal repetitions, in a stage world that envisages the forced replaying of memory as a kind of hell.[20]

Beckett's prime subject, however, is entropy; and so recurrence in all its varied forms in Beckett's *oeuvre* nearly always involves diminution or decline. Thus, even in the production option Beckett approved for *Play*, the second time round may be rendered a degree weaker, the light less strong, the voices lower (p. 160). The implication, as always, is not a prospect of termination, but endless lessening, like a repeating decimal or a hyperbolic curve approaching its zero asymptote.

For all the difference in dramatic method and politics, there is something similar in the return to the beginning in Brecht's *Mother Courage and Her Children*, with its wagon once more on the move against the cyclorama, and Courage's introductory singing commercial recalled in the marching song coming from the soldiers—though the wagon is now battered and depleted, and Courage is hauling it alone. The recurrence suggests being bound to an endless labour in a prospect of unending desolation. But as we have already seen, there is more at work in this complex evocation of the opening than mere circularity. There is not just depletion but finality in the spectacle of a mother (so designated) now stripped of all her children. And yet, in a contrary sense, the soldiers' song with its repeated chorus—on the one hand ironic but on the other revivifying—is a resurrection anthem, a reminder of seasonal renewal, a call like that in Bach's great chorale, 'Sleepers Awake'.

> The spring is come! Christian, revive!
> The snowdrifts melt, the dead lie dead!
> And if by chance you're still alive
> Its time to rise and shake a leg.[21]

Brecht, for all his claims to a dramaturgy that is like a demonstration—as even in his 'one thing after another'—is never really that simple; and his most lasting and challenging plays are those that allow an audience to see and respond in more ways than one.

The shape of the action is often susceptible to such diagrammatic figuration, but even without the geometry, represented events, notably death and marriage, have been more than enough to register as 'conclusive,' and provide the expected satisfactions of closure for most of the plays that come under the rubrics of Tragedy and Comedy. And there are other effective ways of providing the sense of an ending, some that seem to open out rather than close down, and that operate in the realm of feeling and perception rather than through the bare structure of events. There is a structure of emotion and response as well. The end of Chekhov's *Uncle Vanya*, for example, as Sonya projects the future for herself and Vanya, of enduring through their daily labours until they find rest and peace, has such an effect, of enlarging and universalizing. It transforms local experience into a feeling about the human condition, an expansion like that which comes through Gabriel Conroy's visionary westering reflections at the end of Joyce's great story 'The Dead'. It is the antithesis of the da capo recurrence that denies transcendence and constricts the ring of possibilities in mundane repetition. As an enlargement and exaltation of consciousness beyond the local and the particular, such expansion has affinities with the emotion that we often associate with the greatest of tragedies, and with the apotheosis that Evreinov's Director so blithely recommends, where play or protagonist is taken (as in Shaw's description of the end-movement of Major Barbara in the play of that name), 'right up to the skies'.[22]

Finally, there is the play whose shape in retrospect implies shapelessness, in that in the end it eschews resolution, revelation, transformation, the feeling of having arrived. It is not that expectation is here deceived in some surprising reversal; it is ignored or even insulted. Nor are we offered even the formal satisfaction of da capo repetition, or entropic recurrence. Instead, we are left with a shape that is deliberately no shape, but is intended to represent chaos; not symbolically, but mimetically. I would argue Shakespeare's *Troilus and Cressida* is such a play, as measured by its outcomes. There is something like an epilogue, signalling the end, where Pandarus, in character, registers his complaints directly to the audience, and bequeaths it his diseases. But there is no closure. Menelaus and Paris, 'the cuckold and the cuckold-maker', fight, but to no conclusion. Troilus, betrayed by Cressida, seeks revenge on her Greek lover Diomedes on the field, but there is no showdown; having lost Cressida, Troilus merely loses his horse as well. Hector, having bested Achilles in fair fight, is killed like an animal, his corpse insulted, but there is no retribution on Achilles and his murderous gang, and no moment of enlarged understanding. The war will go on, unheroically, and so will the general disorder. 'Lechery, lechery, still wars and lechery', says the splenetic Thersites, 'Nothing else holds fashion' (V. iii. 193–4). More destruction is coming, we know, but for now even catastrophe is withheld as a shaping conclusion. War, lechery, and futility remain the general condition, and there is no end in sight.

7

The Action of Words

At the end of Georg Büchner's tragedy of the French Revolution, *Danton's Death* (1835), the bereaved wife of the executed Dantonist Camille Desmoulins wanders on to the Place de la Révolution and sits on the steps of the guillotine. Her mind astray, she sings a chapbook verse on Death, whereupon:

A PATROL *enters.*

A CITIZEN. Ho! Who's there?

LUCILLE (*reflective, and then as if making a decision, suddenly*). Long live the King!

The Citizen retorts, 'In the name of the Republic!' and Lucille is immediately surrounded and led away.[1]

What has happened? Lucille has decided to join her husband, and so she cries, 'Long live the King!' But Lucille is no Royalist—indeed, she has no politics—and the King has been dead for more than a year. What the words *say* is not the point. What the words *do*, is. Shouting the slogan is a gesture whose meaning—linked to time, place, and circumstance—lies in the feeling that drives it and in its intended effect; its effect on those who hear it, and ultimately on the speaker herself.

That a slogan whose declarative content is so beside the point should conclude *Danton's Death* is altogether fitting. Büchner's Danton, whose mighty voice had earlier both inspired and saved the Revolution, has now had to be prodded into action—meaning into public speech and forensic argument—to save himself; but he has left it too late, and the Jacobin machine silences him. The play shares his disaffection with the formulas and rhetorical abstractions of public discourse, of which, however, there is a great deal; a discourse whose alternative, in the orchestration of the play, is the private voice that speaks of and from a naked and irremediable solitude. But even the scene of the Dantonists' execution—treated as theatre by the crowd—has some of the victims, as they mount the scaffold, attempting to make what one of them has called 'phrases for posterity', memorable rhetorical gestures. Of these, none save perhaps Danton's ironic reproof to an officious executioner—'Do you think you can prevent our heads from kissing in the basket?'—and his final silence is as effective or decisive or indeed as eloquent as Lucille's suicidal cry.[2]

The lesson in Lucille's affirmation is that the action of dialogue in drama lies not so much in what the words say as in what they do. It follows that while they need not mean what they say, they nevertheless can be meaningful. Among the more notable contributions in modern language theory has been the articulation of the notion of the speech act, whereby an utterance is to be understood, not simply as a proposition that may be true or false, or as the just representation of a thought, or as the direct expression of one's feelings, but as embedded in a set of circumstances, a particular situation and occasion, having a social character and as like as not an agenda. Not coincidentally, roughly the same period—mid-twentieth century—saw the elaboration, in acting theory and critical practice, of the notion of the subtext.

The notion of the subtext—a charge in the words beyond and beneath what they seem to say, a region, like the invisible four-fifths of the iceberg, where the true force of what is said is purported to lie—was almost necessitated by another development: a shift in the conventions of dialogue under the pressure of the appetite for prosaic Realism. Earlier than the nineteenth century, the watchword of 'truth to Nature' dwelt amicably with conventions of stage speech that embraced much stylistic variety, including blank verse, rhyme, all the elaborations of wit and rhetoric, and most important, an assumption of commensurate expressibility. Characters could and would say what they had it in them to say, and what the situation called for. Hence the magnificent tirades, disputations, ruminations, badinage, and often high poetry, of drama. Such a convention sorted well with a theory of acting that rested on the expression of the passions and (in comedy at least) the heightened externalization of character. Both the convention and the theory, however, would soon cease to serve in a climate where, for example, the reflections of George Eliot's Dinah Morris in *Adam Bede* (1859), a novel of village lives, might pass for a truism. Dinah is feeling sorry for a friendly dog. 'Poor dog! . . . I've a strange feeling about the dumb things as if they wanted to speak, and it was a trouble to 'em because they couldn't. . . . they may well have more in them than they know how to make us understand, for we can't say half what we feel, with all our words.'[3]

Now there is hardly anything in the theatre more apt to change than what holding the mirror up to nature means for acting. Each generation at least since Garrick was complimented on the realism of its performances compared to its predecessors, though contemporary visual representations and early recordings of actors so celebrated usually fail to convince us. Nevertheless, changes in taste and attitude concerning subject matter and its rendering altered assumptions about dramatic language and its expressive possibilities, bringing it closer to everyday speech. All this was well in train when, late in the nineteenth century, with expectations for dramatic speech responding to a subject matter much closer to common life, Tolstoy took it upon himself to write an improving play for a popular audience, accessible even to a benighted peasantry. In *The Power* [or *Domain*] *of Darkness* (1886), a grim cautionary tale of adultery, murder, incest, infanticide, and despair, Tolstoy fashions a language that plausibly reproduces characteristics of the common speech—its workaday vocabulary, its abruptness, its solecisms, its hostility to abstraction, its heavy infusion of proverbial sayings, formulaic exchanges, liturgical scraps, abusive vulgarity, and concrete analogy with a barnyard flavour. Its speakers, however, experience passion, greed, wilfulness, remorse with an intensity and on a scale in no way inferior to that of the articulate warriors, princes, legendary queens, caught in comparable nets of desire and consequence. It is that intensity and scale which must percolate through the constraints on language and the sordid circumstances, in action, and with speech that functions as action. And so they do, for example after Nikita, racked with remorse, tries to hang himself at his stepdaughter's wedding, and then confesses purgatively and almost ritually, bowing and asking forgiveness, first of the 'Orthodox *Mir*' (the commune), and then, individually and serially, of those his sins have injured. He even takes on the sins of others as his own.[4]

Tolstoy's Nikita, ending in unconscious emulation of Christ, begins as a callow peasant Don Juan, sleeping with his ailing peasant employer's wife, and easily persuaded to abandon the young woman he had previously seduced and promised to marry. At this point there is no reason not to take the vacancy and brutality of his speech as all there is to him. When the neglected Marina insists on a meeting, he replies to her use of his name:

NIKITA. Well, what about Nikita! Here's Nikita. What do you want? Get out of here.
MARINA. So, I see, you want to get rid of me, want to forget.
NIKITA. What's there to remember? . . . I didn't go out to you. Means, I don't want to see you, simple as that. So, go on.[5]

By the end of the scene, however, Nikita, left alone, expresses some confusion: 'It's all somehow mixed up. I love these women like sugar, but if you go too far with them there's trouble!' That confusion and consequent uneasiness—for which he lacks adequate words—bespeak his limitations, but also leave open the possibility of something more. As for Marina, Nikita asks when trying to shake her loose, 'And why keep talking about nothing?' But Marina finds, within the resources of the common tongue and Tolstoy's mimetic convention, the means to convey much of her feeling and understanding. She uses unguarded directness, the simplest diction for the plainest truth, antiquated phrase, pulp cliché, pithy antithesis that smacks of peasant fatalism and cynicism:

MARINA. So it's the end, means that what was is gone. You tell me to forget! Well, Nikita, remember. I valued my maiden honor more than eyesight. You ruined me for nothing, deceived me. Didn't pity an orphan (*cries*), got rid of me. Killed me,

you did, but still I don't have it in for you. God be with you. You find someone
better, you'll forget; find someone worse, you'll remember . . . (p. 394)

As dramatic discourse read or overheard, it is less aspiring than Tamburlaine's
blank verse periods (invoked below), but it is by no means ineffective in its
rueful expression of love and loss. And because there are intimations of a
depth of feeling *beyond* the verbal resources she is able to deploy, we are all
the more certain that Nikita is making a mistake.

Perhaps most telling with respect to the naturalistic premise for dramatic
speech that Tolstoy here adopts is his treatment of the character Akim, who is
the moral compass of Tolstoy's village world, the spokesman for what is true
and right and good. Here the gap between what this spokesman knows and
feels and his power of expressing it in words is made shockingly and ironically
egregious. As Nikita's father, Akim attempts ineffectually to counter the sly,
evil counsel of his wife Matryona concerning their son and Marina. Matryona
makes fun of Akim's stumbling aphasia, and then dismisses his objections as
gibberish—'hot air'.

AKIM (*interrupts*). No, it's not hot air. I mean, you take it all your way, 'bout the girl
or 'bout yourself, you take it your way, the way it seems better to you, but God, I
mean, now, He'll turn it all his way. This, too, that is. (p. 388)

Akim is the closest thing to the voice of Tolstoy, who even puts into his
mouth a Tolstoyan critique of capital and interest as well as of pragmatic
voluntarism. But Tolstoy takes it as given that where eloquence would be
'realistically' implausible, it is better avoided. The result is that Akim's insights
and profundities are clothed in the hallmarks of a sacred simplicity and in his
expressive disability. They emerge, as it were, in spite of the words rather than
as embodied in the words.

The conventions of mimetic realism came to the fore in a theatre bent
on the representation of ordinary lives in apparently ordinary circumstances—husbands and wives instead of kings and usurpers, urban flats
and suburban living rooms rather than courts and castles, domestic rather
than public spaces. As realized in dialogue for the stage, its limitations foster,
on the one hand, the premise of a subtext, to supply what the language can
no longer handle directly and to hint at that within which passeth show; and,
on the other hand, an assumption that language is constitutive, and what
you speak (are able to speak) is what you are. Where the issue is joined is in
plays that attempt to put on the stage a modern lumpenproletariat, speaking
an impoverished dialect mostly confined to ritual phrase and the formulas
of aggression and appetite. O'Neill tried the experiment, as in *The Hairy Ape*
(1921); but no one has succeeded in carrying it further than Edward Bond in

Saved (1965), his rendering of the fruits of a cumulative history of cultural and emotional deprivation in the urban wasteland. The scandal and sensation of *Saved*, forbidden the public stage (like Tolstoy's play) and even prosecuted, was the drawn-out spectacle of an infant tormented and stoned to death in its pram. Unlike the horrific and hardly less graphic murder of a newborn infant in *The Power of Darkness*, the crime is enacted before our eyes; and it is gratuitous rather than motivated, an act of casual cruelty by a clutch of young hooligans in a park, fuelled as much by boredom as by excited, competitive, transgressive sadism. Fred, who is reluctantly drawn into the frenzy (and who also happens to be the father of the murdered child, like Nikita), is the one participant identified and sentenced. On his release from prison, he is met in a café by his friends, among them Len, who boards with the dysfunctional family of the dead child's mother, Pam, and is irretrievably attached to her. Len asks Fred, 'What was it like?'

FRED. I tol' yer.
LEN. No, before.
FRED. Before what?
LEN. In the park.
FRED. Yer saw.
LEN. Wass it feel like?
FRED. Don't know.
LEN. When yer was killin' it.
FRED. Do what?
LEN. Wass it feel like when yer killed it?

Len having gotten the whole question out, other conversations intervene. He resumes:

LEN. Whass it like, Fred.
FRED (*drinks*). It ain' like this in there.
LEN. Fred.
FRED. I tol' yer.
LEN. No yer ain'.
FRED. I forget.
LEN. I thought yer'd a bin full a it. I was—
FRED. Len!
LEN. —curious, thass all, 'ow it feels t'—
FRED. No!
He slams his fist on the table.
LEN. Okay.
FRED. It's finished.
LEN. Yeh.

FRED (*stands*). What yer wan' a do?
The juke box starts.
LEN. Nothin'.
FRED. Wass 'e getting' at?
LEN. It's finished.[6]

Fred has no remorse to express. As he points out, 'I were'n the only one.' As
with most of those in the play, his language in the default mode runs to a
defensive-aggressive banter that gives nothing away; but there is no indication
that there is anything much to give. Len is an exception in that his attachment
to Pam, his ability to listen, his concern for others' feelings, give evidence of an
inner life for which words and articulated concepts are not the measure. Nor
is he quite alone. In the penultimate scene, Pam's marginalized father, Harry,
drops his taciturn hostility and reaches out to Len in something like a paternal
heart-to-heart. And there is enough indication of stubborn vitality and suffering in loss in the other members of this Hobbesian nuclear family to discredit
a response that simply equates them with the violence, nastiness, and poverty
of their verbal and occasionally physical behaviour. It is nevertheless telling
that the last scene, conveying a near approach to domestic harmony, is a scene
almost entirely in stage directions. Len is engaged in repairing a chair broken in
a recent eruption of violence, which Bond himself (outside the play) points to as
something positive, a straw to clutch at.[7] On the other hand, everyone present
is solipsistically engaged—clearing up, reading the *Radio Times*, filling in the
coupon for the football pools; careful to avoid conflict, but certainly not interacting. The sustained effect is tranquil, even harmonious—a 'social stalemate'
in Bond's description. The enabling condition is that it is nearly speechless.[8]

7.1. EXPRESSING, IMPELLING, REVEALING

What the words do in drama may have a divided agenda, acting to different
purpose for those on stage and those looking on. For those speaking and
listening inside the world of the play, what the words do will be specific to
time, place, and situation. For those experiencing the play from outside, what
the words do will have a function or functions specific to the making of plays.
When Shakespeare's Enobarbus, blunt, jaded, and cynical soldier that he is,
launches his famous set-piece description of Cleopatra on the river of Cydnus,
where Antony first saw her, he is responding to his immediate auditors and
thickly laying it on. Fresh from Egypt with Antony, he finds himself with his
Roman counterparts who are eager to hear about the wonders and delights of
his exotic foreign service. He obliges:

ENOBARBUS. I will tell you.
    The barge she sat in, like a burnished throne
    Burned on the water . . .

And so forth (*Antony and Cleopatra*, II. ii. 196 ff.). Like the eager audience on the stage, those seeing and reading the play will be dazzled by the glorious picture, including the fanciful hyperbole that conveys the emotions of the original riverside spectators. But for those of us offstage, at one or two removes, the speech and the scene that contains it will have other functions as well. For one thing, we have already encountered Cleopatra in the flesh and in action, so that the dazzling account of Enobarbus will amplify and qualify what we have already seen, and be verified and qualified in turn. For another, the scene serves as a breather in the action, bridging to the subsequent appearance of the virtuous Octavia, Caesar's sister and Antony's new-made wife. The preemptive contrast laid down by Enobarbus prepares us for Antony's immediate resolve, politics notwithstanding, to return to Egypt: 'I' th' East my pleasure lies.' And finally the description leaves an indelible impression that re-emerges in Cleopatra's final epiphany and apotheosis as she prepares for death ('Show me my women like a queen. Go fetch | My best attire. I am again for Cydnus | To meet Mark Antony' (V. ii. 223–5)).

The work of words in the economy of the play—that external frame of reference—can be generalized according to function. One can distinguish, for example, between narration and enactment, whose alternation and interweaving is marked in some Japanese drama, and makes for a fluid and effective medium in a number of modern plays, including Wilder's *Our Town* (1938), and Michael Frayn's drama of the cold war and German politics *Democracy* (2003) as well as his earlier *Benefactors* (1984). Brian Friel's *Faith Healer* (1980) is a successful experiment in pure narration—four monologues by three characters shaping a progression that is entirely dramatic. Or one could distinguish between the dialogic and the reflective, as in those Greek plays where choral commentary frames and accompanies the action. But from the perspective of the reader as of the hearer, the words are there in the main to *express*, to *impel*, to *reveal*—express thought and feeling; impel (or defer) changes in condition, situation, and relationship; reveal motives, causes, antecedents, the inner truth or logic of events. And when it comes to expressing, impelling, and revealing, there is some affinity between the things words do and the shape they take, between function and form. If expression full blown finds its most efficient vehicle in monologue (soliloquy, aria, tirade), impulsion tends to work best through the back-and-forth of dialogue. Revelation is less particular, given the fact that the whole of a play is a progressive revelation, direct and indirect, intentional and inadvertent, true, false, and ambiguously misleading.

Expressing. A dramatic convention of expressibility is one thing; the notion that everything in God's creation (including Divinity itself) is expressible, is something else. But during the centuries and in those theatres where the convention reigned, even the not uncommon trope asserting the inexpressibility of the highest feelings could rise to the occasion, never at a loss for words. So Torquato Tasso, in his lyrical pastoral drama *Aminta* (1573), has his chorus speak of Love as loosening the tongues of its servants into a beautiful and abundant eloquence. Yet:

> often (O divine
> And wondrous deed of thine!)
> In passion-broken words,
> And a confused saying,
> The struggling heart shall best
> Leap forth and be expressed,
> And more avail than rhetoric's whole displaying.

Meanwhile, even the supposed failure of language to convey the full tide of passion is most exquisitely expressed:

> Thy very silence wears
> The face of ended prayers.[9]

Over a decade later (1587), Marlowe's Tamburlaine, turning from grimmest slaughter to muse on the divine Zenocrate, asks in a famous set-piece soliloquy:

> What is beauty, saith my sufferings, then?
> If all the pens that ever poets held
> Had fed the feeling of their masters' thoughts,
> And every sweetness that inspir'd their hearts,
> Their minds, and muses on admired themes;
> If all the heavenly quintessence they still
> From their immortal flowers of poesy,
> Wherein as in a mirror we perceive
> The highest reaches of a human wit;
> If these had made one poem's period,
> And all combin'd in beauty's worthiness,
> Yet should there hover in their restless heads
> One thought, one grace, one wonder at the least,
> Which into words no virtue can digest.[10]

'Virtue' here indicates capacity, the power to do and say, with which Tamburlaine is so remarkably endowed. The congruence between his largeness of soul, the heroic grandeur that earns him the epithet Tamburlaine the Great, and his capacity to express himself in 'high astounding terms' (Prologue) is underlined early in the play, when Mycetes, whose throne this Scythian shepherd will soon appropriate, seeks to manifest an appropriate anger:

Brother Cosroe, I find myself aggriev'd,
Yet insufficient to express the same,
For it requires a great and thund'ring speech.
Good brother, tell the cause unto my lords;
I know you have a better wit than I. (I. i. 1–5)

Marlowe, cannily subversive as always, exploits the established decorum that would relegate peasants to clownishness and endow nobles with eloquence as confirmation of a Providential disposition in the social order. Not birth but endowment fits this shepherd for the place of the king; and the measure of fitness, the measure of 'virtue' in this dramatic embodiment of the historic Timur, is his expressive power. His first great victory (after shedding his shepherd's gear to reveal armour and cutlass beneath) is winning over the Persian general Theridamas, with a force twice as large as his own, by sheer persuasive eloquence and presence. 'Won with thy words and conquered with thy looks,' Theridamas yields 'myself, my men and horse to thee' (I. ii. 228–9).

But it is nevertheless a *convention* of expressibility that is at work in Marlowe's play, whose ultimate limit is not the capacity of the characters, but of the playwright speaking through them. So Cosroe, who displaces Mycetes with Tamburlaine's help and then is in turn displaced, can appear to find the words to express the ineffable experience of dying itself (II. vii. 42–52). Moreover, though there is hardly anything he can't do with words, Tamburlaine the character (like Marlowe the playwright) shows a limitless mastery of symbolic expression as well. In a fearsome stroke of psychological warfare, for example, Tamburlaine uses spectacle—dress, tenting, pennons, and accoutrements—to signal his intentions when laying siege to Damascus: *white* the first phase; *scarlet* the second, and fatal *black* the third. And earlier, when the devious Agydas attempts to work on captive Zenocrate (whose escort he was) to undermine her new-kindled love for Tamburlaine, and he has the misfortune to be overheard, Tamburlaine speaks his piece without a word (III. ii. 65 ff):

Tamburlaine *goes to her and takes her away lovingly by the hand, looking wrathfully on* Agydas, *and says nothing.*

Agydas, however, left alone, expresses, first his own inward state ('Surpris'd with fear of hideous revenge, | I stand aghast'), and then—in words—what Tamburlaine has 'wrapp'd in silence of his angry soul':

Upon his brows was portray'd ugly death,
And in his eyes the fury of his heart,
That shine as comets, menacing revenge,
And casts a pale complexion on his cheeks.

Then, after an extended epic simile of storm and shipwreck expressing *both* Tamburlaine's elemental rage and his own abysmal terror (ll. 76–87), Agydas receives his sentence:

> Enter Techelles *with a naked dagger.*

Here too Agydas articulates the message:

> It says, 'Agydas, thou shalt surely die,
> And of extremities elect the least:
> More honor and less pain it may procure
> To die by this resolved hand of thine
> Than stay the torments he and heaven have sworn.'
>
> (ll. 95–9)

With everything that needs saying doubly expressed, he takes the path of honour and prudence, and uses the knife to stab himself.

Cordelia is the first instance I at least have met in drama where the gap between feeling and capacity for its expression in words is taken seriously, as more than a paradoxical rhetorical trope, and is embodied in the character itself. In her consistent inarticulateness yoked with what we read as true depth of feeling, she remains an exception to the conventions of dramatic discourse for perhaps two and a half centuries. The anomaly surfaces in the complications of the opening scene. At the division of the kingdom between the sisters, Cordelia appears certainly unwilling, but also apparently unable to suit her father's whim and play along with the game of earning a share proportional to the love she can put into words. (Equal shares have in fact already been scrupulously determined.) But her disability reappears in all its poignancy in the heartbreaking scene of her reunion with Lear as he emerges shakily from sleep and madness (IV. vii). There, seeking recognition and blessing, Cordelia can only reply to her father's humbled tentatives monosyllabically: 'And so I am, I am'; 'No cause, no cause,' reiteration and wordlessness itself serving to convey the overwhelming emotion in the absence of commensurate language.

It is in fact Lear's plainly wrong-headed adherence to the dramatic convention, his expectation that his daughters will provide expressive language commensurate with their love, that precipitates his ruin in the first place—that and his petulant rage at having his ceremonial playlet spoilt. In the scene of division, as her elder sisters grossly pile it on, Cordelia lets us know in asides—her love being 'More ponderous than my tongue'—that she is incapable of doing the same ('What shall Cordelia speak? Love, and be silent').[11] So, when Lear asks her, 'What can you say to draw | A third more opulent than your sisters? Speak,' she replies 'Nothing, my lord.' And when she deigns to defend herself, the import of her statement is less in what the words directly convey than in their situated action, as response, as assertion, with their underburden of implication.

LEAR. Nothing will come of nothing: speak again.
CORDELIA. Unhappy that I am, I cannot heave
  My heart into my mouth. I love your majesty
  According to my bond, no more nor less. (I. i. 90–3)

Part of what she says is directed at her sisters, and perhaps at the complaisant witnesses of their performance. To heave one's heart into one's mouth implies something that ought to make one retch; that makes *her* retch. And her sisters—encouraged by their father—have done this thing with appetite. (Goneril even frames her transcendental hyperboles by invoking the ineffability trope, for 'A love that makes breath poor and speech unable.') 'According to my bond, no more nor less' is directed to her father, who is being asked to understand—as in some corner of his mind he must—that it is a most sacred and compelling tie that is meant, strong in love and obligation, and that to live up to the terms of such a bond is no mean achievement. That Cordelia then goes on to explain herself by arguing the matter rationally and analytically rather than expressively is no help. Lear states the essential question, even if he is deaf to the very thing he would wish to hear: 'But goes your heart with this?' he asks, meaning with language so coldly reasoning. What Cordelia's words actually do is not what they are intended to do, at least where her father is concerned. They do not open a way for Lear to accept what is truly in her heart but not in her mouth. Instead, they make things worse. He will not hear what it is not in her nature or her capacity to express directly. Construed instead as expressing heartlessness, the words precipitate Lear's casting her off.

Expression is the playwright's means of conveying the action within. But the words put in the mouths of the actors serve to express more than what belongs to the character's immediate experience and response. In a play far more than in life, the words spoken express and evoke who and what you are. That is so even where a character is given to self-deception or to deceptive self-advertising, or is aphasic by convention or temperament. A principal burden on dramatic speech is characterological, to establish and particularize identity. So, in the formative era of a professional theatre and drama in Italy, the actor-playwright Angelo Beolco, or 'Ruzzante', opened his play, *Il Reduce* (1523), by announcing:

RUZZANTE. Well, here I am at last! In Venice! The place I've been yearning for worse than a spindle-shanked, empty-bellied old mare yearns for the sweet green grass! What I need is a rest, and a chance to build up my muscles, and to get back to my wife, Gnua. She's living here now. To hell with war, and battlefields, and soldiers! You won't catch me on any battlefields again! I've had enough of those drums beating in my ears. No more trumpets! No more call to arms! And no more getting scared to death! . . . They're not going to get me again, and if they do it'll be in the backside . . . Here I am, safe and sound, and I can hardly believe it. Hey, suppose I'm just dreaming all this! That'd be a blow! What do you mean, dreaming? Didn't I get on board that ship at Fusina? I'm me, aint I? Sure as God, I am. Didn't I dedicate myself to the Holy Virgin as a good little footslogging soldier? Well, that's one little vow I'm taking back. But suppose I'm not really me? Suppose I got killed in combat? So, now I'm a ghost! Oh, that'd be a great one! But, uh, uh! Ghosts don't get hungry! I'm me, all right. Me, myself, and I'm alive.[12]

In telling us what he is feeling and thinking and what he is up to, Ruzzante is asserting who he is and what he is, and perhaps telling us more about that than he knows. He is establishing himself as a presence, a distinctive individual about whom we can entertain distinct expectations. Moreover, though vividly individual with his own particular history (there is a lot more to his account of himself than I have quoted), he shares in a common type, that of the blustering soldier, with classical antecedents and a glorious succession, whose apogee is no doubt Falstaff. His evocation of tribe and type makes him easier to represent and to grasp; and within that evocation there is plenty of scope for something new and individual. It is no different with the language of the play, this one or another.

In almost any play, the dramatis personae share in a common tongue: a style, a diction, a poetics, belonging to a given time, place, genre, or playwright, that one can identify as 'Spanish Golden Age', or 'comedy of manners', or 'Pinteresque' (a coinage he despises). But speech individuated and personalized still remains the playwright's and the actor's primary instrument for character creation, even in those theatres where much of the work is done by the use of fixed 'masks' and stock types, and by the conventionalized accents of class, or region, or nation, or gender. Without those helps, speech more than ever has to carry the signature that supports individuality, as for example in the theatre of the actress and author Anna Deavere Smith, where her idea is to take individuals directly from life. To bring them to the stage, she looks to make 'rhythmic transcriptions and pay attention to the music of the speech'.[13] Her premiss, she wrote, was that 'If we were to inhabit the speech pattern of another, and walk in the speech of another, we could find the individuality of the other and experience that individuality viscerally.'[14]

It is especially in the words that character either directly declares itself, or gives itself away. Shaw observed that, in the classic tradition, many of his stage characters are endowed with a self-knowledge and a power to give it expression that would make them prodigies in ordinary life—the dustman Alfred Doolittle in *Pygmalion*, for example.[15] But then, to be abnormally blind to oneself—like Henry Higgins—is no less in the classic tradition than to be preternaturally self-aware. A character like John Tanner in Shaw's *Man and Superman* manages somehow to be both. Additionally, there are those who lie about themselves, consciously or unconsciously—a disjunction between signifier and signified that generates the perennial comic figure of the Hypocrite, a name that associates him, unfairly if etymologically, with the blameless profession of the actor.

If speaking allows characters to express themselves, to vent feelings and, as characters, put themselves into words, it is also how characters give themselves away, whether inadvertently or despite attempts to suppress, deceive, or conceal; whether to other figures in the play or exclusively to the audience. In fact giving oneself away, in the wake of the demise of a convention of commensurate expressibility and with the triumph of the modern psychology of the unconscious, becomes the standard recourse of the modern theatre. Not that it is anything new. It may be seen at its broadest in a character like Sir Anthony Absolute in Sheridan's *The Rivals* (1775), in his own eyes a mild-tempered, generous, and considerate father, who, at his son's demurral from his fatherly plans to marry him off, immediately explodes: 'I'll disown you, I'll disinherit you, I'll unget you!' Later, reflecting, he fulminates:

No—I'll die sooner than forgive him. Die, did I say? I'll live these fifty years to plague him. At our last meeting, his impudence had almost put me out of temper. An obstinate, passionate, self-willed boy! Who can he take after?[16]

Again, the Philosopher whom M. Jourdain hires to remedy his education in Molière's *Le Bourgeois Gentilhomme* (1670) offers himself as a model of dispassionate stoicism to his argumentative fellow instructors, until he feels his own discipline challenged, whereupon he falls into violent abuse and physical assault.

Subtler forms of giving oneself away are essential to the comedy of many of Molière's characters. If the playwright prepares us for the oddities of a figure like Orgon by what is said about him beforehand (standard practice at the time), it is in the action of his own words that his character comes to life. The obsessed paterfamilias of Molière's *Tartuffe* (1664/9), Orgon is oblivious to what is odd and indeed alarming in his fixation on the outrageous religious hypocrite, Tartuffe; but his madness shows through when, on his first entrance, returned from a journey, he enquires of his servant, Dorine, how the household has got on in his absence. She reports the illness of his wife:

DORINE. Madame had a bad fever, two days ago,
   And a headache that really brought her low.
ORGON. Yes. And Tartuffe?
DORINE.   Tartuffe? Fit as a fiddle:
   Red mouth, pink cheeks, and bulging at the middle.
ORGON. Poor fellow! (I. iv. 231–5)[17]

And so on, through several more rounds, ending always with the same refrain (*Le pauvre homme!*) as Madame's condition gets worse and Tartuffe's appetite enlarges. When Orgon tells his concerned brother how he first encountered Tartuffe in church to convince him of Tartuffe's worthiness, he gives away, not only his own gullibility, but Tartuffe's campaign of ingratiation and gross insincerity, imperceptible to Orgon, but in his words made evident both to us and to his onstage auditor:

ORGON. Ah, if, that day we met, you'd been on hand,
   You'd feel as I do now—you'd understand.
   Each day he came to church, meek as you please,
   And, right across from me, fell on his knees;
   He caught the eye of every person there,
   Such warmth and zeal he put into his prayer;
   His transports were extreme, his sighs profound;
   Each moment he would stoop and kiss the ground;
   And when I left, he always went before
   To offer me holy water at the door. (I. v. 281–90)

At the other end of the spectrum is the uninhibited speaking of who and what you are. Such frankness ignores the norms of social hypocrisy and the respectable self-editing and motivational cosmetology that we ordinarily practise and take for granted. Consequently we laugh, as when W. S. Gilbert's Sir Joseph Porter tells us how he earned his promotions by having 'polished up the handle of the big front door'; or when one of Gilbert's sweet young things articulates her innocent mercenary expectations. Gilbert's self-exhibitors, who often preserve the *tones* of social propriety and polite hypocrisy while giving the game away, belong to the world of his *Palace of Truth* (1870), a pre-Sullivan fantasy whose premiss is an enchanted locale where everyone who speaks says what is really on his or her mind, though without knowing they are doing so. A number of Wilde's figures seem to have passed through the Palace of Truth, albeit in full possession of their faculties; but then, that could be said of Richard of Gloucester soliloquizing, and of Falstaff arguing the case for cowardice, and perhaps of that other self-aware comedian, Iago, explaining his motivations. Except that, as Coleridge long ago observed, Iago's explanations are too many to tell us who he is. Iago anticipates his fellow artist Harold Pinter, who carries his understanding of the reliability of language and the workings of subtext to the textual vanishing point. Not that the words themselves disappear. In an early statement on his craft, Pinter writes that the language his characters speak, like that we also speak, 'is a highly ambiguous business. So often, below the word spoken, is the thing known and unspoken.' But from speech acts rooted in the habits of evasion, unreliability, and defensive obstruction, 'a language arises . . . where under what is said, another thing is being said'.

As a consequence, the act of speaking is rife with its nominal opposite. In effect,

There are two silences. One when no word is spoken. The other when perhaps a torrent of language is being employed. . . . The speech we hear is an indication of that which we don't hear. It is a necessary avoidance, a violent, sly, anguished or mocking smoke screen which keeps the other in its place. When true silence falls we are still left with echo but are nearer nakedness. One way of looking at speech is to say that it is a constant strategem to cover nakedness.[18]

Pinter's take on how words are used and what they do implies a distinction of great import for the craft of playwriting: the distinction between character as inner essence and character as vital presence. The language whose proper action is *not* to express, but to conceal or confuse, disconcert one's interlocutors and gain an advantage over them, or even hide vacuity and incoherence from oneself, may at the same time establish a vivid dramatic personality. Goldberg is one such fast-talking monologist in Pinter's *The Birthday Party* (1958); Lenny is another in *The Homecoming*. The truth or falsity of what they say about themselves—Lenny's intimidating anecdotes of misogynistic violence, Goldberg's florid, folksy reminiscences of happy childhood and domestic comfort—is not an actual dramatic issue; nor is the truth or falsity of anything merely *said* in Pinter (anything we don't see for ourselves) decidable. As to the 'real' Goldberg, we are on surer ground in the appalling moment when words fail him:

And you'll find—that what I say is true.
Because I believe that the world . . . (*Vacant.*). . . .
Because I believe that the world . . . (*Desperate.*). . . .
BECAUSE I BELIEVE THAT THE WORLD . . . (*Lost.*). . . .
    He sits in chair.[19]

Goldberg is half of a team that appears in the seaside boarding house where Stanley, the unkempt protagonist, is living in anonymity. In the end, Goldberg and his partner McCann take Stanley away, having earlier provoked his violent breakdown. Neither the organization they seem to be working for, nor Stanley's prior history (though there are plenty of conflicting hints about it), nor what Stanley may be hiding from and why, is even remotely clear. What is clear is that the result of the team's verbal battering—words functioning as jackhammers—is to reduce the ultimately cleaned-up, dressed up, nicely shaven Stanley, ready to be carted off, to a lobotomized silence.

And here we are at the point where functional distinctions, between *expressing, impelling, revealing*, blur. Not to express by means of a torrent of expression is using words effectively to conceal. Using words to intimidate, to dominate, to seduce, and to silence in the guise of self-expression means using them to impel, that is, to effect, or to create the conditions for change.

Impelling. The eloquence of mime notwithstanding, there is good reason to take as the basic stuff of drama, as drama stripped to its essentials, the interaction of voices in dialogue. Even in the received account of the origins of Greek tragedy, where the first actor (*hypocrites*, or 'interlocutor') emerges from the chorus, it is the dialogue of actor and chorus leader that effects the transition from dithyramb to drama; and it is drama that we are talking about, not static impersonation or bare mimetic display. Aristotle, defining Tragedy as 'an imitation of an action', stipulates that it be 'in language', and 'in the form of action, not of narrative', which implies the progressive interplay of enacted dialogue (*Poetics*, VI). More recently, having collected six brilliant monologues written for television under the title *Talking Heads*, Alan Bennett remarks that although some of them could have been written 'as plays proper', the fact is they were not. Though they are dazzling examples of characters who, in speaking, give themselves away (they are 'telling a story to the meaning of which they are not entirely privy'), they do so, he notes, without other presences, other perspectives, 'room for qualification and extenuation'—without dialogue, in short—leading Bennett to declare, 'In this sense to watch a monologue on the screen is closer to reading a short story than watching a play.'[20] Accordingly, when Edward Albee decided to try his wings as a playwright in *The Zoo Story* (written 1958), a play that is almost an exercise in essential drama, it was as an extended dialogue between two strangers, whose increments, indirections, prolongations, and deferrals lead to the culminating violent act cum revelation ('sometimes a person has to go a very long distance out of his way to come back a short distance correctly').[21] Similarly David Mamet's apprentice plays are nearly all in two-handed dialogues, leading to his tour-de-force four-hander, *Sexual Perversity in Chicago* (1974), which embodies much of its progression in a series of discrete duologues. And when Beckett, pursuing a long-term programme of whittling away the elements of drama to see what he could do without, wrote *Krapp's Last Tape* (1958) as a single-character play, it was nevertheless in the form of an encounter between Krapp and his younger selves, resurrected as voices with the help of a tape recorder.

Dialogue for the most part presumes difference, in perspective, attitude, situation, information, and above all in motivating impulse. Difference makes for friction, resistance, detour. But as in an electrical circuit, it also makes for directional flow. It is in eliciting these differences and negotiating them that dialogue provides the impulse of the action and becomes its vehicle. So much is evident in Aristotle's model play *Oedipus Tyrannus*, where the protagonist's desire, to find out, to solve the riddle, advances through a series of conversations, overcoming resistance (from Tiresias, Jocasta), eliciting information (from the two shepherds), and revising explanation, until the action is complete and there is nowhere left to go. At the same time, by engaging our interest in the play of differences, dialogue keeps us occupied while the outcomes are deferred. Both functions are evident in a dialogue (a scene) from Mamet's vivisection of the trials and triumphs of high-pressure real-estate salesmen, *Glengarry Glen Ross* (1983). As the back-and-forth moves towards impelling a significant action, the resistance seeks to keep the dialogue inconsequential. In the dialogue, the embittered Dave Moss has launched a speculative fantasy of robbing the real-estate office, for which he and Shelley Aaronow work, of its valuable lists of high-quality prospects. As the fantasy begins to sound more concrete, Aaronow is suddenly alarmed. Moss says he has identified a potential buyer for the leads.

AARONOW. You haven't talked to him.
MOSS. No. What do you mean? Have I talked to him about *this*? (*Pause.*)
AARONOW. Yes. I mean are you actually *talking* about this, or are we just . . .
MOSS. No, we're just . . .
AARONOW. We're just "*talking*" about it.
MOSS. We're just *speaking* about it. (*Pause.*) As an *idea*.
AARONOW. As an idea.
MOSS. Yes.
AARONOW. We're not actually *talking* about it.
MOSS. No.
AARONOW. Talking about it as a . . .
MOSS. *No.*
AARONOW. As a *robbery*.
MOSS. As a "robbery"?! No.

Aaronow remaining suspicious, Moss again assures him, 'We're just talking.'

AARONOW. Because you know, it's a *crime*.
MOSS. That's right. It's a crime. It is a crime. It's also very safe.
AARONOW. You're actually *talking* about this?
MOSS. That's right.[22]

Between *talking* (with serious open intent, and with an eye to action) and not talking (keeping one's counsel) there is evidently a whole spectrum of intermediate practices, including 'just talking', where dialogue aims at being inconsequential and leading nowhere, and also talking with a compelling unspoken agenda operating under the words. As the protagonist puts it in Arthur Miller's *After the Fall* (1964), suddenly seeing the light, 'Oh. We're not talking about what we are talking about, are we?'[23]

Much early drama took liberally from other realms of argument and debate—the forum and the law courts, for example. Rapid exchange in argument, as in a verbal fencing match, took on a high degree of formalization in Greek drama—and in its Senecan echo, which in turn so influenced the

Elizabethans—as sustained passages of what is called *stichomythia*. Not that such exchanges were likely to be as conclusive as the staging of actual swordplay; but as the verbal duels created or released tensions, elaborated or resolved differences, an audience might find an analogous pleasure in their forensic virtuosity, whether as wit, argument, or passages of mutual insult and recrimination. Though deployed for many purposes, the numerous variants have enough in common to be called 'the skirmishing style'.

When Hamlet, on his mother's summons, comes to her chamber, they slip into just such a pattern, marked by the enchained statement and retort inherited from classical drama:

HAMLET. Now, mother, what's the matter?
QUEEN GERTRUDE. Hamlet, thou hast thy father much offended.
HAMLET. Mother, you have my father much offended.
QUEEN GERTRUDE. Come, come, you answer with an idle tongue.
HAMLET. Go, go, you question with a wicked tongue. (III. iv. 8–12)

Whereupon, shocked by the accusing word 'wicked'—so at odds with the situation of a son called on the carpet before his mother and queen—Gertrude breaks off the exchange.

Elsewhere, when Hotspur voices his impatience with the mystifications of Owen Glendower, his Welsh partner in rebellion, the blank verse exchange follows such a pattern, though more freely and expansively:

GLENDOWER. I say the earth did shake when I was born.
HOTSPUR. And I say the earth was not of my mind
    If you suppose as fearing you it shook.
GLENDOWER. The heavens were all on fire, the earth did tremble—
HOTSPUR. O, then, the earth shook to see the heavens on fire
    And not in fear of your nativity. (*1 Henry IV*, III. i. 19–24)

After Hotspur further elaborates his naturalistic view and Glendower his supernatural claims, they resume :

GLENDOWER. I can call spirits from the vasty deep.
HOTSPUR. Why so can I, or so can any man;
    But will they come when you do call for them? . . .

Their partner Mortimer pleads for 'no more of this unprofitable chat'. But such 'unprofitable chat' (here a kind of bear baiting) has amused and engaged us, in stroke and counterstroke. And beyond the pleasure of the sport, the exchange serves to suggest the instability, and even unnaturalness, of the combination of forces in rebellion, while it gives further scope to the imprudent Hotspur's quirky appeal, which in turn makes poignant his capsule tragedy.

Very evident in these passages is how word and phrase pick up on word and phrase. In one of the many letters admonishing and instructing his German translator, Shaw wrote, 'Half the art of dialogue consists in the *echoing* of words—the tossing back & forwards of phrases from one actor to another like a cricket ball.'[24] Shaw is speaking to the art and artifice of dialogue in general; but such statement and rejoinder, thrust and counter-thrust, catchword volley and return, have an especially rich descent in exchanges informed, less with anger or idea, than with erotic tension and competitive wit. When Beatrice and Benedick scuffle in Shakespeare's *Much Ado about Nothing*, and so become the archetype of the witty, quarrelsome lovers of romantic comedy, her uncle warns a stranger:

LEONATO. You must not, sir, mistake my niece. There is a kind of merry war betwixt Signior Benedick and her: they never meet but there's a skirmish of wit between them. (I. i. 55–7)

Admittedly, there is less wit than insult in their first exchange, but the skirmish soon gets down to wordplay:

BENEDICK. What, my dear Lady Disdain! Are you yet living?
BEATRICE. Is it possible disdain should die, while she hath such meet food to feed it as Signior Benedick? (I. i. 109–11)

For much of the comic repertory, with only the broadest farce excluded, the action of language is in this line of descent. From the Restoration 'Comedy of Manners' (where it is especially privileged), to Wilde, Maugham, Coward, Albee, Ayckbourn, Stoppard, Simon (to stay with English-language practitioners), and the ubiquity of laugh-track sitcom, the skirmishing style, using irony, insult, witty mistaking, with its signature catch-word repetition and variation, met expectations for comic engagement. As with any language practice, there are large and characteristic differences between adepts. In Wilde's society comedy-dramas, for example, the more self-conscious exchanges are liberally salted with epigrams, many of them memorable enough to become hackneyed, as among these aristocratic men-about-town in *Lady Windermere's Fan* (1892). Fielding a reproach that he has been talking scandal, the youngest and most worldly replies:

CECIL GRAHAM. . . . My dear Arthur, I never talk scandal. *I* only talk gossip.
LORD WINDERMERE. What is the difference between scandal and gossip?
CECIL GRAHAM. Oh! Gossip is charming! History is merely gossip. But scandal is gossip made tedious by morality.

After a great deal of the same, the most romantically inclined declares:

LORD DARLINGTON. What cynics you fellows are!
CECIL GRAHAM. What is a cynic? (*Sitting on the back of the sofa*)
LORD DARLINGTON. A man who knows the price of everything and the value of nothing.

CECIL GRAHAM. And a sentimentalist, my dear Darlington, is a man who sees an absurd value in everything, and doesn't know the market price of any single thing.

LORD DARLINGTON. You always amuse me, Cecil. You talk as if you were a man of experience.

CECIL GRAHAM. I am. (*Moves up to front of fireplace*)

LORD DARLINGTON. You are far too young!

CECIL GRAHAM. That is a great error. Experience is a question of instinct about life. I have got it. Tuppy [*the oldest among them*] hasn't. Experience is the name Tuppy gives to his mistakes.[25]

Among the names that characterize such dramatic discourse is the sometimes dismissive term 'persiflage'. Not long after Wilde's great successes, W. B. Yeats, ruminating on the languages available to drama in the light of the banality of contemporary speech, observed: 'We have, indeed, persiflage, the only speech of educated men that expresses a deliberate enjoyment of words: but persiflage is not a true language. It is impersonal; it is not in the midst but on the edge of life; it covers more character than it discovers: and yet, such as it is, all our comedies are made out of it.'[26]

Noel Coward is a good deal less epigrammatic than Wilde. But his society comedies of sophisticates and squares, where the skirmishing can be both bloodier and more erotically charged than in Wilde, are perhaps the apogee of the drama whose hallmark is the sustained stichomythic exchange, ranging from insult to persiflage. In *Private Lives* (1930), one of Coward's best, Amanda and Elyot, once stormily married, discover that they are honeymooning in adjoining suites of the same Riviera hotel. Having then quarrelled with their new partners respecting a speedy departure, they emerge on their adjoining terraces:

AMANDA. What are we to do?

ELYOT. I don't know.

AMANDA. Whose yacht is that?

ELYOT. The Duke of Westminster's I expect. It always is.

AMANDA. I wish I were on it.

ELYOT. I wish you were too.

AMANDA. There's no need to be nasty.

ELYOT. Yes there is, every need. I've never in my life felt a greater urge to be nasty.

AMANDA. And you've had some urges in your time, haven't you?

ELYOT. If you start bickering with me, Amanda, I swear I'll throw you over the edge.

AMANDA. Try it, that's all, just try it.

ELYOT. You've upset everything, as usual.

AMANDA. I've upset everything! What about you?

ELYOT. Ever since the first moment I was unlucky enough to set eyes on you, my life has been insupportable.

AMANDA. Oh, do shut up, there's no sense in going on like that.

ELYOT. Nothing's any use. There's no escape, ever.
AMANDA. Don't be melodramatic.
ELYOT. Do you want a cocktail? There are two here.
AMANDA. There are two over here as well.
ELYOT. We'll have my two first.

The abrupt shift from the 'melodramatic' (exaggerated despair) to prosaic invitation (no sense in wasting good champagne cocktails) reframes the hostility and the threat of violence, and moves the action forward to the next phase, the dialogue whose result is, predictably, the couple's revived passion and elopement. At the end of the act, as the two newly abandoned spouses, puzzled and disconsolate, meet for the first time on their adjoining terraces, Sibyl accepts one of the remaining pair of cocktails from Victor, and toasts 'absent friends'. Then, as they sit *pensively sipping their cocktails and looking at the view*, Coward slips an echo into the dialogue, to shape a close to this phase of the action, and to carry us forward by raising expectations concerning Sibyl and Victor (expectations that go nowhere):

SIBYL. . . . It's awfully pretty isn't it? The moonlight, and the lights of that yacht reflected in the water—
VICTOR. I wonder who it belongs to.
THE CURTAIN SLOWLY FALLS[27]

'Persiflage' implies both sophistication and a banter or raillery that is effervescent and inconsequential. But clearly 'the skirmishing style' can include much more, and usually does. Though common in natural discourse, and characteristic of the verbal interaction of certain groups—academics and street gangs, for example—it is ubiquitous in the language of drama, and constitutes the medium in which Pinter's characters can jockey for dominance, and Bond's lexically deprived proletarians conduct their Hobbesian warfare, no less than that in which Etherege's courtiers can conduct their affairs and Wilde's *flâneurs* display their plumage.

Out of difference comes motion, but also delay. The result of an all-out skirmish can be impasse, or even failure, where the impulse towards transformation or resolution is unable to overcome the resistance in the participants or the circumstances. For the drama of *not* putting something into words also belongs to the action of dialogue, as in the poignant scene in Chekhov's *The Cherry Orchard* where Lopakhin does *not* speak to Varya (Varvara) at the moment of general diaspora, for all that he apparently intends to. Here the action is in what is *not* happening under what is being said. Mme Ranevsky has forthrightly contrived to bring the moment about. Lopakhin, she points out, seems to be looking for a wife. 'She loves you, you're fond of her, and I haven't the faintest idea why you seem to avoid each other. It makes no sense to me.'

LOPAKHIN. It makes no sense to me either, to be quite honest. It's a curious business, isn't it? If it's not too late I don't mind going ahead even now. Let's get it over and done with. I don't feel I'll ever propose to her without you here.

MME. RANEVSKY. That's a very good idea. Why, it won't take more than a minute. I'll call her at once.

Mme. Ranevsky calls Varya and clears the scene, while Lopakhin waits, uneasily, '*with a glance at his watch*'.

(. . .*After some time* VARYA *comes in.*)

VARYA (*spends a long time examining the luggage*). That's funny, I can't find it anywhere.

LOPAKHIN. What are you looking for?

Varya's search for 'it' among the luggage is her face-saving excuse for being there. Both know the purpose of the meeting, which is for Lopakhin to speak. When he doesn't—Lopakhin's remarks on travel arrangements, and so on, are all to postpone speaking—Varya comes back to the luggage. When he still doesn't speak, but instead reflects on the weather, the embarrassment is terrible—it fills the pauses.

LOPAKHIN. . . . . Three degrees of frost, I should say.

VARYA. I haven't looked. (*Pause.*) Besides, our thermometer's broken. (*Pause.*)

(*A voice at the outer door*: 'Mr. Lopakhin!')

Blessed with an excuse to escape, Lopakhin goes out quickly, while Varya sits on the floor, quietly sobbing. When Mme Ranevsky returns to learn what has happened, there is no need to explain:

MME. RANEVSKY. Well? (*Pause.*) We'd better go.[28]

Lopakhin's not speaking doesn't mean that nothing is said, or that in the dialogue nothing is being done. The words delay, provide cover, distract, and that is work. Even before Lopakhin can escape, Varya's final remark signals the bitter knowledge that the moment is over ('Besides, our thermometer's broken'). But critical throughout the scene is our knowledge of what remains unspoken, the point to which all that is said and all that is done or not done refers.

Speaking and not speaking of a matter of great moment are in fact not that far apart, and drama may lie in one or the other, or even in both at once. Lopakhin, in many ways the most complicated and interesting character in *The Cherry Orchard*, doesn't explain himself or his failure to speak, nor do we assume he could even if he wanted to. He is not less believable for his opacities, as a dramatic character or a human representation. As with Lopakhin, so with the verbal medium wherein Chekhov's characters interact and express themselves: the ambiguities, disjunctions, irrelevancies, tics, upwellings, and latencies complement modern conceptions of self and agency. Indeed, infused with a music of their own, they have furnished the template for a new and distinctive dramatic discourse in the modern theatre.

Nevertheless, no amount of resistance to reductive explanation relieves audiences of the ingrained appetite to discover what motivates a Lopakhin. One earlier episode offering at least a clue to his *not* speaking at the critical moment with Varya comes near the beginning of the play, as he joyfully greets Mme Ranevsky and her entourage on her return from her long stay abroad to the home of her childhood, the estate where Lopakhin's people also lived, in very different circumstances. Lopakhin had come down on purpose in order to meet the party at the station but then had fallen asleep, the first instance in a besetting pattern of failed good intentions. Now, as he tells Mme Ranevsky, he must run away:

LOPAKHIN. I have to leave for Kharkov soon, about half past four. What a nuisance. I'd like to have seen a bit more of you and had a talk. You're just as wonderful as ever . . . This brother of yours calls me a lout of a peasant out for what I can get, but that doesn't bother me a bit. Let him talk. You just believe in me as you used to, that's all I ask, and look at me in the old way, with those wonderful, irresistible eyes. Merciful heavens! My father was a serf, belonged to your father and your grandfather before him. But you—you've done so much for me in the past that I've forgotten all that and love you as a brother. Or even more.

MME. RANEVSKY. I can't sit still, I really can't. (*Jumps up and walks about in great excitement.*) I'll die of happiness. Laugh at me if you want, I'm silly. My own dear little book-case. (*Kisses the book-case.*) My own little table—(Act I, pp. 248–9)

Lopakhin here has crossed a line, whose eroded authority but continuing legacy he feels and resents as much as anyone. But if he is momentarily carried away, Mme Ranevsky instantly starts from the intensity and the impropriety of his near declaration. She cannot acknowledge the embarrassing excess, but instead, in her own excess of joy, lavishes her affection on the furniture. It sobers Lopakhin, and brings him back to business. In the later scene, with all this history of class and geography of feeling, and with Ranevskaya herself just beyond the door, how can he manage to settle for Varya? He fails in his good intentions as he fails in his desire to save the estate for Mme Ranevsky and her brother. Instead—the two of them proving impervious to his urgings and incapable of acting to any purpose under modern conditions—he saves it for himself, at the price of the one thing that once so distinguished the estate, the cherry orchard. He fails to save the estate as he failed to meet the train and as he fails to speak to Varya, where his not speaking despite his good intentions becomes less of a puzzle in the light of his earlier giving himself away in his enthusiasm, and Mme Ranevsky's swift non-response, cutting him off before the thing said could no longer be ignored or denied.

Revealing. The dialogue that impels by raising difficulties, articulating dissonances, framing questions, is also that which reveals and even, sometimes, resolves. The moment of revelation is often the moment of highest drama, as Sophocles knew so well when he has Oedipus and the Herdsman—from whom Oedipus is forcing the last piece of information that will establish his true identity—pause at the edge for an added emphasis, an emphasis that speaks to the condition of the audience no less than that of the characters:

HERDSMAN. O God, I am on the brink of frightful speech.
OEDIPUS. And I of frightful hearing. But I must hear.[29]

Sometimes the revelation is more abruptly declarative. 'Stop, Gerald, stop!' says Mrs Arbuthnot at the climax of the third act (of four) of Wilde's *A Woman of No Importance* (1893); 'He is your own father!' Though part of what was billed as 'a New and Original Play of Modern Life', the line, in its naked melodrama, lets itself in for burlesque.[30] The revelation is direct, between mother and son. But as a revelation of fact and relationship, it is no surprise to an already informed audience, whose interest will be in the charged situation, now changed at a stroke. Gerald has recently been offered a position by Lord Illingworth, who fathered and abandoned him and his mother years earlier. Gerald's mother, whom he loves dearly, is deeply opposed to this dazzling good fortune, though he cannot understand why. With the revelation, everything is made clear, and all is changed. But even here, it is not what the words say that impels their saying, but rather what they do. Mrs Arbuthnot has no wish to tell Gerald who his father is, or to inform him of his illegitimacy. She speaks the words to prevent him from killing Illingworth, who in his vanity and cynicism has just molested the young American Gerald loves; and indeed, the announcement works—it stops Gerald in his tracks. The immediate dramatic meaning, once more, is in what the words do in their immediate circumstances. What they say then translates into what they do in relation to all that follows.

On the one hand there is what words do in plays, and on the other there is how they do it. Much that is said is said by indirection, and much that is revealed in speech is unintentional. The antonymic pairs, 'direct and indirect', 'intended and unintended', are not equivalent. Innuendo, for example, is indirect and intended, whether practised by tea-taking Wildeans or by the supposedly plain-spoken Iago.[31] Irony, on the other hand, may be intended or unintended: unintended when Oedipus unwittingly speaks the truth about himself (the famous 'Sophoclean irony'); intended when Martha comments on George's response to her gross insult in Edward Albee's *Who's Afraid of Virginia Woolf?* (1962):

MARTHA. Uh . . . you make me puke!
GEORGE (*Thinks about it . . . then . . .*) That wasn't a very nice thing to say, Martha.

MARTHA. That wasn't *what*?

GEORGE. . . . a very nice thing to say.

MARTHA. I like your anger. I think that's what I like about you most . . . your anger.[32]

George's understatement is no less ironic than Martha's sarcasm, their contrasting rhetorical styles being very much in keeping with their distinctive characters, yoked in a marriage of contraries.

Irony entails the unstated, or even misstated, but understood. Irony also permits differential understanding, between speaker and hearer, and between speaker, hearer, and over-hearer, namely the audience. In fact, irony implies a kind of subtext, something unspoken or something indirectly spoken which the text superficially denies. The function of *revealing* through what is spoken here includes its opposite, the still unspoken—what the unconditioned words do not or will not or cannot say. It is another form of resistance in the discourse, complicating what the actors are asked to do with the words, a negative element whose limiting extreme is silence.

Silence is the complement of the action of words, and often—especially in the modern theatre where, in the final revelations, answers are *not* forthcoming—its product. In *The Birthday Party*, the action of words, as Goldberg and McCann employ them on Stanley, third-degree fashion, is not to elicit information, but to confuse and unbalance their target, and to subdue him. The measure of its efficacy is the production of silence (or its equivalent, in a strangulated, incoherent sound). And if Stanley is thus reduced to silence in *The Birthday Party*, so is Lucky in the second act of *Waiting for Godot*. (His speaking in the first act, where his principal action was 'to think', took the form of a torrent of language, a tirade, whose effect was to irritate his auditors past bearing.) The action of language in Ionesco's *The Lesson* is precisely to reduce the Professor's hopeful student to a speechless groaning misery; and the climax of the preparations in Ionesco's *The Chairs* is the appearance of the Orator who is deaf and dumb. This is not the silence that ensues when the most word-conscious of Shakespeare's tragic heroes, in a play that often questions their efficacy, finally ceases in mid-sentence with much (he believes) unsaid, and 'the rest is silence'. And it is a world away from Racine's monumental *Phèdre*, whose incremental patterned action is first, the breaking of silence (Phaedra's to her nurse and confidante Oenone, Phaedra's to Hippolytus, Hippolytus' to Aricia, Phaedra's to Theseus), and then the keeping of silence (by Hippolytus, Phaedra, Aricia), with consequences that become manifest in the catastrophe and the final revelations.

The action of naming—that is, putting something into words—can have force over and above the immediate shock or revelatory value of what is spoken. In the first act of Racine's *Phèdre*, for example, naming marks the beginning of the end, the release of the juggernaut that rolls forward, through speaking and not speaking, to the catastrophe. After pressing Phaedra hard to break her 'silence so inhuman' on the cause of the grief that is killing her, Oenone guesses at the identity of the forbidden love for whom her mistress is pining, taking her cue from Phaedra's circumlocutions:

PHAEDRA.   Now hear the crowning horror.
  I love . . . I shake, I tremble at the fatal name,
  I love . . .
OENONE.   Whom?
PHAEDRA.   You know this Amazon's son,
  This prince whom I myself for so long have oppressed?
OENONE. Hippolytus? Great Gods!
PHAEDRA.   It's you who said his name. (I. iii)

C'est toi qui l'a nommé. Naming Hippoytus, Phaedra's stepson, has let the incestuous passion that horrifies her loose from its subterranean labyrinth (like Phaedra's own emergence into daylight to start the scene); to take body in the outer world, like the monster that later comes out of the sea to destroy Hippolytus as he attempts to flee. Less disastrously, in Turgenev's *A Month in the Country*, when Natalia puts a name to what is making everyone behave so peculiarly towards her son's young and oblivious tutor, it has a similar precipitating effect. It opens Beliayev's eyes to himself and his feelings, and breaks up the community of this country-estate summertime world. The word once spoken, the disturbance named, the revelation made, is not something one can take back. The world is changed, and for good.

7.2. *LAPSUS LINGUAE*

Often characters who may not entirely understand themselves understand each other very well, in the things that are being said or not said and in the gestural aspect of the dialogue. But the action of words does not depend on their efficiency as carriers of meaning. What are strictly speaking their inefficiencies play a part in the making of drama as well. In the language fitted for the stage, beyond the transparent duplicities of indirection, innuendo, irony, flirtings with the improper or the impolitic (or what is meant by the risqué), is the speech that misleads, deliberately or otherwise. A good barefaced lie will do much to precipitate an action, as in many a melodrama and comedy of imposture. But a lie becomes more interesting when it is insinuated, as in *Othello*, or when it involves words and actions that are misconstrued, and when its consumers participate in its creation and elaboration—like the 'audience' in Cervantes's *Retablo* interlude, or Othello as he interprets Iago's conversation with Cassio from afar, or misinterprets Desdemona's pleadings for Cassio's pardon. From misconstruing the ambiguities of an oracular prophecy to mistaking the recipient of a love letter, a staple of the confusion that powers the plot in a vast body of drama is misunderstanding the words—through egotism, innocence, dullness, ingenuity, malicious misleading (Macbeth and the witches) and credulous self-delusion (Malvolio and his letter).

At its simplest, it is a matter of mishearing or misspeaking. As such, it produces the fateful error whereby Ruth, the former nursery maid in W. S. Gilbert's *The Pirates of Penzance*, bound the infant Frederic to the wrong nautical profession. Instructed to apprentice him to a pilot, but being unfortunately a trifle hard of hearing,

> I took and bound this promising boy apprentice to a *pirate.*

Quite apart from the hazards of deafness, language gives enormous scope to error when not checked by context or redundancy. Later in *The Pirates of Penzance*, Gilbert improves on Ruth's narrative of misunderstanding, though to less disastrous effect. General Stanley, to save his many nubile wards from enforced marriage to the Pirates, appeals to the villains' softer sides by (falsely) declaring himself an orphan. The Pirates have heard such protestations before, but are incapable of resisting them.

PIRATES (*disgusted*). Oh, dash it all!

[PIRATE] KING. Here we go again!

GENERAL. I ask you, have you ever known what it is to be an orphan?

KING. Often!

GENERAL. Yes, orphan. Have you ever known what it is to be one?

KING. I say, often.

ALL (*disgusted*). Often, often, often! (*Turning away.*)

GENERAL. I don't think we quite understand one another. I ask you, have you ever known what it is to be an orphan, and you say "orphan." As I understand you, you are merely repeating the word "orphan" to show that you understand me.

KING. I didn't repeat the word often.

GENERAL. Pardon me, you did indeed.

KING. I only repeated it once.

GENERAL. True, but you repeated it.

KING. But not often.

GENERAL. Stop: I think I see where we are getting confused. When you said "orphan," did you mean "orphan"—a person who has lost his parents, or "often"—frequently?

KING. Ah! I beg pardon—I see what you mean—frequently.

GENERAL. Ah! You said often—frequently.

KING. No, only once.[33]

Though we are not at the end of the pitfalls Gilbert's characters find in a turn of phrase, such mistakings delay rather than derail, and sometimes even facilitate an appropriate comic outcome. But when not in comedy, the consequences can be grave. A reflection of the protagonist in Heinrich von Kleist's disturbing Romantic tragedy, *Penthesilea* (1808), condenses under the aegis of a slip of the tongue a whole vast universe of misunderstanding, between peoples and cultures as between individuals trapped in their subjective realities.

In *Penthesilea*, Kleist dramatizes the intrusion of an Amazon army from distant Scythia into the neat binary logic of the war between Greeks and Trojans.[34] In this pioneering dramatic challenge to Enlightenment rationality and universalism (Man in the essentials everywhere the same), the Amazons, driven by their singular cultural and religious imperatives, have ritually swarmed from the hive to seize in battle the brave male warriors who will then father the next generation of warrior women. In the thinking of the Amazons, this act of war is the necessary preliminary to the act of love. Encountering these fierce strangers on the field and drawn to the challenge of the Amazon queen, the mighty Achilles finds himself out of his depth. Nor, after a series of battlefield encounters charged with eroticism, can Penthesilea—improperly fixated upon Achilles—understand his incomprehension and enthusiastic brutality. When he does finally catch on, it is too late; through pain and frustration she has gone mad. Consequently, as he confidently strips off his armour and throws away his weapons to meet Penthesilea in love, she looses her dogs upon him and then joins them in the carnage.

Later, having returned to herself, and becoming aware of what she has done, she puts it into words:

> Surely I kissed him? Or did I tear him? Speak!
>
> .   .   .   .
>
> So—it was a mistake. Kissing—biting—
> Where is the difference? When we truly love
> It's easy to do one when we mean the other.

The difference in sound—between *Küsse* and *Bisse*— is even less in German, an easy slip of the tongue:

> (*disengages herself and falls on her knees before the body*)
> Poor man, of all men poorest, you forgive me?
> It was a slip—believe me!—the wrong word—
> I can't control my too impetuous lips.
> But now I tell you clearly what I meant:
> This, my belovèd, this—and nothing more.
>   *She kisses him.*[35]

That Kleist articulates such slippage, not only between word and word, but between word and deed, in a play still written in the high poetic form associated with complete and commensurate expression for the passions and sentiments, is no mere anomaly. For in Kleist's hands the verbal and dramatic textures are marked throughout by the vivid ephemera of thought, speech, and behaviour, by the accidental and the non-essential, including repetition, loss of attention, disjointed syntax, incomprehension, and outright failure of expression—as when Achilles attempts to explain matters to his fellow Greeks. Trying to find the words that can communicate his belated understanding of the Other, he has to give it up, while Diomede, sputtering, is stopped cold in his incredulity:

ACHILLES . . . So then I sent her—
DIOMEDE.   Madman!
ACHILLES.   He'll not listen!
   What he has never seen, in all the world,
   In all his life, with those blue eyes of his,
    That he'll not grasp—he cannot—even in thought.
DIOMEDE. Then you—? You mean?—You will—?
ACHILLES (after a pause).   What will I do?
   What is this monstrous thing that I will do? (Scene 21)

Having challenged Penthesilea to meet him once more in mortal combat, but this time, he believes, only as a matter of form, Achilles is confident in his new knowledge. Oblivious to the import of the Amazon's name and its history[36]—despite having heard it from Penthesilea's own lips—he pronounces one of the most blinkered instances in the literature of the stage of that kind of differential understanding between the character speaking and the audience overhearing qualifying as 'dramatic irony':

        She will not harm me, I tell you! Sooner far
        Would her mailed arm mangle her own fair bosom
        And cry: "Triumph!" when her heart's blood spurts forth,
        Than it would rage against me!

What his new knowledge has failed to include is the final mystery and final solitude, in Kleist's dramatic world, of another's mind and heart.

The inadvertent substitution of one word—a near homonym—for another usually makes for laughs on the stage. It is the familiar device, often with delicious off-colour resonances (and often with an appeal to class snobbery) that takes its name from Richard Brinsley Sheridan's Mrs Malaprop ('. . . an aspersion upon my parts of speech! . . . Sure, if I reprehend any thing in this world it is the use of my oracular tongue, and a nice derangement of epitaphs!').[37] The device of sustained misapprehension, like that over orphan/often, has a still more ancient pedigree, and it frequently falls into the rapid exchanges of stichomythia. In the form called *quiproquo* [*sic*], or this-for-that, where each interlocutor mistakes what the other is talking about, it is a device that has a particular appeal for Tom Stoppard among contemporaries, a playwright whose dramatic worlds are full of moments that can be understood or explained in more ways than one. *Jumpers* (1972), whose population includes language philosophers, is almost a tissue of such sustained misunderstandings—as when the moral philosopher George Moore, upset because his rabbit has gone missing, talks to Crouch the porter, who has witnessed a murder the night before and thinks that George's wife is involved.

GEORGE. You knew about it?
CROUCH. I was there, sir. Doing the drinks. It shocked me, I can tell you.
GEORGE. Who killed him?
CROUCH. Well, I wouldn't like to say for certain . . . I mean, I heard a bang, and when
   I looked, there he was crawling on the floor . . .
   (GEORGE *winces*.)
   . . . and there was Miss Moore . . . well—
GEORGE. Do you realize she's in there now, *eating* him?
CROUCH (*pause*). You mean—*raw*?
GEORGE (*crossly*). No, of course not!—*cooked*—with gravy and mashed potatoes.
CROUCH (*pause*). I thought she was on the mend, sir.

—and their sympathetic exchange goes on until it finally trips over an unambiguous phrase and comes crashing to the ground.[38]

Dialogues with Inspector Bones, with George's wife Dorothy, with Sir Archibald Jumper, logician, physician, and politician, similarly take place in two or more registers at once; and the same is true for much else in Stoppard's dramaturgy, not only for what we hear but often for what we see. Stoppard makes comedy out of cognitive uncertainty and unstable point of view, as in an Escher grid or the famous duck-rabbit drawing of the psychologists. And he uses it to engage wider matters, even in *Jumpers*, where it carries into issues of moral relativism and political expediency, and where a character—Dorothy—can be shattered by the reversal of perspective entailed in seeing the earth from the moon. That champion of a discourse based in realism in the theatre, William Archer, writing for would-be playwrights early in the last century, is full of scorn for comedies that keep destined lovers apart through 'some trumpery misunderstanding', which, 'in the most aggravated cases', is a mere matter of words. 'This ancient trick becomes the more irritating the longer the *quiproquo* is dragged out.'[39] It has been one of Stoppard's many distinctions that, in resurrecting a comedy of language, such sustained bouts of mutual misconstruction, while funnier than ever, serve to sharpen the challenges of an ontologically and epistemologically unstable world.

Meanwhile, if speakers in a dialogue, however articulate and intelligent, can produce such triumphs of sustained confusion, it can happen that in the *absence* of lexical content the interlocutors construe each other's meaning perfectly, and their wordless dialogue prove efficacious as action. Chekhov again provides a most telling example, in *Three Sisters* (1901). Colonel Vershinin, stationed in the remote provincial town that is the provisional home of the Prozerovs, is a talker; and Masha, married to a dull and pedantic schoolmaster, is first drawn to him by his 'philosophizing', flights into a future that will compensate for one's sufferings in the benighted present and validate keeping the flame of culture and civility alive. Vershinin has earlier declared his feelings for Masha; but it is in the third act, with part of the town on fire and in the exhilaration of crisis, that they arrive at a mutuality of confessed and accepted love, at perfect understanding. Vershinin has once more launched into a vision of the fineness of life in the future, and has ended in a brief burst of song from Tchaikovsky's *Eugene Onegin*:

> ... (*Sings.*) 'To Love all ages are in thrall, its transports bless us one and all' ... (*Laughs.*)
> MASHA. Tram-tam-tam ...
> VERSHININ. Tam-tam ...
> MASHA. Tra-ra-ra?
> VERSHININ. Tra-ta-ta. (*Laughs.*)

Here they are interrupted by others coming from the fire. But before leading these away, Vershinin resumes the syllabic dialogue:

> VERSHININ. Tram-tam-tam?
> MASHA. Tram-tam.
> VERSHININ (*laughing, to Solyony*). Let's go into the salon.

In the first exchange, the sender specifies and the receiver acknowledges the code; then Masha asks her question, and Vershinin answers, happily. When they resume, it is Vershinin who asks the question, and Masha who answers affirmatively. The exchange is complete, and so is understanding.[40] As confirmation (for the audience), Masha then declares, for the first time, to her sisters, in an uncontainable overflow of emotion, her impassioned, encompassing, and reciprocated love. As a final confirmation (for themselves), Vershinin, now presumably having left the house, is heard from offstage: 'Tram-tam-tam!'—a strong affirmative, as is the reply:

> MASHA (*rising, in a loud voice*). Tra-ta-ta!

And then she leaves, having just said she would join him.

The form of the love duet, the dialogue of two separate voices that join together, is also its action. A more complicated and circuitous example, where the action of the dialogue eclipses entirely whatever the words happen to mean, occurs in Brian Friel's *Translations,* some time after its complex linguistic landscape is established so disconcertingly in the opening scene. Such duets, culminating in a union of hearts and voices, are rife in drama. Often there is a resistance to be overcome, usually lying in the reluctance of one or both partners, or in awareness of transgression, or of imminent danger. Mozart and Da Ponte's duet for Don Giovanni and Zerlina, 'Là ci darem la mano' (Let's join hands), gives the essential template for such a dialogue as a successful seduction, with its alternating expressions of male desire and female ambivalence giving way to voices harmoniously united. Musical expression is especially apt for such a task, at least according to Shaw, because the words themselves in their lexical character are of so little account. The 'unfortunate Shakespear', he argues, obliged to 'make his words musically arranged mean something to the intellect as well as to the feeling,' could not make Juliet say:

> O Romeo, Romeo, Romeo, Romeo, Romeo;

and so on for twenty lines. He had to make her, in an extremity of unnaturalness, begin to argue the case in a sort of amatory legal fashion . . . Now these difficulties do not exist for the tone poet. He can make Isolde say nothing but 'Tristan, Tristan, Tristan, Tristan, Tristan,' and Tristan nothing but 'Isolde, Isolde, Isolde, Isolde, Isolde,' to their hearts' content without creating the smallest demand for more definite explanations . . . Nay, you may not only reduce the words to pure ejaculation, you may substitute mere roulade vocalization, or even balderdash, for them, provided the music sustains the feeling which is the real subject of the drama . . . [41]

As it happens, the encounter, convergence, and submergence of the voices of Tristan and Isolde in Wagner's orchestral night has less to do with seduction than with consummation. The same is true of the mischievous duet between Kilroy and the Gypsy's daughter (her virginity renewed at every full moon) in Tennessee Williams's *Camino Real* (1952):

> (*He delicately lifts a corner of her veil. She utters a soft cry. He lifts it further. She cries out again. A bit further . . . He turns the spangled veil all the way up from her face.*)
> KILROY. I am sincere.
> ESMERALDA. I am sincere.
> KILROY. I am sincere.
> ESMERALDA. I am sincere.
> KILROY. I am sincere.
> ESMERALDA. I am sincere.
> KILROY. I am sincere.
> ESMERALDA. I am sincere.
> (*Kilroy leans back, removing his hand from her veil. She opens her eyes.*)
> Is that all?
> KILROY. I am tired.[42]

The resistance in *Tristan and Isolde* is of a higher order, having to do with the persistence of unassimilated ego and the threat of daylight and reason in the build to ecstatic transcendence. The resistance in the love duet in *Translations* is no less formidable, for it is rooted in language itself.

In the stage world that *Translations* defines in its opening scene, Gaelic and English are rendered as English. In the second act, second scene, Lieutenant Yolland of the Royal Engineers, attached to a cartographic survey, and Maire, a restless local beauty, escape from a dance in the schoolhouse. Neither speaks the other's language. They run on stage hand in hand, laughing and in apparent conversation:

MAIRE. O my God, that leap across the ditch nearly killed me.
YOLLAND. I could scarcely keep up with you.
MAIRE. Wait till I get my breath back.
YOLLAND. We must have looked as if we were being chased.

And then suddenly they become self-conscious, of themselves and of their situation. '*Their hands disengage. They begin to drift apart.*' There is a pause and a growing disconnection:

MAIRE. The grass must be wet. My feet are soaking.
YOLLAND. Your feet must be wet. The grass is soaking.

Words and meaning are nearly the same; Maire and Yolland are still on the same wavelength. But their speeches are inversely parallel, not responsive. It is no longer a dialogue. After another pause and a further drifting apart, they must start from the very beginning:

YOLLAND. (*Indicating himself*) George.
  (MAIRE *nods:* Yes-yes. *Then*)
MAIRE. Lieutenant George.
YOLLAND. Don't call me that. I never think of myself as Lieutenant.
MAIRE. What-what?
YOLLAND. Sorry-sorry? (*He points to himself again.*) George.
  (MAIRE *nods:* Yes-yes. *Then points to herself.*)
MAIRE. Maire.

They try to extend the reach of their words, through raised voice and staccato emphasis (Yolland), schoolbook Latin (Maire), the names of the four elements in English (Maire), and finally in an English sentence that Maire delivers from memory, '*as if English were her language—easily, fluidly, conversationally*':

MAIRE. Shhh . . . George, in Norfolk we besport ourselves around the maypoll.
YOLLAND. Good God, do you? That's where my mother comes from—Norfolk. Norwich actually.

He runs on, realizes, stops, and stares; and Maire wonders if she hasn't said something dirty.

At this point Maire, feeling the hopelessness, turns and moves slowly away. Yolland, desperate, begins reciting some of the Gaelic place names his revisionary cartographic work has taught him. Maire stops and begins to respond antiphonally, reversing movement. The meaning is now not at all in the geography, but in the music, and the linkage of the speeches, name calling forth name:

MAIRE. Carraig an Phoill.
YOLLAND. Carraig na Ri. Loch na nEan.
MAIRE. Loch an Iubhair . . .

As they progress to general topographic features—'Mullach', 'Port', 'Tor', 'Lag'—'(*She holds out her hands to* YOLLAND. *He takes them. Each now speaks almost to himself/herself.*).' Their intercut monologues then slide into a dialogue whose convergence and iterations are the expression of a union of mind and heart:

YOLLAND. [if you could understand me] I would tell you . . .
MAIRE. Don't stop—I know what you're saying.
YOLLAND. I would tell you how I want to be here—to live here—always—with you—always, always.
MAIRE. 'Always'? What is that word—'always'?
YOLLAND. Yes-yes; always.
MAIRE. You're trembling.
YOLLAND. Yes, I'm trembling because of you.
MAIRE. I'm trembling too. (*She holds his face in her hand.*)
YOLLAND. I've made up my mind . . .
MAIRE. Shhhh.
YOLLAND. I'm not going to leave here . . .
MAIRE. Shhh—listen to me. I want you, too, soldier.
YOLLAND. Don't stop—I know what you're saying.
MAIRE. I want to live with you—anywhere—anywhere at all—always—always.
YOLLAND. 'Always'? What is that word—'always'?
MAIRE. Take me away with you, George.
(*Pause.*
Suddenly they kiss.)

The opacities of language, extreme in division and difference in this place and time, have lost their power to impede, have become transparent to feeling, and the dialogue turns into a progressive speech-act whereby two are made one.

Shaw, who persistently claimed musical models for his work, nevertheless insisted on the primacy of language, with its capacity for argument, as what differentiates the play from other performative and expressive arts—a distinction given force by the birth and efflorescence of the silent film. But though he early aligned himself with a theatre of contemporary relevance like that of Ibsen, and even defended his own methods as those of a 'Dramatic Realist', he never lost sight of the art or artifice that differentiates the language of the stage from that of ordinary life. That difference is as marked in the mimetic vernaculars of Pinter, Albee, Bond, as in the colloquies of Wilde, Stoppard, and Shaw himself. 'My method of getting a play across the footlights is like a revolver shooting: every line has a bullet in it and comes with an explosion,' he wrote to his German translator, whose tendency was to substitute squibs.[43] The spoken words have work to do: 'On the stage every speech must provoke its answer and make the audience curious to hear it,' he wrote in his ninety-second year. 'Every word that digresses and breaks the chain of thought, however splendid, must be ruthlessly cut.'[44] Consequently, when he explained that 'Half the art of dialogue consists in the *echoing* of words,' he had in mind much more than 'the tossing back & forwards of phrases' in repartee. Unhappy with his translator's habit of missing echo and interplay, Shaw admonished him, 'I remember every word [my characters] say, and keep alluding to these sayings pages after you have forgotten them. My stage effects are based on that.' Failure to catch the echo in a barbed retort by the witty General Burgoyne, for example, in Shaw's melodrama of the American Revolution, *The Devil's Disciple* (1897), deprived it of all its value 'as shewing the man's character', and of its force as an exit speech which 'brings down the house in England.' All that remained was a speech 'with no point, no sense, no fun in it'.[45]

But such a craftsman's awareness of functional artifice, and how the demands of the medium differentiate speech in the theatre from speech in the street, left something out, harder to identify, and Shaw knew it. He had been present at the memorable debacle of Henry James's play, *Guy Domville* in 1895, and even wrote a shrewdly defensive review. A quarter of a century later, amplifying an article in the *Times Literary Supplement* on 'The Printed Play', Shaw ventured an explanation for the progressive failure of James's theatrical ambitions in the course of acknowledging the double claim on a playwright who also publishes.[46] 'In preparing a play for publication the author's business is to make it intelligible to the reader. In preparing it for performance he has to make it intelligible to a spectator and listener. The last quality is the one in which a writer who has always worked for publication alone is likely to fail in direct proportion to his inveterate practice and his virtuosity.' James's failure, he writes, was a matter of 'audible intelligibility'. There is 'a literary language which is perfectly intelligible to the eye, yet utterly unintelligible to the ear even when it is easily speakable by the mouth. Of that English James was master in the library and slave on the stage.' Shaw continues:

I cannot give any rule for securing audible intelligibility. It is not missed through long words or literary mannerisms or artificiality of style, nor secured by simplicity. Most of the dialogues that have proved effective on the English stage have been written either in the style of Shakespeare, which is often Euphuistic in its artificiality, or in that of Dr. Johnson, which is, as Goldsmith said, a style natural only to a whale . . . Speech does not differ from literature in its materials. 'This my hand will rather the multitudinous seas incarnadine' is such a polysyllabic monstrosity as was never spoken anywhere but on the stage; but it is magnificently effective and perfectly intelligible in the theatre. James could have paraphrased it charmingly in words of one syllable and left the audience drearily wondering what on earth Macbeth was saying.

James and other temporarily stage-struck novelists might have succeeded, Shaw suggests, 'if only they had understood that as the pen and the *viva vox* are different instruments, their parts must be scored accordingly'. Capturing the *viva vox* is the trick. It happens when actor and playwright have the gift—as Anna Deavere Smith puts it—'to inhabit the speech pattern of another, and walk in the speech of another,' so that not just the actor, but audience *and* reader can 'find the individuality of the other and experience that individuality viscerally'.

8

———

Reading Meanings

In the second act of Chekhov's *Three Sisters*, Vershinin has just let fly one of his characteristic meliorist riffs on happiness deferred for the sake of the life to come, and his fellow officer, Tusenbach, counters with the view that life will always be the same. Look at the cranes, he says; they fly, and will continue to fly, whatever ideas, great or small, wander into their heads, and no matter what philosophers happen to turn up among them. 'They may philosophize as much as they like, so long as they keep flying.'

MASHA. Isn't there some meaning?
TUSENBACH. Meaning . . . Look out there, it's snowing. What's the meaning of that?

Many feel that way about plays, including a number of playwrights. Brendan Behan, according to his brother, was accosted after the first night of *The Hostage* by someone asking, 'What was the message of your play, Mr. Behan?' 'Message? Message?' said Brendan, 'what the hell do you think I am, a bloody postman?'[1] More rhapsodically, Tennessee Williams, seeking to put into words the soul of his art, wrote:

The color, the grace and levitation, the structural pattern in motion, the quick interplay of live beings, suspended like fitful lightning in a cloud, these things are the play, not words on paper, nor thoughts and ideas of an author, those shabby things snatched off basement counters at Gimbels.[2]

Like snow, like the mindless and beautiful flight of the crane, a play *is*. To ask what a play *means* is to reduce it.

As for audiences, with some justification they tend to be suspicious of plays that patently have an axe to grind, or let the author's thoughts and ideas get in the way of 'the structural pattern in motion, the quick interplay of live beings'. Shaw gives a voice to the feeling in his play *Misalliance* (1910), where the self-satisfied, regular sort of a chap Johnny Tarleton proclaims:

If I buy a book or go to the theatre, I want to forget the shop and forget myself from the moment I go in to the moment I come out. Thats what I pay my money for. And if I find that the author's simply getting at me the whole time, I consider that he's obtained my money under false pretences. I'm not a morbid crank: I'm a natural man; and, as such, I don't like being got at.[3]

And yet, Johnny Tarleton is just the sort of person to be upset if he found that he hadn't a clue to what *the play* that he was seeing or reading was getting at. For being 'got at' surely includes unsettling departures from the usual ways a play makes its points and conveys its meanings, and would certainly include challenges to the things one takes for granted in the theatre, in life, in society, so that they seem to make no sense. In such case, an exasperated Johnny Tarleton would be apt to ask, 'What does it all mean?' and not getting an answer, perhaps, like the future Edward VII at an early performance of Shaw's *Arms and the Man,* declare the author mad. 'Meaning' for such playgoers means being able to accommodate new matter in familiar frames of reference, being able to interpret what is happening and what is said within and with the help of those frames of reference. There is a problem, then, when the play sets out to challenge or change the frames of reference.

Bert Lahr acted Estragon in the first New York production of *Waiting for Godot*, a play that has now exercised several generations of interpreters seeking to articulate its meaning, including countless students meeting it as a set text. Lahr famously declared he didn't understand a word of it, yet his performance was brilliant, for it was precisely the words that he did understand—in their action, as part of a situation or an exchange evoking routines familiar from vaudeville and farce or absurdist revues; and as expression, of frustration, appetite, bewilderment, resentment. Lahr understood what the words *did*, and therefore what they meant on the level of interaction. But what the play as a whole was supposed to mean—what it wished to say about life and the world, or when and where it was happening, or how the characters got to be who they were, why they were waiting and for whom, and why it was that 'Godot' never came—that was something else.[4]

A play then evidently 'means' in many ways—and through various means. And meaning of the kind a puzzled playgoer seeks when asking, after a *Godot*-like experience, 'But what does it all mean?' is often not to be had, at least not in the form of a summary statement or a 'moral', such as 'You can't fight City Hall' (i.e. 'Fate,' 'the Gods,' etc.); 'What goes around, comes around'; 'Murder will out'; 'No man is an island'; 'Life is a dream'. Meaning instead may be manifold, rich and complex and paradoxical, or elusive and ambiguous, as in life. But then, a play is not life; and consequently, even when we recognize the lineaments of experience in the text and in 'the quick interplay of live beings', and taste the primal pleasures of mimesis, mirroring is not enough. The cranes in flight, when framed in the perspective of the theatre, or even within the camera's field of view, become something else. Shaw, as usual, put the case in its strong form:

Holding a Mirror up to nature is not a correct definition of a playwright's art. A mirror reflects what is before it. Hold it up to any street at noonday and it shews a crowd of people and vehicles and tells you nothing about them. A photograph of them has no meaning. They may be in love with one another, they may intend to murder one another. They may be husbands and wives, parents and children, or doctors and patients, in the most comic or tragic relations to one another; but the mirror or photograph tells you nothing of all this, and cannot give the playwright any material whatever. Shakespeare's mirror [in Hamlet's advice to the players] was for the actor, to teach not to saw the air and look like nothing on earth. The playwright has more to do than to watch and wave: the policeman does that much; but the playwright must interpret the passing show by parables.[5]

Making and experiencing a play entails at a minimum selection and arrangement, and, nearly always, shaping and interpretation; or rather, shaping towards interpretation. How that is done is our subject—not *what* plays mean, but *how* they mean. How they mean varies according to scale; and it varies by vehicle, from direct statement, debate, illustrative action, to metaphor, parable, and other forms of indirection. In terms of scale, at one end there is the constituent word, or image, or action with a resonance, a resonance that can come from allusion outside the script, or accrue through recurrence and variation in the script. At the other end is the shape of the whole as the embodiment of a comprehensive idea. As for the varieties of vehicle, these may be divided into what I will term *rhetorical* means and *poetic* means, the one heavily (though not exclusively) discursive, explanatory and argumentative, the other variously parabolic. Often they work together.

8.1. THEMATICS

A number of the plays I will talk about have suffered or earned classification as 'plays of ideas', but by no means all of them. The tag is a loose one, often attaching to plays chiefly because they seem to argue with the received wisdom, as well as to plays that actually attempt to set out or embody a philosophic thought. I will begin with a play that has escaped such labelling, but nevertheless is much concerned with ideas, with eliciting and examining a set of related concepts intended to engage an audience's interest, and whose meaning as an action would be much impoverished without that vital aspect. The play is Lope de Vega's *Fuente Ovejuna*, or *The Sheep Well* (before 1618), its title the name of the village that is the true protagonist of the play, but also evocative of a ballad familiar at the time, commemorating a historical occurrence, and of a vernacular saying meaning nobody in particular can be held accountable. 'Fuente Ovejuna did it.'

   Lope's play presents the revolt of the inhabitants of the village of Fuente Ovejuna against their abusive feudal overlord, the Commander of the military order of the Knights of Calatrava, and his subsequent slaughter. The action is collective, and the villagers, having withstood torture designed to elicit the names of the leaders and perpetrators, are ultimately pardoned by their most Catholic Majesties, Ferdinand and Isabella, and the village taken under direct royal government. The play opens with the Commander and two of his followers in the house of the youthful Master of the Order, waiting impatiently for him to appear. The Commander fumes, with touchy pride:

COMENDADOR. Does he know it is I
     Fernàn Gómez de Guzmàn?
FLORES. Don't be astonished. He's only a boy.
COMENDADOR. If my name means nothing to him
     Is he not aware that I am the Order's senior Commander?
ORTUÑO. The fault lies with his councilors
     Who have no use for being courteous.

On this cue, the focus of the conversation becomes courtesy, as a social practice and a bond.

COMENDADOR. That will win him little love.
     Courtesy is the key to good will,
     While the surest way to enmity
     Is a stupid discourtesy.
ORTUÑO. If the discourteous person knew
     How all must detest him—
     Even those who seek to kiss his feet—
     Rather than be the least bit discourteous
     He'd sooner die.
FLORES. How bitter it is to suffer such an insult!
     Discourtesy between equals is a folly,
     And towards inferiors sheer tyranny;
     But all that hardly counts here—
     He is only a boy, as yet ignorant
     Of what it means to be loved.[6]

After this discriminating analysis, the Commander speaks the judgemental clinching word: that the obligations of the sword of knighthood and the cross of the Order should have been enough to teach the young man courtesy.

The action of this scene is simply waiting. Our expectations are primed for the appearance of the young Master, and our attention directed to how, as head of the Order, he will behave to his subordinate. He appears, and behaves with impeccable courtesy: warm, apologetic, respectful of age and experience, grateful for past services. The Commander meanwhile is unmannerly and overbearing, full of himself and his due even as he was in his impatient attendance. The dialogue on courtesy, then, has done more than fill the time. Besides generating expectations and effecting an ironic relation between speech and behaviour on the part of the Commander, it opens the way to what may be called the thematic structure of the play, the conceptual armature that also offers an interpretive framework for channelling the action and making it meaningful.

Flores has been especially cogent in defining courtesy as behaviour within a hierarchical social order, where there are obligations downward as well as between equals. When the Commander finally gets around to his business with the Master of the Order, newly released from tutelage, it is to urge him to take arms against Ferdinand and Isabella, in support of Portuguese claims to Castile. A dubious role for a crusading order, it is also the ultimate in discourteous behaviour, as an act of rebellion against a superior, fostering chaos through the whole civil order. It brings into play two complementary issues: the force that binds societies and individuals together, already touched on twice in the conversation on courtesy, namely love; and the value that speaks to the integrity of the individual, both in oneself and within these reciprocal social relations, namely honour.

These are the three terms whose articulation develops the thematic structure that gives meaning, beyond the bare human drama, to the action of *Fuente Ovejuna*. Each is developed in what is in effect a formal discussion or debate: first that on courtesy, as we have seen; then on the nature of love; then on the question of honour. A debate on love among peasants, where the literary models are aristocratic and pastoral, makes for some exploitable incongruity; but the arguments are cogent. And when it comes to honour, the peasant voice comes through as profoundly serious and dignified. On the matter of honour, argument is joined on an issue of exceptional interest in Lope's world: Can there be such a thing as peasant honour? The stakes are made vivid in the dramatic context of the Commander's cool public demand of the Mayor of Fuente Ovejuna that he make his daughter available. In welcoming the Commander and his henchmen to the village square just before this outrage, Esteban, the Mayor, has stated the proposition that his social superiors then so blatantly disregard: that only those who have honour themselves are capable of rendering honour where it is due; and conversely, that to dishonour others is to dishonour oneself. True honour, then, is not a thing apart from true courtesy, the proper behaviour of rank to rank. They are interdependent.

The debate on love is less fraught and more formal. Mengo, who belongs to the ubiquitous line of comic figures, usually venal, called the *gracioso*, propounds the notion that there is no such thing as love, but only self-love and its gratifications. As the argument develops, love evolves into a universal principal of harmony or concord (*concierto*); while self-love (also *amor natural*) similarly takes on grander colours. Mengo puts the question to Laurencia, the object of the Commander's lust, and to this point in the play virginally independent: 'And do you love?'

LAURENCIA. My personal honour [*Mi proprio honor*].

Love and honour are here brought into conjunction, like love and courtesy earlier, and honor and courtesy in the action to come.

In the action, Frondoso, Laurencia's peasant suitor, challenges the Commander at arrow point, at the risk of his own life, to save her from the rape of body and honour. We see another of the peasant women assaulted and dragged off for a gang rape, and her defender (Mengo) brutally beaten for his pains. We see the village betrothal of Laurencia and Frondoso, all warmth and harmony, and its violent disruption, the groom arrested, the Mayor flogged, his daughter seized and carried off. In the revolt, all normal hierarchical relations—not only of social degree, but of gender—are turned upside down, so that Laurencia, bruised, torn, and dishevelled, transformed into a virago, resolves the irresolute male Council, while the village women, united in arms, take a fierce part in the massacre. In the revolt, all 'courtesy' in and between ranks has been dissolved in disorder; but out of it comes an unprecedented form of concord, in the indiscriminate unity of voice and action. As Frondoso reminded the Commander when the latter freed him for use as an emissary, 'it is love that has moved them'—love, and violated courtesy, and outraged honour. In the serial torture (the successive voices of the peasants on the rack are heard from offstage), the solidarity of the village turns out to be both a manifestation of concord (love) and an act of self-preservation, self-love which in its most creditable form issues in honour. As the examining judge reports, three hundred of the villagers put to the severest torture, not excluding children of 10, valorously replied as one to the question, 'Who did it?', 'Fuenteovejuna'.

To recapitulate: Courtesy, the appropriate behaviour in and between ranks, is abused, quenching Love and violating Honour. The consequence is the collapse of order. But out of this chaos emerges a new concord and a new order, partly a restoration (the Order returned to its original mission and purpose) and partly a transformation, with a new and direct connection between the monarchy and the *pueblo* (the village, the people). The end of the play—an epiphany of sorts—reconciles the King and the Queen with the defeated and repentant Master, and brings the villagers into the royal presence where they speak their piece and are pardoned, the village now coming literally under the royal aegis. In as much as there is a new relation forged in the political realm, with a consolidating monarchy displacing feudal structures, the play becomes a drama of instauration—like Aeschylus' *Oresteia*, for example, and Corneille's *Le Cid*. This adds to the local events of *Fuente Ovejuna* another layer of meaning, another degree of parabolic force, as registering a critical moment of change, inaugurating the order that is.

However subtly invoked and extensively elaborated, the elements in Lope's thematic structure are adduced directly. In creating a framework for interpretation, these are 'rhetorical' means rather than 'poetic', the latter where the work of channelling meaning is done by analogy and inference as opposed to argument. If the first tends to the discursive and dialectical, the second is metaphoric and parabolic. 'Midway between the unintelligible and the commonplace,' as Aristotle explained, 'it is metaphor which most produces knowledge'.[7] Practically, it can provide familiarity and concreteness for something awkward, abstract, or esoteric; or conversely it can serve to jolt something out of its stale familiarity. Whether by saying or doing, but in any case by way of analogy, it can evoke recognition, insight, resonance, and a form for grasping the immediate moment and the unfolding design. It *points* a meaning, but by inference and indirection. For example, when Christy Mahon looks into the mirror, and finds there a prepossessing reflection never seen before 'in the old cracked mirror we had beyond', the action and his comment speak, not to the difference in the quality of the glass, but to how one's view of oneself can vary according to how one is regarded by others. Not all mirrors are made of glass. Christy doesn't understand this yet, nor is he conscious of the mirror's metaphoric bearings. But the episode, both dramatically concrete and cognitively indirect, offers an insight, points to a meaning, in what has been happening to Christy as, for the first time in his life, he experiences praise and admiration.

Christy's encounter with the mirror is brief; and the metaphoric point having been made, the play has no further use for mirrors. It can also happen that a play in its entirety takes on the character of a metaphor, as the embodiment in concrete but parabolic form of a thought, an argument, a comprehensive view. The whole play then—premisses, action, dramatic unfolding—becomes the vehicle for an implicit tenor or purport. Jean-Paul Sartre's *No Exit* is such a play, and I will return to it.

But first, to set against Lope's use of a thematic structure to organize meaning in *Fuente Ovejuna*, we might look at another play from the same author where it is predominantly recurrent metaphor that signposts the action and informs understanding. In Lope's Italianate tragedy, *El Castigo sin Venganza* (*Not Vengeance, but Punishment*, 1631), the play opens with the Duke of Ferrara on one of his night-time forays. A notorious rake who has avoided marriage, but now has a noble bride on the way, he is especially anxious not to be recognized. One of his pimping servants, Riccardo, sees a chance to wax eloquent:

> Under the cover of a disguise
> All things are licensed.
> Even the sky can assume a disguise,
> What else is the veil [*el velo*]
> In which night wraps it?
> A bejeweled cape
> That is the heavens' disguise.[8]

He elaborates on the cloak-embellishing moon and stars, and the Duke asks him if he is losing his mind. By way of explanation, the talk turns to poetry and the strained use of metaphor by the modern school, one of whom named the moon 'the cottage cheese of the sky'. Lope is cultivating his audience's amusement at such extravagance, but at the same time, in calling attention to metaphor, he is telling us something about his play and its own metaphoric art.

Acting under a cloak, wrapping truth in a veil, are metaphoric renderings of the principal action of the play, most notably the catastrophe. On the way to that catastrophe, the metaphor is reinforced and enriched by calling attention to speech that uses indirection both to conceal and reveal, and to actions like that of the Duke's son Federico when he attempts to conceal transgressive love by paying court elsewhere. But the opening of the play marshals another metaphor as part of its lattice of indirect signification. The disguised Duke on the prowl in the night-time streets encounters two women. One declines to admit him at such an hour, even when told that it is the Duke 'come in disguise to make you a fine lady'. A witty woman, she manages not only to excuse herself, but to launch a veiled and scorching reproach. She denies that the Duke, though notorious for living in libertine vice, would so unworthily disgrace himself, being now reformed and on the eve of marriage. She defends the Duke, and berates his servants for slander. The second woman is simply a voice emanating from a house where actors are rehearsing a play. The Duke overhears the famous Italian actress 'Andrelina' (the real Isabel Andreini) speaking lines on the torment of memory, which turns him melancholy and sends him home afraid of what else he might hear. It is at this point that the Duke invokes a familiar metaphor that also will accrete and insinuate meaning as it resurfaces in the play:

Don't you know, Riccardo,
That a play is a mirror
Wherein the foolish, the wise, the old,
The young, the rough, the gallant, the king, the governor,
The maiden, the housewife
May learn by example
Concerning life and honor?

This is a mirror of a different cast than either Shaw's mirror as photograph or that mirror, socially and subjectively conditioned, in Synge's *Playboy*. As reflecting truths that *los señores* would often prefer not to hear, it stands in opposition to the metaphor of action under a cloak or veil—though it is worth remembering that seeing by reflection is also a form of indirection.

El Castigo sin Venganza, while based on real events, also recapitulates the classical triangle of Theseus, Phaedra, and Hippolytus.[9] Pressed to marry and beget a legitimate heir, the Duke sends Federico, his much-loved by-blow, to fetch his noble bride from Mantua. Meeting the young and beautiful Casandra on the road amid romantic perils, Federico and his future stepmother find much to admire in each other. The marriage takes place; but then, despite his reformist resolutions, the Duke reverts to his rakish tastes and neglects the proud and passionate Casandra. Consequently, when he is called to command in the Papal wars, leaving Federico in charge, his wife and son become lovers.

On the Duke's triumphant return, his new dignities once more prompting personal reform, he is alerted by an anonymous letter to the crime against his honour. Bent on vindication, but fearful of exposing the disgrace to public knowledge, and claiming to act, not for revenge, but as the instrument of God's castigation of the sin, he contrives the deaths of Casandra and Federico under a veil:

> The infamous Casandra I left
> Bound hand and foot
> Covered with a silken cloth [*un tafetán*]

—gagged and unconscious as well. When Federico appears, the Duke tells him it is an enemy who has conspired against his life who is thus bound in a chair, identity concealed for the sake of public order, and commands Federico to be his executioner. Federico obeys, with misgivings. While he is about his task offstage, the Duke summons his guards and courtiers and declares Federico has killed Casandra to prevent his displacement by a legitimate heir. Entering then with bloody sword, Federico, appalled and bewildered, begins to speak: 'Going to uncover the face of the traitor you told me of, I found . . .'. But his father cuts him off and commands his slaughter:

FEDERICO. Oh father! Why are they killing me?
DUKE. In the tribunal of God, traitor,
    You will be told the cause.

Though the Duke's vengeance is covert, the success of his camouflage is by no means secure. Several witnesses know more than they should, from Federico's *gracioso* servant Batín to the anonymous letter writer. And Aurora, Federico's earlier love whom he subsequently tried to use as a cloak, knows the truth of the dishonouring adultery. Led one day to the vicinity of Casandra's boudoir, she looked into a crystal mirror and discovered Federico 'measuring the roses of Casandra with his lips'. Horrified, she fled, but not before following—at love's behest, and before the mirror itself seemed to cloud over—every offensive detail of the reflected scene. The worthy Marquès who is her current suitor then moralizes:

> The glass in which you saw her
> Will be the mirror of Medusa
> To this new Circe.

Like the obscuring veil, the mirror metaphor has resurfaced more than once since the first scene, and other telling chains of metaphor run through the play and its poetry. Batín's Act I parable of a lion subduing the wildness of a horse, for example—as marriage to Casandra was supposed to do for the Duke—sets in train a recurring motif in which the beautiful, untamed horse and the powerful and deadly lion seem to exchange referents. But the play's overarching, shaping, and informing metaphors juxtapose action under a veil and the mirror as a reflection and a revelation of truth. The final word, echoing the Duke's earlier homily on the play as a mirror in which all 'may learn by example | Concerning life and honor,' belongs to Batín, speaking directly to the audience:

> And here
> Good senate, ends this tragedy
> Of punishment without vengeance,
> Once a prodigy in Italy,
> Now an example for Spain.

But the lesson in the mirror for Spain is not altogether direct; and there is a final face of truth that strives, as the play ends, to emerge from under its veil. Just before Batín's innocuous *plaudite*, the Duke asks to see his dead son with the dead Casandra. Here again a curtain is drawn to reveal that still-life tableau. The Duke then speaks confusedly of punishment and justice, and then, 'Courage fading, and overwhelmed by tears,' expresses his grief. The Duke loved his son, the fruit of his dissipations, above all things. The retribution he has wrought at the behest of his wounded honor, a vengeance cloaked and dissembled as God's justice, has fallen most terribly on himself.

8.2. PARABLE AND 'CONCEIT'

Metaphoric refractions can illuminate an action and direct our understanding as well as our feeling. But it is also the case that the play as a whole can function as a metaphor where the abstract and the abstruse are made concrete. I mean something more here, or something different, than that the plight of Hamlet, or the sufferings of Lear, or the star-crossed paths of Romeo and Juliet may be felt as emblematic of the human condition. I have in mind plays where the dramatic representation integrally embodies ideas or arguments one might expect to be developed discursively. Such plays do more than illustrate, and they do more than offer an example of what, in chorus or commentary, can be generalized. It is harder to separate what they are from what they mean; they *are* what they mean, embodied argument and illustration at once. Sartre's *No Exit* (1944) is such a play; but so is the anonymous *Everyman* (fifteenth century), Havel's satirical *The Memorandum* (1965), Pirandello's *Six Characters in Search of an Author* (1921). If we think of these plays as 'plays of ideas', they are parabolic rather than discursive (the two primary ways of dramatizing thought) and so at the core more akin to poetry than to rhetoric. That is not to say that they exclude 'the action of words'—the drama in argument and the play of language—or forgo rhetorical objectives: to win over an audience and move or persuade it to adopt the speaker's take on things.

There is a distinction to be made between ideas in the drama and a dramatic idea. Having two strangers who are about to murder or mate with each other discover that they are brother and sister is a dramatic idea. Seating a policeman on the watch and the fugitive patriot he seeks on either side of a barrel, and letting their talk stray to the accidents of life that put them on opposite sides is also a dramatic idea, but with a difference. In its inventive situational premiss and its visual condensation, Lady Gregory's *The Rising of the Moon* (1907) also has that quality of expanded metaphor found in each of the 'plays of ideas' I mention above. In all of these, the play arises out of what one author calls 'a conceit', which can be construed as the concrete embodiment of a thought that gives it dramatic presence, akin to what T. S. Eliot so usefully named an 'objective correlative' for the feeling that drives a poem or a play.[10] Among the virtues of Sartre's *No Exit* (*Huis clos*), a play of great formal strength and concentration with a dramatic logic of classical stringency, is that the conceit succeeds on both counts. That is, it serves not only as parabolic analogue for the thought—an argument about personal freedom and responsibility—but also as direct evocation of how it feels to be unfree, or damned in *this* life.

The conceit places three persons, initially strangers, with only each other for company, within the confines of a room in hell. They are of course dead. The room, furnished in the heavily ornate style of a Second Empire hotel, significantly lacks only one thing, aside from windows: a mirror. As the first to enter discovers, there are no Dantesque torments in prospect; but also, there is no sleep, no darkness, no relief from oneself—just 'life without a break'. The three are a man and two women: Garcin, a pacifist journalist executed for fleeing in wartime, preoccupied with his motives; Inez, a lesbian with a taste for giving pain; Estelle, a pretty, self-centred vamp in need of male attentions. Inez is the first to grasp and state the premiss of their situation: do-it-yourself economy of labour, as in a restaurant cooperative :

Wait! You'll see how simple it is. Childishly simple. Obviously there aren't any physical torments . . . And yet we're in hell. And no one else need come. No one. We'll stay in this room together, the three of us, for ever. . . . I mean that each of us will act as torturer of the two others.[11]

There is a resistance, or counter-action, an attempt to defeat the situation, first by withdrawing into silence and isolation, then by 'helping' each other find distraction or reassurance. But their failure is inherent in the fit, or misfit, of their interlocking egos, an impasse of unsatisfied need and fruitless dependency whose revelation is complete when the door springs open and none is willing to leave.

The action of the play is threefold: a retrospective uncovering of the truth under the bland initial cover stories (a progressive mining and stripping, as in Ibsen); a repeat, in present company, of the defining actions in each character's previous existence (Garcin has been a woman-abusing simulacrum of manliness; Inez, a sharp-tongued, self-hating, sadistic spoiler of other people's happiness; Estelle, a self-serving compunctionless murderer; and all now show themselves the same); and finally—while the memory of their lives fades from the earth and they are left with only themselves—the systematic elimination of all notional avenues of evasion and escape from the hell they now constitute for each other.

The conceit that governs the play and embodies its fundamental thought gives scope to an elaboration of the issues of freedom and dependency. Garcin argues that each person has a motivating desire—his was manliness. It was not just a dream of heroism; 'I chose it. One is whatever one wants to be.' Inez replies that it is only 'what one *does* and nothing else' that counts, that ultimately decides what it was that one really wanted. Garcin claims that he died prematurely, before he had a chance to do his proper deeds. Inez counters that one always dies too soon or too late. 'And nevertheless, that was your life; finished. The line is drawn; now add up the sum. You are your life and nothing else.' Both have a point, Garcin in rejecting a blind determinism that would foreclose agency and pre-empt choice, Inez in insisting on the identity of character and deed—the life you live when given your chances. Life means the books are still open. Hell is when the account is closed and the freedom to choose what you are is all used up.

There is another dimension to hell in Sartre's embracing metaphor, one that has registered on audiences most memorably (and perhaps reductively), because spoken as an aphorism, and because it seems so perfectly embodied in the conceit of the room and its inhabitants. It bears on the matter of authenticity in and for oneself, as well as on the nature of freedom and dependency. The line is spoken by Garcin, and here one should understand that there is no real difference for him between his previous condition and his posthumous one. Like Estelle, he depends for validation on the mirror of other eyes. That inner vacancy, that compromised authenticity, already put him among the damned. He sums up the situation in a life so lived: 'No need for gridirons. Hell—it's other people.'

A parabolic conceit, like that in *No Exit*, is manifestly invention, as distinct from mimesis or the illusion of a direct mirroring of ordinary life. It both clarifies and concretizes, and as such works particularly well where the ideas themselves, in their untowardness or complexity, gravitate towards paradox and a density of implication that are among the hallmarks of poetry. Not that plays structured on such a dramatic conceit have no use for rhetorical strategies. Indeed, the conceit itself may take the form of such a strategy. Jean Giraudoux's *Siegfried* (1928) for example, a key to much of his work, explores national character, national feeling, 'national destinies', and engages the ideology of nationalism in the catastrophic twentieth century through the rhetorical device of postulating a hypothetical extreme, embodying in its premiss the hypothetical limiting case.

The conceit of the play draws on a powerful focus of patriotic sentiment in the aftermath of the First World War, the symbol of the Unknown Soldier, but here found alive on the battlefield, blasted out of anything that can identify him—uniform, papers, memory, language. As the play opens, he is now (1921) Chancellor Siegfried, steering a troubled Germany into acceptance of a new model constitution; but he may also be the French poet Paul Forestier, engaged before the Great War in bringing romantic (Teutonic) mystery and emotion back to life in the French language and tradition. Utterly stripped of identity, he holds in himself complementary national identities that—as in Plato's Aristophanic parable—strive towards wholeness.

Pirandello's *Six Characters in Search of an Author*, with a title that encapsulates its startling conceit, incorporates an unusual form of *reductio ad absurdum* to make its final point. The play ultimately self-destructs. The conceit, its fictive premiss, has 'Characters', who are the creations of art, and ordinary mortals, who work in the theatre, present and interacting in the same physical space. Abandoned by their author, the Characters invade a theatre seeking to have their drama realized. Meanwhile, topics having to do with fixation and mutability in art and life, how these are antithetical but also convergent, and how they affect each other's claims on reality, enter the discourse. In the end, however, when one of the Characters is found drowned in the fake stage fountain, and another shoots himself, apparently for real, Pirandello's fictive premiss collapses:

LEAD ACTRESS (. . . *grief-stricken*). He's dead! Poor boy! He's dead! Oh what an awful thing!

LEAD ACTOR (. . . *laughing*). What do you mean, dead! It's fiction! pretense! Don't believe it!

OTHER ACTORS FROM THE RIGHT. Fiction? Reality! reality! He's dead!

OTHER ACTORS FROM THE LEFT. No! Fiction! fiction!

THE FATHER (*crying out over all*). What do you mean, fiction! Reality, reality, gentlemen! Reality!

—and despairing, he disappears behind the scenes, as have the other Characters, leaving the Manager at the end of his tether, crying, 'Fiction! reality! The hell with it all! Light! Light! Light!'[12] Not only has the premiss of the play—played out as far as it will go—collapsed in contradiction, but so have (parabolically) the certainties that separate the mind-created worlds of imagination and the tangible, everyday world of experience.

Taking up the conceit of an earlier play, to discredit or reverse it and sometimes to burlesque it, is often the mark of a vigorous theatre with an engaged audience. When the intention is critical, taking up the conceit becomes instrumental in a rhetoric of rebuttal, undermining the outlook and assumptions of the prior play, but occasionally enriching how both plays mean. Brecht is a case in point when he does it to himself. The work in question was the wonderful little chamber opera for which Kurt Weill supplied the music, known in its first form as *Der Jasager*, or *He Who Says Yes* (1929–30). Based on a Japanese original, the drama concerns a young boy who joins a knowledge-seeking expedition (*Forschungsreise*) over the perilous mountains in order to fetch medicine for his ailing mother.[13] When his strength fails and he is unable to continue, rather than ask the expedition to turn back, the boy assents to being hurled to his death according to an ancient 'Great

Custom' (*ein große Gebrauch*). The emotional climax of the piece, poignant and moving, is the boy's wistful and prolonged '*Ja*'.

Written for performance by and for students, and promoting the idea of selfless solidarity with the collective good, the piece stimulated objections from the young audience at the Karl Marx School near Berlin. (It also elicited praise from conservative, nationalist reviewers.) And so Brecht promptly wrote a counter-play called *Der Neinsager,* or *He Who Says No* (1930), in which the boy refuses to go quietly. When reminded of his pre-contract, to agree to whatever might befall him, he declines to be held to his word: 'He who says A, does not have to say B. He can also realize that A was false.' He asks instead that the expedition turn back, and inaugurate 'a great new custom . . . the custom to reflect on each new situation'. It would be a custom that challenges the blind authority of custom.

Brecht, understanding the advantages of dialectical argument where meaning, or the conclusion to be drawn, becomes the dramatic issue, had it in mind that the plays be performed in tandem on all future occasions. But he also seems to have revised the original *Jasager* for such occasions, to strengthen its now severely undermined case. In the current authoritative version of *Der Jasager*, the situation that pits the individual and a private (if domestic) good against the collective and the general good loses its almost abstract simplicity.[14] The expedition now is for medicine for the whole city, not for spiritual or scientific enlightenment, whose urgency is less compelling. The critical difficulty of the encumbered expedition's passage along a narrow ledge is stressed and staged, as a failed attempt to bring the sick boy along. The Great Custom, with its ritual demand of the subject's assent, is modified, in that the sick person is now to be left behind, and it is the boy who asks that he be killed quickly rather than be left to suffer and die alone. The students are compelled to this harsh duty by recognizing the reasonableness of the request, and it is *their* 'yes' that now becomes significant, their assent to a collective responsibility, overcoming a pained natural reluctance. In helping the boy to his death—carried out with tender solicitude—they exercise their compassion even as they accept the necessity inherent in the objective situation. Their actions are no longer governed by custom and tradition, but by reason—reason resistant to sentiment, but not divorced from humanity. As a progression, then, of statement, counter-statement, and statement reframed, the three plays constitute a dialectical series addressing an issue that was to trouble much of the European left between the wars. And for those purposes, Brecht commandeers an exotic dramatic conceit and, ignoring any indigenous implications and turning it to his own purposes, first advances, then reverses, then revises a meaning.

Like Brecht in the next century, Ibsen was more than capable of arguing
with his own inventions, though other dramatists were to show themselves
willing to save him the trouble. Ibsen in fact seems to have found inspiration
in counterstatement, in a generative call and response between his plays, even
before his momentous shift from versified poetic drama to 'the very much
more difficult art of writing the straightforward, plain language spoken in
real life', in plays reflecting on aspects of the contemporary scene.[15] Ibsen's
Brand (1865), published as 'a dramatic poem' for readers, but subsequently
performed despite its daunting length, projects a heroic figure of rigid
idealism, of uncompromising will and priestly vocation, whose harsh demands
on himself and others are the drivers of tragic consequence. *Peer Gynt*
(1867), its match in scale and its complement in poetry, is a panoramic
extravaganza with a protean antihero, forever elusive and forever transforming,
whose volatility and comic verve are the fully realized opposite of Brand's
monumental seriousness. *Peer Gynt*, Ibsen himself declared, 'is the antithesis
of *Brand*'.[16]

A *Doll's House* also called up an answer, from Ibsen to start, though the
dialogic response to its basic conceit, of the nice little domestic plaything (as
Nora appears to be) who, awakened to her situation and herself, slams the
doll's-house door on the way out, has had a remarkable extended history.
Ibsen categorically declared, 'After Nora, Mrs. Alving had to come.'[17] Having
begun work on another play, *An Enemy of the People*, he set it aside because
Ghosts (1881) had 'forced itself upon me now with such urgency that I could
not let it alone'.[18] When Nora slams the door, it is the answer to Torvald
Helmer's spark of hope that she might one day return to the domestic enclave.
With Mrs Alving, Ibsen makes the thought experiment, 'Well, what if Nora
had come back?' Mrs Alving is a Nora who (persuaded by the alarmed Pastor
Manders) does come back, who accepts and performs her communally defined
'duty' as a wife and mother, and we see the consequences.

Captain Alving is of course no *homo domesticus* like Torvald Helmer; and
neither is the Captain who is the title figure in Strindberg's *The Father* (1887).
Strindberg's play offers a tendentious 'counter-truth'[19] to Ibsen's *Ghosts*, with
aspects of *A Doll's House* and *The Wild Duck* thrown in. He makes the challenge
explicit by putting it in the mouth of the Doctor, caught in the middle of the
deadly contest between the Captain and his wife, Laura. The Doctor assures
the Captain that he is there to hear both sides.

CAPTAIN. I thought you were quite satisfied with one side.
DOCTOR. You're wrong. And I should like you to know, Captain, that when I heard
    that Mrs. Alving blackening her late husband's memory, I thought what a damned
    shame it was that the fellow should be dead.[20]

As in *Ghosts*, but rather more directly, Strindberg's husband and wife are in a power struggle for the soul of a child. As in *The Wild Duck*, but rather more brutally, the household founders on the pre-DNA issue of paternal uncertainty. As in *A Doll's House*, power in the household entails infantilizing a spouse. But where it is Nora in *A Doll's House*, before she wakes to her situation, who is infantilized, it is the Captain in *The Father*, after he is strait-jacketed like a swaddled child, and reduced to taking comfort on the lap and at the breast of his old nurse.

Shaw's *Candida* also enters into the conversation, again by turning the tables. In the Morell household, as we have seen, it is Candida's cosseted preacher husband who is finally reduced to the child sitting at his wife's feet and learning his lesson, while it is Candida's poet lover who breaks the confines of the domestic enclave and, in a punctuating moment, goes out the door and into the night. And in a further extension of the dialogue, Ruth in *The Homecoming* comes home, reversing Nora's trajectory, and displacing male authority in a new/old domestic configuration wherein, enthroned, she rules the roost. And so the dialogue, launched in modern drama by *A Doll's House,* on the nature of power and autonomy in domestic relations, goes on.[21]

8.3. MAKING A CASE

Rhetoric—the art of expressive discourse—and the art of acting were hardly distinguished for long stretches, as generations of handbooks and treatises attest; and rhetoric's forms and (even more to the point) its objectives left their mark on that which needs to be acted, the players' scripts. The object of rhetoric is to persuade, and incidentally to win over its auditors to the speaker no less than to his views. The long set speech and the passages of forensic argument and debate so characteristic of the dramatic heritage are not intrusions into the medium of drama, but integral to the art. And in such classics as Goethe's *Egmont* (1788) and Shaw's *Saint Joan* (1923), scenes of debate serve as high points of dramatic interest *because* they are about meaning. In the fourth act of Goethe's historical tragedy, set in the Spanish Netherlands of the sixteenth century, the indigenous Count Egmont walks into a trap, set for him by the Duke of Alba who is bringing coercive rule to these restless provinces. But before the trap is sprung, Alba, probing for disloyalty to Spain, engages Egmont in an extended debate on the nature of freedom and government, posing autocratic and absolute rule by an external power that knows best against a self-governing and indigenous polity and society that respects individuality. Goethe rigs the debate, of course, to favour the latter, as much through the management of sympathy for and against the interlocutors as through the intrinsic merit of the arguments, and the issue speaks, not just to the sixteenth century, but to a contemporary audience between the American and the French revolutions. Neither debater refutes the other, but the course of their argument develops and sharpens the differences in their assumptions and ideas. The last word, however, is with Egmont. Under sentence of death and awaiting execution, he wins for the future, first as represented by the heart and mind of Alba's own son, then in a dream vision where Freedom—a radiant goddess with the face of his beloved mistress—crowns him with laurel and gestures an ultimate victory. Finally, with only the dread Spanish infantry filling the background, he accepts his martyrdom and speaks defiance, rallying his forces and in effect exhorting the audience of another day to follow his example and his devotion to that yet unrealized embodied ideal, *Freiheit!*

As a history play purporting to dramatize the forces as well as the personalities of a distant time, *Egmont* not only articulates the issues but takes sides. It finds and offers a meaning in these past events, a meaning for the present; and in so far as it is a political meaning, it is rhetorical in the larger sense. It seeks to persuade. If the history of literary censorship shows a settled conviction on the part of established authority that the theatre is a dangerous place, it is in recognition of the drama's capacities as rhetoric, not to mention its need to evoke immediate response from an audience. Art, for prudential reasons and on aesthetic grounds, has periodically disclaimed such kinetic effect, and assigned works that could conceivably move audiences to action to the Gehenna of Bad Art. Yet a play that can alter perceptions, feelings, even convictions, is hardly the worse for having that power. In the end, though it is useful to distinguish rhetorical from poetic strategies for generating meaning, the one is not to be confused with propaganda any more than the other is to be reduced to mere aestheticism.

Like *Egmont*, Shaw's *Saint Joan* is a history play where the interest goes beyond costume and character. Given Joan's rude shock to the system of fourteenth-century life, her course is appropriately marked by bouts of argument and persuasion, culminating in the forensics of the trial scene (heavily indebted to the historical record). It is however an earlier, unhistorical scene, a scene that seems all talk and all argument, that addresses the meaning of the string of more or less historical episodes that trace Joan's meteoric course. Supposed to occur before her high-water mark in bringing off the coronation of a French king at Rheims (and before her fatal capture), it is the only scene without Joan. But for Sybil Thorndike, the first Saint Joan, that 'three-handed scene between Cauchon, Warwick and de Stogumber [was]the pith and essence of what the play means'.[22]

The scene is a prolonged discussion in which three different voices argue their distinctive points of view, and converge on the necessity of destroying Joan. The Bishop (Cauchon) interprets her as a threat to the universality and authority of the Church in claiming for her conscience and her inspiration a direct relation to God. The Earl names this religious heresy 'Protestantism'. The Earl (Warwick) sees her as a threat to the whole feudal order, in replacing the subject's allegiance to his lord with direct allegiance to the King, the steward of a realm of speakers of a common tongue located in a continuous geography. The Bishop names this secular heresy 'Nationalism'. The third voice, that of the English Chaplain and chauvinist de Stogumber, reads Joan simply as a monstrous rebel against Nature (her womanhood), Authority, and God-given English hegemony. His voice in particular articulates the likely reception of the heretic visionary (often sanctified after the fact) in the process that initiates historical change.

Though the action of the debate as drama is in the articulation of difference, and then the finding of common ground for a final unified resolve, its real achievement is to read a larger historical meaning into the events of the play, intending to offer the audience something more, or at least something other, than a romantic pageant of action and suffering, heroic attainment and heroic martyrdom. In the discursive interplay of these institutionally representative and two-thirds warrantably historical figures, and in the anachronistic boldness of their articulated viewpoints, Joan's drama is given weight, or 'meaning', as signifying the emergence of new forces in the sweep of history, and as touching on the nature of historical agency and the historical process itself.

Meaning, as Brendan Behan asserted, is not to be confused with message. But meaning in some form is hard to avoid, and when rhetorically developed it tends to emerge in dialogue and debate (which suits the primacy of dialogue in drama), in conflict and contrast between typified characters, in paradigmatic arrays of character and incident, in illustrative exemplification, and in the structures that typically shape argument—demonstration and refutation, progression through contradiction to some higher or deeper resolution, or to terminal impasse, and to the collapse of some initial premiss. But one, rather more basic, aspect of rhetorical practice in the specification of meaning deserves notice. In those handbooks on speechmaking and the art of persuasion, nothing is more important than the art required in selection and deployment (or in handbook terms, invention and arrangement); and selection precedes deployment. At the most elementary level, what a play means depends on what is put in and what is left out.

Selection and deployment go into the making of any work of art, even those aspiring to unqualified randomness. But their part in specifying meaning is especially to the fore where there is an established factual base with a claim for inclusion or acknowledgement. As usual, there are wide differences. In a play like *Saint Joan*, where history has already been mythologized, the playwright has to come to terms with an obligatory set of enshrined 'memorable' events, and the choice is between a panoramic chronicle that deploys them sequentially (Shaw's Shakespearian choice in *Saint Joan*), and a focused drama that endows one notable episode with emblematic or comprehensive significance (Caesar's Egyptian interlude in Shaw's *Caesar and Cleopatra*). In contrast, a play like Rolf Hochhuth's *The Deputy* (1963), an investigative 'docudrama' concerning the role of Pope Pius XII during the Holocaust, has a much freer hand in selection and deployment, through which it makes its case. A work that provoked a considerable international scandal in its time, and inspired a genre and a method of which it is the most notable example, it also exemplifies the problems, or paradoxes, of a drama whose documentary approach implies a detached historical objectivity, but whose ultimate character is forensic, making the case for the prosecution. And to that end it is artfully inventive, mingling fictive means with non-fictive representation, including montage, condensation, composite and symbolic character, recurrent pattern, telling juxtapositions, invented scene and action, and expressionistic effects. It thus seeks to elicit a meaning from and in the historical events, a meaning moral and political and ultimately metaphysical. And it seeks to bring its audience, through emotion and insight, not simply into a condition of understanding and acceptance, but to conviction and judgement. A play like *The Deputy*, however, raises questions that reach beyond 'How does a play mean' (and how does *this* play mean). It does so because, at the deepest level, finding a meaning is what this play is about. It is about finding a meaning, not just in the Holocaust as an isolated historical event, but in a world, a universe, in which such events can take place.

Deputation—standing in for another by designation—takes more than one form in this play, whose title insists on the function. The ultimate challenge, dramatized and debated and thrust at the audience, is not to the Deputy as such—in title the Vicar of Christ—but to his Principal. How could God allow it? To find an answer would be to escape the gaping alternative of nihilism, of meaninglessness, argued by the darkest voice in the play (a demonic figure extrapolated from the notorious Dr Mengele). Raising the *question* of meaning, the play in the end cannot resolve it. The audience is left, not satisfied, nor appeased, nor released and restored to itself, but with the playwright's unappeasable moral rage and frustration to deal with; frustration at the impossibility of offering an adequate answer, an adequate object, an adequate form for the historical evil that the play anatomizes and wishes to understand.

8.4. NATURALIZED SYMBOLISM

At a telling moment in *The Deputy*, Father Riccardo Fontana, SJ, a member of the Vatican Secretariat, pins a yellow star on his cassock—

> This star which every Jew must wear
> as soon as he is six years old,
> to show he is an outlaw—I shall wear it too.[23]

The badge is symbolic, both in its historical origins and in its reassigned use by the Nazi authorities; and to a further degree so is its use by Riccardo, declaring his solidarity with the victims of the death factories, his action given resonance by the legend of the King of Denmark doing likewise in behalf of his citizens. After Riccardo's departure, the Pope, who has stained his fingers with ink in the agitation of the scene, washes his hands in a basin of water, and then dries them, proclaiming his blood innocence. This action also, of course, is symbolic, though without explicit decoding, associating Pius with Pilate in the Gospels.[24]

One can argue that every speech with meaningful reverberations beyond the literal, every gesture that sums up or reveals, every telling juxtaposition and representation, every comprehensive action that provides closure or denies it, is symbolic to a degree, even in the most naturalistically inclined modern drama. But the great effort in the dominant modern strain that defers to the conventions of mimetic realism has been to naturalize its symbolism, to make it plausible, even unremarkable, by the standards of ordinary experience. This is a far cry from the undissembled, ostentatious symbolism of both a good deal of earlier drama, and of the challenging modernist counter-current to mimetic realism. There is no veil of plausibility, for example, in Strindberg's *A Dream Play* (1901), which (after a cloud-world Prologue) opens before a 'Growing Castle' crowned by a great flower bud against a backdrop of giant hollyhocks; and ends with the castle aflame before a wall of enquiring and anguished human faces as '*the flower bud on the roof opens into a giant chrysanthemum*'. Whereas the meaning of the Pope's plausible Pilate-like gesture is exceedingly plain, the same cannot be said for Strindberg's striking conception, for all its resonant suggestion. (We learn, however, that the castle is rooted in earth amid piles of straw and dung, and aspires upwards. The moment of consummation, in flames and blossoming, coincides with the release of the Daughter of Indra from her incarnate earthly sojourn, etc.)

'Meaning' in the experience of a play is often lodged primarily in the sense that things have come together, that all the elements, whatever the difficulties, have fallen into place. The feeling is enhanced by what seem to be signs of an aptness beyond the dictates of character, the accidents of circumstance, and the logic of cause and consequence—an aptness that, carried to a certain point, invites us to attach to some workings-out the label of 'poetic justice'. Neither the seal of an uncanny aptness nor the utility of signification by poetic (symbolic) means was easily abandoned in the theatre of prose realism. The consequence was a resort to naturalized symbolism, along with an overt, often critical incorporation of the human propensity to symbolic reading of the ordinary and the everyday. Even before Ibsen and Chekhov—the masters of having it both ways—such symbolic reading comes under scrutiny, in tension with a post-Enlightenment naturalism and humanism.

In the work of the canonical playwrights of modern mimetic realism and their predecessors, it often happens that reading symbolic meanings into natural phenomena is problematized, while at the same time symbolic suggestion is naturalized, by displacing the onus of symbol making from the playwright on to the characters. An early instance is in Friedrich Hebbel's pioneering tragedy of private life (*Ein bürgerliches Trauerspiel*, as it is self-consciously subtitled), *Maria Magdalene* (1844). Klara, the daughter of the family, is prone to a symbol-making powered by guilt and shame. She has been brutally seduced, and her bullying seducer challenges her reaction to the young man, once her dearest companion, now returned from some years at the university:

LEONARD. Then why did you blush when he saw you again?
KLARA. I thought he was looking at the mole on my left cheek, to see if it had gotten larger. You know, that's what I always imagine when someone stares at me so fixedly, and then I always blush. It seems to me then, while anyone looks at it, as if the mole were growing larger.[25]

Thinking her guilt emblazoned on the body, Klara's involuntary fancy and its articulation anticipate the end of the century's revolutionary investigations of such tricks of the mind and such symbolic displacements. Hebbel has a lot more to say about both pragmatic rationalism and symbolic think-ing in a traditional world under assault by competitive individualism. He dramatizes the destruction of a paradigmatic family, whose pride is in its modest respectability, at a point of cultural crisis where traditional communal values, enforced through the paternalistic rigours of a shame culture, are discarded; or else they are introjected, as in the case of Klara, who persis-tently reads her internalized guilt into the omens and events of her narrow world.

One way of naturalizing symbolism within the conventions of realism is to make explicit all that can be problematic in this way of creating meaning. The issues reach beyond playmaking to the human propensity to raise objects into a fetishized shorthand, to displace feelings on to them, and to read objects and events for their coded messages. Alexander Ostrovsky, Russia's most important playwright before Chekhov, moves these matters into the foreground in *The Storm* (1859). It is the best known of his eighty-odd plays, which are the backbone of the Russian classic repertory. A complete man of the theater whose *oeuvre* constitutes a Balzacian anatomy of the society of his time—petty merchants, social climbers, tradesmen, swindlers, hard-up gentry, actors, serfs—Ostrovsky appealed to a burgeoning taste for the sentiment of the real, often with a critical or satirical edge, sometimes angry, usually humane and compassionate. The central figure in *The Storm* is Katerina Kabanova (as in Janáček's notable opera of that name), a romantic innocent living in the Volga provinces under the thumb of her tyrannical mother-in-law. She is aroused to a great passion for a similarly oppressed young man in a neighbouring household, falls briefly into rapturous sin, and finally drowns herself, after a public confession at the height of the storm that gives the play its name. The eponymous storm claims priority as the dominant poetic emblem in the play, and of course it incorporates in its resonant symbolism the burst of mutual passion that strikes the lovers and disrupts the oppressive stagnation of family and community life. But the storm is also a natural event, and as such it not only attracts interpretation in the play, but invites argument over its interpretability. As the literal storm gathers in the fourth act—where the play comes to its crisis—promenaders seek shelter in the arcade of a ruined building overlooking the Volga, and there the self-taught artisan-mechanic Kuligin shocks the tight-fisted domestic tyrant Dikoí, the irascible male counterpart of Katerina's mother-in-law and part of the benighted merchant gerontocracy that darkens the play. Kuligin deplores, in a region of frequent thunderstorms, the absence of lightning rods.

DIKOÍ. But what is a thunderstorm in your opinion, eh? Come on, tell me.
KULIGIN. It's electricity, sir.
DIKOÍ. (*stamping his foot*) Electricity be damned! Now, aren't you a blackguard? Don't you know that a thunderstorm is sent us as a punishment to make us repent of our sins? And you've the impudence to propose to fight it with some blasted steel rods and sticks and I don't know what else. What are you, a Tartar?

Later, with the storm about to break, Kuligin admonishes the sheltering crowd:

What is there to be afraid of, I ask you? Every little blade of grass, every flower, is now rejoicing, and we hide ourselves, terrified out of our wits, as though expecting some terrible calamity to befall us. The thunderstorm will kill me! Why it's not a storm at all. It's a blessing! Yes, a blessing! You're afraid of everything. If the northern lights appear in the sky, do you run out into the streets and admire that miracle of nature? With gratitude in your hearts for God's great wisdom, for 'from the north a dawn ariseth'—no! You're thrown into a panic. You try to invent all sorts of fearful omens. You start whispering to each other: 'What does it signify? A war or a pestilence?' A comet appears . . . You tremble all over with terror! You've transformed every grand spectacle of the heavens into a nightmare. What a people! Lord, what a people![26]

Katerina, who is full of irrational fears and imaginative fantasies, has shown her special terror of thunderstorms in the first act, when, after disclosing her unrealized passion to her husband's sister, Varvara, the sound of thunder from an approaching storm sends her into a panic. It is not so much being killed by the lightning that she fears, as being carried off suddenly, in mid-sin, to appear before God. In the fourth act, having taken shelter with the others in the arcaded ruin, her terrors are increased by the consciousness of sin, the pious persecutions of an elderly gentlewoman who atones for her colourful past by attacking youth and beauty, and the remains of a wall painting showing the Gehenna of Fire. In a paroxysm of fear, she declares her sin 'before God and You' to her mother-in-law and husband, and, as the storm bursts in a great clap of thunder, falls unconscious in her husband's arms.

Ostrovsky uses the storm for dramatic, indeed operatic, effect as well as for symbolic condensation, an epitome of the action. But he also brings such uses into question in the dialogue between an enlightened (and spiritualized) naturalism and a supernaturalism mired in morbid fears and apocalyptic dread. In doing so, he at least partly naturalizes his dominant metaphor. On a more modest scale, he integrates a naturalistic premiss with symbolic uses through foregrounding elements of the strictly mundane, filtered through an imaginative sensibility. The most vividly wrought is the key to the gate of the enclosed back-garden of the Kabanov household, which Varvara filches and gives to Katerina in her brother's absence on a business trip. The key will provide Katerina with the chance to meet alone with the man she is so drawn to, and with an escape, however temporary, from the oppressive confines of the domestic prison. Katerina's maiden fantasies were of flying free, like a bird or a soul unencumbered, but her first impulse is to reject the key to her cage in fright. Then, left alone, in a long soliloquy in which she ruminates on her present and her future, key in hand, she moves from saying that she should throw it into the river so no one could find it—'It burns my hand like a piece of live coal'—to the impulse to conceal this instrument of temptation, to the declaration, 'Why am I deceiving myself? Even if I were to die for it, I must see him. Why pretend to myself? Throw away the key? Not for anything in the world!' (p. 117). It is the character's intense focus on this object that elevates it to a symbol and charges it with meaning; but it is also the psychological drama it precipitates that naturalizes its function.

The displacement of symbol-making on to the characters themselves, and also its critique, so oddly legitimating, are very much on the minds of the two most profoundly influential of the shaping spirits of the modern drama, namely Ibsen and Chekhov. So, for example, in Ibsen's *The Wild Duck* (1884), it is the ideal-monger Gregers Werle who loads symbolic significance on the captive wild duck in the Ekdals' loft, applies it to the Ekdals themselves, and proposes the symbolic sacrifice that Hedvig, the child, transfers to herself. It is the child who observes, at the beginning of the process, that she thought that when Gregers spoke of wounded ducks and clever retrievers, 'he meant something else'.

GINA [her mother] What could he mean?
HEDVIG. I don't know. But I felt as though he meant something different from what he was saying all the time.[27]

In the end, investing the wild duck and its fate with symbolic meaning, like Gregers' missionary work for 'the claim of the ideal', proves disastrous.

That other iconic water fowl of the modern theatre, Chekhov's seagull in the play that bears its name, starts out as an ordinary figure of speech. Nina, speaking of her attraction to the bohemian Sorin estate, with its actors, writers, theatricals, tells the young Treplev, 'I am drawn to this place, to this lake, as if I were a seagull.' Later, when an unhappy Treplev, carrying a gun and a dead seagull, lays the bird at Nina's feet, she asks, 'What does this mean?' Treplev declares, 'Soon I shall kill myself in the same way,' and attributes his malaise to Nina's recent coolness. Nina, however, repudiates his cryptic declarations:

You've grown so irritable lately, and most of the time you've been talking unintelligibly, in a sort of symbolic way. And now this seagull here is apparently another symbol, but—you must forgive me—I don't understand it. . . . (*Puts the seagull on the seat*).[28]

Nina has in fact been drawn to the older, successful writer, Trigorin, who finding her alone, responds to her interest with flattering confidences about his own insecurities and dissatisfactions as a writer. He complains of his practice of cannibalizing life and experience. Then, noticing the dead bird, he begins making notes:

An idea suddenly came into my head. A subject for a short story: a young girl, like you, has lived beside a lake from childhood. She loves the lake as a seagull does, and she's happy and free as a seagull. But a man chances to come along, sees her, and having nothing better to do, destroys her, just like this seagull here. (p. 151)

Trigorin's embryonic story alters Treplev's seagull symbolism, again associating its fate—and now by implication himself—with Nina. Synthesizing

the found elements in the moment—the girl, the gull, the unspoken attraction—his idea is proleptic of what is to come. But in the event, the recruiting
of symbols and the symbolism itself are pointedly undercut, to almost comic
effect. When Trigorin returns to the place of his inspiration two years later,
he is told by the bailiff that there is something waiting for him—a gull that
Treplev once shot, 'and you asked me to get it stuffed for you'. Trigorin replies,
'I don't remember. (*Pondering.*) No, I don't remember' (p. 176). As for Nina,
who has suffered greatly in the interval, largely through Trigorin, but who has
also found her vocation, she ultimately repudiates the seductive symbolism
that, in her fatigue and distraction, has seemed to threaten her mind: 'I'm
a seagull. . . . No, that's not it. I'm an actress' (p. 180). The bailiff actually
produces the stuffed bird for the forgetful Trigorin before the play is out; and
it is at that moment that we hear the shot with which Treplev kills himself.
Not in the end as strong as Nina, Treplev's initial self-pitying, destructive, and
faintly ridiculous conscription of the dead seagull into serving as a symbol for
himself, both the slayer and the slain, is by his own action fulfilled.

8.5. WHERE IT ALL COMES TOGETHER (PERHAPS)

'Meaning' as an attribute of the play can be taken in stride, on the page or on
the boards, as long as the play is sufficiently orthodox for its time and place. But
'meaning' becomes an issue when the playmaking or the play's take on things
is sufficiently heterodox. Modern drama is marked by the taste for an overt
heterodoxy, critical of established institutions and attitudes, even of the regular
ways of seeing and knowing. Titles tell us something, as in the case of such
critical overviews as Robert Brustein's *The Theatre of Revolt* (1964) or Austin
Quigley's *The Modern Stage and Other Worlds* (1985). The notion of a 'Drama
of Ideas' as a distinct category, where what used to be called 'the Argument'
of the play refers less to Aristotle's prime element, the 'plot', than to what he
deemed less important, the 'thought', is essentially a modern invention. And
here as in other respects, it was the brilliant eighteenth-century critic of the
drama and the arts, Gotthold Ephraim Lessing, who set the course for the
drama of ideas, that is to say, drama offering an expository demonstration of
heterodox thought—expository in the discourse, demonstrative in the fable
and the action.

Lessing provided a model. If one were to ask the question of Lessing's
seminal play, *Nathan the Wise*, 'What is this play about?' a different *kind* of
answer would be required than if one were to ask, 'What is *Othello* about?'
Nathan the Wise (1779), standard in the German classic repertory except

during the Hitler years, is also a virtual handbook of how plays mean. The play is set in Jerusalem, sacred to the three great monotheistic religions, during the rule of Saladin (late twelfth century). As one character puts it, 'The whole world comes together here' (III. x. 57).[29] The plot concerns Rachel [Recha], the daughter of Nathan who is a rich merchant and Jew, and a disaffected Knight Templar on parole who saved Rachel from a fire during Nathan's absence on his mercantile travels. Meanwhile Saladin, the great warrior sultan who had retaken Jerusalem, both generous and short of cash, concocts a plan with the help of his clever sister to extract money from Nathan by arousing his confessional anxieties. The argument of the play, and its exemplary rhetorical force, is a negative criticism of the exclusionary intolerance of the established religions, and a positive adumbration of something better: a religion of humanity, universal in its embrace, free of dogma and superstition, open and accepting towards any number of religious practices and affinities. To that end, the play employs direct discourse, using sympathetic characters in dialogue with opponents and each other; parabolic representation of various kinds; and the shape of the action itself, both in its progressive and comprehensive aspects.

Parabolic representation is an elastic term; and here it may include the array of characters—the paradigm of the three religions in the three chief male characters, and the representation of dogmatic intolerance and popular credulity in the upholders of Christian exceptionalism—as well as the symbolic action. But at the heart of the play is an actual parable, the story of the three rings that Lessing lifted from Boccaccio and improved upon. The trap Saladin sets for Nathan is in pretending, as a seeker, to consult him on which of the three religions, in Nathan's considered wisdom, is the true one. Seeing the danger, Nathan answers with a story. He tells of a father who had promised a priceless ring to each of three greatly loved sons. The ring, passing through many generations always to the favourite son, not only conveyed primacy in the house, but had the hidden power 'that he who wore it, | Trusting its strength, was loved of God and men' (III. vii. 21–2). Not able to disappoint any of his sons, the father in secret has two other rings made, impossible to distinguish from the original. He conveys a ring to each son, along with his blessing, and dies. In the ensuing turmoil, the three sons turn to the courts, but their secular judge is wise enough to know that, absent the father, he cannot settle the matter with a judgement. Instead he offers counsel: that each should believe his ring to be the true one, and, in emulation of their father's inclusive love, strive with the others to demonstrate its intrinsic beneficent power.

The point of the parable is soon obvious during the telling; and to Saladin's objections—such as that the 'rings' (the religions) *do* differ, if not in divine origin, then in detail—Nathan has answers: all the religions are grounded in history and depend on faith, and for their adherents are part of an inheritance it makes little sense to exchange. The result, for the action, is not just that Nathan gets off the hook (he soon freely offers to advance the money Saladin needs). More significant, there is a recognition, as between persons of like mind, two co-religionists in an open, inclusive, enlightened religion of Man. Nathan's apocryphal judge has suggested, ironically, that in a thousand thousand years someone wiser than he might be prepared to judge the true ring from results, and Nathan has invited Saladin to step into that role. But instead, Saladin '*rushes to him and seizes his hand, which he retains to the end of the scene*'.

> NATHAN. What is the matter, Sultan?
> SALADIN.   Nathan, dear Nathan!—
>   The thousand thousand years your judge assigned
>   Are not yet up.—His judgment seat is not
>   For me.—Go!—Go!—But be my friend.
>
> (III. vii. 151–4)

Earlier, the Templar and Nathan have come to a similar recognition, against all probability. The Templar, who is proud, prickly, and suspicious, rebuffs Nathan's grateful advances, especially mistrusting one so manifestly of those who first called themselves 'the chosen people'. But in making that point, the Templar shows himself equally at odds with exclusive and coercive Christian claims, in that contested Jerusalem where, he notes, pious frenzy has revealed itself in blackest form. As he starts to go, Nathan stops him:

> NATHAN. Ha! You know not how much closer
>   I now shall cling to you.—O come, we must,
>   We must be friends! Disdain my nation [*Volk*] as much
>   As ever you will. We neither of us chose our nation.
>   Are we our nation? What's it mean, 'a nation'?
>   Are Jew and Christian sooner Jew and Christian
>   Than Man? Ah! If only I have found in you
>   One more for whom it is enough to bear the name
>   Of Man!
> TEMPLAR. Yes, by God, you have, Nathan!
>   You have!—Your hand!
>
> (II. v. 103–12)

Nothing remains but for a similar recognition between the Templar and Saladin to occur. Saladin—who is reminded of the Templar's existence by Nathan—had earlier spared him from execution because of some fancied resemblance to a lost brother. Now he asks the Templar freely to remain with him, 'as Christian, Muslim, all one!'

SALADIN (*offering him his hand*) A word?
TEMPLAR (*grasping it*) A man!

(IV. iv. 39–40)

This series of recognitions, based on affinities in mind and spirit, structures the progressive action, and collectively inaugurates the bonds of fellowship in a religion of Man. To the main supports of this armature are added reinforcements: a Sufi—Saladin's Treasurer—who is more than half Parsee; a Christian Friar who subverts the rabid inclinations of the Patriarch of Jerusalem, and who declares of Nathan, 'By God, a better Christian never lived!' while Nathan says, 'What makes me for you | A Christian, makes yourself for me a Jew!' (IV. vii. 145–7). Sittah, Saladin's clever sister, and Rachel herself, carefully and lovingly educated by Nathan to think as well as feel, are also of the company, if less paradigmatically. But this pattern in the action is not *the plot*, which concerns the obstacles, seemingly of religion, to the match between Rachel and the Templar; the mortal danger to Nathan, personified in the Patriarch, in the revelation that the child Nathan raised as his own was born a Christian; and a final resolution that features, not a kinship of the spirit but of the flesh, literal kinship as in countless tragedies and comedies from Sophocles and Menander to Sam Shepard.

Rachel, we learn, was put into Nathan's care by her Frankish (European) father, one Wolf von Filnek, three days after Nathan had lost his wife and seven sons, burned to death in a Christian pogrom. The infant's mother dead and Wolf soon killed in battle, Nathan raised her as his own, crying to God, 'for seven, *one* at least in return' (IV. vii. 143). The Templar bears the family name of Rachel's dead mother, von Filnek's wife; and in the upshot turns out to be Rachel's brother, raised in Germany by his maternal uncle. And Wolf von Filnek turns out to be not a Frank, but the wayward, romantic brother of Saladin himself and Sittah. The last scene is an extended recognition scene of another kind, as all is revealed and (allowing for the Templar's understandable consternation) all fall seriatim into each other's arms until, '*Amid silent embraces on all sides, the curtain falls.*' The plot has produced a nearly universal multiple kinship among the principals, a literalizing metaphor for the larger human kinship and ideal ties of love that the play wishes to instil, in mind and heart, as its comprehensive meaning. Only Nathan is left out in the genealogy, an irony that raises him, however, in his generosity of spirit, to a universal fatherhood and selfless sanctity, as one set apart.

At one point in the play the Templar, in distress at Nathan's inexplicable resistance to the match after so much encouragement, goes to the Patriarch and puts the case of a Jew raising a baptized Christian as a Jewess and his daughter. The Patriarch, scenting blood, wants to know if the case is real or hypothetical—a mere 'pastime of the mind [*ein Spiel des Witzes*]'. If the latter,

> Then I'd urge my Lord to try
> The theater where such things *pro et contra*
> Could be discussed with general applause.
>
> (IV. ii. 59–61)

The Patriarch doesn't seem to share the Church's long-standing suspicion of the theatre, as a temple of disorder and dangerous suggestion. Hypotheticals enacted—and what else is a play in performance—are sufficiently inconsequential to him to permit indulgence in the play of mind. Otherwise, he insists on the primacy of dogma and decree. His model for a play, however, is an academic exercise with an audience like spectators at a tennis match, applauding each dexterous return, but not invested in meaning or truth. Lessing, who had become embroiled with the Lutheran Chief Pastor of Hamburg on the issue of his orthodoxy, had been forbidden to publish on religious matters without the express sanction of the government. For Lessing, his play *Nathan the Wise* was continuing the argument by other and indeed more potent means. He writes with rhetorical intent; that is, not simply to enlist his audience in a game, engage its interest, its emotions, its appreciation, and leave it essentially unchanged. He contrives a play with an agenda designed to inform, convince, and persuade, by dramatic means: characters sympathetic and antipathetic; a schema from melodrama and romance, of perils and affinities; audience surrogates who need to learn; forensic dialogue; overt parable and a parabolic action; a signifying plot as metaphor. The play means to get at you in that obvious way Johnny Tarleton found so annoying. That is obvious, however, only because its meanings, in its time and place, were not such as could be taken for granted and swallowed whole. Like much heterodox drama, social, political, metaphysical, it has more to explain, more to demonstrate, more to do, in order to say *what* it means, and even to convince. But *how* it means is another matter, and for that, art, imagination, poetic force, embodied insight, and dramatic ingenuity are what count, here as elsewhere, to make the difference between the work of a master and that of a hack, between, as it were, a hawk and a handsaw.

9

Primal Attractions

In one version of a talk that Tom Stoppard delivered in various university settings, he describes a moment in 'a celebrated production of *The Tempest* at one of the Oxford colleges', one he himself never saw, but many times heard recalled by people he worked with. Others have written about it, as an experience so enthralling that it has stayed with them all their lives. As Stoppard tells it:

This production of *The Tempest* took place in the open air in the early evening, and when it became time for Ariel to leave the action of the play he turned and he ran up the stage, away from the audience. Now the stage was a lawn, and the lawn backed on to a lake. He ran across the grass and got to the edge of the lake, and he just kept running, because the director had had the foresight to put a plank walkway just underneath the surface of the water. So you have to imagine: it's become dusk, and quite a lot of the artificial lighting has come on, and back there in the gloom is this lake. And Ariel says his last words and he turns and he runs and he gets to the water and he runs and he goes splish splash, splish splash, right across the lake and into the enfolding dark, until one can only just hear his footsteps making these little splashes, and then ultimately his little figure disappeared from view. And at that moment, from the further shore, a firework rocket was ignited and just went whoosh into the sky and burst into lots of sparks. All the sparks went out one by one and Ariel had gone. This is the thing: you can't write anything as good as that. If you look it up, it says, 'Exit Ariel.'[1]

Stoppard's talk was called 'The Event and the Text', and his point is that the thing he has described, in its circumstances, in its effect as experienced, is not in the text, nor could it be. The text, 'the book of the play', certainly prepares for a moment of release in which we can share, and has made room for its poignancy and interest, but it cannot provide the wonder. Even if Shakespeare had still been alive when *The Tempest* reached print, and had supplied his Folio editors with something as elaborate as James Barrie's novelistic stage directions and as good as Stoppard's evocation of the vanishing, it would not, could not be the same thing.[2]

When we read a play, some of its qualities are as available in the text as in 'the event': the brilliance of the conceit in Aristophanes' *Lysistrata*, let us say, where the women of Athens and Sparta go on a sex strike until the men see reason and stop killing each other; the aptness and ingenuity of Volpone's comeuppance in Ben Jonson's play, where the swindler who fleeces his greedy victims and finds cover for his lusts by pretending to be dying, is fleeced in turn by being declared dead. The witty interchanges of Mirabel and Millamant, the impassioned proclamations of Tamburlaine, the insults of Thersites, the outrageous rationalizations of Falstaff, can also offer intrinsic pleasures directly via the reading, if with valences shifted somewhat from when performed. But some aspects of what the play is written to provide are not available in the reading, except as a spectral promise, because so intrinsically bound up with what happens when we are an audience; and these by-and-large are those primal attractions that give the theatre its perennial draw, and make plays written for the theatre different from the literature that is sufficient unto itself and need concern itself only with serving the competent reader.

9.1. MIMESIS AND MAGIC

Deep in the forest of these primal attractions is the appetite for wonder, as in Ariel's release and evanescence in that open-air Oxford performance. What the audience sees, so apt and so magical, doesn't seem possible. When Anna Deavere Smith, playwright-performer, asked Kenneth Feld, CEO of the circus that calls itself The Greatest Show on Earth, 'What are your criteria for a terrific act?' his answer was, 'You get the audience to ask, "How did you do that?"' And closely related, it is 'to deliver the unexpected'.[3] And yet the appetite for wonder can find satisfaction in less spectacular form, starting with the pleasure in imitation itself—the falsehood that seems true. In the long critical conversation about the nature of drama, imitation—*mimesis*— has a wide-ranging application, and even in its fountainhead, Aristotle's *Poetics*, it means a great deal more than simple mimicry. But at foundation level—and that for the moment is where we are—it starts with impersonation. An actor mimics a figure from life, or a recognizable type, or a way of speaking or doing (falling down drunk, for example), perhaps exaggerating some traits to assure easier recognition. There is no separating the one from the other, mimesis from recognition, connecting what is enacted with something that lies elsewhere, something the audience has brought to the play. The wonder breaks out where the imitation seems closest to what is already present in our minds, and the pleasure is often expressed in laughter, as by children, perhaps because at bottom there is something illogical, magical, in this fracturing of identity through enactment.

The magic of mimesis is prone to camouflage itself in a drab coat in the theatre that aspires to a reflection of ordinary life; but the magic appears in its nakedness in that other engine of primal wonder in the dramatic event, *transformation*. Transformation is inherent in the actor's assumption of other selves, and in turning the playing space into the world of the play, but it also inheres in the action that makes drama out of the change from one state of affairs at the beginning of a play, to another in the middle, and still another at the end. Aristotle's 'turn', or *peripeteia*, sometimes rendered as 'transformation of the situation', points to that species of change. Transformation lies in something becoming other than it is or seems; and whereas many, if not most, plays construct a rationale for such magic, domesticating it so to speak, some forms of theatre and some playwrights take an opposite tack. They emphasize the wonder, and adopt the illusionistic mystification of the stage magician: now you see it, now you don't; watch this goose become a swan. As an aspect of the dramatic event and the scripts that support it, transformation has many faces and takes many forms, from the conceptual to the sensational. In its most literal form, it makes its appeal in the theatre of spectacle, spectacle proving, in its long history, the most consistently seductive of the theatre's primal attractions. In the nineteenth century, it made its mark in the so-called 'transformation scene', the climactic moment in Pantomime and Extravaganza where the scene became a fantastic glittering wonderland before the audience's very eyes. But the 'realistic' complement of such fantasy magic, the convincing imitation of scenes from life—waterfalls, horse races, shipwrecks, conflagrations—was no less an appeal to the appetite for wonder, and no less a conjuration and transformation of the stage.

Finally, somewhere between mimesis and magic in the cabinet of wonder, and partaking of both, is the pleasure in sheer virtuosic performance—virtuosity in speaking, singing, leaping, duelling, and personating; and while personating, virtuosity in lying, seducing, intimidating, escaping, out-talking, out-foxing, out-suffering. The exhilaration in witnessing such performance can only emerge in reading where the playwright—at least momentarily a Shakespeare, a Congreve, a Molière, a Chekhov—so handles the words and the action that we perceive their potential and respond accordingly; respond to such *authorial* virtuosity, so evocative on the page of a fulfilling realization in the performed event. In the past, some Romantic critics, however immersed in the theatre and theatregoing, declared a preference for reading plays because the event so often fell so unattainably short of what they imagined as an ideal performance, fully commensurate with the text. (It didn't help that at the time the actual performance-texts of their test case, Shakespeare, strayed so far, through cuts and revisionary enhancements, from those texts edited and designed to be read as literature.) What abstention from the theatre on such grounds forgoes, however, is all that comes out of the performers' necessity of particularizing, concretizing, enacting and inhabiting the words on the page; and it forgoes something more, that grace beyond any reasonable expectation in the Oxford version of 'Exit Ariel'. It is not the realization of a quintessential ideal performance that produces it, but an inspiration only discoverable in the actualized event.

Delight in the virtuosity of the performance and the acting and staging skills it entails plays an exemplary role in another modern production of *The Tempest* that has become legendary. This *Tempest*, staged by the great Italian director Giorgio Strehler, also survives in report. Here is how the late Bernard Beckerman, an inspired teacher and acute thinker about the workings of theatre and drama, describes the scene of Ariel's first appearance (I. ii), which ultimately prepares for the moment of Ariel's release:[4]

> To introduce Ariel, Strehler draws upon the traditional spectacle of flying. In response to Prospero's cry, 'Approach my Ariel! Come,' Ariel descends from the flies upon a wire, but wonder of wonders, lands deftly in Prospero's right hand, then flits to the other hand, then onto Prospero's shoulder, and finally comes to rest in the magician's right hand again. This seemingly improbable feat is carried out with such delicacy and ease that it never arouses a qualm of incredulity. It is merely astonishing and exhilarating. (pp. 591–2)

Beckerman credits the success of this entrance to the timing and skill of the actors, and notes that the slightness of the actress who plays Ariel has something to do with it—for as in a theatre tradition, 'it is an actress who portrays the spirit, although the first impression one has is of an asexual being'. There is no attempt to deceive the audience in the flying. The wonder lies in the grace and 'naturalness', the achieved illusion of weightlessness:

> Despite the obviousness of the wire that supports her, the actress manages the movements with such aplomb that the illusion is complete. It is of course a special kind of illusion. No one mistakes the entrance for an image of actual flying. Instead, Strehler gives us the idea of an illusion, tempting us with the attractiveness of that illusion while he shows us openly the mechanism by means of which it is achieved. That type of demonstrated illusionism is very close to what the magician does, though for a different purpose. Whereas the magician tries to mystify us, Strehler demonstrates through convincing artifice the insubstantiality of Ariel.

Except when descending as the Harpy that spoils Prospero's disappearing feast, Ariel flies in again only for her last entrance, at Prospero's call, and then unspectacularly:

> Ariel . . . dropped directly to the stage floor at the end of a line. Prospero bade her farewell: 'to the elements | Be free, and fare thee well.' He unhooked Ariel from the line. They gazed at each other, and then Ariel looked out to the audience—not at it,

Figure 10. Enter Ariel on a wire at Prospero's summons, while Miranda sleeps, in Giorgio Strehler's production of Shakespeare's *The Tempest*, Act I, Scene ii. Piccolo Teatro di Milano, 1977–8. Photo, Luigi Ciminaghi.

but through it and beyond it. Never before in this production had a character faced the audience so directly. Ariel crawled over the footlights, across several rows of flats coming up to stage height to represent the sea, and with her eyes ever on freedom before her passed through the audience and beyond it. In this simple way Ariel gained release to freedom through us.

The effect was more than thrilling. It was transforming, giving us a true sense of the freedom we ourselves possess. (p. 592)

The direction of Ariel's exit—opposite to that of Ariel's Oxford vanishing over the lake into darkness and fireworks—makes for the audience's awareness of itself, and of the working aspects of the theatre: footlights, flats, and above all wire and release, with Ariel, spirit in the act of aspiring and breaking free, wading through and seeing beyond the material encumbrances. It appears to involve us in a more complicated emotion and experience than the Oxford liberation; but it too comes out of much that was explicit and implicit in what has preceded this moment, and it feeds in turn into what is still to come: Prospero's epilogue, where the Globe Theatre and everything else stand subject to an inescapable dissolution, which is also dis-illusion. Speaking of Strehler's *Tempest* as a whole, Beckerman observes that '[t]heatrically, it combines stage history and contemporary techniques into a purely personal idiom. Emotionally, it arouses a feeling of naïve wonder at the same time that it creates for the spectator a palpable impression of restraint and release. Intellectually, it provides a subtly resonant model of interplay between illusion and reality, an interplay in which the audience's presence is a necessary factor' (p. 591). And so at the end,

Just as Prospero asked the audience's indulgence to set him free, the wings fell askew, and the border above remained suspended at an odd angle across the face of the stage, a mute symbol of the theatre's and illusion's collapse. In this way Strehler dramatized the dissolution of the 'cloud-capped towers . . . [and] the great globe itself.' (p. 593)

And in this way the audience also took its release from the scene of wonders.

When Prospero, who had had plenty of time to nurse his grudges, has '*strange shapes*' bring in a banquet for the famished castaways and then makes it disappear with sound effects, it is not only the characters who are targeted for sudden fright and mystification. The unusual stage direction reads: '*Thunder and Lightning. Enter Ariel (like a Harpy) claps his wings upon the Table, and with a quaint device the Banquet vanishes.*'[5] As others have observed, the description seems written more from an audience perspective than a production perspective, conveying effect rather than providing technical directions (as in the vaguely indicated 'quaint device').[6] It should also be noted that the noise and the spectacle both enhance the effect and—as in a magician's performance—help cover the mechanics of how it is done. In what follows, the Harpy-Ariel terrorizes his captive audience by telling them their concealed sins, and then '*vanishes in Thunder'*, whereupon the strange shapes enter to soft music and mockingly dance out the table. Over all this, Prospero presides, *'on the top (invisible)'* to the onstage witnesses of his magic, but not of course to the real audience.

The wonder laced with terror with which Prospero's magic afflicts his victims rests on the sensation of the uncanny; and some of that sensation, made safe at one remove, will still have its effect on the audience proper. But for that audience the wonder in this stage magic is also informed by the virtuosity of the illusion, including the 'quaint device', in an art that at once displays and conceals its art. As in the case of a parlour magician, we know there is a trick and we ask, 'How did he do it?' Meanwhile the magician has shown us there is nothing up his sleeve.

The pleasure in virtuosity and the pleasure in illusion, or magic, are deeply entangled in each other, as no one knew better than Jean Cocteau. His plays make much of both, and if several among them are themselves manifestos on art, as is the Modernist habit, he also declares himself in a brief sketch of an American acrobat and his routine, called 'Le Numéro Barbette'. What Cocteau finds entrancing is the sheer virtuosity of the acrobat—whose art is one of presentation, but not ostensibly of representation—in an act that entails metamorphosis. For Barbette is also a female impersonator who performs his stunts on tightrope and trapeze as a woman, though with strength and skills characteristically male. 'Barbette substantiates the Greek legends about young men changed into trees, into flowers: an antidote to their easy magic,' Cocteau writes. But he adds:

Do not forget: we are under the theatre's lights, inside that magic box where truth has no currency, where nature has no value, where the short are made tall and the tall can shrink, where the only realities are feats of prestidigitation whose difficulty the public never suspects.[7]

Between stunts, Cocteau tells us, Barbette performs a little scabrous scene as a woman in her boudoir, 'a real masterpiece of pantomime'. The ultimate tour de force, however, comes at the end, when Barbette pulls off her wig and reveals himself. But even then, 'The truth, too, must be translated, must be heightened to keep on an equal footing with the lie.' Accordingly, Barbette *'acts the part of a man'*—rolls his shoulders, swells his muscles, struts and shambles—the performance, Cocteau suggests, of a master of 'this apparatus of enchantments, of emotions, of skills that trick our senses and our souls' (p. 94). That is, 'Barbette' gives herself/himself away, but most artfully, exposing the trick as theatre without reducing its virtuosity or making it less marvellous.

Cocteau's appetite for magical transformations that are equally feats of technical virtuosity (and so sometimes tread the edge of too much) drew him to the making of movies. But the limitless capabilities of film magic, from the fantasies of Méliès at the beginnings of French cinema to the marvels of Hollywood's Industrial Light and Magic, lack something that emanates from the feat that takes place, not on the screen, but before the naked eye. With a living performer, there is still more of wonder in the question, 'How did you do that?' than plain technical curiosity. In his plays, Cocteau's achievement is to incorporate the magic with what is fundamentally and distinctively theatrical. For example, in *The Knights of the Round Table* (1937), the principal character, the imp, Ginifer, who is the magician Merlin's servant, appears in all three acts making mischief, but in a borrowed shape—as the 'false' Gawain, the 'false' Guinevere, the 'false' Galahad. He is an autonomous character with distinctive traits—a penchant for vulgar speech, for example, which can give him away—but he is performed by the three actors who are otherwise the 'true' Gawain, Guinevere, and Galahad. As a character, he is vividly present, but his role is assigned no actor of its own. On the other hand, the magic of his transformation is a *faux-naïf* version of any actor's self-transformation in assuming a role.[8] Brecht also evokes an absent character entirely through performance by the actors in several other roles in *The Measures Taken* (1930). But in Brecht's case, the actors who, turn and turn about, play the part of their absent, previously executed comrade, do so without ever abandoning their own primary roles. There is no *magic* involved; just show-and-tell, demonstration by enactment before a tribunal. Still, it is no less a tour de force.

In Cocteau's *Orpheé* (1926)—whose ultimate concerns are with poetry and its inspirations, along with its enemies and false friends—the Surrealist horse that taps out messages is of course inhabited by an actor, and much of the magic partakes of equally indigenous tricks of the stage. At one point Heurtebise, the itinerant glazer who is really an angel in disguise, has a chair moved out from under him and remains standing on air. The door to the Underworld is a solid full-length mirror through which Death enters with her helpers, in order to take the poisoned Euridice below, and through which (with the help of Death's rubber gloves) Orpheus, seeking to recover her, will plunge and disappear. After Orpheus is dismembered by the vengeful Bacchantes, his head is flung on to the stage, and it speaks. When the police come, Heurtebise, under suspicion,

> . . . *moves quickly to Orpheus' head. Picks it up. Places the head on the pedestal and then opens the door wide so that it covers the pedestal from view. It is at this moment that the actor playing Orpheus substitutes his own head for the papier-mâché replica. The Commissioner enters, followed by his clerk.*[9]

After Heurtebise disappears via the mirror, the pedestalled head answers the oblivious Commissioner's questions until that functionary notices that his suspect has vanished.

CLERK. Magic!

COMMISSIONER. Magic . . . magic! There's no such thing.

He paces the stage.

I refuse to believe in magic. An eclipse is an eclipse. A table is a table. An accused is an accused. Now, one thing at a time. That door . . .

CLERK. Impossible, sir. If he went out that door he'd have jostled my chair.[10]

When they leave, the Clerk, after another substitution, takes the head off the pedestal and carries it from the room.

When Cocteau published his play, he prefaced it with notes on 'Costumes', 'Décor' (including a sketch and floor plan), and in particular, 'Notes on *mise en scène*', or staging. The setting he describes as reminiscent of 'a prestidigitator's *salon*'. The notes on the staging explain for the curious reader, and any would-be producer, how the tricks are to be managed. They include Heurtebise and the chair; the talking head substitutions; the disappearance of Euridice before our eyes (when, after she is recovered from the Underworld, Orpheus breaks the condition and looks at her), on stages with and without suitable traps; and Death's business with a live dove, which suddenly appears in her hand and then is released into the air during the operations that claim the spirit of Euridice. (The scripted scene also includes much hocus pocus with electrical apparatus, gesture, and action, including—as in a magic show—borrowing a watch from a member of the audience.) Cocteau explains these matters because, as he insists, they are integral to the play; but that means integral to the designed experience of the play in the theatre, including a delight in wonder and in the virtuosity that provokes the question, 'How did you do that?' In the absence of direct experience, he *tells* us 'how'—a compensatory gesture, perhaps, designed to enhance the reader's pleasure, as well as annotate the score as a guide to performance. Cocteau's awareness of what might be missed in his art when it can only be derived from the page appears in a letter he wrote to a friend telling him how touched he was 'to know that you like *Orphée* in book form. I was afraid that away from the footlights all that would remain of it would be like the remnants of submarine plants found on the sand, or what is left of dreams on waking.'[11]

For the final transformation—in the vein of epiphany and apotheosis— Cocteau supplies a transfiguration of the stage wherein eternal poetry and domestic bliss are constellated into one.

The walls of the room fly upward, out of view. Orpheus and Euridice, guided by Heurtebise, step out of the mirror. They look around, as if seeing the room for the first time. They sit at the table. Euridice motions to Heurtebise to sit on her right. All smile. They are the image of contentment.

Taking wine together, they stand for grace: Orpheus's prayer of thanks to God 'for having made a heaven of our home', and to poetry, 'since I worship poetry and poetry is what you are' (p. 150).

Considerably bolder—more playful, more impertinent, and more shocking in its time—was Cocteau's *Les Mariés de la Tour Eiffel* (*The Eiffel Tower Wedding Party*, 1921), a comedy-ballet with two actors costumed as phonographs, complete with horn, who narrate the action and do all the voices. In Cocteau's preface to the published libretto—where he declares his much-cited intention to substitute a 'theater poetry' for the usual 'poetry in the theater'—he simply amplifies what he calls the manifesto of the play itself, with its joyous impudence, its surreal logic, its aggressive deployment of the modern devices of mechanical reproduction for seeing and hearing (camera and phonograph), its indecorous, opportunistic inclusiveness ('God's share', Cocteau called it, as in found art), its revelling in commonplace and cliché only to reframe and transform them. Aside from the Eiffel Tower itself—Modernity's answer to Notre Dame—whose steel-girdered first platform is the setting, with '*a birds-eye view of Paris*', the dominant presence on the scene is a hugely scaled-up camera whose extended body forms a corridor into the wings, and whose lens opens to permit entrances and exits. A fugitive ostrich, trailed by a hunter (who inadvertently shoots down a radiogram), turns out to have escaped from the camera when the photographer invited his subjects to look at the birdie. The camera's malfunctioning has a certain logic: instead of an orthodox taking-in of the subject, the subjects are let out with no telling in advance what they will be. When the resident photographer has the wedding party arrange itself for a group portrait, for example, he (though not the wedding party) is sadly disappointed when he snaps the picture:

> *A Trouville Bathing Beauty comes out of the camera. She wears a one-piece bathing suit, carries a landing net and a creel slung over one shoulder. Colorful lighting. The wedding party lifts its arms to heaven.*
> PHONO I. Oh the pretty postcard!
> *Dance of the Bathing Beauty.*[12]

This eruption of popular postcard art, charming and harmlessly naughty, has its complement later in the piece in a satire of the pretensions of the upscale world of art dealers and collectors.

The camera has other surprises in store: a very large child who greets his future Mama and Papa, and is universally exclaimed over as the image (*le portrait*) of various members of the wedding party, and who then cries to feed the Eiffel Tower as one does the animals in the zoo; a lion who eats the General and then goes back into the camera carrying a spurred boot in its maw. Apparently this is too much for the camera, which will regurgitate the General, much chastened; but not until after the photographer persuades the ostrich (the original offender) back into the camera with the pardonable fiction that it is a get-away cab. This restores the camera to its normal function, and the photographer announces that 'at last I am able to take your photograph peacefully . . . Don't move.' It is this frozen tableau that the art dealer sells the collector as 'The Wedding Party'. (He then commissions a photograph of the same group, but only for publicity purposes, giving an extra turn to the assault on the parameters of art, and its enthusiastic commodification.)

But the satirical burlesque of the art world, however broad and amusing, takes a back seat in the ending to more primal pleasures. Cadence and the sense of completion come with the carrying through of the bizarre logic of the play, so fertile in surprise, and it comes in an ingenious final transformation. With the camera now working as it should, taking a picture means taking *in* the subject. And so, led by the bride and groom, the members of the wedding party peel off in pairs, and—rather as into a Noah's Ark—'*cross the stage and disappear into the apparatus*'. It is now the monument's closing time, and the hunter comes rushing in, frantic to make the last train. But the photographer tells him the gates are shut—'Not my fault. Look—your train—there she goes!'

The camera starts moving towards the left, its bellows stretching out behind it like railway coaches. Through the openings the wedding party can be seen waving handkerchiefs, and, underneath, their feet in motion.

Curtain

Camera has been morphed into train, a transformation, if not plausible, yet not wholly arbitrary. There are serendipitous elements of unexpected analogy here, as in the witty similitudes of the Metaphysical Poets or the transformations of the settings and their elements in the dream logic of Strindberg's *A Dream Play*. The transformation into a train is magical, but it is the kind of stage magic that gives itself away. We see how it is done, but the wonder and delight remain, in the wit, aptness, and surprise of the transformation and the virtuoso panache of its performance.

9.2. THE PLEASURE OF PRIVILEGED WITNESS

If awe is a religious emotion that may occasionally migrate to the theatre, wonder is native and aboriginal. No audience is ever so jaded that it will not respond to the magic in imitation and transformation, and to the authentic skills, ingenuities, and, perhaps at a distant remove, the hint of unsanctioned powers in the performers and the performance. The script creates opportunities for wonder and pleasure; and not the least of these is the pleasure of privileged witness.

Witness can be dangerous, however. The perils of inadvertent witness are a staple of the crime story and the political thriller, where the animus of a covert power, like 'the Organization', or 'the Firm', has been aroused. There is a deeper current of warning and dread in the storytelling of nations about the perils of unauthorized seeing. Tiresias is both empowered and eventually blinded as a consequence of coming upon two serpents engendering.[13] Pentheus in *The Bacchae* is torn to bits by the Maenads when he spies on their sacred mountain revels, entrapped through his prurient curiosity by Dionysus himself. Sophocles' Oedipus feels obliged to put out his own eyes, having looked upon what he should not, and so as not to look upon what he cannot. And 'if there were a means to choke the fountain | of hearing I would not have stayed my hand . . . seeing and hearing nothing.'[14] Two of Noah's three sons are cursed for looking on their father's nakedness. Many are blighted, maddened, alienated, or at least gravely imperilled, by seeing ghosts, faery recreations, animals in their privacies.[15] Semele is destroyed through her demand to see Zeus in his divine effulgence, Moses is spared by being allowed to see only the back parts of God as he passes by, Peeping Tom is struck blind and made a byword for his transgression. Medusa turns those who behold her to stone, but is finally overcome, notably through the invention of *indirect* seeing.

It is especially what lies outside ordinary seeing and hearing—gods, demons, kings, heroes, ghosts, totemic animals in their secret nature—that requires some buffering mithridatic protection to be safely seen and heard. And so it is that while historically most of the world's theatre has been in no way narrowly mimetic, but designed to open a channel to other, esoteric realms, it is a channel laced with protections. That is why the cultural performance of drama typically entails a special occasion, a special licence, a special locale, and a specially vetted and authorized audience. Whether it is the *kiva*, or the *polis* (or at least its male citizenry, in a place and time dedicated to Dionysus), or the community of believers on Corpus Christi day, or the community of ticket-holders who have paid for their privilege, some form of authorization and conferred immunity is attached to the witnessing—the participatory witnessing—of what otherwise it might once have been thought dangerous to see.

On the other hand, plays notoriously let loose on the stage passions and appetites that society finds troublesome, much to the discomfort of generations of moral and societal guardians. Unregulated libido and aggression in broad farce; consuming love and violent hate in tragedy, melodrama, and romance; challenges to the justice, reason, and legitimacy of the way things are and the powers that be, voiced in plays of all stripes, have raised more concern in the censors, official and unofficial, than the imaginative literature found between covers. That has been so even when such literature is the printed text of a play forbidden performance. It is true that performances have touched off riots, and in at least one documented case a revolution;[16] and it is no doubt true, though hard to document, that performances have inspired various forms of subsequent misbehaviour, and also, possibly, of noble emulation. When Bluntschli, the fugitive enemy soldier in Shaw's *Arms and the Man*, shows concern that his unwilling hosts will turn him in, impassioned patriots that they are, Raina asks, 'Have you ever seen the opera of Ernani?'

RAINA. I thought you might have remembered the great scene where Ernani, flying from his foes just as you are tonight, takes refuge in the castle of his bitterest enemy, an old Castilian noble. The noble refuses to give him up. His guest is sacred to him.
THE MAN. (*quickly, waking up a little*) Have your people got that notion?[17]

And Yeats famously wondered, reflecting on the Easter Rebellion of 1916, about the possible effect of his and Lady Gregory's stirring patriotic play of 1902, *Cathleen ni Houlihan*:

> Did that play of mine send out
> Certain men the English shot?[18]

Still, these effects for good or ill are for the most part indirect and residual rather than reflexive and immediate. And that is because they too are qualified in the first instance by 'the pleasure of privileged witness'. Among the greatest of the primal attractions, it is fundamental to the audience's relation to the stage; and while actors, playwrights, and directors, especially in the contemporary theatre, will often challenge complacent enjoyment of the privilege with happy results, it is something audiences are loath to surrender, even when they are persuaded of Artaudian values, seek out Theatres of Cruelty that can strip off insulating integuments, and go so far as to embrace attempts at participatory theatre.

Privileged witness usually entails assigned, segregated spaces for playing and witnessing; but the physical separation is less significant than another kind of distance, conferring immunity from what is happening before our eyes, and excusing us, in dire (or enticing) circumstances, from intervention. There is Desdemona, being strangled or smothered . . . But after all, 'it is only a play'. And there lies the paradox: of an imaginative engagement which can be intense, coexisting with a detachment, an externality, that actually frees us in our involvement with what is so immediately present—libido and aggression, reckless love and violent hate, the satisfactions of retributive justice, the hero's hubris in challenging the gods, the trickster's cleverness in getting away with it.

Sophocles, as conscious of his audience as of his actors in their roles, brings it all into focus in that brief, climactic exchange (already noted) in *Oedipus*

Tyrannus. Oedipus has been dogged in pursuing the truth and assembling the pieces that will tell him who he is, and consequently what he has done. Now the last piece is about to fall into place. The audience has known all along what is about to be revealed, and by now it is anticipated by Oedipus himself. In their anticipations they are now one. Sophocles marks the dramatic moment, a moment long deferred and inexorably approached:

HERDSMAN. O God, I am on the brink of frightful speech.
OEDIPUS. And I of frightful hearing. But I must hear.[19]

And then we go over the brink together. But while this is Oedipus' catastrophe, our own immunity holds. Our position of privileged witness has brought us into intimacy with (in contemporary terms) the worst thing that could possibly happen to a man: to kill one's father and sleep with one's mother, however inadvertently; with what it feels like to make the discovery, and to realize that one has brought it on oneself while trying to evade it. Oedipus has passed from the summit of life and fortune to the deepest abyss; and we, however shaken, remain where we sit.

There are some distinct advantages in being outside, a mere spectator, with undertones that have a psychological appeal, and no doubt vary from person to person: a subliminal touch of comfort, perhaps, that the lightning has struck elsewhere; a subterranean tremor of dread, that such things happen and who is to say who might not be next? But for now one has the pleasure of witness from a position of safety, whose foundation is the knowledge that enactment is here representation only, something we are able to experience without suffering the weight of the pain, ridicule, retribution, responsibility, that is inseparable from such actions in other circumstances.

And yet there is much more to the authentic theatre experience, whose aura, one would hope, informs and inspires the reading of plays; more than a timid or anaesthetized voyeurism. The greatest pleasure and the greatest performances are where the insulating vicariousness is penetrated, and we, reader and audience, are so caught up in the play that we are stirred to the depths, feel others' pain, or share their delight. To be reached in this way is exhilarating, and quite another thing from what happens when a play (in Tarleton's phrase) 'gets' at us—when the audience feels ridiculed or patronized or insulted and (occasionally with riotous effect) roused to resentment. Even then, with the audience deputizing as target, a clever playwright can enlist our masochism and guilts, or play on our vanities to allow us to associate ourselves with the cleverness and the critique. One form of virtuosity is to walk a satirical line between giving amusement and giving offence, to sting and back off; a version of the risqué that flirts with aggression rather than sexuality. It still has elements of an erotic (if dangerous) game, where in theory a little pain adds to the pleasure.

As we have seen, playwrights and directors regularly play at breaking the bounds, spilling the action into the audience chamber, and regularly seek to co-opt the audience, thrusting upon it a role (e.g. as 'audience') in the play. On the audience side, there is a residual resistance to such intrusive disregard of audience 'space', a dissonance often resolved, however, in laughter, which can be cathartic as well as insulating. But also on the audience side, perhaps at a deeper level, is a primal counter-impulse, whose redirection depends on a modicum of acculturation as to what plays are. It is the impulse we hear of, mostly in anecdote, to plunge right in: to defend the beleaguered heroine, attack the villain by rushing the stage, warn the hero of the trap he is walking into. In melodrama, which initially found its audiences among the less jaded and where the emotions are powerful, the impulse was more likely to manifest itself, sublimating into the release of cheers, boos, and hisses—a release in which any moderately sophisticated audience at a modern revival will happily share. But the impulse survives elsewhere, as in a phenomenon observed during the initial run of Edward Albee's sophisticated domestic tragicomedy, *Who's Afraid of Virginia Woolf?* (1962). When George bethinks himself of that crushing blow in his duel with his wife Martha of a telegram announcing their (imaginary) son's death, ejaculations of deep dismay would be heard in the audience ('Oh, no!'). That many in the audience, like George's hapless auditor on the stage, did not know that the child was imaginary certainly helped.

It is of course an awareness of the imaginary, representational reality of the events and dramatis personae on the stage, as in the text, that keeps our participation in check, and excuses us from humane or other interference. And yet we are, one way or another, involved. And, when all is said and done, the more involved, the better we like it. But the difference between the audience member who feels the pathos and the peril of the heroine and the one that rushes the stage can be thought of as the difference between dreaming, when the motor system is turned off, and sleepwalking, where some inner monitor has failed to open the switch.

The inability to separate the actual from the imaginary, the lived from the represented, has often been ridiculed (as in *Don Quixote, The Knight of the Burning Pestle, Le Bourgeois Gentilhomme*) and sometimes stigmatized—as in the Player's offer, in *Rosencrantz and Guildenstern Are Dead*, to put on 'a private and uncut performance', for a mere handful of guilders, of 'The Rape of the Sabine Women':

>   . . . Get your skirt on, Alfred—
> *The* BOY *starts struggling into a female robe.*
>   . . . and for eight [guilders] you can participate.

GUILDENSTERN *backs*, PLAYER *follows*.
    . . . taking either part.
GUILDENSTERN *backs*.
    . . . or both for ten. (p. 26)

Guildenstern, revolted, '*smashes the* PLAYER *across the face*'. As in Genet's *The Balcony*, the confusion of reality and representation opens the way to the pornographic. On the other hand, being able to stand apart from the performance, both in the actor's representation and the audience's reception of role and action, was the centrepiece in Brecht's transforming idea of the theatre in the later twentieth century; an idea that rejected theatre as a confection or a placebo, and led back into reality by engaging the understanding. Between getting lost in the play and standing apart from it, however, is a territory where these fields overlap, not so much neutralizing as additively reinforcing each other, compounding in a third state of involved witnessing. It is in this range of experience that the interactions of the audience with the enacted, embodied script can reach their fullest potential.

I want to give one final example, less for what it clarifies and explains than for what it opens for troubled consideration concerning the nature of theatre, the relation between script and performance, and the sufficiency or permeability of the pleasures and protections in privileged witness.

In the late 1980s and 1990s, the catastrophic impact of the AIDS epidemic in America produced a spate of plays that outed what was, for mainstream society, a pariah subject, to be avoided or kept under wraps. At the disease's intractable height in America, John Jesurun produced a rewriting of Sophocles' *Philoktetes*, a version responsive to the sufferings of the AIDS generation, but with Vietnam resonances, and broader, existential interests as well. In Sophocles' play, Philoktetes has been marooned on a barren island for the past ten years, left there by his fellow Greeks on the way to Troy when they could not bear his cries or the stench of his festering, incurable wound, his rotting foot 'diseased and eaten away with running ulcers'.[20] Now, thanks to a prophecy that Troy will never be won without Philoktetes and his bow of Hercules, Odysseus has brought Neoptolemus, son of the dead Achilles, to lure him back. In the production of Jesurun's adaptation (1994), Philoktetes was played initially by the dying actor Ron Vawter, ravaged and emaciated, visibly afflicted with Kaposi's sarcoma and various infectious disorders. When the ambassadors, having secured the bow but not Philoktetes or his forgiveness, are preparing to leave, the deeply conflicted Neoptolemus—young, healthy, and beautiful—asks, insists, on a kiss goodbye.

PHILOKTETES. For what? For why?
　　He who drinks from my mouth will be as I am.
NEOPTOLEMUS. Kiss me.

And after some resistance, '*They kiss.*'[21] What must have been its effect, with the audience aware of the actor's condition—its reality, not just its appearance—and in view of the pervasive fear, the paranoid state of alarm over anything to do with AIDS, reported in so many incidents at the time? Even with an actor simply in makeup, the effect would have been shocking and powerful. Would not the knowledge of the reality of the terrible disease, and belief in the concomitant, unquantified peril in the action, jar an audience out of its receptivity, provoke rejection of the play as play and withdrawal of participatory assent in its unfolding, destroy all vestige of pleasure and privilege in the pleasure of privileged witness?[22]

The territory where being able to get lost in the play and being able to stand apart from it overlap is as pertinent to the reader's optimal experience as it is to the playgoer's. Where one capacity is forgone or denied, both are impoverished. As for the play itself, it works best where there is a similar convergence of something designed to be seen from outside and something both grasped and felt from within. Let Yeats have the last word, or at least ask the last question:

After all, is not the greatest play not the play that gives the sensation of an external reality but the play in which there is the greatest abundance of life itself, of the reality that is in our minds?[23]

Between inside and outside, strange and familiar, self and other, it is the play that provides the bridge.

Notes

NOTES TO CHAPTER 1, 'INTRODUCTION'

1. Later readers came to expect the play on the manuscript page to come surrounded on all four margins with explanatory notes, or 'scholia', an accumulation of wrestlings with the text and interpretations of the ancient Greek. And readers became accustomed to brief summaries of the plot at the head of the play, a practice continued in various forms into the early modern period.
2. Sydney Grundy, *A Pair of Spectacles* (1890), in George Rowell (ed.), *Nineteenth-Century Plays* (London: Oxford University Press, 1953), 550, (Act III).
3. Dion Boucicault, *The Colleen Bawn* (1860), in Rowell (ed.), *Nineteenth-Century Plays*, 210 (ii. vi).
4. *Plays Pleasant and Unpleasant*, ii. *Pleasant Plays*, Standard Edition (London: Constable, 1931), 3.
5. 'Shakespeare: A Standard Text', *Times Literary Supplement* (17 Mar. 1921), 178; repr. in Bernard F. Dukore (ed.), *Bernard Shaw: The Drama Observed* (University Park, Pa.: Pennsylvania State University Press, 1993), iv. 1369.
6. Repr. in *Samuel Johnson on Shakespeare*, ed. W. K. Wimsatt, Jr. (New York: Hill and Wang, 1960), 40.

NOTES TO CHAPTER 2, 'BEGINNINGS'

1. Brian Friel, *Translations* (London: Faber and Faber, 1984), 15–16.
2. Thomas Hardy, *The Dynasts: A Drama of the Napoleonic Wars, in Three Parts, Nineteen Acts, & One Hundred and Thirty Scenes*, Part First (London: Macmillan, 1904), Preface, p. x.
3. N. Graham Nesmith, 'Arthur Laurents', *Dramatist* (May/June 2003), 11.
4. *King Henry V*, ed. J. H. Walter, The Arden Shakespeare (London: Methuen, 1954), iii, Chorus, 34–5. James Shapiro points out that there is a great deal of systematic dissonance between the elevated tone and expectations of the choral interludes and the often venal, sometimes nasty, frequently ruthless, and altogether more familiar action that is played out in their wake. See *A Year in the Life of William Shakespeare: 1599* (New York: HarperCollins, 2005), 92–4.
5. *Saint Joan*, Standard Edition (London: Constable, 1932), 163.
6. To Ernest Thesiger (18 Mar. 1924), *Collected Letters, 1911–1925*, ed. Dan H. Laurence (New York: Viking, 1985), 872.
7. Tom Stoppard, *Arcadia* (London: Faber and Faber, 1993), 47.

8. Eugène Ionesco, *Four Plays*, tr. Donald M. Allen (New York: Grove Press, 1958), 8.

9. 'The Tragedy of Language', in *Notes et contre-notes* (Paris: Gallimard, 1962), 159.

10. From a journal kept during the writing of the play, *Notes et contre-notes*, 160.

11. *Offending the Audience* [*Publikumbeschimpfung*], tr. Michael Roloff, in *Kaspar and Other Plays* (New York: Farrar, Straus and Giroux, 1969), 9–11.

12. Luigi Pirandello, *Maschere nude* (Milan: Mondadori, 1978), i. 'Premessa dell'Autore', [p. 29]; tr. Eric Bentley in *Naked Masks* (New York: Dutton, 1952), 209. The three plays, two of them further discussed below, are *Six Characters in Search of an Author*; *Each in His Own Way*; and *Tonight We Improvise*.

13. Michael Frayn, *Noises Off* (New York: Anchor Books, 2002), 168.

14. Jean Genet, *The Blacks: A Clown Show*, tr. Bernard Frechtman (New York: Grove Press, 1960), 84–5.

15. Nikolai Evreinov, *Samoe glavnoe*; also in English trans. as *The Chief Thing*. The translation used here is by Christopher Collins, from *Life as Theater: Five Modern Plays* (Ann Arbor: Ardis, 1973).

16. O'Neill adepts will recognize a foreshadowing of Hickey in *The Iceman Cometh*, whose missionary zeal, however, is the reverse of Fregoli's. Hickey, the travelling salesman, wishes to cure the denizens of Harry Hope's hotel of their various 'pipedreams'. In Russian drama, Fregoli has a remote kinship with Luka in Gorky's *Lower Depths*, who, with his evangelist-physician's name, encourages the escapist illusions of the flop-house inhabitants, with dubious results.

17. The term 'psychodrama' has a specific meaning as a psychoanalytic and therapeutic technique pioneered by J. L. Moreno. I use it here with other intent, as a broad term for plays where subjective reality is objectified by theatrical means.

18. Its fountainhead was the late Latin poem, Prudentius' *Psychomacheia* (*c*.400 AD), but an analytical model of the soul and its faculties in contention appears at least as early as Plato's allegory of the Charioteer with the ill-matched horses in the *Phaedrus*.

19. *A Morality of Wisdom, Who Is Christ*, in *The Macro Plays: The Castle of Perseverance, Wisdom, Mankind*, ed. Mark Eccles, Early English Text Society, 262 (London, New York: Oxford University Press, 1969).

20. Brian Friel, *Philadelphia, Here I Come!* (New York: Farrar, Straus, 1965), 11.

21. Appropriately, the classic science-fiction film based on *The Tempest*, MGM's *Forbidden Planet* (1956), explains the embodied projection of murderous feelings in monstrous (Caliban) form on this islanded world (with a Prospero, Miranda, and robot Ariel) as 'Monsters from the Id'. And the theatre critic Ben Brantley writes of a recent production of *The Tempest* at Shakespeare's Globe Theatre, London (with Mark Rylance as Prospero and directed by Tim Carroll), 'there seems to be little question that everything that happens occurs in one man's mind', while the play is 'a Jungian exploration of the psyche at war with itself' (*New York Times*, 6 July 2005).

22. Henrik Ibsen, *Peer Gynt*, tr. Michael Meyer (Garden City, NY: Doubleday, 1963), 106.

23. *The Theatre of the Soul: A Monodrama in One Act*, tr. Marie Protapenko and

Christopher St John, in *Chief Contemporary Dramatists*, 3rd ser., ed. Thomas H. Dickinson (Boston: Houghton Mifflin, 1930), 517–26. The title is also translated as *Corridors of the Soul*, the borrowed Russian word coming from coulisses, for behind the scenes.

24. In Freud's account, these are: *condensation*—fusing elements with a shared attribute, omitting others or decomposing them; *displacement*—of accent or content; *plastic representation*—or 'transformation of latent thought, as expressed in words, into perceptual forms, most commonly visual images'; and a *secondary elaboration* that binds the fragmentary and divergent into apparent coherence. From *The Interpretation of Dreams*, in *The Basic Writings of Sigmund Freud*, tr. and ed. A. A. Brill (New York: Modern Library, 1938), Ch. 6; augmented by Freud's *A General Introduction to Psychoanalysis*, tr. Joan Riviere (Garden City, NY: Doubleday, 1953), Eleventh Lecture.

25. *Six Plays of Strindberg*, tr. Elizabeth Sprigge (Garden City, NY: Doubleday, 1955), 193.

26. *A General Introduction to Psychoanalysis*, 149.

27. *The Emperor Jones*, in Eugene O'Neill, *Complete Plays, 1913–1920* (New York: Library of America, 1988), 1045.

28. Miller has written, 'The first image that occurred to me which was to result in *Death of a Salesman* was of an enormous face the height of the proscenium arch which would appear and then open up, and we would see the inside of a man's head.' Introduction to Miller's *Collected Plays* [vol. i] (New York: Viking, 1957), 23–4.

29. In contrast, in Miller's later play, *After the Fall* (1964), there is no such contest between inner and outer realities in the premises of the stage world. Instead, the opening direction states unequivocally, '*The action takes place in the mind, thought, and memory of Quentin*', and the symbolic setting and the stage rules are shaped accordingly. *Collected Plays*, ii (New York: Viking, 1981), 127.

30. Repr. in W. B. Worthen (ed.), *Modern Drama: Plays/Criticism/Theory* (Fort Worth, Tex.: Harcourt Brace, 1995).

31. John Osborne, *Inadmissible Evidence* (New York: Grove Press, 1965), 9.

32. Erik H. Erikson, *Young Man Luther (New York: Norton, 1962)*.

33. John Osborne, *Luther* (New York: New American Library, 1961), 24 (i, ii).

34. Part of a 'Conversation', in Jonathan Kalb, *Beckett in Performance* (Cambridge: Cambridge University Press, 1991), 240.

NOTES TO CHAPTER 3, 'SEEING AND HEARING'

1. Brecht, *Collected Plays*, v, ed. Ralph Manheim and John Willett (New York: Vintage, 1972), 200–1.

2. A spectacular, immensely successful adaptation of Part One by Irving's house dramatist, W. G. Wills.

3. From Ben Brantley's review of the New York transposition of the RNT (London) production, *New York Times* (7 Mar. 2003), pp. E1, E6.

4. Judith Malina and Julian Beck, *Paradise Now: Collective Creation of the Living Theatre* (New York: Random House, 1971), 78–80.

5. *The Oxford Ibsen*, v, tr. and ed. Walter McFarlane (London: OUP, 1961), 286. In Somerset Maugham's deft comedy *The Constant Wife* (1926), where he takes Ibsen a step further (or perhaps back), Constance tells her philandering but possessive husband that, having achieved the economic independence the ethics of the situation require, she is now off to a holiday in Italy with an adoring male companion. Amazed and hapless, he splutters his outrage at such sauce-for-the-gander as the play moves to a close:

CONSTANCE (*At the door*). Well, then, shall I come back?
JOHN (*After a moment's hesitation*). You are the most maddening, wilful, capricious, wrong-headed, delightful and enchanting woman man was ever cursed with having for a wife. Yes, damn you, come back.
(*She lightly kisses her hand to him and slips out, slamming the door behind her.*)

W. Somerset Maugham, *Six Comedies* (Garden City, NY: Doubleday, 1937), 451.

6. *The Quare Fellow and The Hostage* (New York: Grove Press, 1964), 83.

7. Royal National Theatre, London (1993), directed by Stephen Daldry and brilliantly embodied by the designer, Ian MacNeil.

8. *Mary Stuart: A Tragedy*, tr. Sophie Wilkins (Great Neck, NY: Barron's Educational Series, 1959), 158–9 (v. x).

9. Brecht, *Collected Plays*, v. 83 (Sc. 13).

10. *Coriolanus*, ed. Philip Brockbank, The Arden Shakespeare (London: Methuen, 1976), v. iii. 180–3; the direction as in the First Folio.

11. Arthur Schnitzler, *La Ronde (Reigen)*, tr. Carl Richard Mueller, in *Masterpieces of the Modern Central European Theatre*, ed. Robert W. Corrigan (New York: Collier, 1967), Sc. 4.

12. Anton Chekhov, *Five Plays*, tr. Ronald Hingley, Oxford World Classics (Oxford: Oxford University Press, 1998), 247 (Act I).

13. Tirso de Molina [Gabriel Téllez], *El Burlador de Sevilla y Convidado de Piedra*, in *Comedias*, i, ed. Américo Castro, ser. Clásicos Castellanos (Madrid: Espasa-Calpe, 1967), 226–7.

14. *Götz von Berlichingen, mit der eisernen Hand*, I. in *Dramen* (Cologne: Könemann, 1997), 36–7 (I. v).

15. *The Collected Plays of W. B. Yeats* (New York: Macmillan, 1963), 184–5, 191.

16. Luigi Pirandello, *Maschere nude* (Milan: Mondadori, 1978), i. 54. This is the play as Pirandello revised it. An earlier version (like some English translations) forgoes the masks, and suggests instead distinguishing the Characters by showing them in an unearthly light.

17. *The Picture of Dorian Gray* (1891), ch. 2.

18. *Galileo* in *Collected Plays*, v (Sc. 12).

19. *Heartbreak House*, Standard Edition (London: Constable, 1931), 129–30 (Act III).

20. Victor Hugo, *Théâtre complet*, ed. J.-J. Thierry and Josette Mélèze (Paris: Gallimard, 1963), i. 1499.

21. In the family tree of such sexualized tokens, Ruy Blas's blood-stained lace descends in a straight line from the similarly spotted ribbon sustaining the erotic flirtation between the adolescent page Chérubin and the Countess Almaviva in Beaumarchais's *Marriage of Figaro* (1784).

22. *The Complete Plays of John M. Synge* (New York: Random House, 1935), 83.

23. From the somewhat simplified version of the scene in Paul Selver's translation, repr. in *Contemporary Drama: Nine Plays*, ed E. Bradley Watson and W. Benfield Pressey (New York: Scribner's, 1941), 194, 199. For a fuller recent translation by Peter Majer and Cathy Porter, see Karel Čapek, *Four Plays* (London: Methuen, 1999).

24. Prosper says to the absent Suzanne, 'Ah, you'd like to be clever . . . and swipe my letter American style! [*Ah! tu veux ruser. . . et m'escamoter ma lettre à l'américaine!*]' *Les Pattes de mouche*, ed. W. O. Farnsworth (Boston: D. C. Heath, 1911), ii. i.

25. '*l'air assez cabotin*' say the stage directions, with the artist's dress and facial hair of '*a typical painter or poet of the nineteenth century . . . while the invisible characters must have the greatest possible reality, the Orator should appear unreal.*' Eugène Ionesco, *Théâtre* i (Paris: Gallimard, 1954), 174.

26. *Œuvres complètes de Molière*, ed. M. Félix Lemaistre (Paris: Garnier, 1946), vol. iii, p. 122 (ii. i.).

27. *L'Imposteur, ou le Tartuffe*, in *Œuvres complètes*, vol. ii (ii. iv; iv. iv–vii).

28. How one underlines or qualifies such symbolism in production is a different matter, interestingly aggravated where there are unresolved issues of authorial intention and audience response. See the discussion and illustration of Brecht's play in Ch. 6, below.

29. *The Infernal Machine*, tr. Albert Bermel, in *The Infernal Machine and Other Plays* (New York: New Directions, 1963), 94–6.

30. *Candida*, in *Plays Pleasant and Unpleasant*, ii, Standard Edition (London: Constable, 1931), 76.

31. *The Homecoming* (New York: Grove Press, 1966), 80–2.

NOTES TO CHAPTER 4, 'THE USES OF PLACE'

1. See the description and discussion in Jonathan Kalb's *Beckett in Performance* (Cambridge: Cambridge University Press, 1991), 77–82. 'It unquestionably suggests a specific time and place—an American city, probably New York, after nuclear holocaust' (p. 81).

2. *Endgame* (New York: Grove Press, 1958), 1.

3. *The Shadow of a Gunman* (1923), evoking the guerrilla war of 1919–21; *Juno and the Paycock* (1924); and *The Plough and the Stars* (1926). The latter two are discussed in what follows.

4. Sean O'Casey, *Collected Plays* (London: Macmillan, 1967), i. 36.

5. *The Visit; a Tragi-Comedy* [*Der Besuch der Alten Dame: eine Tragische Komödie*], tr. Paul Bowles (New York: Grove Press, 1962), 67.

6. *The Birthday Party and The Room* (New York: Grove Press, 1961), 109.

7. Eugène Ionesco, *Amédée, The New Tenant, Victims of Duty*, tr. Donald Watson (New York: Grove Press, 1958), 27–8. The full French title is *Amédée ou Comment s'en débarrasser*.

8. Anton Chekhov, *Plays*, tr. Elisaveta Fen (Baltimore: Penguin Books, 1966), [249].

9. Jean Racine, *Athaliah*, in *Five Plays*, tr. Kenneth Muir (New York: Hill and Wang, 1960), 235 (I. i. 1–5).

10. See Rosalind in Shakespeare's *As You Like It*: 'Time travels in divers paces with divers persons. I'll tell you who Time ambles withal, who Time trots withal, who Time gallops withal, and who he stands still withal' (III. ii. 302–5).

11. Thornton Wilder, *The Long Christmas Dinner & Other Plays in One Act* (New York: Coward. McCann and New Haven: Yale University Press, 1931), [1].

12. Stoppard, *Arcadia* (London: Faber and Faber, 1993), 15.

13. Tom Stoppard, interview, *The Village Voice* (New York), 4 Apr. 1995.

14. Alan Ayckbourn, *Time of My Life* (London: Faber and Faber, 1993), 100.

15. E. P. Basté Grangé and X.-A. de Montépin, *Les Frères Corses; or, The Corsican Brothers. A Dramatic Romance in Three Acts and Five Tableaux. Adapted from the Romance of* M. DUMAS (London: Samuel French, n.d.), 20. This English text is a reasonably straightforward translation, with a few adjustments that reflect the staging of Charles Kean, who, like Charles Fechter in France (the original Louis and Fabien) and later Henry Irving in England, played the double role.

16. This side of things, and the politics of modernity versus traditionalism, are much more developed in Dumas's novella, which adopts a non-fictional, reportorial frame and sometimes verges on the ethnographic.

NOTES TO CHAPTER 5, 'THE ROLE OF THE AUDIENCE'

1. *King Richard III*, ed. Antony Hammond, The Arden Shakespeare (London and New York: Methuen, 1981), 148–9.

2. In Hesketh Pearson, *The Life of Oscar Wilde* (London: Methuen, 1946), 224, as reported from shorthand notes taken in the theatre. For other versions, see Richard Ellmann, *Oscar Wilde* (New York: Knopf, 1988), 366.

3. 'The Marvellous Pageant', in *The Interludes of Cervantes*, ed. and tr. S. Griswold Morley (Princeton: Princeton University Press, 1948; repr. Greenwood Press, 1969), 159.

4. *The Knight of the Burning Pestle*, ed. John Doebler, Regents Renaissance Drama ser. (Lincoln, Nebr.: University of Nebraska, 1967), 'Induction', ll. 1–35.

5. Ben Jonson, Beaumont's contemporary, stages a hilarious anti-theatrical assault in *Bartholomew Fair* (1614) where a Puritan divine, Zeal-of-the-Land Busy, rushes in among the (stage) spectators of a profane puppet show, and gets into an argument—which he loses, hands down—with the leading wooden-head of the company.

6. Introduction, *Forty Years On and Other Plays* (London: Faber and Faber, 1971), 10.

7. *Rosencrantz & Guildenstern Are Dead* (New York: Grove Press, 1967), 63 (Act II).

8. *The Persecution and Assassination of Jean-Paul Marat as Performed by the Inmates of the Asylum of Charenton under the Direction of The Marquis de Sade*, tr. Geoffrey Skelton, verse adap. Robin Mitchell (New York: Atheneum, 1965), 100.

9. *The Blacks: A Clown Show*, tr. Bernard Frechtman (New York: Grove Press, 1960), 9–10.

10. Tieck, *The Land of Upside Down*, tr. Oscar Mandel and Maria Kelsen Feder (Rutherford, NJ: Fairleigh Dickinson University, 1978), 37–8. In the standard texts of *Die verkehrte Welt*, the rising of the curtain is preceded by an extraordinary *Symphonie* where the various musical sections are rendered entirely as language. See Ludwig Tieck, *Werke in vier Bänden*, vol. ii, ed. Marianne Thalmann (Munich: Winkler Verlag, 1964), 273–5.

11. As elaborated in the English text. The German text reads, more simply, '*Der Vorhang geht auf. Das Theatre stellt ein Theatre vor* [*The curtain rises. The theatre represents a theatre*]'. *Werke*, vol. ii. 275.

12. Author's 'Premise', in *Naked Masks*, ed. Eric Bentley (New York: Dutton, 1952), 209.

13. *Chiascuno a suo modo*, in *Maschere nude* (Milan: Mondadori, 1978), i. [121]–2.

14. *Major Barbara*, Standard Edition (London: Constable, 1931), 316. (III. i).

15. Letter of 4 Nov. 1895, to Golding Bright, in *Advice to a Young Critic and Other Letters by Bernard Shaw*, ed. E. J. West (New York: Crown Publishers, 1955), 41. The performance of *Mrs Warren's Profession* was long blocked by the Lord Chamberlain in England, so that its audience was actually its readership.

16. *Widowers' Houses*, Independent Theatre Edition (London, 1893), 117–18.

17. *Widowers' Houses*, in *Plays Pleasant and Unpleasant*, vol. i, Standard Edition (London: Constable, 1947), 42 (Act II).

18. *Heartbreak House*, Standard Edition (London: Constable, 1931), 132 (Act III).

19. From a brief manifesto on the theatre (1935), quoted in Edward Mendelsohn, *Early Auden* (New York: Viking, 1981), 263.

20. A celebrated retort by General Cambronne on the field of Waterloo to the demand that he surrender, which has both an official (heroic) and (as here) demotic version.

21. Chekhov wrote to his then editor and friend A. S. Suvorin (4 June 1892): 'I have an interesting idea for a comedy, but I have not thought of an ending yet. He who invents a new ending for a play will usher in a new era! Those damned endings are the very limit! The hero has either to marry or to shoot himself: there is no other way.' (Quoted in *The Seagull Produced by Stanislavsky*, ed. S. D. Balukhaty, tr. David Magarshack (New York: Theatre Arts Books, 1952), 16–17.) In Chekhov's *Ivanov* (1887), the protagonist takes out a revolver, '*rushes offstage and shoots himself*'. In The *Seagull* (1896), the sound of a shot offstage is dismissed, but produces the famously understated curtain line, 'The fact is, Konstantin Gavrilovich has shot himself . . . '. In *Uncle Vanya* (1899)—a revision of the earlier *Wood Demon* (1889) where Vanya shoots himself in the third act and the Astrov figure gets to marry Sonya in the end—Vanya instead tries to shoot the Professor and misses, and no one gets the partner he or she desires. In *Three Sisters* (1901)

'*the hollow sound of a gunshot is heard in the distance*', and the news comes that, not 'the hero', but Irina's worthy though unloved fiancé, the Baron, has been killed in a duel. In *The Cherry Orchard* (1904), the minor figure Epihodov shows a pistol, but there is no shot or suicide; only the sound of the axe in the orchard and the breaking string.

22. 'Epistle Dedicatory', *Man and Superman*, Standard Edition (London: Constable, 1952), pp. viii–ix.

23. Shaw's original ending has Eliza departing with no intention of returning, and the only kiss her Pygmalion, Henry Higgins, gets is from his mother. When Shaw returned to the theatre for the hundredth performance, he found that the notable actor-manager Herbert Beerbohm Tree as Higgins 'had hit on the idea of throwing flowers to Eliza in the brief interval between the end of the play and the fall of the curtain, thus letting the audience know that a marriage would shortly take place between the professor and the flower-girl' (Hesketh Pearson, *Beerbohm Tree: His Life and Laughter* (New York: Harper & Brothers, 1956), 182). Apparently Tree went even further. Before Eliza goes, Higgins loads her with commissions, including buying him a pair of gloves. When the play was later presented in New York, the producer wrote that he had restored to the play a line that Tree had added in London as the final speech—'the line bringing Eliza back for the size of the gloves . . . Frankly, I was *afraid* to omit the line. I felt it would have an enormous commercial value with sentimental America' (Dan H. Laurence, quoting the executive head of Liebler & Co., in Shaw's *Collected Letters, 1911–1925* (New York: Viking, 1985), 253). Shaw countered such efforts by adding a postscript to the published play explaining how and why Eliza married the nonentity Freddy Eynsford Hill and not Higgins. The contest over the ending continued nevertheless, with Shaw losing out in Gabriel Pascal's excellent film version, and of course in *My Fair Lady*.

24. J. L. Styan's name for a dominant strain in modern drama. See *The Dark Comedy: The Development of Modern Comic Tragedy*, 2nd edn., (Cambridge: Cambridge University Press, 1968). *Playboy* citations are from *The Complete Works of John M. Synge* (New York: Random House, 1935).

25. David H. Greene and Edward M. Stephens, *J. M. Synge 1871–1909* (New York: Collier Books, 1961), 255.

26. Ibid. 257–8.

27. Peter Nichols, *Joe Egg* (New York: Grove Press, 1967), 9.

28. E. Martin Browne, *The Making of T. S. Eliot's Plays* (Cambridge: Cambridge University Press, 1969), 36. Browne, who produced and directed, writes, 'This sermon has always been the best-remembered scene of the play, the one which comes instantly to the mind of almost everyone who thinks of it' (p. 47).

29. *Waiting for Lefty* (New York: Dramatists Play Service, [n.d.]), 31.

30. From a 1961 interview, quoted in Margaret Brenman-Gibson, *Clifford Odets, American Playwright* (New York: Atheneum, 1981), 315–16. Cf. Harold Clurman's memoir of The Group Theater, *The Fervent Years* (New York: Hill and Wang, 1957), 138–9: 'Audiences and actors had become one.'

31. *The Main Thing*, in Nikolai Evreinov, *Life as Theatre: Five Modern Plays*, tr. and ed. Christopher Collins (Ann Arbor: Ardis, 1973), 66.
32. *The Entertainer* (New York: Bantam, 1967), 109.
33. *The Balcony*, tr. Bernard Frechtman, rev. version (New York: Grove Press, 1966), 95–6.
34. From David Magarshack's translation, modified, in *The Storm and Other Plays* (New York: Hill and Wang, 1960), 82. Magarshack notes that the famous words to the audience were an inspired addition in an 1842 revision for publication (p. ix).
35. *The Firebugs* [*Herr Biedermann und die Brandstifter*], tr. Michael Bullock (New York: Hill and Wang, 1985), 50–1; pub. in Britain as *The Fire Raisers* (London: Methuen, 1962).
36. *The Bedbug*, tr. Max Hayward, in *Three Soviet Plays*, ed. Michael Glenny (Harmondsworth: Penguin Books, 1966), 75.

NOTES TO CHAPTER 6, 'THE SHAPE OF THE ACTION'

1. *Six Characters in Search of an Author*, tr. Edward Storer, in *Naked Masks*, ed. Eric Bentley (New York: Dutton, 1952), 260.
2. 'On the Tragic Art' (1792), *Essays Æsthetical and Philosophical* (London: George Bell, 1875), 356.
3. From *Eugene O'Neill: A Documentary Film*, directed by Ric Burns. Typescript, Steeplechase Films, 2004, p. 18.
4. Nikolai Evreinov, *Life as Theatre: Five Modern Plays*, tr. and ed. Christopher Collins (Ann Arbor: Ardis, 1973), 117–18.
5. Quoted in Mark Lawson, 'A False Start, and then it all Came Together', *Guardian* (16 Aug. 1997).
6. 'Originally the idea was just that Marlene was 'writing off' her niece, Angie, because she'd never make it; I didn't yet have the plot idea that Angie was actually Marlene's own child.' From a 1984 interview, published in *The Bedford Introduction to Drama*, 3rd edn., ed. Lee A. Jacobus (Boston: Bedford Books, 1997), 1413.
7. From a letter of 24 May 1923 published as 'Mr. Shaw on Mr. Shaw', *New York Times* (12 June 1927), sec. 7, p. 1.
8. See e.g. his observations in 'Two Ways of Playing Mother Courage', included in his *Collected Plays*, v, ed. Ralph Manheim and John Willett (New York: Vintage, 1972), 387–8. Brecht writes (endorsing Helene Weigel's performance), 'The merchant-mother became a great living contradiction, and it was this contradiction which utterly disfigured and deformed her'.
9. For example, in Scene 5, with the wagon stopped in a devastated village, the Chaplain needs linen to bind the wounds of a peasant family. Courage refuses to part with her fine officers' shirts, but in the original, protesting all the while, she reluctantly parts with one shirt after another, action at odds with word: '(. . . *she rips up another shirt*) I'm not giving anything, you can't make me, I've got to think of myself'. As the scene ends, '*Mother Courage goes on ripping up shirts.*' In the revised version, Kattrin has first to threaten her mother with a board, and then, as

Courage remains adamant, '(*The chaplain picks her up from the step* [of the wagon] *and puts her down on the ground. Then he fishes out some shirts and tears them into strips.*' *Collected Plays*, v. 391–2, 175–6.

10. Ivan Turgenev, *A Month in the Country*, tr. Richard Freeborn, The World's Classics (London: Oxford University Press, 1941), 79 (Act III).

11. In Calderón de la Barca's allegorical play, *The Great Theater of the World* (1642), 'the Author' (i.e. producer and presenter) is no less than God. The initial stage direction reads, '*Enter the* AUTHOR *in a starry mantle and nine rays of light grouped in threes* [*potencias*] *on his hat* [*Sale el* AUTOR *con manto de estrellas, y potencias en el sombrero*]', tr. Mack Hendricks Singleton, in *Masterpieces of the Spanish Golden Age*, ed. Angel Flores (New York: Rinehart, 1957), 368.

12. *Old Times* (London: Methuen, 1971), 32 (Act I).

13. Michael Frayn, *Copenhagen* (London: Methuen, 1998), 3.

14. *Cain*, III. i. 465 ff., in *The Complete Poetical Works of Byron* (Boston: Houghton Mifflin, 1933), 653–4.

15. *Antigone*, tr. Elizabeth Wycoff, in *Sophocles I*, in *The Complete Greek Tragedies*, ed. David Grene and Richmond Lattimore (Chicago and London: University of Chicago, 1954), pp. 187–91. In a later edition with the translation by Grene (1991), the less freely rendered last lines read:

> See what I suffer and who made me suffer
> because I gave reverence to what claims reverence.

16. Athol Fugard, John Kani, and Winston Ntshona, *The Island*, in W. B. Worthen (ed.) *Modern Drama: Plays/Criticism/Theory* (Fort Worth, Tex.: Harcourt Brace, 1995), 674.

17. The phrase, 'the principle of thematic recurrence', occurs in Joseph Kerman's discussion of *Otello* in his seminal *Opera as Drama* (New York: Vintage Books, 1959), 157. He treats the 'central use' of such recurrence in Verdi and Wagner. See especially on *Otello* and *Tristan*, 154, 158, and 212.

18. *Four Plays by Eugene Ionesco*, tr. Donald M. Allen (New York: Grove Press, 1958), 42.

19. *Proust* (1931; New York: Grove Press, 1957), 71.

20. *Collected Shorter Plays* (New York: Grove Weidenfeld, 1984), 157. Here—as in perusing a musical score—the divergence between reading and performance is acute. The reader is most unlikely to obey the da capo injunction in the stage direction; but the knowing reader will wish to consider how the stipulated repetition can and will work.

21. *Collected Plays*, v., 210, 136–7. In production, Brecht emphasized the circularity. He noted in his 'Model' that 'the wagon is hauled off a completely empty stage recalling scene I. Mother Courage described a complete circle with it on the revolving stage, passing the footlights for the last time' (p. 384).

22. From a letter giving a sketch of the incomplete play, written to seduce the actress Eleanor Robson into imagining herself in the role. Shaw writes, 'I am half tempted

to take the play right up to the skies at the end because there is a sort of desecration in your marrying even your poet. However that is not human; so I daresay I will be able to get the marriage on to the right plane by a twist of my finger if you will pray for me often enough'. Eleanor Robson Belmont, *The Fabric of Memory* (New York: Farrar, Straus & Cudahy, 1957), 39, from a letter of 4 July 1905. In the play Barbara will marry her poet, but not before, in Shaw's stage direction, '*She is transfigured*', in her renewed calling to do God's work.

NOTES TO CHAPTER 7, 'THE ACTION OF WORDS'

1. In *Georg Büchner: Complete Plays and Prose*, tr. Carl Richard Mueller (New York: Hill and Wang, 1963), p. 71 (IV. ix).
2. Büchner had precedent for Lucille's effective speech gesture. At least one contemporary memoirist, very likely among Büchner's sources, spoke of having seen more than ten women who, not up to taking poison, 'cried out "*Vive le Roi*," and by that means charged the abominable tribunal with the task of ending their days. Some not to survive a spouse, others a lover, others through loathing of life, almost none through royalist fanaticism.' Honoré Riouffe, *Memoires d'un détenu, pour servir à l'histoire de la tyrannie de Robespierre* (Paris [London?], 1795), 69. It is worth pondering the affirmative mood of the phrase, when presumably 'A bas la Révolution' would have been equally effective.
3. *Adam Bede*, in *The Works of George Eliot*, Cabinet Edition (Edinburgh and London: Blackwood, 1878), i. 175.
4. Tolstoy based his peasant speech on the dialect of the Tula region where he lived. Heretofore dialect in drama was traditionally and nearly universally attached to comic characters. To make plebeian dialect the verbal medium for a full-length play, and a deeply serious one at that, had a certain shock value in itself. However, Tolstoy was not alone in this era of dramatic ferment. Gerhart Hauptmann wrote his landmark play *The Weavers* (1892), set in the 1840s, in Silesian dialect originally, but then nervously changed it into standard German for a Berlin production. The Irish playwrights Synge and Lady Gregory found in dialect a poetic resource, liberating rather than restrictive, and extended it beyond comedy in, for example, Synge's *Riders of the Sea* (written 1902) and *Deirdre of the Sorrows* (1909), and Lady Gregory's *The Gaol Gate* (1906). Even so, George Moore, an uncompromising realist in fiction, felt differently when it came to a proposed collaboration on a Celtic tragedy with the third force in the new Irish theatre, W. B. Yeats. Moore reports himself saying that dialect 'would render the heroic characters farcical. "Folk is always farce. It is not until the language has been strained through many brilliant minds that tragedy can be written in it."' (George Moore, *Ave* (New York: Appleton, 1911), 360–1.
5. *The Power of Darkness; or, 'If One Claw is Caught, the Whole Bird is Lost'*, I. xix. I draw here on F. D. Reeve's translation in *An Anthology of Russian Plays*, i. *1790–1890* (New York: Vintage, 1961), 394.
6. Edward Bond, *Saved*, in *Plays: One* (London: Eyre Methuen, 1977), 113–14 (Sc. 10).

7. Note to *Saved*, in *Plays: One*, 309.
8. The American playwright James A. Herne, himself a pioneer of naturalistic acting, also took the logic of naturalistic speech to its limiting extreme in the remarkable ending of his eminently successful play, set in Maine (where the regional style is supposedly laconic), *Shore Acres* (1892). Herne there provides a diminuendo close like the endings Chekhov favoured, but with no music or distant sound effects. He leaves us one remaining character, Uncle Nat, shutting down the scene and fastening up for the night, musing on all that has happened and what is likely to be. The stage direction reads, '*His thoughts are reflected in his face, but not a word is spoken. The scene is played in absolute silence.*' He sinks into his rocking chair, rises, moves to various points—window, stove, door, stairs—but his action and expression are 'business'—parallel or expressive accompaniment—rather than a pantomime substitute for language. The script asks for an extensive play of mood and feeling, with the focus of Nat's reflections often intelligible, but sometimes not—as in the direction, '*For a moment he is lost in thought.*' The words that key most of the thought are set down as if in monologue, but as *not* to be spoken, and yet furnishing and elaborating the content. The scene is in effect the full dramaturgic expression of what naturalistic acting can provide where the premiss is the incommensurateness of speech with feeling and thought. The words appear as the mere trace of thought and emotion, a rubric, a scaffolding. Herne's bold venture is to pull away the scaffolding and ask the enactment to stand on its own. See *Shore Acres and Other Plays*, ed. Mrs James A. Herne (New York: Samuel French, 1928), 120–1.
9. *Aminta: Favola Boschereccia*, tr. Leigh Hunt, as *Amyntas*, repr. in *The Genius of the Italian Theater*, ed. Eric Bentley (New York: New American Library, 1964), 175 (II. iii).
10. *Tamburlaine the Great, Parts I and II*, ed. John D. Jump (Lincoln, Nebr.: Univ. of Nebraska, 1967), 84–5 (I. v. i. 160–73). On 'Inexpressibility Topoi', see Ernst Robert Curtius, *European Literature of the Latin Middle Ages*, tr. Willard Trask (Princeton: Princeton University Press, 1973), 159–72. As Curtius notes, 'From the time of Homer onwards, there are examples in all ages.'
11. The asides are sometimes cut, as in a fine 2003 production with Christopher Plummer as Lear, Jonathan Miller directing. This is a mistake, unless the point is to ensure that Cordelia's subsequent declarations, that she has nothing to say, be taken as wilful stubbornness, even petulance, like that of her father.
12. Translated by Angela Ingold and Theodore Hoffman as *Ruzzante Returns from the Wars*, in *The Classic Theater I: Six Italian Plays*, ed. Eric Bentley (New York: Doubleday Anchor, 1958), 61–2.
13. Greg Tate, 'Bewitching the Other: In *Fires in the Mirror*, Anna Deavere Smith Wears Her Words', *The Village Voice* (New York) (21 July 1992), 98.
14. 'Introduction', *Fires in the Mirror* (New York: Anchor, Doubleday, 1993), p. xxvii.
15. 'Mr. Shaw on Mr. Shaw', *New York Times* (12 June 1927).
16. Richard Brinsley Sheridan, *Plays,* Everyman's Library (London: Dent, 1949), 36 (III. i).

17. *Tartuffe and Other Plays*, tr. Donald M. Frame (New York: New American Library, 1967), 249.

18. 'Writing for the Theatre' (speech at the National Student Drama Festival, 1962), repr. in *The New British Drama*, ed. Henry Popkin (New York: Grove Press, 1964), 578–9.

19. *The Birthday Party and The Room* (New York: Grove Press, 1961), 80 (Act III).

20. Alan Bennett, *Single Spies: Two Plays about Guy Burgess and Anthony Blunt & Talking Heads: Six Monologues* (New York: Summit Books, 1990), 79–80.

21. Edward Albee, *The Zoo Story, The Death of Bessie Smith, The Sandbox* (New York: Coward McCann, 1960), 25.

22. David Mamet, *Glengarry Glen Ross* (New York: Grove Press, 1954), 38–40.

23. Arthur Miller, *After the Fall* (New York: Viking, 1964), 60 (Act I).

24. Letter of 15 Jan. 1903, *Bernard Shaw's Letters to Siegfried Trebitsch*, ed. Samuel A. Weiss (Stanford, Calif.: Stanford University Press, 1986), 36.

25. *Lady Windermere's Fan*, in *The Importance of Being Earnest and Other Plays*, ed. Peter Raby, Oxford Drama Library (Oxford: Clarendon Press, 1995), 43, 45 (Act III).

26. W. B. Yeats, 'The Play, the Player, and the Scene' (1904), in *Plays and Controversies* (New York: Macmillan, 1924), 120–1. The tendency to deplore such pleasurable deployment of heightened dialogue and rhetorical amplitude in the name of 'true language', or 'Nature', is already manifest in Macaulay, who writes, in arguing the excellence of Machiavelli's *Mandragola* at the expense of Congreve and Sheridan, 'The sure sign of the general decline of an art is the frequent occurrence, not of deformity, but of misplaced beauty. In general, tragedy is corrupted by eloquence, and comedy by wit.' From his *Edinburgh Review* essay of 1827, 'Machiavelli', in *Critical and Miscellaneous Essays*, rev. edn. (New York: Appleton, 1896), i. 81.

27. *Three Plays by Noel Coward*, introd. Edward Albee (New York: Dell, 1965), 204, 213.

28. Anton Chekhov, *Five Plays*, tr. Ronald Hingley, Oxford World's Classics (Oxford: Oxford University Press, 1998), 290–2 (Act IV).

29. Tr. David Grene, in *The Complete Greek Tragedies*, ed. David Grene and Richmond Lattimore, 2nd edn. (Chicago: University of Chicago Press, 1991), 62.

30. As in Noel Coward's *Hay Fever*, end of Act II.

31. In Wilde's exchanges, even a professedly naive young person is capable of effective innuendo, as when Cecily in *The Importance of Being Earnest* remarks to Gwendolyn, who claims to be engaged like herself to one Ernest Worthing, 'It seems to me, Miss Fairfax, that I am trespassing on your valuable time. No doubt you have many other calls of a similar character to make in the neighbourhood' (Act II, p. 290).

32. Edward Albee, *Who's Afraid of Virginia Woolf?* (New York: Atheneum, 1963), 13–14.

33. *Plays & Poems of W. S. Gilbert* (New York: Random House, 1932), 158–9. The Abbot and Costello vaudeville and radio routine beginning 'Who's on first?',

immortalized in the films *One Night in the Tropics* (1940) and *The Naughty Nineties* (1945), is doubtless the most famous such *lazzo* of comic misunderstanding.

34. The ever rational Odysseus complains:

> Each force in Nature, creates its opposite
> And fights with this; no room for any third.
> What quenches fire will not make water boil
> And turn to steam; likewise the opposite.
> Yet here appears a deadly foe of both,
> That makes fire doubt: should it not flow like water?
> And water: should it haply burn like fire?
> The hard-press'd Trojan, fleeing the Amazon
> Shelters behind a Grecian shield; the Greek
> Defends him from the maiden's blade, and both
> Trojan and Greek are almost forced, despite
> The rape of Helen, to hold each other friends . . .

(*Penthesilea*, tr. Humphrey Trevelyan in Heinrich von Kleist, *Plays*, ed. Walter Hinderer, German Library, xxv (New York: Continuum, 1982), 170 (Sc. 1)).

35. *Penthesilea*, 265–6 (Sc. 24). On *Küsse* and *Bisse*, Penthesilea says, *Das reimt sich*, a reflexive form of 'it rhymes,' meaning they go together, they are in accord. It is not just the words, the signifiers, that here are supposed to rhyme, but the signified; *und wer recht von Herzen liebt, | Kann schon das eine für das andre greifen.*

36. From *a-mazos* in Greek popular etymology, the Amazons being said to have earned their name by cutting off their right breasts to facilitate the use of the bow.

37. *The Rivals*, p. 44 (iii. iii).

38. *Jumpers* (New York: Grove Press, 1981), 76–7.

39. William Archer, *Play-Making: A Manual of Craftsmanship* (Boston: Small, Maynard and Co., 1912), 34.

40. To Olga Knipper, playing Masha, Chekhov wrote: 'Vershinin says 'Tram tam tam'—as a question, and you—as an answer. And it seems such an original thing to you that you say this 'tram-tram' [*sic*] smilingly, and then break into laughter—not loud, just a little laugh' (letter of 20 Jan. 1901). For an incisive account of these exchanges, see David Magarshack, *Chekhov the Dramatist* (New York: Hill and Wang, 1960), 260–1.

41. *Music in London 1890–1894*, Standard Edition (London: Constable, 1950), iii, 133–4.

42. Tennessee Williams, *Plays 1937–1955* (New York: Library of America, 2000), 826.

43. Letter of 17 June 1922, *Bernard Shaw's Letters to Siegfried Trebitsch*, ed. Samuel A. Weiss (Stanford, Calif.: Stanford University Press, 1986), 233.

44. Letter of 5 Aug. 1948, ibid. 449.

45. Letters of 10 Dec. 1902 and 15 Jan. 1903, ibid. 26, 36.

46. 'Mr. Shaw on Printed Plays', *Times Literary Supplement* (17 May 1923), 339. The original article, 'The Printed Play' (10 May 1923, pp. 309–10), crediting Shaw with

pioneering modern textual practice in stage directions and otherwise exceedingly astute, was by Edward Shanks. Shaw's reflections on *Guy Domville* appeared in *Saturday Review* (12 Jan. 1895), repr. in *Our Theatres in the Nineties* (London: Constable, 1954), i. 6–9.

NOTES TO CHAPTER 8, 'READING MEANINGS'

1. Dominic Behan, *My Brother Brendan* (New York: Simon and Schuster, 1965), 159.
2. 'Afterword' to *Camino Real*, in Tennessee Williams, *Plays 1937–1955* (New York: Library of America, 2000), 747.
3. *Misalliance*, Standard Edition (London: Constable, 1953), 130.
4. Lahr's intuitive understanding and gradual finding of himself in the role is admirably chronicled in the chapter on *Waiting for Godot* in John Lahr's biographical memoir of his father, *Notes on a Cowardly Lion* (New York: Knopf, 1969). John Lahr reports that when the director, Herbert Berghof, 'was asked by reporters, "What do you think Mr. Lahr means when he says he doesn't understand the play?" the director's reply would surprise the reporters and even Lahr himself: "I think he understands it better than any critic I've ever read, better than anybody who has ever read about it, and I think he understands it better than Beckett"' (p. 281). That the question of 'meaning' was shifted from play and author to the player's disclaimer ('What do you think Mr. Lahr means?') has its funny side.
5. Letter to Alan S. Downer, 21 Jan. 1948; printed in *Collected Letters, 1926–1950*, ed. Dan H. Laurence (London: Max Reinhardt, 1988), 813. Shaw, an avid photographer, ignores for the moment the capabilities of that art, the effect of framing and selection, and the irresistible inclination in the human mind to make sense of (to find pattern and meaning in) any finite field of perception.
6. For the sake of a requisite literalism, the translation is largely my own. A useful Spanish text may be found in *Diez comedias del Siglo de Oro*, ed. H. Alpern and J. Martel (New York and London: Harper, 1939).
7. *Rhetoric*, III, 1410^b.
8. Félix Lope de Vega Carpio, *El Castigo sin Venganza*, ed. José María Díez Borque, Clásicos Castellanos, NS (Madrid: Espasa-Calpe, 1987), 114. See also Jill Booty's clarifying and insightful prose translation in Lope de Vega, *Five Plays* (New York: Hill and Wang, 1961).
9. The story's dramatic power and interest attracted Euripides (*Hippolytus*), Racine (*Phèdre*), and O'Neill (*Desire Under the Elms*) among others. Lope makes no allusion to the classical avatars of the figures in his triangle, and unlike his principal rivals, he puts his Theseus figure at the apex.
10. See Friedrich Dürrenmatt, 'Problems of the Theatre' (*Theaterprobleme*, 1955), tr. Gerhard Nellhaus, *Tulane Drama Review*, 3 (Oct. 1958), 20–1. Dürrenmatt's word is *der Einfall*, for which there is no easy equivalent. Nellhaus also translates it as 'inventive idea', and one dictionary renders it as 'brain-wave'. Dürrenmatt associates this kind of dramatic invention with the genre of comedy (Aristophanes, he says, 'lives by conceits'), but that is too limiting. Eliot's 'notorious' phrase (as he later characterized it) turned up in his deconstruction of *Hamlet* (1919), which

may be found in *Selected Prose of T. S. Eliot*, ed. Frank Kermode (New York: Harcourt Brace Jovanovich/Farrar, Straus and Giroux, 1975), 45–9.

11. Jean-Paul Sartre, *No Exit and Three Other Plays* (New York: Vintage, 1960), 17–18. I occasionally adopt a more literal rendering than in Stuart Gilbert's elegant translation, from the text in Sartre's *Théâtre* (Paris: Gallimard, 1947). In Britain, the translation was called *In Camera*.

12. *Maschere nude* (Milan: Mondadori, 1978), i. 115. The word is *finzione*, which implies both fiction and wilful deception.

13. The play follows rather closely Arthur Waley's truncated English translation of *Tanikō* (*The Valley-Hurling*), a Noh play that he attributes to Zenchiku, retranslated for Brecht by his collaborator Elizabeth Hauptmann. See Waley's *The Nō Plays of Japan* (New York: Knopf, 1922), 185–93. In *Tanikō*, the boy's motivation for joining the ritual climb (not an expedition) is to pray for his mother.

14. The final version of *Der Jasager*, with *Der Neinsager*, can be found in *Die Stücke von Bertolt Brecht in einem Band* (Frankfurt am Main: Suhrkamp, 1985), 247–54. My reconstruction of the series is not the common view, but depends for evidence on the resistance to textual revision in Weil's music, as found in the excellent rendering of the original *Jasager* recorded in Düsseldorf (MGM E-3270 (1956)), Siegfried Kohler conducting, under the supervision of Lotte Lenya. As performed, the libretto follows the words of the present *Neinsager* until just short of the boy's declaration, 'No! I don't agree,' and then continues with those of the present *Jasager*, omitting the boy's request to the students that he not be left to die alone. Both plays may be found in a translation by Gerhard Nellhaus in *Accent* (autumn, 1946), 14–24.

15. Letter of 25 May 1883, in *Ibsen: Letters and Speeches*, ed. Evert Sprinchorn (New York: Hill and Wang, 1964), 218.

16. Letter of 30 Apr. 1871, ibid. 124.

17. Letter of 24 June 1882, ibid. 208.

18. Letter of 18 June 1881, ibid. 195.

19. How Yeats characterizes the second term in a dialogue between some of his own works in his poem, 'The Circus Animals' Desertion'.

20. *The Father*, in *Six Plays of Strindberg*, tr. Elizabeth Sprigge (Garden City, NY: Doubleday, 1955), 36.

21. Other plays where the conceit revisited is the vehicle of a disputatious rhetorical strategy include Émile Augier's answer to Alexandre Dumas *fils*'s *The Lady of the Camelias* (1852) after its phenomenal, worldwide success. Augier's premiss, in the spirit of a thought experiment, is also a rhetorician's rebuttal of the implicit argument, sentimental and romantic, of the Dumas play. Dumas has his courtesan heroine, Marguerite Gautier, give up the young lover of good family who wants to marry her in a noble sacrifice for love which ends in her death, a death that in Dumas's hands hints at her Christ-like virtues. Augier, in *The Marriage of Olympe* (1855), takes a minor figure from Dumas's play, also a courtesan, and asks the hypothetical question, 'Well, what if the marriage had gone forward?' With a

husband of even higher pedigree, opulent circumstances, an aristocratic family willing to accept her, Olympe is bored. A vital, vivid character, she is stifled by the propriety, the respectability, the codes of behaviour. Her vulgar mother shows up; she takes up with disreputable theatre people; and in her hard-nosed effort to break free of her comfortable cage without forgoing her marital advantages, she precipitates catastrophe. Both plays may be found in translation in *Camille and Other Plays*, ed. Stephen S. Stanton (New York: Hill and Wang, 1957)

22. Sybil Thorndike, 'Thanks to Bernard Shaw', in Raymond Mander and Joe Mitchenson's *Theatrical Companion to Shaw* (London: Rockcliff, 1954), 14.

23. Rolf Hochhuth, *The Deputy* [*Der Stellvertreter*], tr. Richard and Clara Winston (New York: Grove Press, 1964), 217.

24. Hochhuth reports a serendipitous discovery after the fact, justifying the Pope's gesture in this wholly invented scene. He notes in the historical appendix to the printed text that he later found in the memoirs of the Pope's physician that Pius was an obsessive handwasher, disinfecting his hands after every audience.

25. Trans. from the text in Thomas Moody Campbell (ed.), *German Plays of the Nineteenth Century*, (New York: Appleton-Century-Crofts, 1930), 215 (I. iv).

26. David Magarshack (tr.), *The Storm* [*Groza*] *and Other Plays* (New York: Hill and Wang, 1960), 137, 141, slightly altered. The scrap of verse is from 'Evening Meditation on Seeing the Great Northern Lights' by the eighteenth-century scientist, poet, and historian M. V. Lomonosov.

27. Ibsen, *Hedda Gabler and Three Other Plays*, tr. Michael Meyer (New York: Doubleday Anchor, 1961), 185.

28. Chekhov, *Plays*, tr. Elisaveta Fen (Baltimore: Penguin, 1966), 125, 145.

29. I use Bayard Quincy Morgan's respectful if ungainly verse translation, modified when necessary (New York: Frederick Ungar, 1955). Lessing adopted blank verse as his medium, using Shakespeare as his model, much influencing his great German successors.

NOTES TO CHAPTER 9, 'PRIMAL ATTRACTIONS'

1. *Tom Stoppard in Conversation*, ed. Paul Delaney (Ann Arbor: University of Michigan Press, 1994), 200. The actual performance, directed by Nevill Coghill and Graham Binns, took place in the gardens of Worcester College in 1949. Though Stoppard knew it only by hearsay, it left its mark on the script Stoppard later wrote with Marc Norman for the film *Shakespeare in Love* (1998)—showing that Stoppard, like Shakespeare, knows how to take advantage of a good thing. The film ends with Shakespeare writing *Twelfth Night* (with voice-over), intercut with views of Viola walking on '*a vast and empty beach*' away from the shipwreck she has just survived. For the last shot, the script reads:

EXT[ERIOR]. BEACH. DAY.
DISSOLVE slowly to VIOLA, walking away up the beach towards her brave new world.

2. In point of fact, the Folio text, from which all others derive, does not even say, 'Exit Ariel'. Prospero, who has been promising Ariel his freedom at frequent intervals, gives him one last assignment appropriate to a spirit of the air: to see that the refurbished ship taking the castaway King of Naples and his party home, along with Prospero and Miranda, has the benefit of calm seas and auspicious gales:

> My *Ariel*; chicke
> That is thy charge. Then to the Elements
> Be free, and fare thou well.

He thereupon invites the marvelling Italians into his magician's cell to hear his tale, and the stage direction reads, '*Exeunt omnes*'. But Prospero either lingers on or then returns to speak the Epilogue, still in character but (he says) with his magic powers gone. He needs must beg the hands and breath of the audience for the release that will enable him to leave 'this bare Island' (now meaning also the stage) and fill his sails for Naples. Elizabethan scripts were open to variation and accrual in the course of performance and revival, and this playhouse Epilogue could very well have been an afterthought. But in any case, the Epilogue changes the programme with respect to Ariel, relieving him of his assignment, and few modern productions miss the chance to stage his early release.

3. 'Show and Tell', *New York Times* (30 July 2004), p. A19.

4. Strehler's production, initially 1977–8 in the Piccolo Teatro of Milan, continued to evolve in repertory, and then travelled to America in 1984. Beckerman talks about it in 'The Odd Business of Play Reviewing', *Shakespeare Quarterly*, 36 (1986), 588–93.

5. As in the First Folio (1623), spelling regularized, III. iii.

6. The description is arguably in the form given by the scrivener, Ralph Crane, hired to make decent copy for the typesetters from either the author's rough draft or some other playhouse papers. It could reflect Crane's own spectator experience, now rendered with a reader in mind. See Stephen Orgel's edition of *The Tempest*, The Oxford Shakespeare (Oxford and New York: Oxford University Press, 1987), 57–8; and The Arden Shakespeare edition (3rd ser.) of Virginia Mason Vaughan and Alden T. Vaughan (Walton-on-Thames: Thomas Nelson and Sons, 1999), 129–30.

7. In *Professional Secrets: An Autobiography of Jean Cocteau Drawn from his Lifetime Writings*, ed. Robert Phelps, tr. Richard Howard (New York: Harper & Row, 1972), 90, 92.

8. Merlin is the villain of the piece, and is draining the life out of Camelot through his pernicious influence, which includes Arthur's besotted enchantment with the false Gawain. The play has elements of a personal allegory in which magic and its paralysing, phantasmagoric spell also stand in for Cocteau's opium habit.

9. *Orpheus*, tr. John Savacool, in *The Infernal Machine and Other Plays by Jean Cocteau* (New York: New Directions, 1963), 142.

10. *Orpheus*, tr. Savacool, 148. For 'magic' Cocteau's text reads *prodigieux* and *prodige* (a wonder, a marvel).

11. Quoted in Francis Steegmuller, *Cocteau: A Biography* (Boston: Atlantic Monthly/Little, Brown Books, 1970), 383. Cocteau's full text of *Orphée* may be found, along with the script and stills from his thoroughly reimagined film, in an edition by E. Freeman, Blackwell's French Texts (Oxford: Blackwell, 1976).

12. From Dudley Fitts's translation in *The Infernal Machine and Other Plays*, 167, brought closer to the original text found in Cocteau, *Théâtre I* (Paris: Gallimard, 1948).

13. An alternative tradition has him blinded for having seen Athene bathing, like Actaeon, who is transformed and destroyed for coming upon a naked Artemis similarly engaged.

14. *Oedipus the King*, tr. David Grene, in *Sophocles I*, in *The Complete Greek Tragedies*, ed. David Grene and Richmond Lattimore, 2nd edn. (Chicago: University of Chicago Press, 1991), 70 (ll. 1386–90).

15. See the 'Sunshine through the Rain' segment in Kurosawa's film *Dreams* (*Yume*, 1990), where the young boy, heedless of warning, witnesses the foxes' wedding procession.

16. The disturbances that led to Belgium's independence of the Netherlands broke out in Brussels after a performance of Daniel Auber's opera on a libretto by Eugène Scribe, *La Muette de Portici*, on 25 Aug., 1830.

17. Shaw, *Plays Pleasant and Unpleasant*, vol. ii, Standard Edition (London: Constable, 1931), 19.

18. 'The Man and the Echo', in *The Collected Poems of W. B. Yeats* (London: Macmillan, 1963), 393. Unimpressed, Paul Muldoon (channelling Auden) replies:

> . . . "Did that play of mine
> Send out certain men (*certain* men?)
>
> the English shot . . . ?"
> the answer is "Certainly not."
>
> If Yeats had saved his pencil-lead
> would certain men have stayed in bed?

'Wystan', from '7, Middagh Street', in *Poems 1968–1998* (New York: Farrar, Straus and Giroux, 2001), 178. And yet, Yeats and Lady Gregory's play about answering the call of an abused and indomitable nation, *Cathleen ni Houlihan*, had iconic status, and was frequently performed and much read in the years of a new generation's growing up before the Rebellion. One spectator of the 1902 original production (Stephen Gwynn) anticipated Yeats's later auto-interrogation: 'I went home asking myself if such plays should be produced unless one was prepared for people to go out to shoot and be shot.' R. F. Foster, *W. B. Yeats: A Life*, i (Oxford and New York: Oxford University Press, 1997), 262. And while under sentence of death for her part in the Easter Rebellion, the imprisoned Countess Constance Markievicz declared, distinctly echoing the play, 'they shall be remembered forever, and even poor me will not be forgotten'.

19. In *Sophocles I*, tr. David Grene, in *The Complete Greek Tragedies*, ed. David Grene and Richmond Lattimore, 2nd edn. (Chicago: University of Chicago Press, 1991), 62.

20. David Grene's vigorous translation, in *Greek Tragedies*, vol. iii, ed. David Grene and Richmond Lattimore (Chicago: University of Chicago Press, 1960), 47.

21. *Yale Theatre*, 25 (1994), 89–90. The play was produced, along with André Gide's and Heiner Müller's Philoktetes plays, at the Kaaitheater, Brussels, in a series called 'Philoktetes-Variations', directed by Jan Ritsema. The same actors appeared in all three variations. Jesurun's play and the production are discussed in Peter A. Campbell's Ph.D. diss., 'The Postmodern Remaking of Greek Tragedy' (New York: Columbia University, 2003).

22. A production photograph in the printed text shows an intimate (and touching) embrace, but not a mouth-on-mouth kiss.

23. 'The Play, the Player, and the Scene' (1904), in *Plays and Controversies* (New York: Macmillan, 1924), 120.

Bibliography

Albee, Edward, *The Zoo Story, The Death of Bessie Smith, The Sandbox* (New York: Coward McCann, 1960).

—— *Who's Afraid of Virginia Woolf?* (New York: Atheneum, 1963).

Archer, William, *Play-Making: A Manual of Craftsmanship* (Boston: Small, Maynard and Co., 1912).

Ayckbourn, Alan, *Time of My Life* (London: Faber and Faber, 1993).

Beaumont, Francis, *The Knight of the Burning Pestle*, ed. John Doebler, Regents Renaissance Drama ser. (Lincoln, Nebr.: University of Nebraska Press, 1967).

Beckerman, Bernard, 'The Odd Business of Play Reviewing', *Shakespeare Quarterly*, 36 (1986), 588–93.

Beckett, Samuel, *Proust* (1931; New York: Grove Press, 1957).

—— *Endgame: A Play in One Act, followed by Act without Words: A Mime for One Player* (New York: Grove Press, 1958).

—— *Collected Shorter Plays* (New York: Grove Weidenfeld, 1984).

Behan, Brendan, *The Quare Fellow and The Hostage* (New York: Grove Press, 1964).

Behan, Dominic, *My Brother Brendan* (New York: Simon and Schuster, 1965).

Belmont, Eleanor Robson, *The Fabric of Memory* (New York: Farrar, Straus & Cudahy, 1957).

Bennett, Alan, *Forty Years On and Other Plays* (London: Faber and Faber, 1971).

—— *Single Spies: Two Plays about Guy Burgess and Anthony Blunt & Talking Heads: Six Monologues* (New York: Summit Books, 1990).

Bentley, Gerald Eades, *Shakespeare & Jonson: Their Reputations in the Seventeenth Century Compared* (Chicago: University of Chicago Press, 1945), 2 vols.

Beolco, Angelo, *Il Reduce*, tr. Angela Ingold and Theodore Hoffman as *Ruzzante Returns from the Wars*, in *The Classic Theater I: Six Italian Plays*, ed. Eric Bentley (New York: Doubleday Anchor, 1958).

Bond, Edward, *Saved*, in *Plays: One* (London: Eyre Methuen, 1977).

Brecht, Bertolt, *He Who Says Yes* and *He Who Says No*, tr. Gerhard Nellhaus, in 'Bertolt Brecht: Two Plays', *Accent* (Autumn 1946), 14–24.

—— *Collected Plays*, v, ed. Ralph Manheim and John Willett (New York: Vintage, 1972).

—— *Die Stücke von Bertolt Brecht in einem Band* (Frankfurt am Main: Suhrkamp, 1985).

Brenman-Gibson, Margaret, *Clifford Odets, American Playwright* (New York: Atheneum, 1981).

Browne, E. Martin, *The Making of T. S. Eliot's Plays* (Cambridge: Cambridge University Press, 1969).

Büchner, Georg, *Georg Büchner: Complete Plays and Prose*, tr. Carl Richard Mueller (New York: Hill and Wang, 1963).

Byron, George Gordon, 6th Baron, *The Complete Poetical Works of Byron* (Boston: Houghton Mifflin, 1933).

Calderón de la Barca, Pedro, *The Great Theater of the World*, tr. Mack Hendricks Singleton, in *Masterpieces of the Spanish Golden Age*, ed. Angel Flores (New York: Rinehart, 1957).

Campbell, Peter A., 'The Postmodern Remaking of Greek Tragedy', Ph.D. diss. (New York: Columbia University, 2003).

Čapek, Karel, *R.U.R.*, tr. Paul Selver, in *Contemporary Drama: Nine Plays*, ed. E. Bradley Watson and W. Benfield Pressey (New York: Scribner's, 1941).

—— *Four Plays*, tr. Peter Majer and Cathy Porter (London: Methuen, 1999).

Cervantes Saavedra, Miguel de, *The Interludes of Cervantes*, ed. and tr. S. Griswold Morley (Princeton: Princeton University Press, 1948; repr. Greenwood Press, 1969).

Chekhov, Anton, *Plays*, tr. Elisaveta Fen (Baltimore: Penguin Books, 1966).

—— *Five Plays*, tr. Ronald Hingley, Oxford World's Classics (Oxford: Oxford University Press, 1998).

—— and Stanislavsky, K. S., *The Seagull Produced by Stanislavsky*, ed. S. D. Balukhaty, tr. David Magarshack (New York: Theatre Arts Books, 1952).

Chief Contemporary Dramatists, 3rd ser., ed. Thomas H. Dickinson (Boston: Houghton Mifflin, 1930).

Churchill, Caryl, 'An Interview with Caryl Churchill', conducted by Kathleen Betsko, Rachel Koenig, and Emily Mann, in *The Bedford Introduction to Drama*, 3rd edn., ed. Lee A. Jacobus (Boston: Bedford Books, 1997), 1410–14.

Clurman, Harold, *The Fervent Years: The Story of the Group Theatre and the Thirties* (New York: Hill and Wang, 1957).

Cocteau, Jean, *Théâtre I* (Paris: Gallimard, 1948).

—— *The Infernal Machine and Other Plays,* tr. Albert Bermel *et al.* (New York: New Directions, 1963).

—— *Professional Secrets: An Autobiography of Jean Cocteau drawn from his Lifetime Writings*, ed. Robert Phelps, tr. Richard Howard (New York: Harper & Row, 1972).

—— *Orphée: The Play and the Film*, ed. E. Freeman, Blackwell's French Texts (Oxford: Blackwell, 1976).

Coward, Noel, *Three Plays by Noel Coward*, introd. Edward Albee (New York: Dell, 1965).

Curtius, Ernst Robert, *European Literature of the Latin Middle Ages*, tr. Willard Trask (Princeton: Princeton University Press, 1973).

Dürrenmatt, Friedrich, 'Problems of the Theatre', tr. Gerhard Nellhaus, *Tulane Drama Review,* 3 (Oct. 1958), 3–26.

—— *The Visit; a Tragi-Comedy*, tr. Paul Bowles (New York: Grove Press, 1962).

Eliot, George, *Adam Bede*, 2 vols., in *The Works of George Eliot*, Cabinet Edition (Edinburgh and London: Blackwood, 1878).

Eliot, Thomas Stearns, *Selected Prose of T. S. Eliot*, ed. Frank Kermode (New York: Harcourt Brace Jovanovich/Farrar, Straus and Giroux, 1975).

Ellmann, Richard, *Oscar Wilde* (New York: Knopf, 1988).

Erikson, Erik H., *Young Man Luther* (New York: Norton, 1962).

Eugene O'Neill: A Documentary Film, directed by Ric Burns, typescript (New York: Steeplechase Films, 2004).

Evreinov, Nikolai, *The Theatre of the Soul: A Monodrama in One Act*, tr. Marie Protapenko and Christopher St John, in *Chief Contemporary Dramatists*, 3rd ser., ed. Thomas H. Dickinson (Boston: Houghton Mifflin, 1930).

—— *Life as Theater: Five Modern Plays*, tr. and ed. Christopher Collins (Ann Arbor: Ardis, 1973).

Foster, R. F. (Robert Fitzroy), *W. B. Yeats: A Life*, 2 vols. (Oxford and New York: Oxford University Press, 1997–2003).

Frayn, Michael, *Copenhagen* (London: Methuen, 1998).

—— *Noises Off* (New York: Anchor Books, 2002).

Freud, Sigmund, *The Interpretation of Dreams,* in *The Basic Writings of Sigmund Freud*, tr. and ed. A. A. Brill (New York: Modern Library, 1938).

—— *A General Introduction to Psychoanalysis*, tr. Joan Riviere (Garden City, NY: Doubleday, 1953).

Friel, Brian, *Philadelphia, Here I Come!* (New York: Farrar, Straus, 1965).

—— *Translations* (London: Faber and Faber, 1984).

Frisch, Max, *The Firebugs*, tr. Michael Bullock (New York: Hill and Wang, 1985).

Fugard, Athol, Kani, John, and Ntshona, Winston, *The Island*, in Worthen (ed.), *Modern Drama*.

Genet, Jean, *The Blacks: A Clown Show*, tr. Bernard Frechtman (New York: Grove Press, 1960).

—— *The Balcony*, tr. Bernard Frechtman, rev. version (New York: Grove Press, 1966).

Gilbert, Sir William Schwenk, *Plays & Poems of W. S. Gilbert* (New York: Random House, 1932).

Goethe, Johann Wolfgang von, *Götz von Berlichingen, mit der eisernen Hand*, in *Dramen*, Werkausgabe in zehn Bänden, ii (Cologne: Könemann, 1997).

Grangé, E.-P. Basté, and de Montépin, X.-A., *Les Frères Corses; or, The Corsican Brothers. A Dramatic Romance in Three Acts and Five Tableaux. Adapted from the Romance of* M. DUMAS (London: Samuel French, n.d.).

Greene, David H., and Stephens, Edward M., *J. M. Synge 1871–1909* (New York: Collier Books, 1961).

Handke, Peter, *Kaspar and Other Plays*, tr. Michael Roloff (New York: Farrar, Straus and Giroux, 1969).

Hardy, Thomas, *The Dynasts: A Drama of the Napoleonic Wars, in Three Parts, Nineteen Acts, & One Hundred and Thirty Scenes* (London: Macmillan, 1904).

Hebbel, Christian Friedrich, *Maria Magdalene: Ein bürgerliches Trauerspiel in drei Acten*, in Thomas Moody Campbell (ed.), *German Plays of the Nineteenth Century* (New York: Appleton-Century-Crofts, 1930), 212–34.

Herne, James A., *Shore Acres and Other Plays*, ed. Mrs James A. Herne (New York: Samuel French, 1928).

Hochhuth, Rolf, *The Deputy*, tr. Richard and Clara Winston (New York: Grove Press, 1964).

Hugo, Victor, *Théâtre complet*, ed. J.-J. Thierry & Josette Mélèze, 2 vols., Bibliothèque de la Pléiade (Paris: Gallimard, 1963).

Ibsen, Henrik, *Hedda Gabler and Three Other Plays*, tr. Michael Meyer (Garden City, NY: Doubleday, 1961).

—— *The Oxford Ibsen*, v, tr. and ed. Walter McFarlane (Oxford: Oxford University Press, 1961).

—— *Peer Gynt*, tr. Michael Meyer (Garden City, NY: Doubleday, 1963).

—— *Ibsen: Letters and Speeches*, ed. Evert Sprinchorn (New York: Hill and Wang, 1964).

Ionesco, Eugène, *Théâtre*, i (Paris: Gallimard, 1954).

—— *Four Plays by Eugene Ionesco*, tr. Donald M. Allen (New York: Grove Press, 1958).

—— *Amédée, The New Tenant, Victims of Duty*, tr. Donald Watson (New York: Grove Press, 1958).

—— *Notes et contre-notes* (Paris: Gallimard, 1962).

Jesurun, John, *Philoktetes*, in *Yale Theatre*, 25 (1994), 71–91.

Johnson, Samuel, *Samuel Johnson on Shakespeare*, ed. W. K. Wimsatt, Jr. (New York: Hill and Wang, 1960).

Jonson, Ben, *The Complete Plays*, 2 vols., Everyman's Library (London: J. M. Dent and New York: E. P. Dutton, 1910).

Kalb, Jonathan, *Beckett in Performance* (Cambridge: Cambridge University Press, 1991), 240.

Kerman, Joseph, *Opera as Drama* (New York: Vintage Books, 1959).

Kleist, Heinrich von, *Penthesilea*, tr. Humphrey Trevelyan in *Plays*, ed. Walter Hinderer, German Library, 25 (New York: Continuum, 1982).

Lahr, John, *Notes on a Cowardly Lion* (New York: Knopf, 1969).

Lawson, Mark, 'A False Start, and then it all Came Together', *Guardian* (16 Aug. 1997).

Lessing, Gotthold Ephraim, *Nathan the Wise*, tr. Bayard Quincy Morgan (New York: Frederick Ungar, 1955).

Lope de Vega Carpio, Félix, *Fuente Ovejuna*, in *Diez comedias del Siglo de Oro*, ed. H. Alpern and J. Martel (New York and London: Harper, 1939).

—— *Five Plays*, tr. Jill Booty, ed. R. D. F. Pring-Mill (New York: Hill and Wang, 1961).

—— *El Castigo sin Venganza*, ed. José María Díez Borque, Clásicos Castellanos, NS (Madrid: Espasa-Calpe, 1987).

Macaulay, Thomas Babington, *Critical and Miscellaneous Essays*, rev. edn., 7 vols. in 5 (New York: Appleton, 1895–6).

Macro Plays: The Castle of Perseverance, Wisdom, Mankind, ed. Mark Eccles, Early English Text Society, 262 (London, New York: Oxford University Press, 1969).

Magarshack, David, *Chekhov the Dramatist* (New York: Hill and Wang, 1960).

—— (tr. and ed.), *The Storm and Other Plays* (New York: Hill and Wang, 1960).

Malina, Judith, and Beck, Julian, *Paradise Now: Collective Creation of the Living Theatre* (New York: Random House, 1971).

Mamet David, *Glengarry Glen Ross* (New York: Grove Press, 1954).

Mander, Raymond, and Mitchenson, Joe, *Theatrical Companion to Shaw* (London: Rockcliff, 1954).

Marlowe, Christopher, *Tamburlaine the Great, Parts I and II*, ed. John D. Jump (Lincoln, Nebr.: University of Nebraska, 1967).

Maugham, W. Somerset, *Six Comedies* (Garden City, NY: Doubleday, 1937).

Mayakovsky, Vladimir, *The Bedbug*, tr. Max Hayward, in *Three Soviet Plays*, ed. Michael Glenny (Harmondsworth: Penguin Books, 1966).

Mendelsohn, Edward, *Early Auden* (New York: Viking, 1981).

Miller, Arthur, *Collected Plays*, 2 vols. (New York: Viking, 1957, 1981).

—— *After the Fall* (New York: Viking, 1964).

Molière, Jean Baptiste Poquelin, *Œuvres complètes de Molière*, ed. M. Félix Lemaistre, 3 vols. (Paris: Garnier, 1946).

—— *Tartuffe and Other Plays*, tr. Donald M. Frame (New York: New American Library, 1967).

Moore, George, *Ave*, part 1 of *Hail and Farewell* (New York: Appleton, 1911–14).

Muldoon, Paul, *Poems 1968–1998* (New York: Farrar, Straus and Giroux, 2001).

Nesmith, N. Graham, 'Arthur Laurents', *Dramatist* (May/June 2003).

Nichols, Peter, *Joe Egg* (New York: Grove Press, 1967).

Norman, Marc, and Stoppard, Tom, *Shakespeare in Love* (London, Faber and Faber, 1999).

O'Casey, Sean, *Collected Plays*, 4 vols. (London: Macmillan and New York: St Martin's, 1967).

Odets, Clifford, *Waiting for Lefty* (New York: Dramatists Play Service, [n.d.]).

O'Neill, Eugene, *Complete Plays, 1913–1920* (New York: Library of America, 1988).

Osborne, John, *Luther* (New York: New American Library, 1961).

—— *Inadmissible Evidence* (New York: Grove Press, 1965).

—— *The Entertainer* (New York: Bantam, 1967).

Pearson, Hesketh, *The Life of Oscar Wilde* (London: Methuen, 1946).

—— *Beerbohm Tree: His Life and Laughter* (New York: Harper & Brothers, 1956).

Pinter, Harold, *The Birthday Party and The Room* (New York: Grove Press, 1961).

—— 'Writing for the Theatre', repr. in *The New British Drama*, ed. Henry Popkin (New York: Grove Press, 1964).

—— *The Homecoming* (New York: Grove Press, 1966).

—— *Old Times* (London: Methuen, 1971).

Pirandello, Luigi, *Naked Masks*, ed. Eric Bentley (New York: Dutton, 1952).

—— *Maschere nude*, 2 vols. (Milan: Mondadori, 1978).

Racine, Jean, *Five Plays*, tr. Kenneth Muir (New York: Hill and Wang, 1960), 235.

Riouffe, Honoré, *Memoires d'un détenu, pour servir à l'histoire de la tyrannie de Robespierre* (Paris [London?], 1795).

Rowell, George (ed.), *Nineteenth-Century Plays* (Oxford: Oxford University Press, 1953).

Sardou, Victorien, *Les Pattes de mouche*, ed. W. O. Farnsworth (Boston: D. C. Heath, 1911).

Sartre, Jean-Paul, *Théâtre* (Paris: Gallimard, 1947).

—— *No Exit and Three Other Plays* (New York: Vintage, 1960).

Schiller, Friedrich von, *Essays Æsthetical and Philosophical* (London: George Bell, 1875).

—— *Mary Stuart: A Tragedy*, tr. Sophie Wilkins (Great Neck, NY: Barron's Educational Series, 1959).

Schnitzler, Arthur, *La Ronde*, tr. Carl Richard Mueller, in *Masterpieces of the Modern Central European Theatre*, ed. Robert W. Corrigan (New York: Collier, 1967).

Shakespeare, William, *King Henry V*, ed. J. H. Walter, The Arden Shakespeare (London: Methuen, 1954).

—— *The Tempest*, ed. Frank Kermode, The Arden Shakespeare (London: Methuen, 1954).

—— *Mr. William Shakespeares Comedies, Histories, & Tragedies* [London, 1623], *A facsimile edition*, ed. Helge Kökeritz and Charles Tyler Prouty (New Haven: Yale University Press, 1955).

—— *Coriolanus*, ed. Philip Brockbank, The Arden Shakespeare (London: Methuen, 1976).

—— *King Richard III*, ed. Antony Hammond, The Arden Shakespeare (London and New York: Methuen, 1981).

—— *The Tempest*, ed. Stephen Orgel, The Oxford Shakespeare (Oxford and New York: Oxford University Press, 1987).

—— *The Tempest*, The Arden Shakespeare, 3rd ser., ed. Virginia Mason Vaughan and Alden T. Vaughan (Walton-on-Thames: Thomas Nelson and Sons, 1999).

Shapiro, James, *A Year in the Life of William Shakespeare: 1599* (New York: Harper-Collins, 2005).

Shaw, George Bernard, *Widowers' Houses*, Independent Theatre Edition (London, 1893).

—— 'Shakespeare: A Standard Text', *Times Literary Supplement* (17 Mar. 1921), 178.

—— 'Mr. Shaw on Printed Plays', *Times Literary Supplement* (17 May 1923).

—— 'Mr. Shaw on Mr. Shaw', *New York Times* (12 June 1927), sec. 7, p. 1.

—— Standard Edition of the Works of Bernard Shaw, 36 vols. (London: Constable and Company, 1931–50).

—— *Advice to a Young Critic and Other Letters by Bernard Shaw*, ed. E. J. West (New York: Crown Publishers, 1955).

—— *Collected Letters*, ed. Dan H. Laurence, *1874–1897* (New York: Dodd Mead, 1965); *1898–1910* (New York: Dodd Mead, 1972); *1911–1925* (New York: Viking, 1985); *1926–1950* (London: Max Reinhardt, 1988).

—— *Bernard Shaw's Letters to Siegfried Trebitsch*, ed. Samuel A. Weiss (Stanford, Calif.: Stanford University Press, 1986).

—— *Bernard Shaw: The Drama Observed*, ed. Bernard F. Dukore (University Park, Pa.: Pennsylvania State University Press, 1993), 4 vols.

Sheridan, Richard Brinsley, *Plays*, Everyman's Library (London: J. M. Dent; New York: E. P. Dutton, 1949).

Smith, Anna Deavere, *Fires in the Mirror* (New York: Anchor, Doubleday, 1993).

—— 'Show and Tell', *New York Times* (30 July 2004), A19.

Sophocles, *Antigone*, tr. Elizabeth Wycoff, in *Sophocles I* in *The Complete Greek Tragedies*, ed. David Grene and Richmond Lattimore (Chicago and London: University of Chicago, 1954).

—— *Philoctetes*, tr. David Grene, in *Greek Tragedies*, vol. iii, ed. David Grene and Richmond Lattimore (Chicago: University of Chicago Press, 1960).

—— *Oedipus the King*, tr. David Grene, in *Sophocles I*, in *The Complete Greek Tragedies*, ed. David Grene and Richmond Lattimore, 2nd edn. (Chicago: University of Chicago Press, 1991).

Stanton, Stephen S. (ed.), *Camille and Other Plays* (New York: Hill and Wang, 1957).

Steegmuller, Francis, *Cocteau: A Biography* (Boston: Atlantic Monthly/Little, Brown Books, 1970).

Stoppard, Tom, *Rosencrantz & Guildenstern Are Dead* (New York: Grove Press, 1967).

—— *Jumpers* (New York: Grove Press, 1981).

—— *Arcadia* (London: Faber and Faber, 1993).

—— *Tom Stoppard in Conversation*, ed. Paul Delaney (Ann Arbor: University of Michigan Press, 1994).

Strindberg, August, *Six Plays of Strindberg*, tr. Elizabeth Sprigge (Garden City, NY: Doubleday, 1955).

Styan, J. L., *The Dark Comedy: The Development of Modern Comic Tragedy*, 2nd edn. (Cambridge: Cambridge University Press, 1968).

Synge, John Millington, *The Complete Plays of John M. Synge* (New York: Random House, 1935).

Tasso, Torquato, *Aminta: Favola Boschereccia*, tr. Leigh Hunt, as *Amyntas*, repr. in *The Genius of the Italian Theater*, ed. Eric Bentley (New York: New American Library, 1964).

Tate, Greg, 'Bewitching the Other: In *Fires in the Mirror*, Anna Deavere Smith Wears Her Words', *The Village Voice* (New York) (21 July 1992), 98.

Tieck, Ludwig, *Die verkehrte Welt*, in *Werke in vier Bänden*. vol. ii, ed. Marianne Thalmann (Munich: Winkler Verlag, 1964).

—— *The Land of Upside Down*, tr. Oscar Mandel and Maria Kelsen Feder (Rutherford, NJ: Fairleigh Dickinson University, 1978).

Tirso de Molina [Gabriel Téllez], *El Burlador de Sevilla y Convidado de Piedra*, in *Comedias*, i, ed. Américo Castro, ser. Clásicos Castellanos (Madrid: Espasa-Calpe, 1967).

Tolstoy, Lyov Nikolaevich, *The Power of Darkness; or, "If One Claw is Caught, the Whole Bird is Lost"*, in F. D. Reeve (ed. and tr.), *An Anthology of Russian Plays*, 2 vols. (New York: Vintage, 1961).

Turgenev, Ivan, *A Month in the Country*, tr. Richard Freeborn, The World's Classics (London: Oxford University Press, 1941).

Waley, Arthur, *The Nō Plays of Japan* (New York: Knopf, 1922).

Weiss, Peter, *The Persecution and Assassination of Jean-Paul Marat as Performed by the Inmates of the Asylum of Charenton under the Direction of The Marquis de Sade*, tr. Geoffrey Skelton, verse adap. Robin Mitchell (New York: Atheneum, 1965).

Wilde, Oscar, *The Picture of Dorian Gray*, in *Complete Writings of Oscar Wilde*, vol. x (New York: Nottingham Society, 1909).

—— *The Importance of Being Earnest and Other Plays*, ed. Peter Raby, Oxford Drama Library (Oxford: Clarendon Press, 1995).

Wilder, Thornton, *The Long Christmas Dinner & Other Plays in One Act* (New York: Coward-McCann and New Haven: Yale University Press, 1931).

Williams, Tennessee, *Plays 1937–1955* (New York: Library of America, 2000).

Worthen, W. B. (ed.), *Modern Drama: Plays/Criticism/Theory* (Fort Worth, Texas: Harcourt Brace, 1995).

Yeats, William Butler, *Plays and Controversies* (New York: Macmillan, 1924).

—— *The Collected Plays of W. B. Yeats* (New York: Macmillan, 1963).

—— *The Collected Poems of W. B. Yeats* (London: Macmillan, 1963).

Index

Bold numbers denote reference to illustrations.